LIVY

XI

BOOKS XXXVIII—XXXIX

313

LIVY

WITH AN ENGLISH TRANSLATION

IN FOURTEEN VOLUMES

XI

BOOKS XXXVIII—XXXIX

TRANSLATED BY

EVAN T. SAGE, PH.D.

PROFESSOR OF LATIN AND HEAD OF THE DEPARTMENT OF CLASSICS IN THE UNIVERSITY OF PITTSBURGH

CAMBRIDGE, MASSACHUSETTS
HARVARD UNIVERSITY PRESS

LONDON
WILLIAM HEINEMANN LTD

MCMLXXXIII

American ISBN 0-674-99346-2
British ISBN 0-434-99313-1

First printed 1936
Reprinted 1949, 1958, 1965, 1983

Printed in Great Britain

CONTENTS

TRANSLATOR'S PREFACE

This preface should be brief. The Books contained in Volume XI deal with minor matters, and Livy feels himself more at leisure, so that he can include anecdotes and digressions. Another possible consequence is that Livy, having less of moment to relate, felt able to examine details more closely and to compare his sources more consciously. This may be the explanation of the appearance here of the one serious bit of historical criticism to be found in Livy (XXXIX. lii).

The textual problem grows more serious in this Volume. Our best MS., *B*, now breaks off with *inci* (XXXVIII. xlvi. 4). The major difference between my text and that of the latest revision of Weissenborn–Müller is that I have occasionally restored readings of *B*, and I believe that careful examination will reveal more readings which should be received into the text. But there are many indications that the consensus of the minor MSS. is of almost equal value, although we lack the precision of information that is necessary before accepting this as a principle of textual criticism in the case of Livy. It would be fortunate if this were so. But the individual minor MSS. do not always agree among themselves, and I have usually accepted and reported as the reading of ς the reading of the majority of the MSS., so far as I could determine it from the reports accessible to me. In this part of the text I have preferred readings of *M*, where reported, and have restored some without remark. A more difficult question is the relative authority of certain sixteenth-century editions which are presumably based, at least in part, on *M* and possibly on the lost *S*(*pirensis*). The frequent references of Gelenius to "antiqua scriptura," "archetypa," "ex archetypis," "vetusti codices" and the like are exasperating in their suggestion of buried treasures which seem the more valuable as they are at present lost to us. In practice I have followed *M* where it was reported, ς when there was no report of *M*, and have furnished critical notes on passages where ς was preferred to *M* or the sixteenth-century editions or later conjectures were preferred to *M*ς.

My obligations as to index, maps, incidental assistance, and editorial aid and encouragement are unchanged. No repetition of details would prove an adequate expression of my debts.

New bibliography is covered in the notes, which I have tried to make useful from the historical standpoint, as before, and from the literary standpoint as well.

CONSPECTUS SIGLORUM

B = Codex Bambergensis M. IV. 9, s. 11.
F = Codex Bambergensis Q. IV. 27 (Theol. 99), s. 6.
M = Codex Moguntinus deperditus, s. 9 (?).
ς = Codices deteriores et editiones veteres (the most important early editions are cited by name).

BIBLIOGRAPHICAL ADDENDUM (1983)

The following important work includes detailed discussion of Livy 38 and 39 as well as an excellent bibliography:

T. J. Luce, *Livy, The Composition of His History*, Princeton 1977.

Also deserving mention here are:

P. G. Walsh, *Livy, His Historical Aims and Methods*, Cambridge 1961 and

D. W. Packard, *A Concordance to Livy*, 4 vols., Cambridge, Mass. 1968.

INTRODUCTORY NOTE

By the year 189 B.C. a Roman optimist (if such an one existed) might well have said that Rome's eastern difficulties were over: Philip had been reduced to impotence by Flamininus; the Aetolians had been severely punished; now Antiochus had been eliminated as a factor in Asian politics by Scipio. The only other eastern powers demanding consideration, Egypt, Pergamum and Rhodes, were Rome's allies and the last two were deeply in Rome's debt by reason of the projected settlement of Asia. Yet at the same moment a Roman pessimist might have argued just as insistently that her troubles in the east were just beginning. Asia, he would have admitted, presented no threatening problem. Philip had been allowed to regain some of his lost Greek possessions as compensation for his assistance against the Aetolians and Antiochus. The Aetolians had been defeated but not crushed completely, and their fundamental grievance, that they had been ill-treated after the victory over Philip, had not been removed. Perhaps most serious of all was the fact that Rome had no real base of operations east of the Adriatic: this was a theoretically laudable, but practically unfortunate, consequence of her desire to avoid assuming territorial responsibilities in the east.

Within Europe there were numerous situations

any one of which might provoke a war. In the Peloponnesus there was the Achaean–Lacedaemonian problem, since Rome had never pronounced judgment on the Achaean policy after the murder of Nabis. In the north there was the constant hostility of the Aetolians, rendered for the moment more serious because of the recent Macedonian expansion. These were only the most apparent dangers. Whether Rome honestly believed that a conquered nation could remain conquered and submissive after the withdrawal of Roman troops is a question which we are unable to answer; whether she honestly believed that the Greek states were capable, at this time, of self-government is also a question to which there is no answer. I fear that Roman generals, ambitious for triumphs and material rewards, were quite willing to defer as long as possible a definitive settlement in Greece for the sake of the fairly easy victories that were promised.

In Asia, the withdrawal of Antiochus left a multitude of unsolved problems, and the solution of some of these soon appeared to be exceedingly profitable undertakings: the Galatian campaign will serve as a sufficient example.

Another solution of the eastern problem might have been the enlargement of some one state, bound firmly by ties of alliance and dependence to Rome, which could have dominated the eastern Mediterranean and by virtue of her military superiority have maintained peace there. If Rome looked for such a state she failed to find one that could be so enlarged and could still be trusted. There was nothing left for Rome, apart from the cynically brutal course of allowing the eastern states to destroy one another, except to assume the informal protectorate which she does insensibly assume in the years covered by this Volume.

There seems little doubt that public sentiment would have rejected such a settlement as a formal occupation of Greece and Asia had it been proposed in Rome. But, in addition to sincere differences of opinion among Romans, there was an almost unanimous sentiment, which seems to increase in strength, that in some form or other Roman control of the east was necessary. But so great was the Romans' faith in Roman power that they were inclined to cut through diplomatic and political red tape and announce decisions in a form so categorically brief as to be unintelligible to others who were not Romans. One suspects that the Romans talked in riddles so frequently because they were not themselves sure of what they meant. It was easier to let time decide the exact interpretation and to punish the unfortunates who had in the meantime misunderstood.

The Books contained in this Volume record events of a period of transition. With no major enemy to confront her, Rome turns her attention to smaller problems. Little tasks are performed by little men, who strive through partisan politics to make themselves and their achievements seem great.

LIVY

FROM THE FOUNDING OF THE CITY

BOOK XXXVIII

T. LIVI

AB URBE CONDITA

LIBER XXXVIII

A.U.C. 565 I. Dum in Asia bellum geritur, ne in Aetolia
quidem res quietae fuerant, principio a gente Atha-
2 manum orto. Athamania ea tempestate pulso Amynandro sub praefectis [1] Philippi regio tenebatur praesidio, qui superbo atque immodico imperio desiderium
3 Amynandri fecerant. Exulanti tum [2] Amynandro in
Aetolia litteris suorum, indicantium statum Atha-
4 maniae, spes recuperandi regni facta est. Remissique
ab eo nuntiant principibus Argitheam—id enim
caput Athamaniae erat—si popularium animos satis
perspectos haberet, impetrato ab Aetolis auxilio in
Athamaniam se venturum. Non diffidere sibi facile
conventurum [3] cum delectis, quod consilium est [4]
5 gentis, et Nicandro praetore. Quos ubi ad omnia

[1] praefectis ς : praefecto *B*.
[2] exulanti tum ς : exulantium *B*.
[3] venturum. non diffidere sibi facile conventurum *M. Mueller* : uenturum *BM*ς.
[4] est *Madvig* : esset *B*ς.

---

[1] The events here described belong to the previous year.

LIVY

FROM THE FOUNDING OF THE CITY

BOOK XXXVIII

I. While the war in Asia was in progress, there was no peace in Aetolia either,[1] the trouble having been begun by the Athamanian people. Athamania at that time, after the expulsion of Amynander,[2] was held by royal garrisons under the prefects of Philip, and they, by their arrogant and lawless administration, had created a longing for Amynander. Amynander, who was then an exile in Aetolia, was inspired by the letters of his partisans, who described to him the state of affairs in Athamania, with the hope of recovering his kingdom. His agents, too, sent with his reply to the chiefs at Argithea—for this is the capital of Athamania—announced that if he perceived clearly enough the sentiments of his countrymen he would obtain the aid of the Aetolians and proceed to Athamania. They said that he had no doubt that he would easily come to an agreement with the chosen persons[3] who comprise the council of the people and with the praetor Nicander. When B.C. 189

[2] Cf. XXXVI. xiv. 9.
[3] The *apocleti* (XXXV. xxxiv. 2, etc.).

A.U.C. 565 paratos esse vidit, certiores suos subinde[1] facit quo die cum exercitu Athamaniam ingressurus esset.
6 Quattuor primo fuerunt coniurati adversus Macedonum praesidium. Hi senos sibi adiutores ad rem gerendam assumpserunt;[2] dein paucitate parum freti, quae[3] celandae rei quam agendae aptior erat,
7 parem priori numerum adiecerunt. Ita duo et quinquaginta facti quadrifariam se diviserunt; pars una Heracleam, altera Tetraphyliam petit, ubi custodia regiae pecuniae esse solita[4] erat, tertia
8 Theudoriam, quarta Argitheam. Ita inter omnes convenit ut primo quieti,[5] velut ad privatam rem agendam venissent, in foro obversarentur; die certa multitudinem omnem[6] convocarent ad praesidia
9 Macedonum arcibus expellenda. Ubi ea dies advenit, et Amynander cum mille Aetolis in finibus erat, ex composito quattuor simul locis praesidia Macedonum expulsa, litteraeque in alias urbes passim dimissae ut vindicarent sese ab impotenti dominatione Philippi et restituerent in patrium ac legitimum
10 regnum. Undique Macedones expelluntur. Theium[7] oppidum litteris a Xenone praefecto praesidii interceptis[8] et arce ab regiis occupata paucos dies obsi-
11 dentibus restitit; deinde id quoque traditum

[1] suos subinde *H. J. Mueller* : subinde *B.*
[2] assumpserunt ς : consumpserunt *B.*
[3] quae ς : quod *B.*
[4] esse solita ς : *om. B.*
[5] primo quieti *edd. vett.* : prima quietem *B.*
[6] omnem ς : omnes *B.*

he learned that they were ready for any event, B.C. 189 he at once informed his friends on what day he would arrive in Athamania at the head of an army. At first there were four who had conspired against the Macedonian garrison. Each of these chose six assistants to aid in carrying out their plan; then, lacking confidence by reason of their small number, which was better suited to concealment than to action, they added a number equal to that which they had first enlisted. Their number having thus become two and fifty, they divided themselves into four sections; one proceeded to Heraclea, one to Tetraphylia, which was the usual storehouse of the royal wealth, the third to Theudoria, the fourth to Argithea. It had been agreed upon among them all that at first they should move about quietly in the market-place as if they were engaged in transacting private business; that on the appointed day they should summon the whole population to drive the Macedonian garrisons from the citadels. When this day came and Amynander with a thousand Aetolians was at the frontiers, according to agreement the Macedonian garrisons were expelled from the four places at once, and a despatch was sent in all directions to the other towns, summoning them to free themselves from the headstrong rule of Philip and to return to their hereditary and lawful sovereign. On all sides the Macedonians were expelled. The town of Theium, since the despatch had been intercepted by Xeno, the prefect of the garrison, and the citadel had been seized by the king's troops, held out for a few days against the besiegers; finally

[7] Theium *edd. vett.*: telum *Bϛ*.
[8] interceptis *ϛ*: interseptis *B*.

A.U.C. 565 Amynandro est, et omnis Athamania in potestate
erat praeter Athenaeum castellum, finibus Macedoniae subiectum.

II. Philippus audita defectione Athamaniae cum
sex milibus armatorum profectus ingenti celeritate
2 Gomphos pervenit. Ibi relicta maiore parte exercitus—neque enim ad tanta itinera sufficerent—cum
duobus milibus [1] Athenaeum, quod unum a praesidio
3 suo retentum fuerat, pervenit. Inde proximis
temptatis cum facile animadvertisset cetera hostilia
esse, Gomphos regressus omnibus copiis simul in
4 Athamaniam redit. Xenonem inde cum mille
peditibus praemissum Aethopiam occupare iubet,
5 opportune Argitheae imminentem; quem ubi teneri
ab suis locum vidit, ipse circa templum Iovis Acraei
posuit castra. Ibi unum diem foeda tempestate
retentus, postero die ducere ad Argitheam intendit.
6 Euntibus extemplo apparuere Athamanes in tumulos
imminentes viae discurrentes. Ad quorum conspectum constitere prima signa, totoque [2] agmine
7 pavor et trepidatio erat et pro se quisque quidnam
futurum esset cogitare, si in valles subiectas rupibus
8 agmen foret demissum. Haec tumultuatio regem
cupientem si se sequerentur raptim evadere angustias,
revocare primos et eadem qua venerat via referre
coegit signa. Athamanes primo ex intervallo quieti
9 sequebantur; postquam Aetoli se coniunxerunt, hos,
ut ab tergo agmini instarent, reliquerunt, ipsi ab

[1] milibus ς: *om. B.*
[2] signa totoque ς: signatoque *B*: concitatoque *M.*

it also was delivered to Amynander, and all Athamania was in his hands except the fortress of Athenaeum, lying on the borders of Macedonia. B.C. 18

II. Philip, on hearing of the revolt of Athamania, set out with six thousand troops and very quickly arrived at Gomphi. There he left the greater part of his men—for they would not have had strength enough for such hard marching—and with two thousand went on to Athenaeum, which alone had been held by his garrison. Then, when he had quickly learned, by trial of the neighbouring towns, that everything else was unfriendly, he returned to Gomphi and thence, with his whole force united, marched into Athamania. He ordered Xeno to go ahead with a thousand infantry to seize Aethopia, which was favourably situated to threaten Argithea; and when he saw that his men were in possession of the place, he himself encamped near the temple of Jupiter Acraeus. There he was detained for a day by a violent storm, and on the next day began his march toward Argithea. Suddenly as they were advancing the Athamanians appeared, hurrying towards the hills that commanded the road. At the first glimpse of them the advance guard halted and throughout the whole column there was terror and confusion, each for himself considering what would happen if the column were led down into the valleys lying at the foot of the cliffs. This panic compelled the king, who had wished, should his troops follow him, to get through the pass with a rush, to recall the van and retire by the same road by which he had come. The Athamanians at first followed quietly, keeping their distance; after the Aetolians joined them, they left them to harass the column from the

A.U.C. 565
10 lateribus se circumfuderunt, quidam per notas calles
breviore via praegressi transitus insedere; tantumque
tumultus Macedonibus est iniectum, ut fugae magis
effusae quam itineris ordinati modo multis armis
11 virisque relictis flumen traiecerint.[1] Hic finis sequendi fuit. Inde tuto Macedones Gomphos et a
12 Gomphis in Macedoniam redierunt. Athamanes
Aetolique Aethopiam ad Xenonem ac mille Mace-
13 donas opprimendos undique concurrerunt. Macedones parum[2] loco freti ab Aethopia in altiorem
deruptioremque undique tumulum concessere; quo
pluribus ex locis aditu invento expulere eos Atha-
14 manes, dispersosque et per invia atque ignotas rupes
iter fugae non expedientis partim ceperunt partim
interfecerunt. Multi pavore in derupta praecipitati;
perpauci cum Xenone ad regem evaserunt. Postea
per indutias sepeliendi caesos potestas facta est.

III. Amynander recuperato[3] regno legatos et
Romam ad senatum et ad Scipiones in Asiam, Ephesi
post magnum cum Antiocho proelium morantes,
2 misit. Pacem petebat excusabatque sese, quod per
Aetolos recuperasset paternum regnum; Philippum
incusabat.

[1] traiecerint ς: traiecerunt *B*.
[2] parum ς: *om. B*.
[3] recuperato ς: recuperando *B*.

---

[1] Amynander recognizes the necessity of placating Rome even if he does not admit her virtual protectorate over Greece. His own diplomatic status was somewhat uncertain: he had allied himself with the Aetolians and Antiochus (XXXV. xlvii. 8), and for that reason the Romans had consented to Philip's conquest (XXXVI. xiv. 9). It may be assumed that the return of Amynander would automatically restore Atha-

rear and threw themselves upon the flanks, while some, going ahead over familiar trails by a shorter route, blocked the crossing; and such great confusion was caused among the Macedonians that in the fashion of a disorderly rout rather than a march under discipline, leaving behind many weapons and men, they crossed the river. This was the end of the pursuit. From that point the Macedonians returned safely to Gomphi and from Gomphi to Macedonia. The Athamanians and Aetolians came from all sides to Aethopia to destroy Xeno and his thousand Macedonians. The Macedonians, distrusting the strength of the place, withdrew from Aethopia to a hill higher and steeper on every side; from this the Athamanians dislodged them, finding ways to scale it in several places, and as they scattered over pathless country and unfamiliar cliffs that offered no aid to flight, part were captured and part killed. Many, panic-stricken, plunged over precipices; a very few with Xeno escaped to the king. Later a truce was made to give them an opportunity to bury their dead. B.C. 189

III. Amynander, having recovered his kingdom, sent ambassadors both to the senate in Rome and to the Scipios in Asia, since they were tarrying in Ephesus after the decisive battle with Antiochus. He asked for peace and defended himself for having recovered his ancestral kingdom through the aid of the Aetolians;[1] he laid the blame on Philip.[2]

mania to the status of an Aetolian ally, and that Amynander is trying to escape the dangers of such a position.

[2] These charges must have been based on the character of Philip's government after his conquest (i. 2 above), as no other plausible cause for finding fault with him is apparent.

A.U.C. 565

3 Aetoli ex Athamania in Amphilochos profecti
sunt et maioris partis voluntate [1] in ius dicionemque
4 totam redegerunt gentem. Amphilochia recepta—
nam fuerat quondam Aetolorum—eadem spe in
Aperantiam transcenderunt; [2] ea quoque magna ex
parte sine certamine in deditionem venit. Dolopes
5 numquam Aetolorum fuerant, Philippi erant. Hi
primo ad arma concurrerunt; ceterum postquam
Amphilochos cum Aetolis esse fugamque ex Athamania Philippi et caedem praesidii eius accepere, et ipsi
6 a Philippo ad Aetolos deficiunt. Quibus circumiectis
gentibus iam undique se a Macedonibus tutos
credentibus esse Aetolis fama adfertur Antiochum in
Asia victum ab Romanis; nec ita multo post legati
ab Roma rediere sine spe pacis Fulviumque consulem
7 nuntiantes cum exercitu iam traiecisse. His territi,[3]
prius ab Rhodo et Athenis legationibus excitis, ut
per auctoritatem earum civitatium suae preces nuper
repudiatae faciliorem aditum ad senatum haberent,
principes gentis ad temptandam spem ultimam
8 Romam miserunt, nihil, ne bellum haberent, priusquam paene in conspectu hostis erat, praemeditati.
9 Iam M. Fulvius Apolloniam exercitu traiecto cum

[1] uoluntate ς: uoluntatem *B*.
[2] Aperantiam transcenderunt ς: *om. B*.
[3] territi ς: territis *B*.

---

[1] Cf. XXXII. xxxiv. 4.

[2] For Philip's recent acquisition of Aperantia and Dolopia, cf. XXXVI. xxxiii. 7. In the latter case it was a re-conquest, since Dolopia had been freed from Macedonian control in 196 B.C. (XXXIII. xxxiv. 6).

[3] The embassy had been expelled from Italy: cf. XXXVII. xlix. 5–7.

[4] The appointment of Fulvius to Aetolia was reported at XXXVII. i. 8.

From Athamania the Aetolians moved against the Amphilochians, and with the consent of the majority brought the whole tribe under their authority and control. Amphilochia having been recovered[1]—for it had once belonged to the Aetolians—they proceeded with the same hope to Aperantia; this state also surrendered, in large measure without resistance. The Dolopians[2] had never been subjects of the Aetolians, but belonged to Philip. At first they rushed to arms, but after they learned that the Amphilochians were with the Aetolians, that Philip had been driven from Athamania and his garrison destroyed, they too went over from Philip to the Aetolians. Having set up these buffer-states and believing that they were now safe from the Macedonians on all sides, the Aetolians received the news that Antiochus had been defeated in Asia by the Romans; and not long afterwards their envoys returned from Rome with no promise of peace,[3] and brought word that the consul Fulvius with the army had already crossed.[4] Terrified by this information, first summoning embassies from Rhodes and Athens,[5] that through the influence of these states their own prayers, though previously rejected, might obtain easier access to the senate, they sent the leading men of the people to Rome to try the last hope of peace, having given no thought to the avoidance of war until the enemy was almost in sight. B.C. 189

Marcus Fulvius had by now transported his army to Apollonia and was consulting with the chiefs of

[5] These two states were frequently appealed to as peacemakers; for Rhodes, cf. XXVII. xxx. 4; for Athens, cf. XXXVII. vi. 4, where her intervention for Aetolia the preceding year is recorded.

A.U.C. 565 Epirotarum principibus consultabat unde bellum in-
ciperet. Epirotis Ambraciam placebat aggredi, quae
10 tum contribuerat se Aetolis: sive ad tuendam eam
venirent Aetoli, apertos circa campos ad dimicandum
esse; sive detractarent[1] certamen, oppugnationem
11 fore haud difficilem; nam et copiam in propinquo
materiae ad aggeres excitandos et cetera opera esse,
et Arethontem, navigabilem amnem, opportunum ad
comportanda quae usui sint praeter ipsa moenia
fluere, et aestatem aptam rei gerendae adesse. His
persuaserunt ut per Epirum duceret.

IV. Consuli ad Ambraciam advenienti magni
operis oppugnatio visa est. Ambracia tumulo aspero
2 subiecta est; Perranthem incolae vocant. Urbs, qua
murus vergit in campos et flumen, occidentem, arx,
3 quae imposita tumulo est, orientem spectat. Amnis
Aretho ex Athamania fluens cadit in sinum maris ab
nomine propinquae urbis Ambracium appellatum.
4 Praeterquam quod[2] hinc amnis munit, hinc tumuli,
muro quoque firmo saepta erat, patente in circuitu
5 paulo amplius quattuor milia passuum. Fulvius
bina a campo castra, modico inter se distantia intervallo, unum castellum loco edito contra arcem
6 obiecit; ea omnia vallo atque fossa ita[3] iungere

[1] detractarent ς: detrectarent *B*.
[2] quod ς: *om. B*.
[3] ita *ed. Frobeniana* 1535: *om. Bς*.

---

[1] Livy here seems to think that there were no other Roman forces in Greece at this time, and in this he apparently has the support of Polybius (XXII. ix). However, in XXXVII. ii. 7–8 the propraetor Cornelius was instructed to conduct an army to Aetolia, and in XXXVII. i. 4 the presence of an army there was assumed. Livy has, as often, changed sources without warning. The account of the siege of Ambracia follows Polybius closely.

the Epirotes as to where to begin the campaign.[1] B.C. 189
The advice of the Epirotes was to attack Ambracia, which had at this time joined the Aetolians:[2] if, on the one hand, the Aetolians should come to defend it, there were open plains on which to fight; if, on the other hand, they declined an engagement, the siege would not be difficult; for there was both abundance of material close at hand for building mounds and raising other siege-works, and a navigable river, the Aretho, suitable for the transportation of the necessary supplies, flowed past the very walls, and, moreover, summer was at hand, a season adapted to active operations. By such arguments they induced him to lead the army through Epirus.

IV. When the consul arrived before Ambracia, the siege seemed to him to involve great toil. Ambracia lay at the foot of a rugged hill; the natives call it Perranthes. The city, where the wall turns towards the plains and the river, looks west; the citadel, which is situated on the hill, faces east. The river Aretho, rising in Athamania, empties into the gulf of the sea which is called "the Ambracian" from the name of the neighbouring city. In addition to the fact that the river on one side and the hills on the other defended the city, it was also protected by a strong wall, extending in circumference a little more than four miles. Fulvius established two camps on the side of the plain, separated from one another by a moderate distance, and one redoubt on a high spot facing the citadel; all these he planned so to connect by means of a wall and ditch that no

[2] Ambracia had been the capital of Pyrrhus (cf. v. 2 and ix. 13 below), and had later become a member of the Aetolian League.

A.U.C. 585 parat, ne exitus inclusis ab urbe neve aditus foris ad
auxilia intromittenda esset. Ad famam oppugna-
tionis Ambraciae Stratum iam edicto Nicandri
7 praetoris convenerant[1] Aetoli. Inde primo copiis
omnibus ad prohibendam obsidionem venire in animo
fuerat; dein, postquam urbem iam magna ex parte
operibus saeptam viderunt, Epirotarum trans flumen
loco plano castra posita esse, dividere copias placuit.
8 Cum mille expeditis Eupolemus Ambraciam profectus
per nondum commissa inter se munimenta urbem
9 intravit. Nicandro cum cetera manu primo Epirotarum castra nocte aggredi consilium fuerat haud
facili ab Romanis auxilio, quia flumen intererat;
10 dein, periculosum inceptum ratus, ne qua sentirent
Romani et regressus[2] inde in tuto non esset, deter-
ritus ab hoc consilio ad depopulandam Acarnaniam
iter convertit.

V. Consul iam munimentis quibus saepienda[3]
urbs erat, iam operibus, quae admovere muris
parabat, perfectis quinque simul locis moenia est
2 aggressus. Tria paribus intervallis, faciliore[4] aditu
a campo, adversus Pyrrheum quod vocant admovit,
unum e regione Aesculapii, unum adversus arcem.
3 Arietibus muros quatiebat; asseribus falcatis de-
tergebat pinnas. Oppidanos primo et ad speciem

[1] conuenerant ς: conuenerunt *B*.
[2] regressus ς: praegressus *B*.
[3] saepienda ς: *om.* *B*.
[4] faciliore *edd. vett.*: faciliora *B*ς.

---

[1] Probably the palace of Pyrrhus: see the last note.
[2] The *falx muralis* of Caesar (*B.G.* III. xiv. 5). This detail, like those which follow, is derived directly from Polybius (XXII. x).

egress from the city might be allowed the besieged nor ingress from without to a relieving force. At the report of the siege of Ambracia the Aetolians had already assembled at Stratus in response to the edict of the praetor Nicander. It had been their first intention to march from there with their entire force to prevent the siege; then, when they saw that the city was already in large part hemmed in by siege-works, and that the camp of the Epirotes lay on level ground across the river, they decided to divide their forces. Eupolemus with a thousand light-armed troops, setting out for Ambracia, entered the city through the fortifications which had not yet been joined together. It had been the original plan that Nicander, with the rest of the troops, should make a night attack on the camp of the Epirotes, which could not readily be aided by the Romans because the river was between them; later, thinking that there was in the enterprise the danger that the Romans might somehow learn of it and he have no escape to a place of safety, he abandoned that design and turned aside to plunder Acarnania. B.C. 189

V. The consul had by now completed the fortifications by which the town had to be surrounded as well as the siege-engines which he was making ready to move up to the walls, and attacked the ramparts in five places at once. Three of the assaults, equidistant from one another, the approach from the plain being easier, he directed against what they call the "Pyrrheum,"[1] one on the side of the temple of Aesculapius, one against the citadel. He was shaking the walls with battering-rams; he was pulling down the parapets with hooks fixed on poles.[2] The citizens were at first stricken with terror

A.U.C. 565 et ad ictus moenium cum terribili sonitu editos[1]
4 pavor ac trepidatio cepit; deinde, ut praeter spem
stare muros viderunt, collectis rursus animis in arietes
tollenonibus libramenta[2] plumbi aut saxorum stipi-
tesve[3] robustos incutiebant; falces ancoris ferreis
iniectis in interiorem partem muri trahentes asserem
5 praefringebant; ad hoc eruptionibus et[4] nocturnis
in custodias operum et diurnis in stationes ultro
terrorem inferebant.

6 In hoc statu res ad Ambraciam cum essent, iam
Aetoli a populatione Acarnaniae Stratum redierant.[5]
Inde Nicander praetor spem nactus solvendae[6] incepto
forti obsidionis, Nicodamum quendam cum Aetolis
7 quingentis Ambraciam intromittit. Noctem certam
tempusque etiam noctis constituit, quo et illi ab urbe
opera hostium[7] quae adversus Pyrrheum erant
aggrederentur, et ipse ad castra Romana terrorem
faceret, posse ratus ancipiti tumultu et nocte augente
8 pavorem memorabilem rem geri. Et Nicodamus
intempesta nocte, cum alias custodias fefellisset,
per[8] alias impetu constanti perrupisset,[9] superato
brachio in urbem penetrat, animique aliquantum[10]
ad omnia audenda et spei obsessis adiecit et, simul
constituta nox venit, ex composito repente opera
9 est aggressus. Id inceptum conatu quam effectu

[1] editos *edd. vett.* : editus *B*ς.
[2] libramenta ς : libramento *B*.
[3] stipitesue ς : stipites *B*.
[4] et *ed. Frobeniana* 1535 : *om. B*ς.
[5] redierant ς : redierunt *B*.
[6] soluendae ς : *om. B*.
[7] hostium ς : *om. B*.
[8] per ς : et per *B*.
[9] perrupisset *Crévier* : erupisset et *B* : erupisset ς.
[10] aliquantum ς : aliquantulum *B*.

and confusion both at the sight and at the blows which struck the walls with fearful din; then, when they saw the walls still standing, contrary to expectations, they recovered their courage and with the aid of cranes they dropped on the rams masses of lead or stone or stout logs; seizing the wall-hooks with grappling-irons they pulled them inside the walls and broke off the poles; besides, by sallies conducted both by night against the guards of the engines and by day against the outposts they did their part in spreading terror. B.C. 189

While matters before Ambracia were in this state, the Aetolians had now returned to Stratus from the devastation of Acarnania. Then the praetor Nicander, conceiving the hope of raising the siege by a bold stroke, sent a certain Nicodamus with five hundred Aetolians into Ambracia. He appointed a certain night and even an hour of the night when both the troops from the city should attack the enemy's siege-works which faced the Pyrrheum and he himself should cause a panic in the Roman camp, thinking that something memorable could be accomplished by an attack from two directions and with night adding to the terror. And Nicodamus, at dead of night, after eluding some pickets and forcing his way past others by a resolute attack, crossed one branch of the wall[1] and entered the town thereby inspiring in the besieged no small degree of courage for any deed of daring and of hope, and as soon as the appointed night arrived, according to the agreement, he suddenly attacked the siege-works. This venture was more serious in its purpose than in

[1] This was probably a low rampart connecting two of the Roman strong points.

A.U.C. 565

gravius fuit, quia nulla ab exteriore parte vis admota
10 est,[1] seu metu deterrito praetore Aetolorum, seu quia potius visum est Amphilochis nuper receptis ferre opem, quos Perseus, Philippi filius, missus ad Dolopiam Amphilochosque recipiendos,[2] summa vi oppugnabat.

VI. Tribus locis, sicut ante dictum est, ad Pyrrheum
opera Romana erant, quae omnia simul, sed nec
2 apparatu nec vi simili, Aetoli aggressi sunt: alii
cum ardentibus facibus, alii stuppam picemque et
malleolos ferentes, tota collucente flammis acie,
3 advenere. Multos primo impetu custodes oppresserunt; dein, postquam clamor tumultusque in castra
est perlatus datumque a consule signum, arma
capiunt et omnibus portis ad opem ferendam effun-
4 duntur. Ferro ignique gesta res; ab duobus irrito
incepto, cum temptassent magis quam inissent certamen, Aetoli abscesserunt; atrox pugna[3] in unum
5 inclinaverat locum. Ibi diversis partibus duo duces
Eupolemus et Nicodamus pugnantes hortabantur
et prope certa fovebant spe iam Nicandrum ex com-
6 posito adfore et terga hostium invasurum. Haec res
aliquamdiu animos pugnantium sustinuit; ceterum,
postquam nullum ex composito signum a suis accipiebant et crescere numerum hostium cernebant, desti-
7 tuti[4] segnius instare; postremo re omissa iam vix
tuto receptu fugientes in urbem compelluntur,

[1] est ς: *om. B.*
[2] recipiendos ς: *om. B.*
[3] pugna ς: *om. B.*
[4] destituti ς: destitutis *B.*

its result, since no attack was made from outside, B.C. 189 whether because the Aetolian praetor was prevented by fear or because it seemed better to assist the Amphilochians who had just been recovered and whom Perseus, the son of Philip, sent to regain control of Dolopia and the Amphilochians, was attacking with the greatest vigour.

VI. There were Roman works, as has been said before, in three places facing the Pyrrheum, all of which the Aetolians attacked at once, but not with the same equipment or violence: some advanced with flaming torches, others carrying tow and pitch and firebrands, the whole battle-line gleaming with flames. They cut down many of the guards at the first attack; then, when the shouting and the din were heard in the camp and the signal was given by the consul, the Romans seized their arms and from all the gates hastened to the rescue. The battle raged with steel and fire; in two places the Aetolians retired without accomplishing anything, after trying rather than actually beginning an engagement; the severe fighting had concentrated in one place. There in different quarters the two captains Eupolemus and Nicodamus were urging on the fighters and encouraging them with the almost certain hope that Nicander would soon be there according to agreement and would take the enemy in the rear. This assurance kept up for a considerable time the spirits of the fighters; but when they received no signal from their comrades according to the agreement and they perceived that the number of the enemy was increasing, being thus left unsupported, they pressed on less vigorously; finally, abandoning their effort, their retreat being by now scarcely safe, they were driven back into the city

A.U.C. 565 parte operum incensa et pluribus aliquanto, quam ab
ipsis[1] ceciderant, interfectis. Quodsi ex composito
acta res fuisset, haud dubium erat expugnari una
utique parte opera cum magna caede hostium
8 potuisse. Ambracienses quique intus erant Aetoli
non ab eius solum noctis incepto recessere, sed
in reliquum quoque tempus velut proditi ab suis
9 segniores ad pericula erant. Iam nemo eruptionibus,
ut ante, in stationes hostium, sed dispositi per muros
et turres ex tuto pugnabant.

VII. Perseus ubi adesse[2] Aetolos audivit, omissa
obsidione urbis, quam oppugnabat, depopulatus tantum agros Amphilochia excessit atque in Mace-
2 doniam redit. Et Aetolos inde avocavit populatio
maritimae orae. Pleuratus, Illyriorum rex, cum
sexaginta lembis Corinthium sinum invectus adiunctis
Achaeorum quae Patris erant navibus maritima
3 Aetoliae vastabat.[3] Adversus quos mille Aetoli missi,
quacumque se classis circumegerat per litorum am-
4 fractus, brevioribus semitis occurrebant. Et Romani
ad Ambraciam pluribus locis quatiendo arietibus
muros aliquantum urbis nudaverant, nec tamen
5 penetrare in urbem poterant; nam et pari celeritate
novus pro diruto murus obiciebatur, et armati ruinis
6 superstantes instar munimenti erant. Itaque cum

[1] ab ipsis *M. Mueller* : ipsis *Bς*.
[2] adesse ς : *om. B.*
[3] uastabat ς : uastabant *B.*

---

[1] This use of *ab ipsis* (which is itself an emendation) is somewhat unusual, but the interpretation here given seems to be required.
[2] Cf. XXXIII. xxxiv. 11.

in flight, after they had burned part of the siege-works B.C. 189
and killed a considerably larger number of the enemy than they had themselves lost.[1] But if the plan had been carried out according to the agreement there was no doubt that in one place at least the works could have been taken with heavy loss to the enemy. The Ambraciots and the Aetolians who were inside the city not only gave up their attempt for that night, but for the future too, feeling that they had been deserted by their friends, they were more reluctant to face dangers. Henceforth no one took part in sallies, as before, against the outguards of the enemy, but posting themselves along the walls and towers they fought in safety.

VII. When Perseus learned that the Aetolians were approaching, he abandoned the siege of the city he was investing and, merely plundering the fields, withdrew from Amphilochia and returned to Macedonia. The Aetolians too were called away from there by the devastation of their sea-coast. Pleuratus,[2] the king of the Illyrians, sailed into the Corinthian gulf with sixty cruisers and joining the ships of the Achaeans which were at Patrae was laying waste the coast districts of Aetolia. A thousand Aetolians sent against them, wherever the fleet went, following the indentations of the shore-line, would travel by shorter routes and meet them. Also the Romans before Ambracia, by battering at the walls with rams, had to a great extent laid bare the town, but nevertheless could not force their way into it; for with equal speed a new wall was thrown up to replace what had been destroyed and armed men, standing on the ruins, served as a fortification. Accordingly, since visibly applied force was not

A.U.C. 565 aperta vi parum procederet consuli res, cuniculum
occultum vineis ante contecto[1] loco agere instituit;[2]
et aliquamdiu, cum[3] dies noctesque in opere essent,
non solum sub terra fodientes sed egerentes etiam
7 humum fefellere hostem. Cumulus repente terrae
eminens index operis oppidanis fuit, pavidique ne
iam subrutis muris facta in urbem via esset, fossam
intra murum e regione eius operis quod vineis con-
8 tectum erat ducere instituunt. Cuius ubi ad tantam
altitudinem quantae esse solum infimum cuniculi
poterat pervenerunt, silentio facto[4] pluribus locis
9 aure admota sonitum fodientium captabant. Quem
ubi acceperunt, aperiunt rectam in cuniculum viam,
nec fuit magni operis; momento enim ad inane[5]
suspenso fulturis[6] ab hostibus muro pervenerunt.
10 Ibi commissis operibus, cum e fossa in cuniculum
pateret iter, primo ipsis ferramentis, quibus in opere
usi erant, deinde celeriter armati etiam subeuntes
occultam sub terra ediderunt pugnam; segnior deinde
ea facta est intersaepientibus cuniculum, ubi vellent,
nunc ciliciis praetentis nunc foribus raptim obiectis.
11 Nova etiam haud magni operis adversus eos qui in
cuniculo erant excogitata res. Dolium a fundo

[1] contecto ς: collecto *B*.
[2] instituit ς: statuit *B*.
[3] cum ς: *om. B*.
[4] facto ς: *om. B*.
[5] inane ς: inanem *B*.
[6] fulturis *ed. Frobeniana* 1535: furculis *B*ς.

---

[1] The apparent meaning is that the trench of the defenders ran at right angles to the assumed direction of the tunnel. Polybius (XXII. xi) describes the trench as parallel to the city-wall.

progressing well for the consul, he determined to dig B.C. 189
secretly a tunnel in a place formerly covered by his sheds, and for a considerable period, although the work was in progress day and night, not only the men digging beneath the ground but also those who were carrying out the earth went unnoticed by the enemy. Suddenly a rising mound of earth betrayed the work to the townspeople, and, fearing that the walls had already been undermined and a way opened into the city, they began to dig a ditch inside the wall in the direction of that work which had been covered by the sheds.[1] When they came to a depth as great as the bottom of the tunnel could have, they remained silent, and placing their ears against the walls in several places they listened for the sound of the diggers. When they heard this they opened a way straight into the tunnel, nor was this a difficult task; for in a moment they came into the open space where the enemy was supporting the roof on props. The works joining there, as the way was open from the trench to the tunnel, they began to fight, at first with the same tools which they had used in the work, then quickly armed men too came up and engaged in a hidden battle underground; later this fighting became more desultory, since they blocked the tunnel wherever they wished, now with curtains[2] stretched across, now with hastily constructed doors.[3] A new device as well, and one easy of execution, was thought out against the Romans who were in the tunnel. They prepared a cask pierced at the

[2] Literally, garments made of the hair of goats.

[3] Polybius (*l.c.*) says that both sides protected themselves with shields (θυρέους), and it has been suggested that Livy confused this word with θύρας, "doors."

A.U.C. 565 pertusum, qua[1] fistula modica inseri posset, et
ferream fistulam operculumque dolii[2] ferreum, et
ipsum pluribus locis perforatum, fecerunt. Hoc
tenui pluma completum dolium ore in cuniculum
12 verso posuerunt. Per operculi foramina praelongae
hastae, quas sarisas vocant, ad summovendos hostes
eminebant. Scintillam levem ignis inditam plumae
folle fabrili ad caput fistulae imposito flando accende-
13 runt. Inde non solum magna vis fumi sed acrior
etiam foedo quodam odore ex adusta pluma cum
totum cuniculum complesset, vix durare quisquam
intus poterat.

VIII. Cum in hoc statu ad Ambraciam res esset,
legati ab Aetolis Phaeneas et Damoteles cum liberis
mandatis decreto gentis ad consulem venerunt.
Nam praetor eorum, cum alia parte Ambraciam
2 oppugnari cerneret, alia infestam oram navibus
hostium esse, alia Amphilochos Dolopiamque[3] a
Macedonibus vastari, nec Aetolos ad tria simul
diversa bella occursantes sufficere, convocato concilio
Aetoliae principes quid agendum esset consuluit.
3 Omnium eo sententiae decurrerunt, ut pax si posset
aequis,[4] si minus tolerandis condicionibus peteretur;
4 Antiochi fiducia bellum susceptum; Antiocho terra
marique superato et prope extra orbem terrae ultra

[1] qua ς : quasi *B*. [2] dolii ς : dolium *B*.
[3] Dolopiamque *edd. vett.* : dolophiam *B* : dolopiam ς.
[4] aequis ς : aequius *B*.

[1] Livy for some reason omits certain picturesque details given by Polybius (*l.c.*), but otherwise follows him closely. Smoking out an enemy in mine-warfare was a recognized device (Aeneas Tacticus 37), but we need not consider this an example of the early use of chemicals for military purposes: cf. Lamer's review of Vatter, "Giftgase und Gasschutz" (Stuttgart, 1934), in *Phil. Woch.* 55, 1935, 202–204.

bottom, where a pipe of moderate size could be inserted, and likewise an iron pipe and an iron lid for the cask, this lid too being perforated in several places. This cask, filled with light feathers, they placed with its mouth facing the tunnel. They fixed in the holes in the lid the very long spears which they call "sarisae," so as to keep the enemy at a distance. A light spark of flame, placed among the feathers, they fanned by blowing with a smith's bellows placed at the mouth of the pipe. Then, since smoke, not merely abundant in quantity, but, even more, unendurable by reason of the vile stench from the burning feathers, had filled the whole tunnel, scarcely anyone was able to remain within it.[1] B.C. 189

VIII. While affairs were in this condition at Ambracia,[2] Phaeneas and Damoteles came to the consul as ambassadors from the Aetolians, with full power to act, by decree of the people. For their praetor, when he saw that on one side Ambracia was undergoing siege, that on another the sea-coast was endangered by the enemy's ships, that on a third the Amphilochians and Dolopia were being plundered by the Macedonians, and that the Aetolians, rushing here and there to three different wars at the same time, could not hold out, called a council and laid before the chiefs of Aetolia the question of what should be done. The opinions of all tended in this direction—that peace should be sought, on fair terms if possible, if not, on endurable terms: they argued that they had begun the war because of their reliance on Antiochus; when Antiochus was beaten on land and sea and driven virtually beyond the bounds of the

[2] The embassy mentioned in XXXVII. xlix (cf. iii. 6 above) is ignored in the following account.

A.U.C. 565

iuga Tauri exacto quam spem esse sustinendi belli?
5 Phaeneas et Damoteles quod e re[1] Aetolorum, ut
in tali casu, fideque sua esse censerent, agerent;
quod enim sibi consilium aut cuius rei electionem a
6 fortuna relictam? Cum his mandatis legati missi
orare consulem ut parceret urbi, misereretur gentis
quondam sociae, nolle dicere iniuriis, miseriis certe
7 coactae insanire; non plus mali meritos Aetolos
Antiochi bello quam boni ante, cum adversus
Philippum bellatum sit, fecisse; nec tum large
gratiam relatam sibi, nec nunc immodice poenam
iniungi debere. Ad ea consul respondit magis saepe
quam vere umquam[2] Aetolos pacem petere. Imi-
tarentur Antiochum in petenda pace, quem in bellum
8 traxissent; non paucis urbibus eum, de quarum
libertate certatum sit, sed omni Asia cis Taurum
9 montem, opimo regno, excessisse.[3] Aetolos nisi
10 inermes de pace agentes non auditurum se; arma
illis prius equosque omnes tradendos esse, deinde
mille talentum argenti[4] populo Romano dandum,
cuius summae dimidium praesens numeretur, si
pacem habere vellent. Ad ea adiecturum etiam
in foedus esse ut eosdem quos populus Romanus
amicos atque hostes habeant.

[1] e re ς: de re *B*. [2] uere umquam ς: *om. B*.
[3] excessisse ς: excepisse *B*. [4] argenti ς: *om. B*.

[1] It should be noted that this discussion makes no progress towards peace. It was one of the stock grievances of the Aetolians that their services against Philip had been inadequately recognized and rewarded, and this position they still maintain. The final demands of Fulvius are repetitions of those made by Rome in the futile negotiations of 190 B.C. (XXXVII. i. 5), although nothing had been said before about Aetolian disarmament as a condition of peace.

earth, to the other side of the ridges of Taurus, what hope was there of continuing the war? Phaeneas and Damoteles, they said, should do what they judged consistent with the best interests of the Aetolians, considering the straits they were in, and with their own sense of loyalty; for what plan that they could adopt or what choice of action was left them by fortune? The envoys, sent with these instructions, begged the consul to spare the city and to have compassion on a people, once his ally, now driven to the point of madness, they would not say by their wrongs but at least by their misfortunes; the Aetolians had not deserved to suffer any ill fortune, by reason of the war with Antiochus, outweighing the good service which they had rendered previously when they had fought against Philip; neither had liberal gratitude been shown them then nor should excessive punishment be imposed upon them now. To this the consul replied that the Aetolians ever sought peace frequently rather than sincerely. In their plea for peace they should follow the example of Antiochus, whom they had enticed into the war; he had withdrawn not from a few towns about whose liberty there was a question, but from the whole rich land of Asia on this side of the Taurus mountains. He would not, he said, listen to the Aetolians treating for peace unless they were disarmed; they must first turn over their weapons and all their horses, then pay a thousand talents of silver to the Roman people, of which sum half must be paid at once if they wanted to have peace. He would, besides, add this clause to the treaty—that they should regard as friends and enemies the same persons whom the Romans so regarded.[1] B.C. 189

A.U.C. 565

IX. Adversus quae legati, et quia gravia erant, et quia suorum animos indomitos ac mutabiles noverant, nullo reddito responso domum regressi sunt, ut etiam atque etiam quid agendum esset re integra praetorem
2 et principes consulerent. Clamore et iurgio excepti, quam diu rem traherent, qualemcumque pacem referre iussi, cum redirent Ambraciam, Acarnanum insidiis prope viam positis, cum quibus bellum erat, circumventi Thyrreum custodiendi deducuntur.
3 Haec mora iniecta est paci, cum iam Atheniensium Rhodiorumque legati, qui ad deprecandum pro iis
4 venerant, apud consulem essent. Amynander quoque Athamanum rex fide accepta venerat in castra Romana, magis pro Ambracia urbe, ubi maiorem partem temporis exulaverat, quam pro Aetolis
5 sollicitus. Per hos certior factus consul de casu legatorum adduci eos a Thyrreo iussit; quorum
6 post adventum agi coeptum est de pace. Amynander, quod sui maxime operis erat, impigre agebat,
7 ut Ambracienses compelleret ad deditionem. Ad id[1] cum per colloquia principum succedens murum parum proficeret, postremo consulis permissu[2] ingressus urbem partim consilio partim precibus evicit,
8 ut permitterent se Romanis. Et Aetolos C. Valerius, Laevini filius, qui cum ea gente primum amicitiam pepigerat, consulis frater matre eadem genitus,

[1] Ad id *M. Mueller* : id *B*ς.
[2] permissu ς : promissu *B*.

[1] Cf. XXXI. iii. 3, etc.; for the treaty of 211 B.C., XXVI. xxiv. 8.

IX. To these proposals, both because they were severe and because the ambassadors knew that the tempers of their people were fierce and changeable, they made no reply but returned home, that they might again and again consult the praetor and the chiefs as to what was to be done while they were still uncommitted to a decision. They were received with abusive shouts, being asked how long they would drag things out, and were ordered to bring back any sort of peace whatsoever, but when they were returning to Ambracia they were caught in an ambush set beside the road by the Acarnanians, with whom they were at war, and were taken to Thyrreum for confinement. This caused a delay to the peace, although ambassadors of the Athenians and the Rhodians, who had come to intercede for them, were now with the consul. Amynander also, the king of the Athamanians, had come to the Roman camp under a safeguard, more concerned for the city of Ambracia, where he had spent the greater part of his exile, than for the Aetolians. Being informed by them of the misfortune of the ambassadors, the consul ordered them to be brought from Thyrreum; after their arrival the discussion of peace began. Amynander, since this was his particular mission, laboured earnestly to induce the Ambraciots to surrender. When he met with little success in this, approaching the walls and conferring with the chiefs, finally, by permission of the consul, he entered the city, and partly by advice and partly by entreaty he prevailed upon them to entrust themselves to the Romans. The Aetolians too received notable assistance from Gaius Valerius, son of the Laevinus,[1] who had concluded the first treaty of friendship with that people, Gaius being the brother of the consul and B.C. 189

A.U.C. 565

9 egregie adiuvit. Ambracienses prius pacti, ut
Aetolorum auxiliares sine fraude emitterent, aperu-
erunt portas. Dein Aetolis condiciones pacis dictae:[1]
quingenta Euboica ut darent talenta, ex quibus
ducenta praesentia, trecenta per annos sex pensionibus aequis; captivos perfugasque redderent Ro-
10 manis; urbem ne quam formulae sui iuris facerent,
quae post id tempus, quo T. Quinctius traiecisset in
Graeciam, aut vi capta ab Romanis esset[2] aut voluntate in amicitiam venisset; Cephallania insula ut
11 extra ius foederis esset. Haec quamquam spe
ipsorum aliquanto leviora erant, petentibus Aetolis
12 ut ad concilium referrent, permissum est. Parva
disceptatio de urbibus tenuit, quae cum sui iuris
aliquando fuissent, avelli velut a corpore suo aegre
patiebantur; ad unum omnes tamen accipi pacem
13 iusserunt. Ambracienses coronam auream consuli
centum et quinquaginta pondo dederunt. Signa
aenea marmoraeque et tabulae pictae, quibus
ornatior Ambracia, quia regia ibi Pyrrhi fuerat,[3]

[1] Dein Aetolis condiciones pacis dictae *H. J. Mueller*: dein *B*ς.

[2] esset ς: *om. B.*

[3] fuerat ς: fuerant *B.*

---

[1] Her name is unknown. She had apparently married Laevinus after the death of the elder Fulvius, since Polybius (XXII. xii) speaks of Gaius as a young man. Cf. Münzer, *Röm. Adelsparteien* (Stuttgart, 1920), 210.

[2] Cf. XXXVII. xlv. 14 and the note.

[3] This island, like Zacynthos (XXXVI. xxxi–xxxii), now had a strategic value for the Romans, and, since it did not

born of the same mother.[1] The Ambraciots, having B.C. 189 first bargained that the Aetolian auxiliaries should be released in safety, opened their gates. Then terms of peace were given to the Aetolians: they were to pay five hundred Euboean [2] talents, two hundred of these at once and three hundred in equal instalments through six years; they were to restore the prisoners and deserters to the Romans; they were to bring under their jurisdiction no city which since the time when Titus Quinctius had crossed to Greece had either been captured by force by the Romans or had voluntarily entered into friendship with them; the island of Cephallania [3] was to be outside the scope of the treaty.[4] Although these terms were much lighter than they had anticipated, the request of the Aetolians that they should submit them to their council was granted. There was a brief dispute about the cities, since they took it hard that towns which had once been under their control should be torn, as it were, from their body, yet all unanimously agreed that the peace should be accepted. The Ambraciots presented the consul with a golden crown of one hundred and fifty pounds' weight.[5] The bronze and marble statues and the paintings with which Ambracia was more lavishly adorned than the other cities of this region, because the palace of Pyrrhus had been

come under either class of communities just mentioned, is excepted. It had belonged to Aetolia.

[4] These conditions are essentially those given by Polybius (XXII. xiii).

[5] Polybius (*l.c.*) says practically the same thing, although he seems to use στέφανος to mean any sort of complimentary present. In XXXIX. v. 14 Livy says that Fulvius displayed in his triumph golden crowns weighing one hundred and twelve pounds.

A.U.C. 565 quam ceterae regionis eius urbes erant, sublata omnia
14 avectaque; nihil praeterea tactum violatumve.

X. Profectus ab Ambracia consul in mediterranea Aetoliae ad Argos Amphilochium—viginti duo milia ab Ambracia abest[1]—castra posuit. Eo tandem legati Aetoli, mirante consule quod morarentur,[2]
2 venerunt. Inde, postquam approbasse pacem concilium Aetolorum accepit, iussis proficisci Romam ad senatum permissoque ut et Rhodii et Athenienses deprecatores irent dato, qui simul cum iis proficisceretur, C. Valerio fratre ipse in Cephallaniam
3 traiecit. Praeoccupatas aures animosque principum Romae criminibus Philippi invenerunt, qui per legatos, per litteras Dolopas Amphilochosque et Athamaniam erepta[3] sibi querens, praesidiaque sua postremo filium etiam Persea ex Amphilochis pulsum, averterat senatum ab audiendis precibus eorum.
4 Rhodii tamen et Athenienses cum silentio auditi sunt. Atheniensis legatus Leon Hicesiae filius
5 eloquentia etiam dicitur movisse; qui vulgata similitudine, mari tranquillo quod ventis concitaretur aequiperando multitudinem Aetolorum, usus, cum in fide Romanae societatis mansissent, insita gentis
6 tranquillitate quiesse eos aiebat; postquam flare ab Asia Thoas et Dicaearchus, ab Europa Menestas et Damocritus coepissent, tum illam tempestatem

[1] abest *ed. Frobeniana* 1531 : est *B*ς.
[2] morarentur ς : moraretur *B*.
[3] erepta ς : ereptas *B*.

---

[1] Fulvius was later severely criticized for his treatment of Ambracia: cf. xliii. 5 below, and his defence in XXXIX. iv. 11–12. Polybius does not mention this, and Livy may

there, were all removed and carried away; nothing else was touched or harmed.[1] B.C. 189

X. Leaving Ambracia for the interior of Aetolia, the consul encamped near Amphilochian Argos, it being twenty-two miles from Ambracia. There finally the Aetolian ambassadors came while the consul was wondering why they were delaying. Then, when he learned that the council of the Aetolians had approved the peace, having ordered them to go to the senate in Rome and having given permission to both the Rhodians and the Athenians to go with them as intercessors, and appointed his brother Gaius Valerius to accompany them, he himself crossed to Cephallania. The ambassadors found that the ears and minds of the leading men at Rome had already been filled by the allegations of Philip, who, through envoys, through letters, complaining that the Dolopians, the Amphilochians and Athamania had been snatched from him and that his garrisons and finally even his son Perseus had been driven off from the Amphilochians, had made the senate disinclined to hear their petitions. Nevertheless, the Rhodians and the Athenians were listened to in silence. The Athenian ambassador Leon, the son of Hicesias, is said to have created something of an impression by his eloquence; employing the familiar simile of a calm sea which is disturbed by the winds, likening to it the Aetolian populace, he said that as long as they had remained faithful to the Roman alliance they had been quiet with the natural calmness of the race; after Thoas and Dicaearchus began to blow from Asia and Menestas and Damocritus from Europe, then

have inferred it from the later debate as to the triumph of Fulvius.

A.U.C. 565 coortam, quae ad Antiochum eos sicuti in scopulum intulisset.

XI. Diu iactati Aetoli tandem, ut[1] condiciones pacis
2 convenirent, effecerunt. Fuerunt autem hae.[2] "Imperium maiestatemque populi Romani gens Aetolorum conservato sine dolo malo; ne quem exercitum, qui adversus socios amicosque eorum ducetur, per
3 fines suos transire sinito, neve ulla ope iuvato; hostes eosdem habeto quos populus Romanus, armaque
4 in eos ferto, bellumque pariter gerito; perfugas fugitivos captivos reddito Romanis sociisque, praeterquam si qui capti, cum domos redissent, iterum capti sunt, aut si qui eo tempore ex iis capti sunt qui tum hostes erant Romanis, cum intra praesidia Romana
5 Aetoli essent; aliorum qui comparebunt intra dies centum Corcyraeorum magistratibus sine dolo malo tradantur; qui non comparebunt, quando quisque
6 eorum primum inventus erit, reddatur; obsides quad-

[1] ut *ed. Frobeniana* 1535 : ut ad *B*ς.
[2] hae ς : haec *B*.

---

[1] Polybius (XXII. xiv) quotes this speech at greater length and with more direct application. However, he credits the speech to Damis, and a philosopher of that name is said to have been at some time a resident of Athens. The corruption in the text of Polybius at this point probably makes it impossible to explain the variation in names between Livy and Polybius.

The mischief-makers named were mainly responsible, according to both Livy and Polybius, for the Aetolian alliance with Antiochus: cf. the Index to Volume X.

[2] The terms here given are in essence those given by Polybius (XXII. xv). The formal beginning appears to be that regularly employed in *foedera non aequa*, *i.e.* treaties between a politically superior and a politically inferior state. It is thus interpreted by Cicero (*Balb.* 35).

that storm had arisen which had dashed them upon Antiochus as upon a rock.[1] B.C. 189

XI. After long agitation the Aetolians finally succeeded in obtaining an agreement on the terms of peace. These were the conditions:[2] "The people of the Aetolians shall uphold the sovereignty and dignity of the Roman people without fraud;[3] they shall permit no army which is being led against the allies and friends of the Romans to cross their borders and shall aid such an army in no way; they shall regard as enemies the same persons whom the Romans so regard, shall take up arms against them and make war upon them in company with the Romans; they shall restore deserters, runaways and captives to the Romans and their allies, except such prisoners as were captured a second time after they had returned to their homes, or such as were captured from those who were enemies to the Romans at that time when the Aetolians were associated with the Roman forces,[4] and any of the others who shall be discovered within one hundred days to the magistrates[5] of the Corcyraeans without fraud; those who shall not be discovered shall be turned over as soon as each of them is found; they shall deliver

[3] *Dolus malus* is technical and legal; its implication is the intent to injure or deceive another.

[4] The second class of exceptions apparently includes citizens of Rome and allied states who were in arms against their native cities during the period of the active Aetolian alliance with Rome in the Second Macedonian War. But neither the meaning nor the purpose of the clause is entirely clear.

[5] Polybius (*l.c.*) says merely τῷ ἄρχοντι, meaning, probably, a Roman prefect in Corcyra. Livy seems to misunderstand, and there seems to be no point in the demand that these persons be handed over to native magistrates in Corcyra.

A.U.C. 565 raginta arbitratu consulis Romanis dato[1] ne minores
7 duodecim annorum neu maiores quadraginta, obses ne
esto praetor, praefectus equitum, scriba publicus, neu
quis qui ante obses fuit apud Romanos; Cephallania
8 extra pacis leges esto." De pecuniae summa quam
penderent pensionibusque eius nihil ex eo, quod cum
consule convenerat, mutatum; pro argento si aurum
dare mallent, darent,[2] convenit, dum pro argenteis
9 decem aureus unus valeret. "Quae urbes, qui agri,
qui homines Aetolorum iuris aliquando fuerunt, qui
eorum T. Quinctio Cn. Domitio consulibus postve
eos consules aut armis subacti aut voluntate in
dicionem populi Romani venerunt, ne quem[3] eorum
Aetoli recepisse velint; Oeniadae cum urbe agrisque[4]
Acarnanum sunto." His legibus foedus ictum cum
Aetolis est.

XII. Eadem non aestate solum, sed etiam iisdem
prope diebus quibus haec a M. Fulvio consule in
Aetolia gesta sunt, consul alter Cn. Manlius in Gallograecia bellum gessit, quod nunc ordiri pergam.
2 Vere primo Ephesum consul venit, acceptisque copiis
ab L. Scipione et exercitu lustrato contionem apud

[1] dato ς : dando *B*.

[2] darent ς : *om. B*.

[3] ne quem *ed. Frobeniana* 1535 : neque *B*ς.

[4] recepisse velint; Oeniadae cum urbe agrisque *ed. Frobeniana* 1535 : recepissent uel in aetolia x urbes agrosque (*sic*) *B*ς.

---

[1] Polybius (*l.c.*) states the equivalence in terms of *minae*, preserving the ratio of 10 : 1, and adds certain details as to the financial settlement.

[2] Livy and Polybius (*l.c.*) agree on these names, but one or the other name is nevertheless wrong. The colleague of T. Flamininus in the consulship was Sex. Aelius Paetus

to the Romans forty hostages, acceptable to the consul, none younger than twelve years nor older than forty, provided that no hostage shall be a praetor, a commander of cavalry, a public secretary, or one who has previously been a hostage at Rome; Cephallania shall be excepted from the terms of peace." Regarding the sum of money which they were to pay and the instalments thereof, no change was made in the conditions proposed by the consul; "if in place of silver they propose to pay gold, let them do so," it was agreed, "provided that one gold piece shall be the equivalent of ten pieces of silver.[1] Whatever cities, whatever districts, whatever persons have at any time been under the jurisdiction of the Aetolians and have, in the consulship of Titus Quinctius and Gnaeus Domitius or after that consulship,[2] either been conquered by arms or submitted voluntarily to the control of the Roman people, none of these shall the Aetolians essay to recover; the Oeniadae with their city and lands shall belong to the Acarnanians." On these conditions the treaty with the Aetolians was concluded. B.C. 189

XII. Not merely in the same summer, but even practically during the same days when Marcus Fulvius the consul was thus engaged in Aetolia, the other consul Gnaeus Manlius in Gallograecia waged the war which I shall now proceed to describe. The consul arrived in Ephesus in the beginning of spring, and, having taken over the troops from Lucius Scipio

(XXXII. viii. 1), while Domitius was consul in 192 B.C. with L. Flamininus (XXXV. x. 10). Titus was named in the corresponding section of the consul's proposals (ix. 10 above), but it is possible that the senate made this particular condition easier by changing the date from 198 B.C. to 192 B.C.

A.U.C. 565
3 milites habuit, qua collaudata virtute eorum, quod
cum Antiocho uno proelio debellassent, adhortatus
eos ad[1] novum cum Gallis suscipiendum bellum,
4 qui et auxiliis iuvissent Antiochum et adeo[2] indo-
mita haberent ingenia ut nequiquam Antiochus
emotus[3] ultra iuga Tauri montis esset, nisi frange-
rentur opes Gallorum, de se quoque pauca, nec falsa
5 nec immodica, adiecit. Laeti milites cum frequenti
adsensu consulem audiverunt, partem virium Antiochi fuisse Gallos credentes; rege superato nullum
momentum in solis per se Gallorum copiis fore.
6 Eumenen haud in tempore abesse—Romae tum erat
—credere consul, gnarum locorum hominumque, et
7 cuius interesset frangi Gallorum opes. Attalum
igitur fratrem eius accersit a Pergamo, hortatusque
ad capessendum secum bellum pollicentem suam
suorumque operam domum ad comparandum di-
8 mittit. Paucos post dies profecto ab Epheso consuli ad Magnesiam occurrit Attalus cum mille peditibus equitibusque quingentis, Athenaeo fratre[4] iusso
cum ceteris copiis subsequi, commendata iis custodia
Pergami quos fratri regnoque fidos[5] credebat.
9 Consul collaudato iuvene cum omnibus copiis ad

[1] ad *ed. Frobeniana* 1531 : eum *B* : *om.* ς.
[2] adeo ς : ante *B*.
[3] emotus ς : semotus *B* : amotus *M*.
[4] athenaeo fratre ς : athene fratre eius *B*.
[5] fidos ς : eius fidos *B*.

---

[1] By sacrifice to possible hostile spirits; cf. XXXVI. xlii. 2, etc.

[2] The praetorship of Manlius in Sicily (XXXIII. xliii. 5) had been undistinguished, and it is not easy to see the basis for his eulogy of himself. He probably dwelt upon the exploits of earlier Manlii against Gauls, as he does in xvii. 8–9 below.

and purified[1] the army, he delivered a speech to the soldiers in which he gave great praise to their valour because they had ended the war with Antiochus by a single battle, and urged them to undertake a new war with the Gauls, who had not only aided Antiochus with auxiliaries but possessed spirits so untamable that the expulsion of Antiochus beyond the ridges of the Taurus mountains would be in vain unless the power of the Gauls were broken, while as regards himself also he added brief remarks, neither false nor exaggerated.[2] The joyous soldiers listened to the consul with great applause, believing that the Gauls had been only a part of the forces of Antiochus; after the defeat of the king there would be no strength in the Gauls alone and by themselves. The consul believed that Eumenes was away at an unsuitable time—he was then in Rome[3]—as he was familiar with the country and the people and as it was to his interest that the power of the Gauls should be broken.[4] Manlius therefore summoned Eumenes' brother Attalus from Pergamum and urged him to join in the prosecution of the war, and on receiving the promise of the co-operation of himself and his countrymen sent him home to make preparations. A few days later, when the consul left Ephesus for Magnesia, Attalus met him with a thousand infantry and five hundred cavalry, having directed his brother Athenaeus to follow with the rest of the army and having entrusted the guardianship of Pergamum to those men whom he deemed loyal to his brother and the throne. The consul, praising the young man, marched with the B.C. 189

[3] Cf. XXXVII. lii. 1.

[4] Pergamum and the Gauls were traditional enemies xvi. 14 below.

A.U.C. 565 Maeandrum progressus castra posuit, quia[1] vado
superari amnis non poterat et contrahendae naves
erant ad exercitum traiciendum. Transgressi Maeandrum ad Hieran[2] Comen pervenerunt.

XIII. Fanum ibi augustum Apollinis et oraculum;
sortes versibus haud inconditis dare vates dicuntur.[3]
2 Hinc alteris castris ad Harpasum flumen ventum est,
quo legati ab Alabandis venerunt, ut castellum, quod
ab ipsis nuper descisset, aut auctoritate aut armis[4]
3 cogeret iura antiqua pati. Eodem et Athenaeus,
Eumenis et Attali frater, cum Cretense Leuso[5]
et Corrago Macedone venit; mille pedites mix-
tarum gentium et trecentos equites secum adduxe-
4 runt. Consul tribuno militum misso cum modica
manu castellum[6] vi cepit, captum Alabandensibus
reddit.[7] Ipse nihil via degressus ad Antiochiam
5 super Maeandrum amnem posuit castra. Huius
amnis fontes Celaenis oriuntur. Celaenae urbs
caput quondam Phrygiae fuit; migratum inde haud
procul veteribus Celaenis, novaeque urbi Apameae
nomen inditum ab Apama sorore Seleuci regis.
6 Et Marsyas amnis, haud procul a Maeandri fontibus
oriens, in Maeandrum cadit, famaque ita tenet
Celaenis Marsyan cum Apolline tibiarum cantu
7 certasse. Maeander ex arce summa Celaenarum[8]

[1] quia ς : qua *B.*

[2] ad Hieran *ed. Frobeniana* 1531 : phileram *M* : ad ς : *om. B.*

[3] dicuntur ς : dicunt *B.*

[4] armis ς : *om. B.*

[5] Leuso *edd. vett.* : lento *B.*

[6] cum mod. ma. cas. ς : cas. cum mod. ma. *B.*

[7] reddit *ed. Frobeniana* 1535 : redit *B* : reddidit ς.

[8] celenarum ς : caele atrum *B.*

entire force to the Meander and encamped, because B.C. 189
the river could not be crossed by fording and boats had to be collected to ferry the army across. After crossing the Meander they advanced to Hiera Comê.

XIII. There was at this place a venerable shrine of Apollo and an oracle; the priests, it is said, give the responses in verses not without polish. On the second day's march from here they came to the Harpasus river, where ambassadors from Alabanda came with the request that he would compel, either by authority or by armed force, a stronghold which had recently revolted from them to accept its ancient status. There also came Athenaeus, the brother of Eumenes and Attalus, with Leusus the Cretan and Corragus the Macedonian; they brought with them a thousand infantry of different nationalities and three hundred cavalry. The consul, sending a tribune of the soldiers with a force of moderate size, took the stronghold by storm and having captured it turned it over to the people of Alabanda. He himself, not leaving the direct road, pitched camp at Antiochia on the Meander river. The sources of this river spring from Celaenae. The city of Celaenae was once the capital of Phrygia; thence there was a migration to a place not far from old Celaenae, and to the new town was given the name of Apamea, from Apama, the sister of King Seleucus.[1] The Marsyas river also, rising not far from the sources of the Meander, empties into the Meander, and the story runs thus, that at Celaenae Marsyas contended with Apollo in playing on the pipes.[2] The Meander, rising on top of the citadel of Celaenae and flowing through the centre

[1] Apama was actually the wife, not the sister, of Seleucus.
[2] Cf. the similar statements of Xenophon (*Anab.* I. ii. 7–8).

A.U.C. 565

ortus, media urbe decurrens, per Caras primum deinde
Ionas in sinum maris editur qui[1] inter Prienen et
8 Miletum est. Ad Antiochiam in castra consulis Seleucus, Antiochi filius,[2] ex foedere icto cum Scipione
9 ad frumentum exercitui dandum venit. Parva disceptatio de Attali auxiliaribus orta est, quod Romano tantum militi pactum Antiochum ut daretur frumen-
10 tum Seleucus dicebat.[3] Discussa ea quoque est constantia consulis, qui misso tribuno edixit ne Romani milites acciperent priusquam Attali auxilia
11 accepissent. Inde ad Gordiutichos quod vocant processum est. Ex eo loco ad Tabas tertiis castris perventum. In finibus Pisidarum posita urbs est, in ea parte quae vergit ad Pamphylium mare. Integris viribus[4] regionis eius feroces ad bellandum
12 habebat viros. Tum quoque equites in agmen Romanum eruptione facta haud modice[5] primo impetu turbavere; deinde ut apparuit nec numero se[6] nec virtute pares esse, in urbem[7] compulsi veniam
13 erroris petebant, dedere urbem parati. Quinque

[1] editur qui ς: edituri quod *B*.
[2] filius ς: frater *B*.
[3] Seleucus dicebat ς: ut seleucus ducebat *B*.
[4] uiribus ς: urbibus *B*.
[5] modice ς: modico *B*.
[6] se ς: *om. B*.
[7] in urbem ς: deinde *B*.

---

[1] The provisions of the treaty as given by Livy (XXXVII. xlv; cf. lv) say nothing of any such obligation, nor does Polybius mention it. In xxxvii. 7 below Livy again speaks of grain (and now money) owed under the treaty. It may have been taken for granted that Antiochus owed supplies to the Romans until the treaty was formally ratified.

[2] Many of the place-names in the following sections are doubtful, some by reason of corruptions in the text, some,

of the city, then first through Carian and later B.C. 189
Ionian territory, empties into the gulf of the sea which lies between Prienê and Miletus. At Antiochia, Seleucus, the son of Antiochus, came to the consul's camp to furnish the grain to the army in accordance with the treaty[1] made with Scipio. There was a short argument regarding the auxiliaries of Attalus, since Seleucus maintained that Antiochus had bargained to supply grain to the Roman soldiers only. This too was ended by the firmness of the consul, who sent a tribune with the order that no Roman soldiers should receive any grain until the auxiliaries of Attalus should have had their share. Thence he marched to the place called Gordiutichi.[2] From there they came on the third march to Tabae. The city lies on the borders of the Pisidians, on the side which faces the Pamphylian sea. Since the strength of the region was unimpaired, its men were fierce in warfare. At this time too the cavalry, charging the Roman column, threw it at first into no small degree of confusion; then, when it became evident that they were equal in neither numbers nor courage, when driven back into the town they begged pardon for their mistake and were ready to surrender the city. The consul exacted of them twenty-five talents

probably, because Livy did not understand his sources, while others are not mentioned elsewhere. I have been content in general to repeat the names as they are found in the Latin text I have followed, realizing that beyond question many of them are wrong.

The route of the Romans can be followed more easily on the map than through notes. As one traces their course one wonders whether their dominating motive, in selecting the line of march, was the topography of the country, the desire to come to grips with the Galatians as soon as possible, or the profits which quickly began to come in. (See Map 3.)

A.U.C. 565 et viginti talenta argenti et decem milia medimnum
tritici imperata; ita in deditionem accepti.

XIV. Tertio inde die ad Casum amnem perventum; inde profecti Erizam urbem primo impetu ce-
2 perunt. Ad Thabusion castellum imminens flumini
Indo ventum est, cui fecerat nomen Indus ab ele-
3 phanto deiectus. Haud procul a Cibyra aberant, nec
legatio ulla a Moagete, tyranno civitatis eius,
homine ad omnia infido atque importuno, veniebat.
4 Ad temptandum eius animum C. Helvium[1] cum
quattuor milibus peditum et quingentis[2] equitibus
consul praemittit. Huic agmini iam fines ingredienti
legati occurrerunt nuntiantes paratum esse tyran-
5 num[3] imperata facere; orabant ut pacatus fines
iniret cohiberetque a populatione agri militem, et in
6 corona aurea quindecim talenta adferebant. Helvius
integros[4] a populatione agros servaturum pollicitus
7 ire ad consulem legatos iussit. Quibus eadem
referentibus consul "neque Romani" inquit "bonae
voluntatis ullum signum erga nos tyranni habemus,
et ipsum talem esse inter omnes constat ut de poena
eius magis quam de amicitia nobis[5] cogitandum sit."
8 Perturbati hac voce legati nihil aliud[6] petere quam
ut coronam acciperet veniendique ad eum tyranno
potestatem et copiam loquendi ac purgandi se
9 faceret. Permissu consulis postero die in castra

[1] Helvium *ed. Frobeniana* 1535: muluium *B.*
[2] quingentis ς: .x. *B.*
[3] tyrannum ς: tyranni *B.*
[4] integros ς: *om. B.*
[5] nobis ς: *om. B.*
[6] aliud ς: *om. B.*

---

[1] Livy generally uses the Latin term *modius* in reference to quantities of grain (XXXI. xix. 2, etc.); here he more appropriately uses the Greek measure. The *medimnus* was the approximate equivalent of six *modii.*

of silver and ten thousand *medimni*[1] of wheat; on these terms they were received in surrender. B.C. 189

XIV. On the third day from there they came to the Casus river; on their departure thence they took the town of Eriza at the first assault. They came next to Thabusium, a fortress overlooking the Indus river, which derived its name from an Indian[2] who fell from his elephant. They were not far from Cibyra, and no embassy was coming from Moagetes, tyrant of that city, a man faithless and hard to deal with in every way. To test his attitude, the consul sent Gaius Helvius ahead with four thousand infantry and five hundred cavalry. As this column was crossing the frontier ambassadors met them, bringing word that the tyrant was ready to do their bidding; they begged that he would enter their country peacefully and restrain the soldiery from laying waste the land, and brought him fifteen talents in the form of a golden crown.[3] Helvius, promising to keep the farms safe from pillage, ordered the ambassadors to go to the consul. When they delivered the same message, the consul said, "We Romans have no indication of the good-will of the tyrant towards us, and it is well known to all that he is such a person that we must think about punishing him rather than cultivating his friendship."[4] Dismayed by this speech, the ambassadors asked nothing else than that he accept the crown and give the tyrant the opportunity to come to him, to speak and to defend himself. With the permission of the consul the tyrant the next day came

[2] Presumably the driver of the elephant: cf. Polybius I. xl; III. xlvi.

[3] Cf. ix. 13 above and the note.

[4] The characterization resembles that of Polybius (XXII. xvii).

A.U.C. 565 tyrannus venit, vestitus comitatusque vix ad privati
modice locupletis habitum, et oratio fuit summissa
et infracta, extenuantis opes suas urbiumque suae
10 dicionis egestatem querentis. Erant autem sub eo [1]
praeter Cibyram Sylleum et ad Limnen quae ap-
pellatur. Ex his, ut se suosque spoliaret, quinque et
viginti talenta se confecturum, prope ut diffidens pol-
11 licebatur. "Enimvero" inquit consul "ferri iam
ludificatio ista non potest. Parum est non erubuisse
absentem, cum per legatos frustrareris nos; praesens
12 quoque in eadem perstas impudentia. Quinque et
viginti talenta tyrannidem tuam exhaurient? Quingenta ergo talenta nisi triduo numeras, popula-
13 tionem in agris, obsidionem in urbe expecta." Hac
denuntiatione conterritus perstare [2] tamen in perti-
14 naci simulatione inopiae. Et paulatim illiberali
adiectione nunc per cavillationem, nunc precibus et
simulatis lacrimis ad centum talenta est perductus.
Adiecta decem milia medimnum frumenti. Hace
omnia intra sex dies exacta.

XV. A Cibyra per agros Sindensium exercitus
ductus, transgressusque Caularem amnem posuit
2 castra. Postero die et praeter Caralitin paludem
agmen ductum; ad Madamprum manserunt. Inde
progredientibus ab Lago, proxima urbe, metu
3 incolae fugerunt; [3] vacuum hominibus et refertum
rerum omnium copia oppidum diripuerunt. Inde
ad Lysis fluminis fontes, postero die ad Cobula-
4 tum amnem progressi. Termessenses eo tempore

[1] sub eo ς: *om. B.*
[2] conterritus perstare ς: perterritus instare *B.*
[3] incolae fugerunt ς: uincula effugerunt *B.*

---

[1] Polybius (XXII. xviii) calls it Colobatus.

to the camp, clothed and attended in a style inferior B.C. 189 to that of a private person of moderate wealth, and his speech was humble and incoherent, the speech of a man who belittled his own station and lamented the poverty of the cities under his control. Now there were under him, in addition to Cibyra, Sylleum and a city which they call *ad Limnen*. From them, by robbing himself and his subjects, he promised, though hesitatingly, to raise twenty-five talents. "Come, come," replied the consul, "this trifling cannot be endured. It is not enough that you did not blush when, remaining away, you mocked us through your ambassadors; even when here you persist in the same shamelessness. Will five-and-twenty talents drain your tyranny dry? Very well, unless you pay five hundred talents in three days, look forward to the devastation of your lands and the siege of your city." Though terrified by this threat he nevertheless persisted in his stubborn pretence of poverty. And little by little by grudging concessions, now amid much quibbling, now with prayers and feigned tears, he was worked up to the point of paying one hundred talents. Ten thousand *medimni* of grain were added. All this was collected within six days.

XV. From Cibyra the army was led through the territory of the people of Sinda and crossing the Caulares river went into camp. The next day they marched along the marsh of Caralitis; they encamped near Madamprus. As they advanced from there the inhabitants fled in terror from the neighbouring town of Lagum; empty of men and filled with abundance of all things, the town was sacked. Thence they moved to the sources of the Lysis river and next day to the Cobulatus river.[1] Troops from Termessus

A.U.C. 565

Isiondensium arcem urbe capta oppugnabant. Inclusi,
cum alia spes auxilii nulla esset, legatos ad consulem
5 orantes opem miserunt: cum coniugibus ac liberis in
arce inclusos se mortem in dies, aut ferro [1] aut fame
patiendam, expectare. Volenti consuli causa in
6 Pamphyliam devertendi [2] oblata est. Adveniens
obsidione Isiondenses exemit; Termesso pacem
dedit quinquaginta talentis argenti acceptis; item
7 Aspendiis ceterisque Pamphyliae populis. Ex Pamphylia
rediens ad fluvium Taurum primo die, postero
ad Xylinen quam vocant Comen posuit castra. Profectus
inde continentibus itineribus ad Cormasa
8 urbem pervenit. Darsa proxima urbs erat; eam
metu incolarum desertam, plenam omnium rerum
copia invenit. Progredienti praeter paludes legati
9 ab Lysinoe dedentes civitatem venerunt. Inde in
agrum Sagalassenum, uberem fertilemque omni
genere frugum, ventum est. Colunt Pisidae, longe
optimi bello regionis eius. Cum ea res animos fecit [3]
tum agri fecunditas et multitudo hominum et situs
10 inter paucas munitae urbis. Consul, quia nulla
legatio ad finem praesto fuerat, praedatum in agros
misit. Tum demum fracta pertinacia est ut ferri
11 agique res suas viderunt; legatis missis pacti quinquaginta
talentis et viginti milibus medimnum
12 tritici, viginti hordei, pacem impetraverunt. Progressus
inde ad Rhotrinos fontes ad vicum, quem

[1] ferro ς: *om. B.*
[2] devertendi *Drakenborch*: reuertendi *B*ς: diuertendi *M.*
[3] fecit *aut* facit ς: *om. B.*

---

[1] The sites in this sentence cannot be placed, but Manlius has clearly turned north towards his proper route into Galatia.

were at that time besieging the citadel of the B.C. 189
Isiondenses after capturing the town. The besieged, since there was no other hope of relief, sent envoys to the consul asking aid: shut up in the citadel with their wives and children, they were expecting death day by day, to be suffered by either the sword or starvation. Thus the eager consul was offered an occasion to turn aside into Pamphylia. By his arrival he rescued the Isiondenses from siege; on payment of fifty talents of silver he granted peace to Termessus; he did the same for the Aspendians and other peoples of Pamphylia. Returning from Pamphylia, he encamped the first day on the river Taurus, the next at what they call Xylines Comê.[1] Advancing from there by continuous marches he came to the city of Cormasa. Darsa is the nearest town; this he found deserted by the inhabitants through fear, but full of all sorts of supplies. As he marched along the marshes ambassadors came from Lysinoë surrendering their city. Then they entered the country of the Sagalassenes, rich and abounding in all kinds of crops. Pisidians inhabit it, by far the best warriors in this region. This circumstance gave them courage, as well as the fertility of the soil and their large population and the situation of their fortified town in a land where such strongholds were few. Since no embassy met him at the frontier, the consul sent out parties to plunder the fields. Then at last their stubbornness was broken when they saw their property being carried and driven away; sending ambassadors and agreeing to pay fifty talents, twenty thousand *medimni* of wheat and as many of barley, they obtained peace. Then he proceeded to the Rhotrine springs and encamped at a village which they call

A.U.C. 565 Acoridos Comen vocant, posuit castra. Eo Seleucus
13 ab Apamea postero die venit. Aegros inde et inutilia
impedimenta cum Apameam dimisisset, ducibus
itinerum ab Seleuco acceptis profectus eo die in
Metropolitanum campum, postero die Dynias Phry-
14 giae processit. Inde Synnada venit, metu omnibus
circa oppidis desertis. Quorum praeda[1] iam grave
agmen trahens vix quinque milium die toto itinere
perfecto ad Beudos, quod vetus appellant, pervenit.
15 Ad Anabura inde, et altero die ad Alandri fontes,
tertio ad Abbassium posuit castra. Ibi plures dies
stativa habuit, quia perventum erat ad Tolostobogiorum fines.

XVI. Galli, magna hominum vis, seu inopia agri
seu praedae spe, nullam gentem, per quam ituri
essent, parem armis rati, Brenno duce in Dardanos
2 pervenerunt. Ibi seditio orta est; ad viginti milia
hominum cum Lonorio ac Lutario regulis secessione
3 facta a Brenno in Thraeciam iter avertunt. Ubi
cum resistentibus pugnando, pacem petentibus
stipendium imponendo Byzantium cum pervenissent,
aliquamdiu oram Propontidis, vectigales habendo
4 regionis eius urbes, obtinuerunt. Cupido inde eos
in Asiam transeundi, audientes ex propinquo quanta

[1] quorum praeda ς : *om. B.*

---

[1] Both places and names are uncertain.

[2] The names of the Galatian tribes to which Manlius has now come are quite uncertain. I have given them in the forms used in the text.

The defective condition of the text of Polybius deprives us of the opportunity to test the relation between Polybius and Livy in their accounts of the anabasis of Manlius. A war-diary or other special source may be suspected for both.

[3] Livy here digresses to describe the migration of the Gauls to Asia Minor in 278 B.C.

Acoridos Comê.[1] Thither the next day Seleucus came from Apamea. When the consul had sent back thence to Apamea the sick and his useless equipment, receiving from Seleucus guides for the march, he came that day into the country of Metropolis and the following day to Dyniae in Phrygia. From there he marched to Synnada, all the towns in the neighbourhood being deserted through fear. Dragging after him a column which was now overloaded with their booty and barely accomplishing a march of five miles in a whole day, he arrived at Beudos, which they call "the Old." Next he reached Anabura and the following day the sources of the Alander, and the third he encamped at Abbassius. There he maintained his camp for many days because he had come to the frontiers of the Tolostobogii.[2] B.C. 189

XVI. The Gauls,[3] a vast horde of men, whether moved by shortage of land or hope of plunder, feeling assured that no people through which they would pass was their match in war, under the leadership of Brennus came into the country of the Dardanians.[4] There strife broke out among them; about twenty thousand men, with Lonorius and Lutarius as their chiefs, seceded from Brennus and turned aside into Thrace. There, when they had penetrated as far as Byzantium, contending against those who resisted and imposing tribute upon those who sought peace, they occupied for a considerable time the coast of the Propontis, holding as tributaries the cities of the district. Then the desire of crossing into Asia seized them, as they heard from their

[4] Livy omits to mention the visit to Greece and the attack on Delphi (xlviii. 2 below; XL. lviii. 3).

A.U.C. 565 ubertas eius terrae esset, cepit; et Lysimachia
fraude capta Chersonesoque omni armis possessa ad
5 Hellespontum descenderunt. Ibi vero exiguo di-
visam [1] freto cernentibus Asiam multo magis animi
ad transeundum accensi; nuntiosque ad Antipatrum
praefectum eius orae de transitu mittebant. Quae
res cum lentius spe ipsorum traheretur, alia rursus
6 nova inter regulos seditio orta est. Lonorius retro
unde venerat cum maiore parte hominum repetit
Byzantium; Lutarius Macedonibus per speciem
legationis ab Antipatro ad speculandum missis duas
tectas naves et tres lembos adimit. Iis alios atque
alios dies noctesque travehendo [2] intra paucos dies
7 omnes copias traicit.[3] Haud ita multo post Lonorius adiuvante Nicomede Bithyniae rege a By-
8 zantio transmisit. Coeunt deinde in unum rursus
Galli et auxilia Nicomedi dant adversus Ziboetam,
9 tenentem partem Bithyniae, gerenti bellum. Atque
eorum maxime opera devictus Ziboeta est, Bithy-
niaque omnis in dicionem Nicomedis concessit.
Profecti ex Bithynia in Asiam processerunt. Non
plus ex viginti milibus hominum quam decem armata
10 erant. Tamen tantum terroris omnibus quae cis
Taurum incolunt gentibus iniecerunt, ut quas
adissent quasque non adissent, pariter ultimae
11 propinquis, imperio parerent. Postremo cum tres
essent gentes, Tolostobogii Trocmi Tectosages, in

[1] diuisam ς: diuisis *B*.
[2] noctesque trauehendo ς: noctemque trahendo *B*.
[3] traicit *Weissenborn*: traiecit *B*ς.

---

[1] Nicomedes and Ziboetas were brothers, sons of the elder Ziboetas, the first king of Bithynia.

neighbours how rich was this land; and having taken B.C. 189
Lysimachia by treachery and occupied the whole Chersonesus by force of arms they came down to the Hellespont. There, as they saw Asia separated from them by a narrow strait, their souls were even more inflamed with the desire to cross, and they sent messengers to Antipater, the prefect of this coast, regarding the crossing. When this negotiation was dragging out longer than they had expected, another new revolt broke out between the chiefs. Lonorius with the larger part of the men went back to Byzantium whence he had come; Lutarius, when Macedonians were sent by Antipater to spy, under cover of being an embassy, took from them two decked ships and three cruisers. Using these as ferry-boats day after day and night after night, within a few days he transported his entire force. Only a little later Lonorius, with the aid of Nicomedes,[1] king of Bithynia, crossed from Byzantium. Then the Gauls were once more united and aided Nicomedes in the war he was waging against Ziboetas, who held some part of Bithynia. And, principally as a result of their assistance, Ziboetas was conquered and all Bithynia acknowledged the sovereignty of Nicomedes. Setting out from Bithynia they made their way into Asia. Of their twenty thousand men, not more than ten thousand were armed. Nevertheless, they inspired such terror in all the peoples who dwell on this side of the Taurus, those whom they approached and those whom they did not approach, that the most distant and the nearest alike obeyed their orders. Finally, since there were three tribes, the Tolostobogii, the Trocmi, and the Tectosages, they split

A.U.C. 565 tres partes, qua cuique populorum suorum vectigalis
12 Asia esset, diviserunt. Trocmis Hellesponti ora
data; Tolostobogii Aeolida atque Ioniam, Tectosages mediterranea Asiae sortiti sunt. Et sti-
13 pendium tota cis Taurum Asia exigebant, sedem
autem ipsi sibi circa Halyn flumen cepere. Tan-
tusque terror eorum nominis erat, multitudine etiam
magna subole aucta, ut Syriae quoque ad postremum
14 reges stipendium dare non abnuerent. Primus
Asiam incolentium abnuit Attalus, pater regis
Eumenis; audacique incepto praeter opinionem
omnium adfuit fortuna, et signis collatis superior
fuit. Non tamen ita infregit animos eorum ut absis-
15 terent imperio; eaedem opes usque[1] ad bellum
Antiochi cum Romanis manserunt. Tum quoque,
pulso Antiocho, magnam spem habuerunt, quia
procul mari incolerent, Romanum exercitum ad se
non[2] perventurum.

XVII. Cum hoc hoste, tam terribili omnibus regionis eius, quia bellum gerendum erat, pro contione
milites in hunc maxime modum adlocutus est consul:
2 "Non me praeterit, milites, omnium quae Asiam
3 colunt gentium Gallos fama belli praestare. Inter
mitissimum genus hominum ferox natio pervagata
bello prope orbem terrarum sedem cepit. Procera

[1] eaedem opes usque ς: aedem ophesusque *B*.
[2] ad se non ς: ad senatum *B*.

---

[1] Their territory was called Galatia, comprising parts of Phrygia and Cappadocia.

[2] The Seleucid kingdom was weakened by internal dissension and wars with Egypt, but may not have paid tribute regularly.

[3] Cf. XXXIII. xxi. 3.

up into three divisions, according to the states of Asia which each held as tributaries. To the Trocmi the coast of the Hellespont was assigned; the Tolostobogii received by the lot Aeolis and Ionia, the Tectosages the interior parts of Asia. And they exacted tribute from all Asia on this side of the Taurus, but established their own dwellings along the river Halys.[1] And so great was the terror of their name, their numbers being also enlarged by great natural increase, that in the end even the kings of Syria [2] did not refuse to pay them tribute. Attalus, the father of King Eumenes, was the first of the inhabitants of Asia to refuse, and his bold step, contrary to the expectation of all, was aided by fortune and he worsted the Gauls in pitched battle.[3] Yet he did not cow them so thoroughly that they refrained from exercising their power; [4] their strength remained the same until the war between Antiochus and the Romans. Even then, after the defeat of Antiochus, they entertained great hopes that, since they lived far from the sea, the Roman army would not march against them. B.C. 189

XVII. Since war was to be waged with this enemy, so terrible to all the inhabitants of this region, the consul summoned an assembly and addressed the soldiers in about this fashion: "It does not escape me, soldiers, that of all the peoples who inhabit Asia the Gauls stand first in reputation for war. Among peoples of the most unwarlike sort this fierce tribe, travelling up and down in war, has almost made the world its residence. Tall bodies, long

[4] The displays of power which Livy has in mind were probably raids and demands for tribute. Possibly, however, *imperium* should be understood in a geographical sense.

A.U.C. 565 corpora, promissae et rutilatae comae, vasta scuta,
4 praelongi gladii; ad hoc cantus ineuntium proelium
5 et ululatus et tripudia, et quatientium scuta in patrium quendam modum horrendus armorum crepitus,
omnia de industria composita ad terrorem. Sed
haec, quibus insolita atque insueta sunt, Graeci et
Phryges et Cares timeant; Romanis Gallici tumultus
6 assueti, etiam vanitates notae sunt. Semel primo
congressu ad Alliam eos olim fugerunt maiores
nostri;[1] ex eo tempore per ducentos iam annos
pecorum in modum consternatos caedunt fugantque,
et plures prope de Gallis triumphi quam de toto
orbe terrarum acti sunt. Iam usu hoc cognitum
7 est: si primum impetum quem, fervido ingenio et
caeca ira effundunt, sustinueris, fluunt sudore et
lassitudine membra, labant arma; mollia corpora,
molles, ubi ira consedit, animos sol pulvis sitis ut
8 ferrum non admoveas prosternunt. Non legionibus
legiones eorum solum experti sumus, sed vir unus
cum viro congrediendo T. Manlius, M. Valerius
quantum Gallicam rabiem vinceret[2] Romana virtus
9 docuerunt. Iam M. Manlius unus agmine scandentes
in Capitolium detrusit Gallos. Et illis maioribus
nostris cum haud dubiis Gallis, in sua terra genitis,

[1] ad Alliam eos olim fugerunt maiores nostri *Modius*: ad alia olim fugerunt maiores nostros *B*: ad alliam eos olim fuderunt maiores uestri *M*: ad alliam olim fuderunt maiores nostros ς.

[2] uinceret ς: *om. B.*

---

[1] *Tumultus*, which became almost technical for uprisings in Gaul (XXXI. x. 1, etc.), is here used in a different sense, as a summary of what has just preceded.

reddish hair, huge shields, very long swords; in addition, songs as they go into battle and yells and leapings and the dreadful din of arms as they clash shields according to some ancestral custom—all these are deliberately used to terrify their foes. But let Greeks and Phrygians and Carians fear these things to which they are unused and unaccustomed; to Romans Gallic riotings[1] are familiar and their vain displays too are well known. Once, when we first met them at the Allia,[2] our ancestors long ago fled before them; from that time now for two hundred years, terrified like animals they are slain and routed, and more triumphs, almost, have been celebrated over the Gauls than over all the world. This has now been learned by experience: if you bear up under their first onset, into which they rush with glowing enthusiasm and blind passion, their limbs grow lax with sweat and weariness, their weapons fall from their hands; their soft bodies, their soft souls (when passion subsides) are overcome by sun, dust, thirst, so that you need not use arms against them. Not only when matched legion to legion have we learned this, but when fighting man to man alone. Titus Manlius, Marcus Valerius have shown how far Roman valour surpasses Gallic madness. Then Marcus Manlius alone thrust down the Gauls as they climbed in close array to the Capitoline.[3] And those forefathers of ours had to do with true Gauls, born in their own B.C. 189

[2] The river which was the scene of the defeat which led to the capture of Rome (traditionally dated 390 B.C.); cf. V. xxxvii.–xxxix.

[3] The three Romans named were famous for their exploits against the Gauls. The consul is quite willing to have the fact recalled that two of the three were members of his own *gens*.

A.U.C. res erat; hi iam degeneres sunt, mixti, et Gallo-
565 10 graeci vere, quod appellantur; sicut in frugibus
pecudibusque non tantum semina ad servandam
indolem valent, quantum terrae proprietas caelique
11 sub quo aluntur mutat.[1] Macedones, qui Alex-
andriam in Aegypto, qui Seleuciam ac Babyloniam,
quique alias sparsas per orbem terrarum colonias
habent, in Syros Parthos Aegyptios degenerarunt;
12 Massilia, inter Gallos sita, traxit aliquantum ab
accolis animorum; Tarentinis quid ex Spartana
13 dura illa et horrida disciplina mansit? Est[2] gene-
rosius, in sua[3] quidquid sede gignitur; insitum
alienae terrae in id quo[4] alitur, natura vertente se,
degenerat.[5] Phrygas igitur Gallicis oneratos armis,
sicut in acie Antiochi cecidistis,[6] victos victores, cae-
14 detis. Magis vereor ne parum inde gloriae, quam
15 ne nimium belli sit. Attalus eos rex saepe fudit
fugavitque. Nolite existimare beluas tantum recens[7]
captas feritatem illam silvestrem primo servare, dein,
cum diu manibus humanis aluntur, mitescere, in
hominum feritate mulcenda non eandem naturam
16 esse. Eosdemne hos[8] creditis esse, qui patres
eorum avique fuerunt? Extorres inopia agrorum
profecti domo per asperrimam Illyrici oram, Paeoniam inde et Thraeciam pugnando cum ferocissimis

[1] mutat ς: mutant *B*.
[2] Est *Weissenborn*: *om. B*ς.
[3] in sua ς: *om. B*.
[4] quo *ed. Parisina* 1513: quod *B*ς.
[5] natura uertente se degenerat ς: natam uertentes *B*.
[6] cecidistis ς: cedetis *B*.
[7] recens *Ascensius*: recentis *B*: recentes ς.
[8] hos ς: hostes *B*.

---

[1] The characterization given by the Rhodians (XXXVII. liv. 21–22) is quite different and probably more accurate.

land; these now are degenerates, of mixed race, and really Gallogrecians, as they are named; just as, in the case of plants and animals, the seeds have less power to maintain their natural quality than the character of the soil and climate in which they live has power to change it. The Macedonians who hold Alexandria in Egypt, who hold Seleucia and Babylonia and other colonies scattered throughout the world, have degenerated into Syrians, Parthians, Egyptians; Massilia,[1] situated among the Gauls, has acquired something of the disposition of its neighbours; what have the Tarentines retained of that stern and dreadful Spartan discipline? Whatever grows in its own soil, has greater excellence; transplanted to a soil alien to it, its nature changes and it degenerates towards that in which it is nurtured. It is Phrygians,[2] therefore, burdened with the weapons of Gauls, whom, even as you slew them in the battle-line of Antiochus, you will slay, victorious over the vanquished. I am afraid that there will be too little of glory rather than too much of war. King Attalus has often repulsed and routed them. Do not think that it is only beasts which when newly caught first retain that fierceness of their forest life, and then, when long fed by the hands of men, grow tame, but that in moderating the ferocity of men nature does not do the same. Do you believe that these are the same men that their fathers and their grandfathers were? Exiles on account of the poverty of the land, they left home, travelling through the most inhospitable land of Illyricum, then Paeonia and Thrace, fighting with the fiercest tribes, and seized B.C. 189

[2] The Phrygians of Livy's time were proverbially effeminate: cf., *e.g.*, Virgil, *Aen.* IV. 215–216.

A.U.C. 565
17 gentibus emensi, has terras ceperunt. Duratos eos
tot malis exasperatosque accepit terra, quae copia
omnium rerum saginaret. Uberrimo agro, mitissimo
caelo, clementibus accolarum ingeniis omnis illa,
18 cum qua venerant, mansuefacta est feritas. Vobis
mehercule, Martiis viris, cavenda ac fugienda quam
primum amoenitas est Asiae: tantum hae peregrinae voluptates ad extinguendum vigorem animorum possunt; tantum[1] contagio disciplinae
19 morisque accolarum valet. Hoc tamen feliciter
evenit, quod sicut vim adversus vos nequaquam, ita
famam apud Graecos parem illi antiquae obtinent,
20 cum qua venerunt, bellique gloriam victores eandem
inter socios habebitis, quam si servantes antiquum
specimen animorum Gallos vicissetis."

XVIII. Contione dimissa missisque ad Eposognatum legatis, qui unus ex regulis et in Eumenis man-
serat amicitia[2] et negaverat Antiocho adversus
Romanos auxilia, castra movit. Primo die ad
Alandrum flumen, postero ad vicum quem vocant
2 Tyscon ventum. Eo legati Oroandensium cum
venissent amicitiam petentes, ducenta talenta his
sunt imperata, precantibusque[3] ut domum renun-
3 tiarent potestas facta. Ducere inde exercitum
consul ad Pliten intendit; deinde ad Alyattos castra
posita. Eo missi ad Eposognatum redierunt, et

[1] tantum *ed. Frobeniana* 1535: quantum *B*ς.
[2] amicitia ς: inamicitia *B*.
[3] precantibusque ς: precantibus *B*.

---

[1] Such philosophizing seems hardly consistent with the character of Manlius and doubtfully appropriate to the occasion. Perhaps Livy wishes to prepare the reader for his analysis of Asiatic influence in XXXIX. i. and elsewhere,

these lands. Toughened and hardened by so many misfortunes, they were received by a land which could stuff them with its abundance of all things. In a land most rich, under a sky most kindly, among natives mild in disposition, all that fierceness with which they came has grown gentle. You, by Hercules, being men of Mars, must escape and avoid as soon as possible the pleasantness of Asia: such power have these foreign delights to destroy the vigour of the soul; such influence does contact with the habits and character of the natives exert.[1] Yet this turns out well in this respect—that, while their strength against you is vain, still their reputation among the Greeks is the same as that of old, which they had when they came, and you will win, as victors, the same military glory among our allies as if you had conquered Gauls who had preserved their ancient type of courage." B.C. 189

XVIII. Dismissing the meeting and sending envoys to Eposognatus, who alone of the chiefs had both remained loyal to Eumenes and refused to aid Antiochus against the Romans, he moved his camp. The first day he marched to the Alander river, the second to the village which they call Tyscon. When ambassadors from the people of Oroanda had come there asking friendship, he demanded of them two hundred talents and granted them permission to report this at home. Then the consul proceeded to lead the army towards Plitê; next he encamped at Alyatti. There the messengers sent to Eposognatus returned, accompanied by ambassadors of

especially since he holds Manlius responsible for the enervation of his own soldiers and indirectly of Rome. If Polybius had a corresponding speech it is, unfortunately, lost.

A.U.C. 565 legati reguli orantes ne Tectosagis bellum inferret;
ipsum[1] in eam gentem iturum Eposognatum per-
4 suasurumque[2] ut imperata faciant. Data venia
regulo, duci inde exercitus per Axylon quam vocant
terram coeptus. Ab re nomen habet: non ligni
modo quicquam, sed ne spinas quidem aut ullum
aliud alimentum fert ignis; fimo bubulo pro lignis
5 utuntur. Ad Cuballum, Gallograeciae castellum,
castra habentibus Romanis apparuere cum magno
tumultu hostium equites, nec turbarunt tantum
Romanas stationes repente invecti[3] sed quosdam
6 etiam occiderunt. Qui tumultus cum in castra
perlatus esset, effusus repente omnibus portis equi-
tatus Romanus fudit fugavitque Gallos et aliquot
7 fugientes occidit. Inde consul, ut qui iam ad hostes
perventum cerneret, explorato deinde et cum cura
coacto agmine procedebat. Et continentibus itineribus cum ad Sangarium flumen venisset, pontem, quia
8 vado nusquam transitus erat, facere instituit. Sangarius ex Adoreo monte per Phrygiam fluens mis-
cetur ad Bithyniam Tymbri fluvio; inde maior iam
geminatis aquis per Bithyniam fertur et in Propontidem sese[4] effundit, non tamen tam magnitudine memorabilis, quam piscium accolis ingentem
9 vim praebet. Transgressis ponte perfecto flumen
praeter ripam euntibus Galli Matris Magnae[5] a

[1] ipsum ς: et ipsum *B*.
[2] persuasurumque ς: peruasurumque *B*.
[3] inuecti ς: inuectis *B*.
[4] propontidem sese ς: proponti dense se *B*.
[5] magnae ς: *om*. *B*.

---

[1] Assuming with Livy that *Axylon* is a Greek word, it means "woodless."

that chief, who asked him not to make war upon the Tectosagi; Eposognatus himself, they said, would go to that tribe and persuade them to do what was ordered. Granting this favour to the chief, he began to lead the army through the district which is called Axylon. It derives its name from the fact: it not only produces no wood at all but not even thorns or any other food for fire; they use cow-dung in place of wood.[1] While the Romans were encamped near Cuballum, a fortress of Galatia, the enemy's cavalry appeared with great uproar, and not only threw the Roman outguards into confusion by their unexpected attack, but even killed some men. When this disorder was reported in the camp, the Roman cavalry, pouring in haste from all the gates, repulsed and routed the Gauls and killed a considerable number in their flight. Thenceforth the consul, since he realized that he had now encountered the enemy, marched with scouts sent in advance and his column carefully formed. And when, marching without interruption, he had reached the Sangarius river, he determined to build a bridge, since there was nowhere a way to cross it by fording. The Sangarius river, flowing from Mount Adoreus through Phrygia, is joined near Bithynia by the river Thymbres; thence, enlarged by the doubling of its waters, it flows through Bithynia and discharges into the Propontis,[2] being, however, not so remarkable for its size as because it furnishes the inhabitants with vast quantities of fish. When they had finished the bridge and crossed the river and were marching along the bank, *Galli* of the Great Mother from Pessinus B.C. 189

[2] The river actually empties into the Euxine sea. It is now the Sakaria.

A.U.C. 565 Pessinunte occurrere cum insignibus suis, vatici-
nantes fanatico carmine deam Romanis viam belli et
10 victoriam dare imperiumque eius regionis. Accipere
se omen cum dixisset consul, castra eo ipso loco
11 posuit. Postero die ad Gordium pervenit. Id
haud magnum quidem oppidum est, sed plus quam
mediterraneum celebre et frequens emporium.
12 Tria maria pari ferme distantia intervallo habet, ad
Hellespontum, ad Sinopen, et alterius orae litora [1]
qua Cilices maritimi colunt; multarum magnarumque
praeterea gentium fines contingit,[2] quarum commercium in eum maxime locum mutui usus con-
13 traxere. Id tum desertum fuga incolarum oppidum,
refertum idem copia rerum omnium invenerunt.
14 Ibi stativa habentibus legati ab Eposognato venerunt
nuntiantes profectum eum ad regulos Gallorum
15 nihil aequi impetrasse; ex [3] campestribus vicis
agrisque frequentes demigrare et cum [4] coniugibus
ac liberis, quae ferre atque agere possint, prae se
agentes portantesque Olympum montem petere, ut
inde armis locorumque situ sese tueantur.

XIX. Certiora postea Oroandensium legati attu-
lerunt, Tolostobogiorum civitatem Olympum montem [5] cepisse; diversos Tectosagos alium montem,
2 Magaba qui dicatur, petisse; Trocmos coniugibus ac

[1] litora ς : litore *B*. [2] contingit ς : *om. B*.
[3] ex ς : *om. B*.
[4] cum ς : *om. B*.
[5] montem ς : *om. B*.

---

[1] Cf. XXXVII. ix. 9. The Magna Mater had been brought to Rome from Pessinus (XXIX. xi. 7, etc.). The *Galli* were eunuchs devoted to her service.

met them,[1] wearing their ritual ornaments and prophesying in their frenzied chants that the goddess was granting to the Romans the way of war and victory and dominion over this region. The consul said that he accepted the omen and encamped on that very spot. Next day he moved to Gordium. This is not indeed a large town, but is a market visited and frequented more than is usually the case with an inland city. It has three seas about equidistant from it, the Hellespont, the sea at Sinope and the shores of the opposite sea where the Cilicians of the coast dwell; besides, it adjoins the borders of several strong states, and their mutual needs concentrated their intercourse at this place especially. At this time the Romans found it deserted by the flight of the inhabitants, but likewise filled with abundance of all things. While he was maintaining a base there, ambassadors from Eposognatus came reporting that his visit to the chiefs of the Gauls had won no fair response; from the villages and farms in the plains they were moving in large numbers, accompanied by their wives and children, driving ahead of them and carrying what they could carry and drive,[2] and were making for the Olympus mountain, that thence they might maintain themselves by arms and by the situation of the place. B.C. 189

XIX. Later the ambassadors from the people of Oroanda brought surer news, that the tribe of the Tolostobogii had occupied the Olympus range; that the Tectosagi, separated from them, had made for another mountain which was called Magaba; that the Trocmi had left their wives and children among

[2] This combination of verbs is usually used of booty being removed by an enemy: so in xv. 10 above.

A.U.C. 565 liberis apud Tectosagos depositis armatorum agmine [1]
Tolostobogiis statuisse auxilium ferre. Erant autem
tunc trium populorum reguli Ortiago et Combolo-
3 marus et Gaulotus. Iis haec maxime ratio belli
sumendi fuerat, quod cum montes editissimos regionis
eius tenerent, convectis omnibus quae ad usum
quamvis longi temporis sufficerent, taedio se fati-
4 gaturos hostem censebant: nam neque ausuros per
tam ardua atque iniqua loca subire eos et, si cona-
rentur, vel parva manu prohiberi aut deturbari posse,
nec quietos in radicibus montium gelidorum sedentes
5 frigus aut inopiam laturos. Ac cum ipsa altitudo
locorum eos tutaretur, fossam quoque et alia munimenta verticibus iis quos insederant circumiecere.
6 Minima apparatus missilium telorum cura fuit,
quod saxa adfatim praebituram asperitatem ipsam
locorum credebant.

XX. Consul quia non comminus pugnam sed
procul locis oppugnandis futuram praeceperat animo,
ingentem vim pilorum, velitarium hastarum, sagitta-
rum glandesque et modicorum qui funda mitti
2 possent lapidum [2] paraverat, instructusque missilium apparatu ad Olympum montem ducit et a
3 quinque ferme milibus castra locat. Postero die
cum quadringentis equitibus et Attalo progressum
eum ad naturam montis situmque Gallicorum castrorum visendum equites hostium, duplex numerus,
effusi [3] e castris, in fugam averterunt; occisi quoque

[1] agmine ς: agmen *B*.
[2] mitti possent lapidum *ed. Frobeniana* 1535: lapidum possent *B*: mitti lapidum possent ς.
[3] effusi *Kreyssig*: effusus *B*.

the Tectosagi and with their armed forces on the march had decided to aid the Tolostobogii. The chiefs of these three tribes at this time were Ortiago and Combolomarus and Gaulotus. They had adopted this plan particularly for conducting the war—that, when they had occupied the highest peaks in the region, conveying everything there which would be sufficient for their use over however long a period, they would wear down the enemy by exhaustion; for, they were convinced, the Romans would neither venture to climb over such steep and difficult ground, and, if they did attempt it, they could be stopped even by a small force or pushed back, nor would they sit quietly at the foot of cold mountains and endure chill and hunger. And, although the very height of the place was a defence, they also threw a ditch and other fortifications around the summits which they had occupied. They took little forethought for a supply of missile weapons, because they believed that the very roughness of the terrain would furnish stones in abundance. B.C. 189

XX. The consul, because he had foreseen, as a result of reflection, that the fighting would not be done hand to hand but by making attacks from a distance, had prepared a vast quantity of javelins, skirmishers' spears, arrows, bullets and stones of moderate size which could be thrown from slings, and equipped with this supply of missiles he led the army towards the Olympus mountain and encamped about five miles away. The next day, taking Attalus and four hundred cavalry, he set out to survey the character of the mountain and the situation of the Gallic camp, but the cavalry of the enemy, in double his number, rushing out of the camp put him to flight; a few

A.U.C. 565

4 pauci fugientium, vulnerati plures. Tertio die cum
omnibus ad loca exploranda profectus, quia nemo
hostium extra munimenta processit, tuto circumvectus montem, animadvertit meridiana regione
terrenos et placide acclives ad quendam finem colles
5 esse, a septentrione arduas et rectas prope rupes,
atque omnibus ferme aliis inviis itinera tria esse,
unum medio monte, qua terrena erant, duo difficilia
ab hiberno solis ortu et ab aestivo occasu. Haec
contemplatus eo die sub ipsis radicibus posuit castra;
6 postero, sacrificio facto, cum primis hostiis litasset,
trifariam exercitum divisum ducere ad hostem pergit.
7 Ipse cum maxima parte copiarum, qua aequissimum
aditum praebebat mons, ascendit; L. Manlium
fratrem ab hiberno ortu, quoad loca patiantur et tuto
8 possit, subire iubet; si qua periculosa et praerupta
occurrant, non pugnare cum iniquitate locorum
neque inexsuperabilibus vim adferre, sed obliquo
9 monte ad se declinare et suo agmini coniungi; C.
Helvium cum tertia parte circuire sensim per infima
montis, deinde ab occasu aestivo erigere agmen.
Et Attali auxilia trifariam aequo numero divisit,
10 secum esse ipsum iuvenem iussit. Equitatum cum

---

[1] Roughly, the south-east and north-west sides.

[2] It was regarded as especially propitious if the entrails of the first animals sacrificed gave favourable omens: cf. XXXVI. i. 3.

were killed in the flight, a larger number wounded. B.C. 189
The third day he proceeded with his entire force to reconnoitre the ground, and, because no one of the enemy came out beyond the fortifications, he rode in safety around the mountain, and observed that on the southern side the hills were covered with earth and sloped gently up to a certain point, that on the north there were steep and almost perpendicular cliffs, and that although almost everything else was impassable there were three roads, one in the centre of the mountain, where it was covered with soil, two difficult, on the side of the winter rising of the sun and of its summer setting.[1] Having inspected them, he encamped that day at the very base; the following day, having offered sacrifice and obtained favourable omens from the first victims,[2] he divided the army into three columns and began the advance against the enemy. He himself, with the largest part of the forces, made the ascent where the mountain offered the most gradual slope; he directed his brother Lucius Manlius to move forward on the side of the winter rising, as far as the terrain permitted and as he could go in safety; if any dangerous and steep places confronted him he was not to contend against the unfavourable character of the ground or struggle with insuperable obstacles, but to turn aside crosswise over the mountain towards the consul and join his column; his orders to Gaius Helvius, commanding the third contingent, were to go slowly around the base of the mountain and then climb up on the side of the summer setting. The auxiliaries of Attalus he also divided into three sections, and ordered the young man himself to attend him. The cavalry with the

A.U.C. 565 elephantis in proxima tumulis planitie reliquit; edictum praefectis ut intenti quid[1] ubique geratur animadvertant opemque ferre quo postulet res possint.

XXI. Galli ab[2] duobus lateribus satis fidentes
invia esse, ab ea parte quae in meridiem vergeret,
ut armis clauderent viam, quattuor milia fere
armatorum ad tumulum imminentem viae minus
mille passuum a castris occupandum mittunt,[3] eo se
2 rati veluti castello iter impedituros. Quod ubi
Romani viderunt, expediunt sese ad pugnam. Ante
signa modico intervallo velites eunt et ab Attalo
Cretenses sagittarii et funditores et Tralli et Thraeces;
3 signa peditum, ut per arduum, leni gradu ducuntur,
ita prae se habentium scuta ut missilia tantum vita-
4 rent, pede collato non viderentur pugnaturi. Missi-
libus ex intervallo loci proelium commissum est,
primo par, Gallos loco adiuvante, Romanos varietate
et copia telorum; procedente certamine nihil iam
aequi erat. Scuta longa ceterum ad amplitudinem
corporum parum lata, et ea ipsa plana, male[4]
5 tegebant Gallos. Nec tela iam alia habebant

[1] quid ς: quod *B*.
[2] ab ς: et ab *B*.
[3] mittunt ς: mittit *B*.
[4] plana male ς: plana *B*.

---

[1] On the return of Manlius to Rome his critics, Furius and Aemilius, savagely assailed him, partly on account of his conduct of this campaign (xlv–xlvi below). A less prejudiced examination of his tactical dispositions, while recognizing that his advance up the mountain in the face of the enemy was contrary to Roman practice and, under normal circumstances, too rash, judges him entitled to considerable praise as a tactician (cf. Pauly-Wissowa, XIV, col. 1219).

elephants he left in the plain close to the hills; his orders to the prefects were to observe alertly what went on in every quarter and to render assistance wherever the situation should demand it.[1] B.C. 189

XXI. The Gauls, being quite confident that their position could not be approached from the two flanks, in order to block with arms the road on the side which faces the south, sent about four thousand armed men to hold a hill overlooking the road and less than a mile from the camp, thinking that from this, as from a redoubt, they would hinder the approach. When the Romans perceived this they prepared for battle. A moderate distance in front of the standards marched the skirmishers[2] and Cretan archers and slingers furnished by Attalus and the Trallianians and Thracians; the standards of the infantry, moving over difficult ground, proceeded at a slow rate, the men holding their shields before them so as only to ward off missiles, whilst they did not seem disposed to fight at close quarters. The discharge of missiles from a distance began the fighting, which at first was even, the Gauls having the advantage of position, the Romans of variety and a plentiful supply of weapons; as the battle continued there was no longer any equality. Their shields, long, but not wide enough for the size of their bodies and, moreover, flat,[3] offered poor protection to the Gauls. They had at this time no other

[2] The *velites* were usually advance parties thrown out by the legions as a screen; in this case they seem to have been independent units under their own commanders, but the grammar of the sentence is not clear.

[3] The Roman shield presented a convex surface to the enemy and so deflected weapons more successfully.

A.U.C. 565 praeter gladios, quorum, cum manum[1] hostis non con-
6 sereret, nullus usus erat. Saxis nec modicis, ut quae non praeparassent, sed quod cuique temere trepidanti ad manum venisset, ut insueti, nec arte[2] nec
7 viribus adiuvantes ictum, utebantur. Sagittis glande iaculis incauti ab[3] omni parte configebantur[4] nec quid agerent, ira et pavore occaecatis animis, cernebant et erant deprensi genere pugnae in quod
8 minime apti sunt. Nam quemadmodum comminus, ubi[5] in vicem pati et inferre vulnera licet, accendit ira animos eorum, ita ubi ex occulto et procul levibus telis vulnerantur, nec quo ruant caeco impetu habent,[6] velut ferae transfixae in suos temere
9 incurrunt. Detegebat[7] vulnera eorum, quod nudi pugnant, et sunt fusa et candida corpora, ut quae numquam nisi in pugna nudentur; ita et plus sanguinis ex multa carne fundebatur et foediores patebant plagae et candor corporum magis sanguine atro
10 maculabatur.[8] Sed non tam patentibus plagis moventur; interdum insecta cute, ubi latior quam altior plaga est, etiam gloriosius se pugnare putant;
11 iidem, cum aculeus sagittae aut[9] glandis abditae introrsus tenui vulnere in speciem urit, et scrutantes qua evellant[10] telum non sequitur, tum in rabiem et

[1] manum ς : manu *B*. [2] nec arte ς : *om. B.*
[3] ab *ed. Frobeniana* 1535 : et ab *B*ς.
[4] configebantur ς : conficiebantur *B*.
[5] ubi ς : sub *B*. [6] habent ς : *om. B.*
[7] detegebat ς : detegebant *B*.
[8] maculabatur ς : maculatur *B*.
[9] aut ς : *om. B.*
[10] qua evellant *Perizonius* : quae uellent *B* : quae uellant ς.

---

[1] The Gauls were not devotees of the exercise in the open air which tanned the Romans.

weapons than their swords, for which there was no use, since the enemy did not meet them in hand-to-hand conflict. Stones—but not of suitable size, since they had made no preparations in advance, but took each what happened to come to his hand in his hasty search—they did use, but like men untrained in their employment, with neither skill nor strength to add effectiveness to the blow. Arrows, sling-bullets, darts, coming from all sides wounded them unexpectedly, nor did they see what to do, as their minds were blinded by rage and fear, and they were involved in a kind of battle for which they were very ill-adapted. For, as in hand-to-hand fighting, where they can receive and inflict wounds in turn, passion inflames their minds, so when they are struck by light weapons, coming from unseen and distant sources, and when they have no place at which they can charge with blind violence, like wounded animals they rush headlong upon their own friends. The fact that they fight naked makes their wounds conspicuous and their bodies are fleshy and white, as is natural, since they are never uncovered except in battle;[1] so that both more blood flowed from their abundant flesh and the wounds stood out to view more fearfully and the whiteness of their skins was more stained by the black blood. But they are not much disturbed by open wounds; indeed, sometimes they cut away the skin, when the gash is broad rather than deep, and think that thus they gain greater glory in the fight; the same men, when the sting of an arrow or of a bullet that has buried itself in the flesh torments them, having caused a wound small to look at, and, as they search for a way to extract the missile, it does not come out, turning B.C. 189

A.U.C. 565 pudorem tam parvae perimentis[1] versi pestis
prosternunt corpora humi, sic[2] tum passim pro-
12 cumbebant; alii[3] ruentes in hostem undique configebantur et, cum comminus venerant, gladiis a
13 velitibus trucidabantur. Hic miles tripedalem par-
mam habet et in dextera hastas quibus eminus
utitur; gladio Hispaniensi est cinctus; quodsi pede
collato pugnandum est,[4] translatis in laevam hastis
14 stringit gladium. Pauci iam supererant Gallorum,
qui, postquam ab levi armatura superatos se viderunt
et instare legionum signa, effusa fuga castra repetunt
pavoris et tumultus iam plena, ut ubi feminae pue-
15 rique et alia imbellis turba permixta esset. Romanos
victores deserti fuga hostium acceperunt tumuli.

XXII. Sub idem tempus L. Manlius[5] et C. Helvius,
cum, quoad viam colles obliqui dederunt, escendis-
sent, postquam ad invia ventum est, flexere iter in
2 partem montis, quae una habebat iter, et sequi
consulis agmen[6] modico uterque intervallo velut
ex composito coeperunt, quod primo optimum factu
3 fuisset, in id necessitate ipsa compulsi; subsidia enim

[1] perimentis ς: prementis *B*.
[2] humi sic *edd. vett.*: humi sicut *M*ς.
[3] procumbebant; alii *M. Mueller*: procumbebant alii *B*ς.
[4] est ς: *om. B*.
[5] l. manlius ς: *om. B*.
[6] agmen *edd. vett.*: agmen l. manlius c. heluius *B*ς.

---

[1] It would be interesting to know the source of this highly realistic and picturesque description of the manners of the Gauls in battle. One thinks of the apparent relish with which the source which Livy followed in XXXI. xxxiv. 4 described the wounds suffered by Philip's cavalry in an engagement with Roman cavalry, and wonders whether the same person is responsible for the originals of the two passages.

[2] According to XXVI. iv. 4 each man carried seven javelins.

to madness and shame at being destroyed by so small a thing, throw their bodies upon the ground. So in this instance they lay prostrate here and there; some, rushing against the enemy, were wounded from every side, and when they had come to close quarters they were slain by the swords of the skirmishers.[1] This type of soldier carries a three-foot shield and, in his right hand, javelins [2] which he uses at long range; he is also equipped with a Spanish sabre; [3] if he is compelled to fight hand to hand, he shifts his javelins to his left hand and draws his sword. By now there were few of the Gauls surviving, and they, when they saw themselves defeated by the light troops and that the legionary standards were drawing near, in headlong flight sought their camp, which was already full of panic and confusion, as the women and children and the rest of the unarmed crowd were gathered there. The victorious Romans took possession of the hills abandoned by the flight of the enemy. B.C. 189

XXII. About the same time Lucius Manlius and Gaius Helvius, when they had marched up as far as the slopes of the hill admitted of progress, after they had reached the impassable places changed their direction towards that part of the mountain which alone offered a road, and began to follow the consul's column, each at a moderate distance as if by agreement, being compelled by necessity itself to do what would from the first have been the best thing to do; [4]

[3] If Livy speaks with technical accuracy, this was the heavy weapon, adapted to cutting, carried by Roman cavalry; the infantry sword, which was short and adapted to both cutting and thrusting, is called *gladius Hispanus*: cf. XXXI. xxxiv. 4 and the note.

[4] The implied criticism is perhaps that of Polybius, whose account of the battle has been lost.

A.U.C. 565 in talibus iniquitatibus locorum maximo saepe usui
fuerunt,[1] ut primis forte deturbatis secundi et tegant
4 pulsos et integri pugnam excipiant. Consul, postquam ad tumulos ab levi armatura captos prima signa
legionum pervenerunt,[2] respirare et conquiescere
paulisper militem iubet; simul strata per tumulos
5 corpora Gallorum ostentat et, cum levis armatura
proelium tale ediderit, quid ab legionibus, quid ab
iustis armis, quid ab animis fortissimorum militum
expectari? Castra illis capienda esse, in quae
6 compulsus ab levi armatura hostis trepidet. Praecedere tamen iubet levem armaturam, quae, cum
staret agmen, colligendis per tumulos telis ut missilia
sufficerent, haud segne id ipsum tempus consump-
7 serat. Iam castris appropinquabant; et Galli, ne
parum se munimenta sua tegerent, armati pro vallo
constiterant. Obruti deinde omni genere telorum
cum, quo plures atque densiores erant, eo minus vani
quicquam intercideret teli,[3] intra vallum momento
temporis compelluntur stationibus tantum firmis ad
8 ipsos aditus portarum relictis. In multitudinem
compulsam in castra vis ingens missilium telorum
coniciebatur, et vulnerari multos clamor permixtus
mulierum atque puerorum ploratibus significabat.

[1] fuerunt *ed. Frobeniana* 1535: fuerant *BMς*.
[2] peruenerunt ς: uenerunt *B*.
[3] teli ς: *om. B*.

for reserves have often, on such unfavourable terrains, B.C. 189
been of the greatest service, that when the leading troops have perhaps been thrown into disorder the reserves may both shield the defeated and, being themselves fresh, take up the fight. When the leading standards of the legions came to the hills which had been captured by the light troops, the consul ordered the men to take breath and to rest for a little while; at the same time he called their attention to the corpses of Gauls strewn over the hills and asked them what, when light-armed troops had worked such havoc in the fight, was to be expected of the legions, what of regular weapons, what of soldiers of the stoutest hearts? Their camp, he said, remained to be taken, into which the enemy had been driven in confusion by the light troops. Nevertheless, he ordered the light-armed men to lead the advance, and they, while the column was halted, had spent the time by no means idly, in collecting the weapons over the hills, that the supply of missiles might suffice. Now they were approaching the camp, and the Gauls, lest their fortifications should offer them too little shelter, had taken post under arms in front of the rampart. Then they were overwhelmed by missiles of every kind, and the more numerous and the more crowded together they were, the less did any weapon fall without effect, so that in an instant they were driven back within the rampart, leaving only strong guards at the actual gates of the fortifications. A vast quantity of missile weapons was discharged at the throng which had been driven inside the camp, and the shouts mingled with the wails of women and children showed that many were wounded. Against the troops who had

A.U.C. 565
9 In eos qui portas stationibus suis clauserant, legionum
antesignani pila coniecerunt. Iis vero non vulnera-
bantur, sed transverberatis scutis plerique inter se
conserti haerebant; nec diutius impetum Romanorum
sustinuerunt.

XXIII. Patentibus iam portis, priusquam irrumperent victores, fuga e castris Gallorum in omnes
partes facta est. Ruunt caeci per vias per invia;
nulla praecipitia saxa, nullae rupes obstant;[1] nihil
2 praeter hostem metuunt; itaque plerique prae-
cipites per vastam altitudinem prolapsi aut debilitati
exanimantur. Consul captis castris direptione praedaque abstinet militem; sequi pro se quemque et
3 instare et perculsis pavorem addere iubet. Supervenit et alterum cum L. Manlio agmen; nec eos
castra intrare sinit; protinus ad persequendos hostes
mittit, et ipse paulo post tradita captivorum custodia
tribunis militum sequitur, debellatum ratus, si in illo
4 pavore quam plurimi caesi forent aut capti. Egresso
consule C. Helvius cum tertio agmine advenit, nec
continere suos ab direptione castrorum valuit,
praedaque eorum, iniquissima sorte, qui pugnae non
interfuerant, facta est.[2] Equites diu ignari et
5 pugnae et victoriae suorum steterunt; deinde et
ipsi, quantum equis subire poterant, sparsos fuga
Gallos circa radices montis consectati cecidere aut

[1] obstant ς : *om. B.*
[2] facta est ς : *om. B.*

---

[1] The Gauls stood with shields overlapping, and a spear which struck near the edge might fasten two of them together. Caesar (*B. G.* I. xxv. 3) describes more clearly a similar occurrence.

blocked the gates at which they were posted, the B.C. 189 *antesignani* of the legions hurled their spears. The men indeed were not injured by them, but their shields in many cases were pierced and fastened together,[1] nor did they longer resist the attack of the Romans.

XXIII. The gates being now open, before the victors could break in, the Gauls began to flee from the camp in all directions. They rushed blindly along the roads and where there were no roads; no steep rocks, no cliffs, held them back; they feared nothing but the enemy; accordingly many were killed, falling headlong or slipping in weariness over tremendous precipices. The consul, having taken the camp, kept his soldiers from spoil and pillage; he ordered them each to follow as best he could, press the pursuit and increase the panic of the fugitives. The second column, under Lucius Manlius, also came up; he did not permit his men to enter the camp, but sent them at once to pursue the enemy, and he himself followed a little later, having entrusted the guarding of the prisoners to the tribunes of the soldiers, being convinced that the war was over if the largest possible number was killed or captured in that rout. When the consul had gone, Gaius Helvius arrived with the third column and was unable to prevent his men from plundering the camp, and the booty, by a most unjust decree of fate, fell into the hands of men who had had no part in the battle. The cavalry, knowing nothing for a long time of either the battle or the victory of their comrades, remained stationary; later they too, with all the speed of which their horses were capable, pursuing the Gauls as they scattered in flight around the

A.U.C. 565

6 cepere. Numerus interfectorum haud facile iniri
potuit, quia late per omnes amfractus montium
7 fugaque et caedes fuit, et magna pars rupibus inviis
in profundae altitudinis convalles[1] delapsa est, pars
8 in silvis vepribusque occisa. Claudius, qui bis pugnatum in Olympo monte scribit, ad quadraginta
milia hominum auctor est caesa, Valerius Antias, qui
magis immodicus in numero augendo esse solet, non
9 plus decem milia. Numerus captivorum haud dubie
milia quadraginta[2] explevit, quia omnis generis
aetatisque turbam secum traxerant demigrantium
10 magis quam in bellum euntium modo. Consul armis
hostium in uno concrematis cumulo ceteram praedam
conferre omnes iussit, et aut vendidit, quod eius in
publicum redigendum erat, aut cum cura ut quam
11 aequissima esset per milites divisit. Laudati quoque
pro contione omnes sunt, donatique pro merito quisque, ante omnes Attalus summo ceterorum assensu;
nam singularis eius iuvenis cum virtus et industria
in omnibus laboribus periculisque tum modestia
etiam fuerat.

[1] conualles ς : ualles *B*. [2] quadraginta ς : *om. B*.

---

[1] Manlius himself (xlvii. 6 below) says that he captured and killed more than forty thousand of the enemy, and Orosius (IV. xx; he credits the victory to the other consul Fulvius) says that forty thousand were killed. Appian, however (*Syr.* xlii), asserts that there were forty thousand prisoners and that the slain could not be counted. Perhaps the official report of Manlius was used by Claudius.

[2] The vividness of the preceding narrative gives rise to a question as to its sources. Valerius Antias and Claudius are quoted, and in the preceding note I suggest that the latter may have used the official report of Manlius. For some reason or other the Galatian campaign attracted an unusual amount of attention: Hannibal is said to have

base of the mountain, killed and captured them. The number of casualties could not easily be calculated because the flight and slaughter went on far and wide over all the outlying parts of the mountains, and a great number fell from the pathless cliffs into valleys of enormous depth, and some were killed in the forests and thickets. Claudius, who writes that there were two battles on the Olympus mountain, asserts that about forty thousand men were slain;[1] Valerius Antias, who is usually more unrestrained in exaggerating numbers, says that not more than ten thousand fell. The number of prisoners without doubt brought the total up to forty thousand, because they had brought with them their whole population of every class and age, like a people in migration rather than setting out to war. The consul, having burned all the weapons of the enemy in one pile, ordered all his troops to bring in the rest of the booty and either sold that part of the booty which it was his duty to convert to public use or carefully distributed it to the soldiers so as to secure the greatest possible measure of equity. Also before an assembly he praised everyone according to his merits, and Attalus before all, with the complete approval of the rest; for the young man had displayed not only remarkable courage and diligence amid all the toils and dangers, but also modesty of behaviour.[2] B.C. 189

written an account of it (Nepos, *Hann.* xiii. 2), but there is no trace of this. In the note to xv. 5 above I mentioned the generally accepted assumption that Livy had access to a diary of some participant in the campaign: Mommsen once suggested (*Röm. Forsch.* II. 538 ff.) that he was Polybius, but this has not been taken seriously. Whether the sanguinophile source of chap. xxi (see the note to xxi. 12 above) was one of those already mentioned cannot be determined.

A.U.C. 565 XXIV. Supererat bellum integrum cum Tectosagis. Ad eos profectus consul tertiis castris Ancyram, nobilem in illis locis urbem,[1] pervenit, unde
2 hostes paulo plus decem milia aberant. Ubi cum
stativa essent, facinus memorabile a captiva factum
est. Orgiagontis reguli uxor forma eximia custo-
diebatur inter plures captivos;[2] cui custodiae cen-
3 turio praeerat et libidinis et avaritiae militaris. Is
primo animum temptavit; quem cum abhorrentem
a voluntario videret stupro, corpori, quod servum
4 fortuna erat, vim fecit. Deinde ad leniendam indig-
nitatem iniuriae spem reditus ad suos mulieri facit,
et ne eam quidem, ut amans, gratuitam. Certo auri
pondere pactus, ne quem suorum conscium haberet,
ipsi permittit ut quem vellet unum ex captivis
5 nuntium ad suos mitteret. Locum prope flumen
constituit, quo duo ne[3] plus necessarii[4] captivae
cum auro venirent nocte insequenti ad eam acci-
6 piendam. Forte ipsius mulieris servus inter captivos eiusdem custodiae erat. Hunc nuntium primis
7 tenebris extra stationes centurio educit. Nocte
insequenti et duo necessarii mulieris ad constitutum
8 locum et centurio cum captiva venit. Ubi cum
aurum ostenderent, quod summam talenti Attici

[1] urbem ς : in urbem *B.*
[2] captiuos ς : *om. B.*
[3] quo duo ne ς : *om., spat. rel., B.*
[4] necessarii ς : necessia *B.*

---

[1] This city (modern Angora) was important enough later to have the *Res Gestae* of Augustus (*Monumentum Ancyranum*) set up there.

[2] Polybius and others give her name as Chiomara.

XXIV. There remained an entirely new war with the Tectosagi. Setting out against them the consul came on the third day of marching to Ancyra, a famous city in that region,[1] from which the enemy was a little more than ten miles distant. While they were established in camp there, a memorable deed was done by a captive woman. The wife [2] of the chieftain Orgiago,[3] a woman of surpassing beauty, was held under guard among a large number of prisoners; the commander of the guard was a centurion, characterized by both the lust and the greed of the soldier. At first he tried her disposition; when he found it shrinking from voluntary fornication, he did violence to her body, which fortune had made a slave. Then, to quiet her indignation at the injury, he held out to the woman the hope of a return to her own people, but not even that, as a lover might have done, did he grant her for nothing. Having stipulated for a definite quantity of gold, to avoid taking one of his own men as an accomplice, he allowed the woman herself to send as a messenger to her people whomsoever of the prisoners she should choose. He designated a spot near the river to which not more than two of the kinsmen of the captive were to come with the money the following night to receive her. It happened that one of the woman's own slaves was among the prisoners under the same guard. This man, as messenger, the centurion at nightfall conducted beyond the line of sentinels. The following night both the two kinsmen of the woman and the centurion with the prisoner came to the appointed place. While they were displaying the money, which was to amount to an Attic B.C. 189

[3] Probably identical with Ortiago of xix. 2 above.

A.U.C. 565 —tanti enim pepigerat—expleret, mulier lingua sua
stringerent ferrum et centurionem pensantem aurum
9 occiderent imperavit. Iugulati praecisum caput ipsa
involutum veste ferens ad virum Orgiagontem, qui
ab Olympo domum refugerat, pervenit; quem priusquam [1] complecteretur, caput centurionis ante pedes
10 eius abiecit, mirantique cuiusnam id caput hominis
aut quod id facinus haudquaquam mulieris esset, et
iniuriam corporis [2] et ultionem violatae per vim
pudicitiae confessa viro est aliaque, ut traditur, sanc-
titate et gravitate vitae huius matronalis facinoris
decus ad ultimum conservavit.

XXV. Ancyram in stativa oratores Tectosagum
ad consulem venerunt petentes, ne ante ab Ancyra
castra moveret quam collocutus cum suis regibus
esset: nullas condiciones pacis iis non bello fore
2 potiores. Tempus [3] in posterum diem constituitur
locusque, qui medius maxime inter castra Gallorum
3 et Ancyram est visus. Quo cum consul ad tempus
cum praesidio quingentorum equitum venisset nec
ullo Gallorum ibi viso regressus in castra esset, ora-
4 tores idem redeunt, excusantes religione obiecta
venire reges non posse; principes gentis, per quos
5 aeque res transigi posset, venturos. Consul se
quoque Attalum missurum dixit. Ad hoc colloquium utrimque ventum est. Trecentos equites

[1] priusquam ς: prius *B*.
[2] et iniuriam corporis ς: *om. B*. [3] tempus ς: *om. B*.

---

[1] Practically the same story is told by Polybius (XXII. xxi), Plutarch (*Mul. Virt.* 43), Valerius Maximus (VI. i. ext. 2) and Florus (I. xxvii. 6). All probably came from the same ultimate source (the diary mentioned above?), although Plutarch quotes as from Polybius an item not now found in Polybius' own version.

talent—for so great had been the sum agreed upon —the woman in her own language ordered them to draw sword and kill the centurion as he was weighing the money. When they had slit his throat and cut off his head, the woman herself wrapped it in her garment and carried it on her return to her husband Orgiago, who had escaped home from Olympus; before she embraced him she dropped at his feet the head of the centurion, and, when he wondered whose head this was and what this act meant, so unlike that of a woman, she confessed to her husband the violence done to her person and the vengeance exacted for her forcibly violated chastity, and, as the story goes, by the purity and dignity of her life in other respects maintained to the end the glory won by a deed that marked her as a true matron.[1] B.C. 189

XXV. Ambassadors from the Tectosages came to the consul at his base at Ancyra, requesting that he should not move from Ancyra until he had conferred with their chiefs: there were no terms of peace which would not be preferable in their sight to war. The time fixed was for the next day and the place one which seemed approximately half-way between the camp of the Gauls and Ancyra. When the consul had come there at the designated time, attended by a guard of five hundred cavalry, and had returned to his camp without having seen any Gaul there, the same ambassadors returned, apologizing that their chiefs could not come by reason of religious objection; the leading men of the tribe, they said, through whom the business could equally well be transacted, would come. The consul said that he too would send a representative, namely, Attalus. Both parties attended this conference. When

A.U.C. 565 Attalus praesidii causa cum adduxisset, iactatae[1]
6 sunt pacis[2] condiciones; finis rei quia absentibus
ducibus imponi non poterat, convenit uti consul
7 regesque eo loco postero die congrederentur. Frus-
tratio Gallorum eo spectabat, primum ut tererent
tempus, donec res suas quibus periclitari nolebant
cum coniugibus et liberis trans Halyn flumen trai-
cerent, deinde quod ipsi consuli, parum cauto adversus
8 colloquii[3] fraudem, insidiabantur. Mille ad eam
rem ex omni numero audaciae expertae delegerunt
equites; et successisset fraudi ni pro iure gentium,
cuius violandi consilium initum erat, stetisset for-
9 tuna. Pabulatores lignatoresque Romani in eam
partem in qua colloquium futurum erat ducti sunt,[4]
tutius id futurum tribunis ratis, quia consulis praesidium et ipsum pro statione habituri erant hosti
10 oppositum; suam tamen alteram stationem propius
11 castra sescentorum equitum posuerunt. Consul,
affirmante Attalo venturos reges et transigi rem
posse, profectus e castris, cum eodem quo[5] antea
praesidio equitum quinque milia fere processisset
nec multum a constituto loco abesset, repente con-
citatis equis cum impetu hostili videt Gallos venientes.
12 Constituit agmen, et[6] expedire tela animosque
equitibus iussis primo constanter initium pugnae

[1] iactatae *J. F. Gronovius* : iactae *Bς* : actae *M.*
[2] pacis ς : *om. B.*
[3] colloquii ς : consilii *B.*
[4] ducti sunt ς : *om. B.*
[5] quo ς : quod *B.*
[6] et ς : *om. B.*

Attalus had brought up with him a bodyguard of three hundred cavalry, terms of peace were discussed; since a conclusion to the matter could not be reached in the absence of the principals, it was agreed that the consul and the chiefs should meet in that place the following day. The evasiveness of the Gauls had this purpose: first, that they might waste time until they could transport their property, which they did not wish to jeopardize, together with their wives and children, across the river Halys; second, that they were plotting against the consul himself, who had not been sufficiently on guard against treachery at the conference. For this purpose they chose from their entire number a thousand cavalry of tried boldness; and success would have attended their treachery had not fortune stood on the side of the law of nations which they had planned to violate. The Roman foragers and wood-gatherers were led in the direction in which the conference was to be held, the tribunes thinking that this would be safer, since they would have between them and the enemy the consul's bodyguard, placed as a sort of outpost for them; nevertheless, they posted another outguard of their own, consisting of six hundred cavalry, nearer the camp. The consul, on the assurance of Attalus that the chiefs would come and that the business could be settled, set out from camp with the same guard of cavalry as before, and, when he had gone about five miles and was not far from the appointed place, suddenly he saw the Gauls coming, their horses at full gallop, and with the air of enemies. He halted his column, and, ordering the troopers to prepare arms and, minds for the combat, at first he stoutly received the onset of the attack and did not

B.C. 189

A.U.C. 565 excepit[1] nec cessit; dein, cum praegravaret multitudo, cedere sensim nihil confusis turmarum ordinibus
13 coepit; postremo, cum iam plus in mora periculi quam in ordinibus conservandis[2] praesidii esset, omnes passim in fugam effusi sunt. Tum vero instare dissipatis Galli[3] et caedere; magnaque pars oppressa foret ni statio pabulatorum, sescenti equites,
14 occurrissent. Ii procul clamore pavido suorum audito cum tela equosque expedissent, integri pro-
15 fligatam pugnam acceperunt. Itaque versa extemplo fortuna est, versus a victis in victores terror. Et primo impetu fusi Galli sunt, et ex agris concurrebant pabulatores, et undique obvius hostis Gallis erat, ut ne fugam quidem tutam aut facilem haberent, quia recentibus equis Romani fessos sequebantur.
16 Pauci ergo effugerunt; captus est nemo; maior multo pars per fidem violati colloquii[4] poenas morte luerunt. Romani ardentibus ira[5] animis postero die omnibus copiis ad hostem perveniunt.

XXVI. Biduum natura montis per se ipsum explorandа ne quid ignoti esset absumpsit[6] consul; tertio die, cum auspicio operam dedisset, deinde immolasset, in quattuor partes divisas copias educit,
2 duas, ut medio monte duceret, duas ab lateribus, ut
3 adversus cornua Gallorum erigeret. Hostium quod roboris erat, Tectosagi et Trocmi, mediam tenebant

[1] excepit *Perizonius*: cepit *B*: accepit ς.
[2] conseruandis ς: *om. B.*
[3] Galli ς: *om. B.*
[4] colloquii ς: eloquii *B.*
[5] ira *ed. Frobeniana* 1535: *om. Bς.*
[6] absumpsit ς: assumpsit *B.*

[1] Cf. xix. 1 above.

give way; then, when the weight of numbers was bearing him down, he began to retire gradually, preserving the formation of his troops; finally, when there was now more danger in delay than protection in maintaining the formation, all scattered in random flight. Then indeed the Gauls began to pursue and kill the scattered cavalry; and a great part of them would have been destroyed had not the outpost of the foragers, the six hundred cavalry, come up to them. When they had heard from afar the terrified shouts of their comrades and had made ready their weapons and horses, they came upon the rout with their force still fresh. So straightway fortune changed and the panic changed sides, from the vanquished to the victors. And at the first attack the Gauls were routed and the foragers flocked in from the fields and foes faced the Gauls from every side, so that they did not find even flight either easy or safe, since the Romans with fresh horses were pursuing the weary. And so few then escaped; no one was taken prisoner; by far the greatest part paid with their lives the penalty for breaking the faith of a conference. The Romans, their hearts on fire with wrath, advanced the next day with their whole strength against the enemy. B.C. 189

XXVI. The consul spent two days in exploring for himself the character of the mountain,[1] that nothing might be unfamiliar to him; on the third day, after giving his attention to the auspices and then offering sacrifice, he divided his army into four columns and led them out, planning to lead two up the central part of the mountain and to send two from the sides to oppose the flanks of the Gauls. The Tectosagi and the Trocmi, who constituted the

A.U.C. 565 aciem, milia hominum quinquaginta; equitatum,
quia equorum nullus erat inter inaequales[1] rupes
usus, ad pedes deductum, decem milia hominum, ab
4 dextro locaverunt cornu; Ariarathis Cappadoces et
Morzi auxiliares in laevo quattuor ferme milium
numerum explebant. Consul, sicut in Olympo
monte, prima in acie locata levi armatura, telorum
omnis generis ut aeque magna vis ad manum esset,
5 curavit. Ubi appropinquarunt,[2] omnia eadem utrimque
quae fuerant in priore proelio erant praeter
animos et victoribus ab re secunda auctos et hostibus
6 fractos,[3] quia, etsi non ipsi victi erant, suae gentis
hominum cladem pro sua ducebant. Itaque a
paribus initiis coepta res eundem exitum habuit.
7 Velut nubes levium telorum coniecta obruit aciem
Gallorum. Nec aut procurrere quisquam ab ordinibus
suis, ne nudarent[4] undique corpus ad ictus,
audebant, et stantes quo densiores erant hoc plura,
velut destinatum petentibus, vulnera accipiebant.
8 Consul iam per se turbatis si legionum signa ostendisset,
versuros extemplo in fugam omnes ratus
receptis inter ordines velitibus et alia turba auxiliorum
aciem promovit.

XXVII. Galli et memoria Tolostobogiorum cladis territi et inhaerentia corporibus gerentes tela fessique

[1] inaequales ς : aequales *B.*
[2] appropinquarunt ς : appro (*sic, in fine paginae*) *B.*
[3] fractos ς : *om. B.*
[4] nudarent ς : nudaret *B.*

---

[1] A Paphlagonian prince.

strength of the enemy, held the centre of their line B.C. 189 with fifty thousand men; the cavalry, being dismounted since there was no use for horses on the rough cliffs, and numbering ten thousand men, they placed on their right flank; the Cappadocians of Ariarathes and the auxiliaries of Morzius [1] on the left flank amounted to about four thousand men. The consul, as at the Olympus mountain, placed the light-armed troops in the van and made provision that there might be at hand an equally large supply of every kind of weapon. When they approached, everything was the same on both sides as in the former battle except courage, which was increased in the victors by reason of their success and diminished in the enemy because, while they themselves had not been conquered, they considered as their own the disaster suffered by men of their own race. And so from like beginnings the affair had the same end. The discharge of a veritable cloud of light missiles overwhelmed the line of the Gauls. No one dared to rush forward from their ranks lest he expose his body to wounds from all sides, and, standing fast, the more closely they were crowded together the more wounds they received, the attackers aiming, so to speak, at a target. The consul, thinking that if he disclosed the standards of the legions to an enemy already disorganized on its own account they would all at once turn to flight, received within his ranks the skirmishers and the rest of the throng of auxiliaries and moved forward his battle-line.

XXVII. The Gauls, terrified as they were by the recollection of the defeat of the Tolostobogii, carrying weapons fixed in their bodies and wearied both by

A.U.C. 565 et stando et[1] vulneribus ne primum quidem impetum
2 et clamorem Romanorum tulerunt. Fuga ad castra
inclinavit; sed pauci intra munimenta sese recepere;
pars maior dextra laevaque praelati qua quemque
3 impetus tulit fugerunt.[2] Victores usque ad castra
secuti ceciderunt terga; deinde in castris[3] cupiditate
4 praedae haeserunt, nec sequebatur quisquam. In
cornibus Galli diutius steterunt quia serius ad eos
perventum est; ceterum ne primum quidem[4]
5 coniectum telorum tulerunt. Consul, quia ingressos
in castra ab direptione abstrahere non poterat, eos
qui in cornibus fuerant protinus ad sequendos hostes
6 misit. Per aliquantum spatium secuti non plus
tamen octo milia hominum in fuga—nam pugna
nulla fuit—ceciderunt; reliqui flumen Halyn
7 traiecerunt. Romanorum pars magna ea nocte in
castris hostium mansit; ceteros in sua castra consul
reduxit. Postero die captivos praedamque recensuit,
quae tanta fuit quantam[5] avidissima rapiendi gens,
cum cis montem Taurum omnia armis per multos
8 annos tenuisset, coacervare potuit. Galli ex dissi-
pata passim fuga in unum locum congregati, magna
pars saucii aut[6] inermes, nudati omnibus rebus,
9 oratores de pace ad consulem miserunt. Eos
Manlius Ephesum venire iussit; ipse—iam enim
medium autumni erat—locis gelidis propinquitate
Tauri montis excedere properans victorem exercitum
in hiberna maritimae orae reduxit.

[1] et ς: *om. B.* [2] fugerunt ς: fuerunt *B.*
[3] in castris ς: castris *B.* [4] quidem ς: *om. B.*
[5] quantam *ed. Frobeniana* 1531: quanta *B*ς.
[6] saucii aut *ed. Frobeniana* 1535: saucia ut *B*ς.

---

[1] It is improbable that the Taurus mountain could have much effect on the climate of Galatia.

standing and by wounds, did not endure even the first assault and shout of the Romans. Their flight was directed towards their camp, but few found their way within the ramparts; the majority was carried past to right and left and fled wherever the course of each led. The victors, cutting them down from behind, followed as far as the camp; then they remained in the camp in their greed for plunder, nor did anyone pursue. On the flanks the Gauls stood firm longer because the attack was slower to reach them; but they did not endure even the first volley of weapons. Since the consul was unable to tear away from their plundering the troops who had entered the camp, he at once sent those who had been on the flanks to pursue the enemy. Although they followed for a considerable distance, they did not kill more than eight thousand men in the flight, for there was no battle; the rest crossed the river Halys. A large part of the Romans stayed that night in the camp of the enemy; the consul led the rest back to their own camp. The next day he surveyed the prisoners and booty, which was as great as a people most greedy for plunder could amass after holding under armed control for many years everything on this side of the Taurus mountain. The Gauls, assembling in one place after their scattered and disorderly flight, most of them being wounded or unarmed, stripped of everything, sent ambassadors to the consul concerning peace. Manlius ordered them to come to Ephesus; he himself—for it was now mid-autumn—was in haste to get away from regions cold owing to the neighbourhood of the Taurus mountain [1] and led the victorious army back into winter quarters on the sea coast. B.C. 189

A.U.C. 565

XXVIII. Dum haec in Asia geruntur, in ceteris provinciis tranquillae res fuerunt. Censores Romae T. Quinctius Flamininus et M. Claudius Marcellus
2 senatum legerunt;[1] princeps in senatu tertium lectus P. Scipio Africanus; quattuor soli[2] praeteriti sunt, nemo curuli usus honore. Et in[3] equitatu recensen-
3 do mitis admodum censura fuit. Substructionem super Aequimelium in Capitolio et viam silice sternendam a porta Capena ad Martis locaverunt.
4 Campani ubi censerentur senatum consuluerunt; decretum uti Romae censerentur. Aquae ingentes eo anno fuerunt; Tiberis duodeciens campum Martium planaque urbis inundavit.

5 Ab Cn. Manlio consule bello in Asia cum Gallis perfecto, alter consul M. Fulvius perdomitis Aetolis cum traiecisset in Cephallaniam, circa civitates insulae misit percontatum utrum se dedere Romanis
6 an belli fortunam experiri mallent. Metus ad omnes valuit, ne deditionem recusarent. Obsides inde

[1] legerunt *Modius*: perlegerunt *B*ς: elegerunt *M*.
[2] soli ς: solis *B*. [3] et in ς: et *B*.

---

[1] Livy now enumerates briefly events in Rome during the period occupied by the Aetolian and Galatian campaigns. The narrative thus supplements that of XXXVII. lii–lviii incl.

[2] Cf. XXXIV. xliv. 4 and the note. Scipio had received this distinction in 199 B.C. (when he had been one of the censors) and in 194 B.C.

[3] The censors performed the function of revising the list of *equites* and removing from the list such individuals as the facts as they found them warranted.

[4] Neither the meaning of the word nor the situation of the place is quite certain, although if it was near the *vicus Iugarius*

XXVIII. While this was going on in Asia things were quiet in the other provinces. At Rome[1] the censors Titus Quinctius Flamininus and Marcus Claudius Marcellus chose the senate; as *princeps senatus*[2] Publius Scipio Africanus was chosen for the third time; only four senators were passed over, none of whom had held curule office. In the review of the *equites*[3] also the censorship was quite lenient. Contracts were let for the building of a substructure above the Aequimelium[4] on the Capitoline and for the paving with flint of the road from the Porta Capena to the temple of Mars.[5] The Campanians asked the senate for a decision as to where they should be listed by the censors; it was decreed that they should be listed in Rome.[6] There were great floods that year; the Tiber on twelve occasions overflowed the Campus Martius and the level districts of the city. B.C. 189

The war with the Gauls in Asia having been finished by the consul Gnaeus Manlius, the other consul, Marcus Fulvius, after conquering the Aetolians, crossed to Cephallania[7] and sent agents around the island to inquire of the cities whether they preferred to surrender themselves to the Romans or to try the fortune of war. Fear prevailed upon all of them not to refuse submission. Hostages were then requisi-

the work may have been necessitated by the landslide of 192 B.C. (XXXV. xxi. 6).

[5] This temple lay between a mile and two miles outside the Porta Capena on the Via Appia.

[6] These were probably Campanians who had been driven from their homes during the Second Punic War and had settled in other parts of Italy. They were not, however, citizens of the towns in which they resided, and the censors could not take cognizance of them there.

[7] Cf. ix. 10 above and the note.

A.U.C. 565 imperatos pro viribus inopes populi. . . .[1] vicenos
autem Cranii[2] et Palenses et Samaei dederunt.[3]
7 Insperata pax Cephallaniae adfulserat, cum repente
una civitas, incertum quam ob causam, Samaei
8 desciverunt. Quia opportuno loco urbs posita esset,
timuisse se aiebant ne demigrare cogerentur ab
Romanis. Ceterum ipsine sibi eum finxerint metum
et timore vano quietum excitaverint[4] malum, an
iactata[5] sermonibus res apud Romanos perlata ad
9 eos sit, nihil comperti est, nisi quod datis iam ob-
sidibus repente portas clauserunt et ne suorum
quidem precibus—miserat enim sub muros consul
ad temptandam misericordiam parentium populari-
10 umque—desistere ab incepto voluerunt.[6] Oppugnari
deinde, postquam nihil pacati respondebatur, coepta
urbs est. Apparatum omnem tormentorum machina-
rumque travectum ab Ambraciae oppugnatione habe-
11 bat, et opera quae facienda erant impigre milites per-
fecerunt. Duobus igitur locis admoti arietes quatie-
bant muros.

XXIX. Nec ab Samaeis quicquam quo aut opera
aut hostis arceri posset[7] praetermissum est. Duabus
2 tamen maxime resistebant rebus, una,[8] interiorem

[1] *probabilem emendationem huius loci mendosi, multis frustra temptatis, non invenerunt viri docti.*
[2] Cranii *Sigonius*: grannoni *Bς*.
[3] dederunt *ς*: *om. B*.
[4] excitaverint *edd. vett.*: excitauerunt *Bς*.
[5] iactata *ς*: iactatos *B*.
[6] uoluerunt *ς*: *om. B*.
[7] posset *ς*: possit *B*.
[8] una *ς*: unam *B*.

---

[1] The text is hopelessly corrupt, and I have not indicated the lacuna in the translation. It is uncertain whether *pro viribus* goes with *imperatos*, with *inopes*, as I have translated

tioned and supplied by the cities, poor in proportion B.C. 189 to their strength, twenty each by the Cranians, the Palensians and the Sameans.[1] The radiance of unexpected peace had shone upon Cephallania when suddenly one city, the Sameans, it is uncertain for what reason, revolted. Because the city enjoyed a strategic position, they said that they were afraid that they would be compelled by the Romans to move away. But whether they had invented this alarm for themselves and in baseless terror had roused a sleeping evil, or the subject had been discussed by the Romans and reported to them, nothing has been ascertained, except that when they had already given hostages they suddenly closed their gates and not even in response to the prayers of their own people—for the consul had sent some of them to the foot of the walls to stir up pity for their parents and fellow-countrymen—were they willing to abandon their undertaking. Then, when their replies showed no pacific intent, the siege of the city began. He had all the equipment of artillery and siege-engines transferred from the siege of Ambracia, and what works had to be constructed the soldiers zealously undertook. Accordingly, the battering-rams were moved up in two places and the walls attacked.

XXIX. Nor was any measure overlooked by the Sameans by which either the works or the enemy could be interfered with. Nevertheless, their resistance depended mainly upon two things; first, the

it, or with something omitted. Moreover, the fourth city on the island (Thuc. II. xxx. 2; Plin. *N.H.* IV. 54) is not mentioned. Finally, the number of hostages is very large (cf. xi. 6 above), which ill accords with *inopes*, unless the interpretation here given of *pro viribus inopes* is accepted.

A.U.C. 565 semper iuxta validum pro diruto novum obstruentes
murum, altera, eruptionibus subitis nunc in opera
hostium nunc in stationes; et plerumque his proeliis
3 superiores erant. Una ad coercendos inventa, haud
magna memoratu, res est. Centum funditores ab
4 Aegio et Patris et Dymis acciti. A pueris ii more
quodam [1] gentis saxis globosis, quibus ferme harenae
immixtis strata litora sunt, funda mare apertum
5 incessentes exercebantur. Itaque longius [2] certi-
usque et validiore ictu quam Baliaris funditor eo telo
6 usi sunt. Et est non simplicis habenae, ut Baliarica
aliarumque gentium funda, sed triplex scutale, crebris [3]
suturis duratum, ne fluxa habena volutetur in iactu
glans, sed librata cum sederit, velut nervo missa
7 excutiatur. Coronas modici circuli magno ex intervallo loci adsueti traicere non capita solum hostium
vulnerabant, sed quem locum destinassent oris.
8 Hae fundae Samaeos cohibuerunt, ne tam crebro
neve [4] tam audacter erumperent, adeo ut precarentur
ex muris Achaeos ut [5] parumper abscederent et se
cum Romanis stationibus pugnantes quiete spectarent.
9 Quattuor menses obsidionem Same sustinuit.
Cum ex paucis cotidie aliqui eorum caderent aut
vulnerarentur, et qui supererant fessi et corporibus

[1] quodam ς : quondam *B.*
[2] longius *B* (*ex corr.*) ς : longiore *B.*
[3] scutale crebris ς : scuta lecebris *B.*
[4] neue ς : nec *B.*
[5] ut ς : *om. B.*

[1] The corresponding passage in Polybius is lost, and the source of this description is uncertain. A somewhat similar account is found in XLII. lxv. 10, but it does not seem from either that Livy entirely understood what he was describing.

construction of a new wall, equally strong throughout, on the inner side and in place of the wall that was destroyed; second, their sudden sallies, now against the enemy's siegeworks, now against his outguards; and generally in these battles they had the advantage. One device was found to hold them in check, though trivial to mention. A hundred slingers were recruited from Aegium and Patrae and Dymae. These peoples were trained from boyhood, in accordance with a tradition of the race, in hurling with a sling at the open sea the round stones which, mingled with the sand, generally strew the coasts. In consequence they use this weapon at longer range, with greater accuracy and with more powerful effect than the Balearic slinger. Moreover, the sling is not composed of a single strap, like those of the Baleares and other peoples, but the bullet-carrier is triple, strengthened with numerous seams, that the missile may not fly out at random, from the pliancy of the strap at the moment of discharge, but, seated firmly while being whirled, may be shot out as if from a bow-string.[1] Having been trained to shoot through rings of moderate circumference from long distances, they would wound not merely the heads of their enemies but any part of the face at which they might have aimed. These slings prevented the Sameans from making sallies so frequently or so boldly, to such an extent that from the walls they begged the Achaeans[2] to withdraw for a while and in quiet to watch them fighting with the Roman outguards. For four months Same underwent the siege. Since every day some of their small number were killed or wounded and those who remained were wearied

B.C. 189

[2] *i.e.* the slingers.

A.U.C. 565 10 et animis essent, Romani nocte per arcem quam
Cyneatidem vocant—nam urbs in mare devexa in
occidentem vergit—muro superato in forum pervene-
11 runt. Samaei postquam captam partem urbis ab
hostibus senserunt, cum coniugibus ac liberis in
maiorem refugerunt arcem. Inde postero die dediti
direpta urbe sub corona omnes venierunt.

XXX. Consul compositis rebus Cephallaniae, praesidio Samae imposito, in Peloponnesum iam diu
accersentibus Aegiensibus maxime ac Lacedae-
2 moniis traiecit. Aegium a principio Achaici concilii
semper conventus gentis indicti sunt, seu dignitati
3 urbis id seu loci opportunitati [1] datum est. Hunc
morem Philopoemen eo primum anno labefactare
conatus legem parabat ferre, ut in omnibus civitatibus quae Achaici concilii essent in vicem conventus
4 agerentur. Et sub adventum consulis damiurgis
civitatium, qui summus est magistratus, Aegium
evocantibus Philopoemen—praetor tum erat—Argos
5 conventum edixit. Quo cum appareret omnes ferme
conventuros, consul quoque, quamquam Aegiensium
favebat causae, Argos venit; ubi cum disceptatio
fuisset, et rem inclinatam cerneret, incepto destitit.
6 Lacedaemonii deinde eum in sua certamina averte-

[1] opportunitati ς : opportunitate *B*.

---

[1] Cf. XXXII. xxii. 2 and the note.

[2] His fifth term in this office began in the autumn of 189 B.C. Livy habitually uses the Latin word *praetor* for the chief magistrate of foreign states: cf. XXXI. xxiv. 6 and the note.

in both body and mind, the Romans at night, by way of the citadel which they call Cyneatis—for the city slopes towards the sea and faces west—crossed the wall and entered the market-place. When the Sameans realized that part of the city had been captured by the enemy, they took refuge with their wives and children in the larger citadel. Then the next day the city was plundered and all who had surrendered were sold as slaves. B.C. 189

XXX. The consul, having arranged matters in Cephallania and stationed a garrison at Same, crossed to the Peloponnesus, whither the Aegians especially and the Lacedaemonians had long been summoning him. From the beginning of the Achaean League the meetings of the assembly had all been called for Aegium, whether this was a tribute to the importance of the city or the convenience of the place. This custom Philopoemen, in this year for the first time, was trying to break down, and was preparing to propose a law that the meetings should be held in all the cities which belonged to the Achaean League in rotation. And at the approach of the consul, when the *damiurgi* of the cities (they are the chief magistrates)[1] called the meeting at Aegium, Philopoemen —he was then praetor[2]—summoned it at Argos. When it was clear that almost all would assemble there, the consul, although he favoured the cause of the Aegians, also went to Argos; when the argument had begun there and he saw that the Aegian case was weaker, he gave up his purpose.[3] Then the Lacedaemonians diverted his attention to their own

[3] Fulvius had evidently intended to oppose the proposal of Philopoemen at the meeting.

A.U.C. 565 runt. Sollicitam eam civitatem exules maxime habebant, quorum magna pars in maritimis Laconicae orae castellis, quae omnis adempta erat,[1] habitabant.
7 Id aegre patientes Lacedaemonii, ut aliqua liberum ad mare haberent aditum, si quando Romam aliove quo mitterent legatos, simul ut emporium et receptaculum peregrinis mercibus ad necessarios usus esset, nocte adorti vicum maritimum nomine Lan[2]
8 improviso occupaverunt. Vicani quique ibi exules habitabant primo inopinata re territi sunt; deinde sub lucem congregati levi certamine expulerunt
9 Lacedaemonios.[3] Terror tamen omnem maritimam oram pervasit, legatosque communiter et castella omnia vicique et exules, quibus ibi domicilia erant, ad Achaeos miserunt.

XXXI. Philopoemen praetor, iam inde ab initio exulum causae amicus,[4] et auctor semper Achaeis minuendi opes et auctoritatem Lacedaemoniorum,
2 concilium querentibus dedit, decretumque referente eo factum est, cum in[5] fidem Achaeorum tutelamque T. Quinctius et Romani Laconicae orae castella

[1] adempta erat *ed. Frobeniana* 1535: ademptae erant *B*: adepti erant ς.

[2] Lan *ed. Frobeniana* 1535: lamin *B*ς.

[3] lacedaemonios ς: *om. B.*

[4] amicus *ed. Frobeniana* 1535: et amicus *B*ς.

[5] cum in ς: ut in *B*.

---

[1] In 195 B.C. Flamininus had concluded a treaty with Nabis, tyrant of Lacedaemon, in which it was provided, among other things, that Nabis should surrender his holdings on the coast (XXXIV. xxxv–xxxvi); the Achaean League had assumed, without explicit authority, so far as the evidence shows, the enforcement of this provision when, in 192 B.C., Nabis had undertaken to obtain an outlet to the sea (XXXV. xxv–xxx). After the assassination of Nabis by the Aetolians

quarrels.[1] The state was kept in anxiety especially by the exiles, a great part of whom lived in the fortresses along the Laconian sea coast, all of which had been taken away from Sparta. The Lacedaemonians, angered at this, in order that somehow they might possess free access to the sea, if ever they sent ambassadors to Rome or elsewhere, and at the same time that they might have a market and a place for the storage of foreign merchandise for necessary purposes, made an unexpected night attack on the coast town of Las and captured it. The townspeople and the exiles who lived there were at first terrified by this unlooked-for event; then, assembling at daybreak, with a slight effort they expelled the Lacedaemonians. Nevertheless, the panic spread to the whole sea coast, and all the forts and villages and the exiles whose residences were there sent a joint embassy to the Achaeans. B.C. 189

XXXI. The praetor Philopoemen, who had from the very beginning championed the cause of the exiles and had always urged the Achaeans to diminish the power and influence of the Lacedaemonians, gave the complainants an audience before the council, and on his motion a decree was passed that, whereas Titus Quinctius and the Romans had put the fortresses and villages of the Laconian coast under the protection and guardianship of the Achaeans, and whereas,

in the same year, Philopoemen had taken Lacedaemon into the Achaean League (XXXV. xxxvii. 2), where its status was somewhat uncertain. Philopoemen's own policy was definitely anti-Laconian, and the unsettled question of the banished Spartan aristocrats was a continual problem (XXXVI. xxxv. 7). Livy now recounts the history of Achaean–Spartan relations from this time to the holding of the council at which Fulvius was present.

A.U.C. 565 et vicos tradidissent et, cum abstinere iis ex foedere Lacedaemonii deberent, Las [1] vicus oppugnatus esset, caedesque ibi facta, qui eius rei auctores adfinesque essent, nisi dederentur Achaeis, violatum videri
3 foedus. Ad exposcendos eos legati extemplo Lacedaemonem missi sunt. Id imperium adeo superbum et indignum Lacedaemoniis visum est [2] ut, si antiqua civitatis fortuna esset, haud dubie arma extemplo
4 capturi fuerint. Maxime autem consternavit eos metus, si semel primis imperiis oboediendo iugum accepissent,[3] ne, id quod iam diu moliretur Philo-
5 poemen, exulibus Lacedaemonem traderet. Furentes igitur ira triginta hominibus ex factione, cum qua consiliorum aliqua societas Philopoemeni atque exulibus erat, interfectis decreverunt renuntiandam societatem Achaeis legatosque extemplo Cephallaniam mittendos, qui consuli M. Fulvio quique Romanis Lacedaemonem dederent orarentque eum,
6 ut veniret in Peloponnesum ad urbem Lacedaemonem in fidem dicionemque populi Romani accipiendam.

XXXII. Id ubi legati ad Achaeos rettulerunt, omnium civitatium quae eius concilii erant consensu bellum Lacedaemoniis indictum est. Ne extemplo
2 gereretur hiems impediit; incursionibus tamen parvis, latrocinii magis quam belli modo, non terra

[1] Las *ed. Frobeniana* 1535: lace *Bς*.
[2] est ς: *om. B.*
[3] accepissent ς: accepisset *B.*

---

[1] The motion as quoted by Livy has the verbal characteristics of the actual decree. The treaty referred to was with the Romans, not the Achaeans, and the moral and legal right of the latter to enforce it is not unquestioned.
[2] This must be the winter of 189–188 B.C. The details of

although under the treaty the Lacedaemonians were under obligations to let them alone, the village of Las had been attacked and men had been killed there, therefore, unless those who had been principals in and accessories to this act should be surrendered to the Achaeans, the treaty should be deemed to have been violated.[1] Messengers were at once sent to Lacedaemon to demand them. This demand seemed to the Lacedaemonians so insolent and unmerited that if the ancient fortune of the state had continued they would without doubt have immediately taken up arms. The principal cause of the terror which struck them was that, if they once accepted the yoke by obedience to these first commands, Philopoemen would turn Lacedaemon over to the exiles, as he had long been planning. Mad with wrath, then, they killed thirty men of the faction with which Philopoemen and the exiles had shared any other plans, and decreed that the alliance with the Achaeans should be broken off and that ambassadors should at once be sent to Cephallania to surrender Lacedaemon to the consul Marcus Fulvius and the Romans and to implore him to come to the Peloponnesus to receive the city of Lacedaemon under the good faith and protection of the Roman people. B.C. 189

XXXII. When the ambassadors reported this to the Achaeans, with the approval of all the cities which were represented at that council, war was declared upon the Lacedaemonians. Winter[2] prevented the immediate prosecution of the war; nevertheless, their territories were devastated by small raids, more like brigandage than war, not

the chronology are obscure, but the siege of Same must have lasted well into the autumn.

A.U.C. 565

tantum sed etiam navibus a mari fines eorum vastati.
3 Hic tumultus consulem Peloponnesum adduxit,
iussuque eius Elin concilio indicto Lacedaemonii ad
4 disceptandum acciti. Magna ibi non disceptatio
modo sed altercatio fuit, cui consul, cum alia satis
ambitiose partem utramque fovendo incerta respondisset, una denuntiatione ut bello abstinerent,
donec Romam ad senatum legatos misissent,[1] finem
5 imposuit. Utrimque legatio missa Romam est.
Exules quoque Lacedaemoniorum suam causam
6 legationemque Achaeis iniunxerunt. Diophanes et
Lycortas, Megalopolitani ambo, principes legationis
Achaeorum fuerunt qui, dissidentes in re publica,
tum quoque minime inter se convenientes orationes
7 habuerunt. Diophanes senatui disceptationem omnium rerum permittebat: eos optime controversias
inter Achaeos ac Lacedaemonios finituros esse;
8 Lycortas ex praeceptis Philopoemenis postulabat ut
Achaeis ex foedere ac legibus suis quae decressent
agere liceret, libertatemque sibi illibatam, cuius ipsi
9 auctores essent, praestarent. Magnae auctoritatis
apud Romanos tum gens Achaeorum erat; novari
tamen nihil de Lacedaemoniis placebat. Ceterum
responsum ita perplexum fuit ut et Achaei sibi de
10 Lacedaemone permissum acciperent, et Lacedae-

[1] misissent ς: *om. B.*

---

[1] The senate probably intended that the Lacedaemonians should remain members of the Achaean League and that their surrender to Fulvius should be ignored. It seems a fair inference that the Achaeans were not to interfere, as Philopoemen proposed to do, in local Spartan affairs. But Roman fondness for sententiousness in legislation made this decree unpardonably vague, considering the gravity of the situation, and one is tempted to conclude that the senate did not really grasp the arguments and was not greatly interested.

only on land but also by ships from the sea. This disturbance brought the consul to the Peloponnesus; and by his order a council was called at Elis and the Lacedaemonians summoned to take part in the debate. Not only a lively debate took place there but also a violent quarrel, to which the consul, although in other respects, favouring both sides in a spirit of conciliation, he had given ambiguous replies, put an end by the one peremptory demand that they should refrain from war until they had sent ambassadors to the senate in Rome. Both sides sent embassies to Rome. The Lacedaemonian exiles also entrusted their case and their representation to the Achaeans. Diophanes and Lycortas, both from Megalopolis, were chiefs of the Achaean delegation, and they, opposed as they were to one another on public questions generally, at this time also delivered speeches quite inconsistent with one another. Diophanes was for entrusting to the senate the adjudication of all questions: they, he said, would best settle the disputes between the Achaeans and the Lacedaemonians; Lycortas, acting on the instructions of Philopoemen, demanded that the Achaeans be permitted to carry out whatever they had decreed in accordance with the treaty and their own laws, and that the Romans should grant them, unabridged, the freedom of which they themselves were the source. The people of the Achaeans at that time had great influence with the Romans; nevertheless, it was decreed that no change should be made in the status of the Lacedaemonians.[1] The reply, however, was so ambiguous that both the Achaeans accepted it as a concession of freedom of action regarding Lacedaemon and the Lacedaemon- B.C. 189

A.U.C. 565 monii non omnia concessa iis interpretarentur. Hac
potestate immodice Achaei ac superbe usi sunt.
Philopoemeni continuatur magistratus.

XXXIII. Qui veris initio exercitu indicto castra in
2 finibus Lacedaemoniorum posuit, legatos deinde
misit ad deposcendos auctores defectionis, et civitatem in pace futuram si id fecisset pollicentes et
3 illos nihil indicta causa passuros. Silentium prae
metu ceterorum fuit; quos nominatim depoposcerat,
ipsi se ituros professi sunt, fide accepta a legatis vim
4 abfuturam,[1] donec causam dixissent. Ierunt etiam
alii illustres viri, et advocati privatis et quia pertinere
5 causam eorum ad rem publicam censebant. Numquam alias exules Lacedaemoniorum Achaei secum
adduxerant in fines, quia nihil aeque alienaturum
animos civitatis videbatur; tunc exercitus totius
6 prope antesignani exules erant. Hi venientibus
Lacedaemoniis ad portam castrorum agmine facto
occurrerunt; et primo lacessere iurgiis, deinde,
altercatione orta, cum accenderentur irae,[2] ferocissimi
7 exulum impetum in Lacedaemonios fecerunt. Cum
illi deos et fidem legatorum testarentur, et legati et
praetor summovere turbam et protegere Lacedaemonios vinclaque iam quosdam inicientes arcere.[3]

[1] uim abfuturam ς : futuram (*post spat. rel.*) *B*.
[2] irae ς : ira *B*. [3] arcere *Weissenborn* : arceret *B*ς.

---

[1] Elections were normally held in the autumn, and Philopoemen may have been chosen for his sixth term before the embassy to Rome.

[2] The introductory relative gives some support to the view that chap. xxxiii should begin with *Hac* or with *Philopoemeni* above. I have retained the division of the Teubner text.

[3] At this time the Achaeans were deliberately trying to provoke the Lacedaemonians to violence.

ians interpreted it as not granting the Achaeans full authority. This power the Achaeans employed unrestrainedly and tyrannically. Philopoemen was re-elected to the chief magistracy.[1] B.C. 189

XXXIII. He[2] at the beginning of spring called out the army and encamped within the borders of the Lacedaemonians, and then sent ambassadors to demand the men responsible for the revolt and to promise that the state should be at peace if they did this and that those men should suffer no injury without the opportunity to plead their cause in court. The rest kept silent from fear; those whom he had demanded by name declared that they would go on receipt from the ambassadors of a guaranty that they should suffer no violence until they had pleaded their cause. Other well-known men also went with them, both to support them as private citizens and because they knew that their case affected the public interest. Under no other circumstances had the Achaeans taken Lacedaemonian exiles with them to the frontiers,[3] because it was obvious that nothing would offend so much the feelings of the state; on this occasion practically the whole of the advance troops of the army consisted of exiles. They formed in a body and met the Lacedaemonians as they came to the gates of the camp; and at first they assailed them with insults and then, as a quarrel broke out and passions were aroused, the most impetuous of the exiles attacked the Lacedaemonians. When they appealed to the gods and the pledges of the ambassadors, both the ambassadors and the praetor were trying to push the mob aside and to protect the Lacedaemonians and to restrain some who were already binding them with chains. The crowd grew as the

A.U.C. 565

8 Crescebat tumultu concitato turba; et Achaei ad
9 spectaculum primo concurrebant; deinde vociferanti-
bus exulibus quae passi forent et orantibus opem
affirmantibusque simul numquam talem occasionem
habituros si eam praetermisissent; foedus, quod in
Capitolio, quod Olympiae, quod in arce Athenis
10 sacratum fuisset, irritum per illos esse; priusquam
alio de integro foedere obligarentur, noxios puniendos
esse, accensa his vocibus multitudo ad vocem unius,
qui ut ferirent inclamavit, saxa coniecit. Atque ita
decem septem, quibus vincula per tumultum iniecta
11 erant, interfecti sunt. Sexaginta tres postero die
comprehensi, a quibus praetor vim arcuerat,[1] non
quia salvos vellet sed quia perire causa indicta
nolebat, obiecti [2] multitudini iratae, cum aversis [3]
auribus pauca locuti essent, damnati omnes et traditi
sunt ad supplicium.

XXXIV. Hoc metu iniecto Lacedaemoniis im-
peratum primum uti muros diruerent; deinde ut
omnes externi auxiliares, qui mercede apud tyrannos
2 militassent, terra Laconica excederent; tum uti
quae servitia tyranni liberassent—ea magna multitudo
erat—ante diem certam abirent; qui ibi mansissent,
eos prendendi abducendi vendendi Achaeis ius esset;

[1] arcuerat ς : arguerat *B*.
[2] obiecti ς : obiecta *B*.
[3] aversis *edd. vett.* : aduersis *B*ς.

---

[1] Their exact meaning is uncertain.

excitement increased; and first the Achaeans rushed up to see the sight; then the exiles began bitterly to proclaim what they had suffered and to beg for aid, at the same time asserting that they would never have such an opportunity if they let this one slip; the treaty, they said, which had been ratified with religious sanction on the Capitoline, at Olympia, and on the Acropolis at Athens, had been made void by those men;[1] before they were bound anew by another treaty they urged that the guilty should be punished. Then the multitude, inflamed by these words, at the call of one man, who shouted out that they should strike, began to throw stones. And so seventeen of those who had been put into chains in the excitement were killed.[2] The next day sixty-three were arrested whom the praetor had protected against violence, not because he was concerned for their safety but because he did not wish them to be killed without pleading their cause, becoming the victims of an angry mob, and when they had spoken briefly to hostile ears all were condemned and handed over for execution. B.C. 189

XXXIV. Fear having been thus inspired in the Lacedaemonians, it was first ordered that they should destroy their walls; then, that all the foreign auxiliaries who had served under the tyrants for pay should leave Laconian territory; next, that the slaves whom the tyrants had freed[3]—their number was large—should depart before a designated day; if any of them remained the Achaeans were to have the right to seize, carry off and sell them; then, that

[2] This affair was too ingeniously explained by Lycortas in 184 B.C. (XXXIX. xxxvi. 9–16).

[3] Nabis defended this policy in XXXIV. xxxi. 14–18.

A.U.C. 565

3 Lycurgi leges moresque abrogarent, Achaeorum adsuescerent legibus institutisque: ita unius eos corporis fore et de omnibus rebus facilius consensuros.
4 Nihil oboedientius fecerunt quam ut muros diruerent,
5 nec aegrius passi sunt quam exules reduci. Decretum Tegeae in concilio communi Achaeorum de restituen-
6 dis iis factum est; et mentione illata externos auxiliares dimissos ac Lacedaemoniis adscriptos—ita enim vocabant qui ab tyrannis liberati erant—urbe excessisse et in [1] agros dilapsos,[2] priusquam dimitteretur exercitus, ire praetorem cum expeditis et comprehendere id genus hominum et vendere iure
7 praedae placuit. Multi comprehensi venierunt. Porticus ex ea pecunia Megalopoli permissu [3]
8 Achaeorum refecta est quam Lacedaemonii diruerant. Et ager Belbinates, quem iniuria tyranni Lacedaemoniorum possederant, restitutus eidem civitati ex decreto vetere Achaeorum, quod factum erat Philippo
9 Amyntae filio regnante. Per haec velut enervata civitas Lacedaemoniorum diu Achaeis obnoxia fuit; nulla tamen res tanto erat damno quam disciplina

[1] et in *Ussing*: in *B*ς.
[2] dilapsos ς: dilapsus *B*.
[3] permissu ς: persensu *B*.

---

[1] The traditional Spartan constitution had been preserved when Sparta was taken into the Achaean League in 192 B.C. (XXXV. xxxvii. 2). The apparent purpose of the Achaeans at this time was to weaken their military power, although their pretext has a fairer sound.

[2] They were supposed to have been built by the tyrants (XXXIV. xxxviii. 2).

they should annul the laws and customs of Lycurgus[1] B.C. 189
and adjust themselves to the laws and institutions of the Achaeans: thus, they said, they would all become one body and would agree more readily on all matters. They obeyed no command more willingly than the order to tear down their walls,[2] nor were they more reluctant to accept any than the one which required that the exiles be restored. The decree for their restoration was passed at Tegea in the common council of the Achaeans,[3] and when the report was submitted that the foreign auxiliaries had been discharged and that the newly-registered Lacedaemonians—for so they called the men who had been set free by the tyrants—had left the city and had scattered through the country, they ordered the praetor, before the army was dismissed, to go with the light-armed troops and arrest men of this category and sell them under the law governing booty. Many were arrested and sold. Out of this money, with the permission of the Achaeans, they rebuilt a portico at Megalopolis which the Lacedaemonians had destroyed. Also the *ager Belbinates*,[4] which had been wrongfully seized by the tyrants of the Lacedaemonians, was given back to that state under an old decree of the Achaeans which had been passed while Philip, the son of Amyntas, was on the throne.[5] The Lacedaemonian state, thus, so to speak, emasculated, was long at the mercy of the Achaeans; yet nothing did them so much injury as the subversion of the discipline

[3] Since these men had been banished as a result of party strife, their restoration practically assured the progressive weakening of Lacedaemon by internal political conflict.

[4] Probably the territory of the town of Belemina in Tripolis.

[5] This Philip was the father of Alexander the Great.

A.U.C. 565 Lycurgi, cui per octingentos annos adsuerant,
sublata.

XXXV. A concilio, ubi ad consulem inter Achaeos
Lacedaemoniosque disceptatum est, M. Fulvius,
quia iam in exitu annus erat, comitiorum causa
profectus Romam creavit consules M. Valerium
Messalam et C. Livium Salinatorem, cum[1] M.
Aemilium Lepidum inimicum eo quoque anno peten-
2 tem deiecisset.[2] Praetores inde creati Q. Marcius
Philippus M. Claudius Marcellus C. Stertinius C.
Atinius P. Claudius Pulcher L. Manlius Acidinus.
3 Comitiis perfectis consulem M. Fulvium in provinciam
et ad exercitum redire placuit, eique et collegae Cn.
4 Manlio imperium in annum prorogatum est. Eo
anno in aede Herculis signum[3] dei ipsius ex decemvirorum responso, et seiuges in Capitolio aurati a
P.[4] Cornelio positi; consulem dedisse inscriptum est.
5 Et duodecim clipea aurata ab aedilibus curulibus P.
Claudio Pulchro et Ser. Sulpicio Galba sunt posita ex
pecunia qua frumentarios ob annonam compressam
6 damnarunt; et aedilis plebi Q. Fulvius Flaccus duo

[1] cum *ed. Frobeniana* 1535 : *om. Bς*.

[2] deiecisset *ed. Frobeniana* 1535 : decessisset *B* : decessisse ς.

[3] signum ς : *om. B*.

[4] a P. *Sigonius* : ab cn. *Bς*.

---

[1] The numeral cannot be taken too literally, although it is used again in XXXIX. xxxvii. 5 (in the speech of Lycortas).

[2] Livy omits to say how the case was decided. The events described in the preceding chapters (see the note to xxx. 6 above) must all have antedated this meeting, although the chronology is badly confused.

[3] Lepidus had been defeated the preceding year (XXXVII. xlvii. 7).

of Lycurgus to which they had been accustomed for eight hundred years.[1] B.C. 189

XXXV. From the council at which the case of the Achaeans and the Lacedaemonians had been argued before the consul,[2] Marcus Fulvius, since his year was now near its end, set out for Rome to hold the elections and announced the selection as consuls of Marcus Valerius Messala and Gaius Livius Salinator, when he had secured the defeat of his personal foe, Marcus Aemilius Lepidus, who was a candidate that year also.[3] Next the praetors were elected; Quintus Marcius Philippus, Marcus Claudius Marcellus, Gaius Stertinius, Gaius Atinius, Publius Claudius Pulcher, and Lucius Manlius Acidinus. When the elections were over it was decided that the consul Marcus Fulvius should return to the province and the army, and for him and for his colleague Gnaeus Manlius the *imperium* was prolonged for one year. In that year in the temple of Hercules a statue of the divinity himself was installed in accordance with a decree of the decemvirs, and a six-horse chariot of gold was set up on the Capitoline by Publius Cornelius;[4] the inscription read that "one who had been consul had dedicated it."[5] Also twelve gilded shields were set up by the curule aediles, Publius Claudius Pulcher and Servius Sulpicius Galba, out of the money which they had condemned the grain-dealers to pay for hoarding the grain-supply; likewise the plebeian aedile, Quintus Fulvius Flaccus,

[4] Probably Scipio Nasica.

[5] The use of *consul* in such inscriptions would not mean that the donor was consul at the time of the dedication, but merely that he had held the office. The inscription may have existed in Livy's time.

A.U.C. 565 signa aurata uno reo damnato—nam separatim
accusaverant [1]—posuit; collega eius A. Caecilius
neminem condemnavit. Ludi Romani ter, plebei
quinquiens toti instaurati.

A.U.C. 566 7 M. Valerius Messala inde et C. Livius Salinator
consulatum idibus Martiis cum inissent, de re
publica deque provinciis et exercitibus senatum
8 consuluerunt. De Aetolia et Asia nihil mutatum
est; consulibus alteri Pisae cum Liguribus, alteri
9 Gallia provincia decreta est. Comparare inter se aut
sortiri iussi et novos exercitus, binas legiones,
scribere et ut sociis [2] Latini nominis quina dena milia
peditum imperarent et mille et ducentos equites.
10 Messalae Ligures, Salinatori obtigit Gallia. Praetores inde sortiti sunt: M. Claudio urbana, P.
Claudio peregrina iurisdictio evenit; Q. Marcius
Siciliam, C. Stertinius Sardiniam, L. Manlius Hispaniam citeriorem, C. Atinius ulteriorem est sortitus.

XXXVI. De exercitibus ita placuit: ex Gallia
legiones quae sub C. Laelio fuerant ad M. Tuccium
2 propraetorem in Bruttios traduci, et qui in Sicilia
esset dimitti exercitum, et classem quae ibi esset
3 Romam reduceret M. Sempronius propraetor. Hispaniis singulae legiones quae tum in iis provinciis
erant decretae,[3] et ut terna milia peditum, ducenos
equites ambo praetores in supplementum sociis

[1] accusaverant *ed. Moguntina*: accusati erant *B*ς: accu-sauerunt *M*.
[2] sociis ς: socii *B*. [3] decretae ς: decreta *B*.

---

[1] The aediles usually acted in unison.
[2] The meaning must be that each consul was to have six hundred cavalry. The ratio of cavalry to infantry fluctuates so much that emendation of distributive numerals (twelve hundred cavalry for each) is not justified.

after convicting only one defendant—for they had prosecuted independently[1]—dedicated two gilded statues; his colleague Aulus Caecilius condemned no one. The Roman Games in their entirety were repeated three times, the Plebeian Games five times. B.C. 189

Then, when Marcus Valerius Messala and Gaius Livius Salinator had been inaugurated as consuls on the Ides of March, they consulted the senate regarding the general policy and regarding the provinces and armies. No change was made respecting Aetolia and Asia; to one consul was assigned Pisa together with the Ligurians, to the other Gaul, as their provinces. They were directed to arrange between them or to cast lots and to enroll new armies of two legions each and to requisition from the allies of the Latin confederacy fifteen thousand infantry for each and twelve hundred cavalry.[2] The lot gave to Messala the Ligurians and to Salinator Gaul. Then the praetors cast lots: Marcus Claudius received the jurisdiction between citizens and Publius Claudius that between citizens and aliens; Quintus Marcius Sicily, Gaius Stertinius Sardinia, Lucius Manlius Nearer Spain and Gaius Atinius Farther Spain. B.C. 188

XXXVI. Regarding the armies, this was the decision: the legions from Gaul, which had been under the command of Gaius Laelius, to be transferred to Marcus Tuccius the propraetor for service among the Brutti, the army which was in Sicily to be brought home, and the fleet which was there to be conducted to Rome by Marcus Sempronius the propraetor. For the Spains the single legions which were then in those provinces were decreed, and the praetors were allowed to enlist as reinforcements from the allies and to transport with them each three thousand

A.U.C. 566 4 imperarent secumque transportarent. Priusquam in provincias novi magistratus proficiscerentur, supplicatio triduum pro collegio decemvirorum imperata fuit in omnibus compitis, quod luce inter horam tertiam ferme et quartam tenebrae obortae fuerant. Et novemdiale sacrificium indictum est, quod in Aventino lapidibus pluvisset.

5 Campani, cum eos ex senatus consulto quod priore anno factum erat censores Romae censeri coegissent—nam antea incertum fuerat[1] ubi censerentur—petierunt ut sibi cives Romanas ducere uxores
6 liceret et, si qui prius duxissent,[2] ut habere eas et nati ante eam diem uti iusti sibi liberi heredesque
7 essent. Utraque res impetrata. De Formianis Fundanisque municipibus et Arpinatibus C. Valerius Tappo tribunus plebis promulgavit ut iis suffragii latio—nam antea sine suffragio habuerant[3] civitatem—
8 esset. Huic rogationi quattuor tribuni plebis,[4] quia non ex auctoritate senatus ferretur, cum intercederent, edocti populi esse, non senatus, ius suffragium quibus velit impertire, destiterunt incepto.

[1] fuerat ς : erat *B*. [2] duxissent ς : dixissent *B*.
[3] habuerant ς : habuerunt *B*. [4] plebis ς : *om. B*.

---

[1] This eclipse has been dated July 17, 188 B.C. (corrected calendar).

[2] Cf. xxviii. 4 above.

[3] This would grant them, retroactively, *conubium*, a right characteristic of Roman citizenship.

[4] The *municipia* in general enjoyed only the private rights (*commercium* and *conubium*) of Roman citizens: Livy describes their status as *civitas sine suffragio*. This incident illustrates the gradual promotion of the *municipia* to full civic rights.

[5] Measures intended for an assembly were ordinarily, but not necessarily, submitted first to the senate, and those

infantry and two hundred cavalry. Before the new magistrates departed for their provinces a three-day period of prayer was proclaimed in the name of the college of decemvirs at all the street-corner shrines because in the day-time, between about the third and fourth hours, darkness had covered everything.[1] Also a nine-day sacrifice was decreed because (so it was said) there had been a shower of stones on the Aventine. B.C. 188

The Campanians,[2] since, according to the decree which had been passed the year before, the censors compelled them to be assessed at Rome—for previously it had been uncertain where they should be assessed—requested that they should be permitted to take Roman citizens as wives, that any who had already married Roman citizens should be allowed to keep them, and that children born before this day should be legitimate, and capable of inheriting from their fathers.[3] Both requests were granted. Respecting the residents in the municipalities [4] of Formiae, Fundi and Arpinum, Gaius Valerius Tappo, tribune of the people, proposed that the right to vote—for previously the citizenship without the right to vote had belonged to them—should be conferred upon them. When four tribunes of the people vetoed this bill, on the ground that it was not proposed with the sanction [5] of the senate, and they were informed that it was the prerogative of the assembly, not the senate, to bestow the franchise upon whomsoever it desired, they gave up the effort. The bill was passed

which the senate favoured received its *auctoritas*. In this instance the assembly seems to assert its legislative independence of the senate, but Livy's habit of abbreviating his accounts of constitutional debates complicates the problem.

A.U.C. 566

9 Rogatio perlata est ut in Aemilia tribu Formiani et Fundani, in[1] Cornelia Arpinates ferrent; atque in his tribubus[2] tum primum ex Valerio plebiscito censi
10 sunt. M. Claudius Marcellus censor sorte[3] superato T. Quinctio lustrum condidit. Censa sunt civium capita $\overline{\text{CCLVIII}}$ CCCXVIII. Lustro perfecto consules in provincias profecti sunt.

XXXVII. Hieme ea qua haec Romae gesta sunt, ad Cn. Manlium consulem primum, dein[4] pro consule, hibernantem in Asia, legationes undique ex omnibus civitatibus gentibusque, quae cis Taurum montem
2 incolunt, conveniebant. Et ut clarior nobiliorque victoria Romanis de rege Antiocho fuit quam de Gallis, ita laetior sociis erat de Gallis quam de
3 Antiocho. Tolerabilior regia servitus fuerat quam feritas immanium barbarorum incertusque in dies terror, quo velut tempestas eos populantes inferret.[5]
4 Itaque, ut quibus libertas Antiocho pulso, pax Gallis domitis data esset, non gratulatum modo venerant sed coronas etiam aureas pro suis quaeque facultatibus
5 attulerant. Et ab Antiocho legati et ab ipsis Gallis, ut pacis leges dicerentur, et ab Ariarathe rege Cappadocum venerunt ad veniam petendam luendamque pecunia noxam, quod auxiliis Antiochum iuvisset.[6]

[1] et fundani in ς: *om.* *B*.
[2] tribubus ς: tribus *B*.
[3] sorte ς: *om.* *B*.
[4] dein ς: deinde in *B*.
[5] inferret ς: inferet *B*.
[6] iuuisset ς: iuuissent *B*.

---

[1] The *Aemilia* and *Cornelia* were two of the local tribes (ultimately thirty-five in number) to which all Roman citizens were assigned.

[2] Cf. XXXV. ix. 2 and the first note.

[3] Cf. XXXV. ix. 2 and the second note, and the *Periocha* of this Book.

with the provision that the people of Formiae and Fundi should vote in the tribe called *Aemilia* and the Arpinates in the *Cornelia*; and in these tribes they were then for the first time registered under the Valerian plebiscite.[1] Marcus Claudius Marcellus the censor, having been victorious over Titus Quinctius at the drawing of lots, closed the *lustrum*.[2] The number of citizens shown by the census was two hundred and fifty-eight thousand three hundred and eighteen.[3] The *lustrum* having been closed, the consuls set out for their provinces. B.C. 188

XXXVII. During the winter in which these events occurred in Rome, Gnaeus Manlius, who was wintering in Asia, first as consul, then as proconsul, received embassies from all quarters, from all the cities and tribes which live on this side of the Taurus mountain. And while the Roman victory over King Antiochus had been more glorious and more splendid than that over the Gauls, yet the victory over the Gauls afforded the allies more satisfaction than that over Antiochus. The slavery imposed by the king was more endurable than the ferocity of the rude barbarians and the constant and uncertain fear as to whither a storm so to speak would bring the Gauls marauding upon them. Accordingly, since from the overthrow of Antiochus they had received liberty and peace from the defeat of the Gauls, they had not only come to offer congratulations but had brought golden crowns, each in proportion to his ability. Also ambassadors came from Antiochus, and from the Gauls themselves, asking that terms of peace should be stated, and from King Ariarathes of Cappadocia, to ask pardon and to wash away with money his guilt in that he had aided Antiochus with auxiliaries.

A.U.C. 566

6 Huic sescenta talenta argenti sunt imperata; Gallis responsum, cum Eumenes rex venisset, tum daturum iis leges.[1] Civitatium legationes cum benignis responsis, laetiores etiam quam venerant, dimissae.
7 Antiochi legati pecuniam in Pamphyliam frumentumque ex pacto cum L. Scipione foedere iussi advehere;
8 eo se cum exercitu venturum. Principio deinde veris lustrato exercitu profectus die octavo Apameam venit. Ibi triduum stativis habitis, tertiis rursus ab Apamea castris in Pamphyliam, quo pecuniam frumen-
9 tumque regios convehere iusserat, pervenit. Duo milia et quingenta[2] talenta argenti accepta Apameam deportantur; frumentum exercitui dividitur. Inde ad Pergam ducit, quae una in iis locis regio tenebatur
10 praesidio. Appropinquanti praefectus praesidii obvius fuit, triginta dierum tempus petens ut regem
11 Antiochum de urbe tradenda consuleret. Dato tempore ad eam diem praesidio decessum est.[3] A Perga L. Manlio fratre cum quattuor milibus militum Oroanda[4] ad reliquum pecuniae ex eo quod pepigerant exigendum misso, ipse, quia Eumenem regem et decem legatos ab Roma Ephesum audierat venisse, iussis sequi Antiochi legatis Apameam exercitum reduxit.

XXXVIII. Ibi ex decem legatorum sententia foedus in haec verba fere cum Antiocho[5] conscriptum

[1] leges *ed. Frobeniana* 1535: legem *Bς*.
[2] Duo milia et quingenta *Rubens*: mille et quinquaginta *Bς*.
[3] praesidio decessum est *ed. Frobeniana* 1535: decessit praesidio et *Bς*.
[4] oroanda *ς*: *om., spat. rel., B.*
[5] cum antiocho *ς*: *om. B.*

---

[1] Polybius (XXII. xxvi) says that the commander had received no instructions from Antiochus to evacuate the town.

Six hundred talents of silver were demanded of him; B.C. 188
the Gauls were told that when King Eumenes had arrived he would give them terms. The embassies from the cities were sent away with gracious responses and in an even happier mood than when they had come. The envoys of Antiochus were directed to bring to Pamphylia the money and grain agreed upon in the treaty concluded with Lucius Scipio; the consul and the army would come there. Then at the beginning of spring, having purified the army, he set out and reached Apamea on the eighth day. Having spent three days in camp there, in three more marches from Apamea he arrived in Pamphylia, where he had ordered the king's agents to bring the money and grain. Two thousand five hundred talents of silver were received and conveyed to Apamea; the grain was distributed to the army. Then he led the troops towards Perga, which alone in this district was held by a royal garrison.[1] As he approached the commander of the garrison met him, asking for a truce of thirty days in order that he might consult King Antiochus about surrendering the city. The time having been granted for that period, the garrison withdrew. From Perga he sent his brother Lucius Manlius with four thousand men to Oroanda to collect the balance of the money which they had agreed to pay,[2] and he himself, since he had heard that King Eumenes and the ten commissioners had arrived in Ephesus from Rome, ordered the envoys of Antiochus to follow and led the army back to Apamea.

XXXVIII. There in accordance with the decision of the ten commissioners the treaty with Antiochus

[2] Cf. xviii. 2 above.

A.U.C. 566 2 est: "Amicitia regi Antiocho cum populo Romano his
legibus et condicionibus esto: ne quem exercitum,
qui cum populo Romano sociisve bellum gesturus erit,
rex per fines regni sui eorumve qui sub dicione eius
erunt transire sinito, neu commeatu neu[1] qua alia
3 ope iuvato; idem Romani sociique Antiocho et iis
qui sub imperio eius erunt praestent. Belli gerendi
ius Antiocho ne esto cum illis qui insulas colunt neve
4 in Europam transeundi. Excedito[2] urbibus agris
vicis castellis cis Taurum montem usque ad Halyn[3]
amnem, et a valle[4] Tauri usque ad iuga qua in
5 Lycaoniam vergit. Ne qua praeter[5] arma efferto[6]

[1] neu ς: nec *B*. [2] excedito ς: expedito *B*.

[3] Halyn *Budaeus*: tanaim *B*, *fortasse rectius*: accaym, accayn, canym, achanim ς: Taurum *Mommsen*; *de loco toto uid. quae Anglice scripsi.*

[4] a ualle ς: ea ualle *B*: ab ea valle *Viereck, fortasse rectius.*

[5] praeter *Perizonius*: *om. B*ς.

[6] efferto ς: et ferto *B*.

---

[1] In XXXVII. lv–lvi the appointment of this commission was recorded and their functions stated as the adjustment of such details as could be considered only on the ground. There are certain changes in the treaty as stated below and certain discrepancies between it and the text as given by Polybius (XXII. xxvii).

[2] The crucial part of this sentence is lost from the text of Polybius and the MSS. of Livy offer a variety of readings. No combination of emendations has been found which pays due regard to the readings of the Livy MSS. and also gives a definite and easily recognizable boundary. I have therefore translated the text as it is printed in the latest Weissenborn–Mueller revision, although I may have given to *Tauri* a construction differing from theirs. I have chosen this course with full appreciation of the difficulties involved, some of which it seems proper to discuss briefly. The reference to the Halys river seems inappropriate unless it was the intention of the treaty-makers to dispose also of the terri-

was drafted in about this language:[1] "There shall be friendship between King Antiochus and the Roman people on these conditions and terms: the king shall permit no army which shall purpose to wage war with the Roman people or its allies to march through the territories of his kingdom or of his allies, and he shall not aid them with grain or with any other form of assistance; the Romans and their allies shall guarantee the same to Antiochus and to those who are under his control. Antiochus shall have no right to wage war upon those peoples who inhabit the islands nor to cross to Europe. He shall withdraw from the cities, lands, villages and strongholds on this side of the Taurus mountain as far as the Halys river and from the valley as far as the ridges of Taurus where it slopes down into Lycaonia.[2] He shall carry B.C. 188

tories brought to notice by the defeat of the Gauls. But no Tanaïs river is known and a Taurus river must be imaginatively identified. (Livy mentions a river of this name in xv. 7 above, but even if he is correct the position he gives it is wrong.) Furthermore, no natural boundary is provided between the crest of the Taurus range and the Halys river (I presume that this means the portion of the river above the point where it turns north-west near the Cappadocian-Cilician frontier). If a Tanaïs river could be plausibly identified north of the Taurus range, I should be inclined to read . . . *cis Taurum montem usque ad Tanaim amnem, et ab ea valle Tauri usque ad iuga* . . . ("on this side of the Taurus mountain as far as the river Tanaïs and from the valley of this river as far as the crest of Taurus"), although the order in which these geographical points are mentioned seems unnatural. It seems hardly necessary to establish an eastern frontier for Asia. For reviews of recent discussion of these questions see the *Bericht* on Livy by Rau and that on Greek History by Lenschau in *Jahresbericht über die Fortschritte der klassischen Altertumswissenschaft*, 242, 1934, esp. p. 87, and 244, 1934, esp. pp. 120–121, respectively, and Map 3 in this volume.

A.U.C. 566 ex iis oppidis agris castellisque quibus excedat; si qua extulit quo quaeque [1] oportebit recte restituito.
6 Ne militem neu quem alium ex regno Eumenis recipito. Si qui earum urbium cives quae regno abscedunt cum rege Antiocho intraque fines regni eius sunt, Apameam omnes ante diem certam re-
7 deunto; qui ex regno Antiochi apud Romanos sociosque sunt, iis ius abeundi manendique esto; servos seu fugitivos seu bello captos, seu quis liber captus aut transfuga erit, reddito Romanis sociisque.
8 Elephantos tradito omnes neque alios parato. Tradito et naves longas armamentaque earum, neu plures quam decem naves tectas neve plures quam . . . . naves actuarias,[2] nulla quarum plus quam [3] triginta remis agatur, habeto, neve monerem [4] belli
9 causa quod ipse illaturus erit. Ne navigato citra Calycadnum neu Sarpedonium promunturia, extra quam si qua navis pecuniam [5] in [6] stipendium aut
10 legatos aut obsides portabit. Milites mercede conducendi ex iis gentibus quae sub dicione populi Romani sunt Antiocho regi ius ne esto, ne voluntarios
11 quidem recipiendi. Rhodiorum sociorumve quae

[1] quo quaeque *Perizonius*: quae quoque *Bς*.
[2] decem naves tectas neve plures quam * naves actuarias *Madvig*: .X. naues *Bς*: decem naues actuarias *M*.
[3] quam *ς*: quam in *B*.
[4] monerem *Madvig*: minore ea *B*: minorem ex *M*. minorem ea *et* monerem ea *ς*.
[5] pecuniam *ς*: pecunias *B*.
[6] in *Madvig*: *om.* *Bς*.

---

[1] The MSS. of Livy provide for *decem naves actuarias* only. Polybius, however, allows ten decked ships, and it seems necessary then to assume the loss of some words, including a numeral for *actuarias*. For the sake of simplicity,

away nothing but his weapons from these towns, lands and fortresses from which he is withdrawing; if he has removed anything, he shall duly restore it to the place in which each item belongs. He shall harbour no soldier or other person from the kingdom of Eumenes. If any citizens of those cities which are separating from his kingdom are with King Antiochus and within the borders of his kingdom, they shall all return to Apamea before a designated day; whatever persons from the kingdom of Antiochus are with the Romans or their allies shall have the right to depart or to remain; slaves, whether fugitives or prisoners of war, and whatever freemen there are, whether prisoners of war or deserters, he shall turn over to the Romans and their allies. He shall surrender all his elephants and shall acquire no more. He shall surrender also his warships and their rigging, and he shall have not more than ten decked ships nor more than ten merchant vessels,[1] nor shall any of these be propelled by more than thirty oars, nor shall he have a ship of one bank for a war in which he himself shall be the aggressor. He shall not sail beyond the promontories of Calycadnus and Sarpedon, unless a ship is carrying payments of tribute or ambassadors or hostages. King Antiochus shall not be authorized to hire soldiers from those peoples which are under the control of the Roman people, nor even to accept volunteers therefrom. If the Rhodians or the allies B.C. 188

[1] I have assumed in the translation, though I have not ventured to include it in the text, that this numeral was *decem*: anything is a guess, since Polybius mentions neither the *actuariae* nor the *moneris*. The restriction on *moneres* should apply equally to such *actuariae* as could easily be adapted to military uses, so that there may be more corruption in both Livy and Polybius than has been recognized.

A.U.C. 566 aedes aedificiaque intra fines regni Antiochi sunt,
quo iure ante bellum fuerunt, eo Rhodiorum sociorum-
12 ve sunto; si quae pecuniae debentur, earum exactio
esto; si quid ablatum est, id conquirendi cognoscendi
repetendique item ius esto. Si quas urbes quas tradi
oportet ii tenent, quibus Antiochus dedit, et ex iis
praesidia deducito, utique recte tradantur,[1] curato.
13 Argenti probi talenta Attica duodecim milia dato
intra duodecim annos pensionibus aequis—talentum
ne minus pondo[2] octoginta[3] Romanis ponderibus
pendat—et tritici quingenta quadraginta milia
14 modium. Eumeni regi talenta trecenta quinquaginta intra quinquennium dato, et pro frumento
quod aestimatione fit talenta centum viginti septem.
15 Obsides Romanis viginti dato et triennio mutato, ne
minores octonum denum annorum neu maiores
16 quinum quadragenum. Si qui sociorum populi
Romani ultro bellum inferent[4] Antiocho, vim vi
arcendi ius esto, dum ne quam urbem aut belli iure
17 teneat aut in amicitiam accipiat. Controversias inter
se iure ac iudicio disceptanto,[5] aut, si utrisque place-

[1] tradantur ς : tradatur *B*.
[2] pondo ς : *om*. *B*.
[3] octoginta ς : LLXXX *B*.
[4] inferent ς : inferrent *B*.
[5] disceptanto *J. F. Gronovius* : disceptent *B*ς.

---

[1] These provisions are probably included to protect existing rights of individuals under private law.

[2] The demand of Scipio (XXXVII. xlv. 14) was expressed in the equivalent Euboean currency. One-fifth of the sum had already been paid, and this clause mentions only the instalments still due.

[3] Polybius (XXII. xxvi) gives the figure more exactly as one hundred and twenty-seven talents and twelve hundred

own any houses or buildings within the boundaries of the kingdom of Antiochus, they shall belong to the Rhodians or the allies on the same basis as before the war; if any moneys are due, the right to collect them shall exist; if anything has been taken away, the right shall likewise exist to search for, identify and recover it.[1] If any cities which should be surrendered are held by persons to whom Antiochus has entrusted them, he shall withdraw his garrisons from them and shall see that they are duly surrendered. He shall pay twelve thousand Attic talents [2] of tested silver within twelve years in equal instalments—with the proviso that the talent shall not weigh less than eighty Roman pounds—and five hundred and forty thousand *modii* of wheat. He shall pay to King Eumenes three hundred and fifty talents within five years, and in commutation for the grain, on his own valuation, one hundred and twenty-seven talents.[3] He shall give the Romans twenty hostages and shall change them triennially, provided that none of them shall be younger than eighteen years nor older than forty-five years. If any of the allies of the Roman people shall without provocation make war upon Antiochus, he shall have the right to oppose force with force, provided that he shall neither hold any city under the law of war nor receive any into friendship. They shall settle disputes between them by law and legal formula,[4] or, if both states shall desire, by war." B.C. 188

and eight *drachmae*, adding that Antiochus had proposed and Eumenes had agreed to accept this sum in full payment. In XXXVII. xlv. 16 Scipio had insisted on the payment of the grain which was due to Attalus, but both parties have now agreed on compensation in cash.

[4] The clause is borrowed from the Roman *ius civile*.

A.U.C. 566

18 bit, bello." De Hannibale Poeno et Aetolo Thoante et Mnasilocho[1] Acarnane et Chalcidensibus Eubulida et Philone dedendis in hoc quoque foedere adscriptum est et ut, si quid postea addi demi mutarive placuisset, ut id salvo foedere fieret.

XXXIX. Consul in hoc foedus iuravit; ab rege qui exigerent[2] iusiurandum, profecti Q. Minucius Thermus et L. Manlius, qui tum forte ab Oroandis
2 rediit. Et Q. Fabio Labeoni qui classi praeerat[3] scripsit, ut Patara extemplo proficisceretur, quaeque ibi naves regiae essent concideret cremaretque.
3 Profectus ab Epheso quinquaginta tectas naves aut concidit aut incendit. Telmessum eadem expeditione territis subito adventu classis oppidanis recipit.
4 Ex Lycia protinus, iussis ab Epheso sequi qui ibi relicti erant per insulas in Graeciam traiecit. Athenis paucos moratus dies, dum Piraeum ab Epheso naves venirent, totam inde classem in Italiam reduxit.

5 Cn. Manlius cum inter cetera quae accipienda ab Antiocho erant elephantos quoque accepisset donoque Eumeni omnes dedisset,[4] causas deinde civita-
6 tium, multis inter novas res turbatis, cognovit. Et Ariarathes rex parte dimidia pecuniae imperatae beneficio Eumenis, cui desponderat per eos dies filiam,
7 remissa[5] in amicitiam est acceptus. Civitatium autem

[1] Mnasilocho *Drakenborch*: milunosymacho *B*.
[2] exigerent ς: exigeret *B*.
[3] praeerat ς: praeerant *B*.
[4] dedisset ς: dedisset et *B*.
[5] remissa *ed. Frobeniana* 1535: demissam *B*: dimissa ς.

---

[1] Polybius names these men in the clause which Livy quotes as sect. 7 above; cf. XXXVII. xlv. 16–17.

[2] Polybius requires the consent of both parties to such amendments.

[3] Cf. XXXVII. lx.

With regard to the surrender of Hannibal the Carthaginian, and Thoas the Aetolian and Mnasilochus the Acarnanian and Eubulidas and Philo the Chalcidians,[1] there was a clause in this treaty too, and another to the effect that whatever in future it should seem desirable to add, take away, or modify, could be so altered without invalidating the treaty.[2] B.C. 188

XXXIX. The consul swore to observe this treaty; to secure the oath from the king, Quintus Minucius Thermus was sent and Lucius Manlius, who chanced at that time to return from Oroanda. He wrote also to Quintus Fabius Labeo, who was in command of the fleet,[3] to proceed at once to Patara and to destroy and burn the ships of the king that were there. Setting out from Ephesus, he either wrecked or burned fifty decked ships. Telmessus, since the townspeople were alarmed at the unexpected appearance of the fleet, was recovered on the same expedition. From Lycia, ordering the ships which had been left at Ephesus to follow from there, Labeo crossed straight to Greece by way of the islands. Delaying a few days at Athens, until the ships from Ephesus should reach Piraeus, he conducted the entire fleet from there to Italy.

When Gnaeus Manlius, among the other things which were to be received from Antiochus, had received the elephants also and had presented them all to Eumenes as a gift, he next investigated the affairs of the cities, since many were in confusion in consequence of the changes. And King Ariarathes, half of the money which had been demanded of him having been remitted through the good offices of Eumenes, to whom he had about this time betrothed his daughter, was received into friendship. The ten

A.U.C. 566 cognitis causis decem legati aliam aliarum fecerunt
condicionem. Quae stipendiariae regi Antiocho
fuerant et cum populo Romano senserant, iis im-
8 munitatem dederunt; quae partium Antiochi fuerant
aut stipendiariae Attali regis, eas omnes vectigal
pendere Eumeni iusserunt. Nominatim praeterea
Colophoniis, qui in Notio habitant, et Cymaeis et
9 Mylasenis immunitatem concesserunt; Clazomeniis
super immunitatem et Drymussam insulam dono
dederunt, et Milesiis quem sacrum appellant agrum
10 restituerunt, et Iliensibus Rhoeteum et Gergithum
addiderunt, non tam ob recentia ulla merita quam
originum memoria. Eadem at Dardanum liberandi
11 causa fuit. Chios quoque et Zmyrnaeos et Erythrae-
os, pro singulari fide quam eo bello praestiterunt, et
agro donarunt et in omni praecipuo honore habuerunt.
12 Phocaeensibus et ager quem ante bellum habuerant
redditus, et ut legibus antiquis uterentur permissum.
13 Rhodiis affirmata quae data priore decreto erant;
Lycia et Caria datae usque ad Maeandrum amnem
14 praeter Telmessum. Regi Eumeni Chersonesum in
Europa et Lysimachiam, castella vicos agrum quibus
15 finibus tenuerat Antiochus, adiecerunt; in Asia
Phrygiam utramque—alteram ad Hellespontum,
maiorem alteram vocant—et Mysiam, quam Prusia
16 rex ademerat, ei[1] restituerunt, et Lycaoniam et
Milyada et Lydiam et nominatim urbes Tralles

[1] ei *ed. Frobeniana* 1535 : et *Bς*.

[1] Cf. XXXVII. xxvi. 5–6.

commissioners, having looked into the situation of the cities, made different dispositions in different cases. Those which had been tributaries to King Antiochus but had sided with the Roman people were granted freedom from taxation; those which had been partisans of Antiochus or tributaries to King Attalus were all ordered to pay tribute to Eumenes. In addition, they granted freedom from taxation expressly to the Colophonians who live in Notium,[1] to the Cymaeans and the Mylasenians; to the Clazomenians, in addition to immunity, they gave the island of Drymussa as a gift, and to the Milesians they restored what they call the "sacred land," and to the people of Ilium they added Rhoeteum and Gergithus, less as a reward for recent services than in recognition of their descent. This was also the reason for liberating Dardanus. The Chians, Zmyrnaeans and Erythraeans, because of the extraordinary loyalty they had displayed in the war, were rewarded with lands and in addition were treated with every mark of honour. To the Phocaeans they both gave back the lands which they had held before the war and permitted them to live under their ancient laws. The Rhodians were confirmed in the possession of what had been given them by the earlier decree; they received Lycia and Caria as far as the Meander river with the exception of Telmessus. Upon King Eumenes they bestowed, in Europe, the Chersonesus and Lysimachia, the strongholds, villages and lands within the boundaries of Antiochus; in Asia, both Phrygias—the one on the Hellespont, the other which they call the Greater; and they gave back to him Mysia, which King Prusias had taken from him, and Lycaonia and Milyas and Lydia and expressly B.C. 188

A.U.C. 566 17 atque Ephesum et Telmessum. De Pamphylia disceptatum inter Eumenem et Antiochi legatos cum esset, quia pars eius citra pars ultra[1] Taurum est, integra res[2] ad senatum reicitur.

XL. His foederibus decretisque datis Manlius cum decem legatis omnique exercitu ad Hellespontum profectus, evocatis eo regulis Gallorum, leges quibus
2 pacem cum Eumene servarent dixit, denuntiavit ut morem[3] vagandi cum armis finirent agrorumque suo-
3 rum terminis se continerent. Contractis deinde ex omni ora navibus et Eumenis etiam classe per[4] Athenaeum fratrem regis ab Elaea adducta copias omnes
4 in Europam traiecit. Inde per Chersonesum modicis[5] itineribus grave praeda omnis generis agmen trahens Lysimachiae stativa habuit, ut quam maxime recentibus et integris iumentis Thraeciam, per
5 quam iter vulgo horrebant, ingrederetur. Quo profectus est ab Lysimachia die ad amnem Melana
6 quem vocant, inde postero die Cypsela pervenit. A

[1] pars ultra ς : par lustrato *B*.
[2] integra res *ed. Frobeniana* 1531 : integra *B*ς.
[3] morem ς : mores *B*.
[4] classe per ς : classe iper *B*.
[5] modicis ς : *om. B*.

---

[1] Polybius (XXII. xxix) seems to think that the dispute concerned all Pamphylia, not regarding it, as Livy does, as cut in two by the range. It is evident that not even the commissioners, while on the spot, could tell where the western end of the Taurus chain was situated, and one does not see how the senate could be expected to determine that geographical fact. The incident shows how indistinct was the boundary established by the treaty: cf. the note to xxxviii. 4 above. In XLIV. xiv. 3 Pamphylia seems to be free, but otherwise there is no indication of the senate's decision.

With the chapters which deal with the treaty and with the settlement of Asia XXXVII. xlv. and lv.–lvi. should be read.

the cities of Tralles and Ephesus and Telmessus. B.C. 188
When a dispute over Pamphylia broke out between Eumenes and the ambassadors of Antiochus, because part of it was on this side of Taurus and part on the other,[1] the whole question was referred to the senate.

XL. Having published these treaties and decrees, Manlius with the ten commissioners and all the army set out for the Hellespont, summoning thither the chiefs of the Gauls, and stated the terms on which they should observe peace with Eumenes,[2] and warned them that they should discontinue their habit of wandering about under arms and should keep themselves within the boundaries of their own lands. Then, collecting ships from the whole coast, the fleet of Eumenes also being brought up from Elaea by his brother Athenaeus, he ferried all his forces across to Europe.[3] Then, leading a column heavily laden with every sort of booty by short stages through the Chersonese he established a base at Lysimachia, in order that with his pack-animals as far as possible fresh and in good condition he might enter Thrace, the journey through which was generally feared. On the day of his departure from Lysimachia he reached the river called Melas and on the day after that Cypsela. From Cypsela

[2] The legal jurisdiction of either Manlius or the *legati* is not clear. Rome acquired no territory from the Galatians and recognized no Galatian interest in the treaty with Antiochus. Nevertheless, Rome had a moral responsibility for all Asia and particularly for the kingdom of Eumenes, the nearest neighbour and the traditional enemy of the Galatians.

[3] Appian (*Syr.* 43), who abridges the account of the return journey of Manlius, criticizes severely the decision to return by land rather than by sea, and emphasizes the services rendered to Scipio by Philip (XXXVII. vii. 16).

A.U.C. 566

Cypselis via decem milium fere silvestris angusta
confragosa excipiebat, propter cuius difficultatem
itineris in duas partes divisus exercitus, et praecedere
una iussa, altera, magno intervallo cogere agmen,
media impedimenta interposuit; plaustra cum
7 pecunia publica erant pretiosaque alia praeda. Ita
cum per saltum iret, Thraecum decem haud amplius
milia ex quattuor populis, Astii et Caeni et Maduateni et Coreli, ad ipsas angustias viam circumse-
8 derunt. Opinio erat non sine Philippi Macedonum
regis fraude id factum; eum scisse non alia quam per
Thraeciam redituros Romanos, et quantam pecu-
9 niam secum portarent. In primo agmine imperator
erat, sollicitus propter iniquitatem locorum. Thraeces nihil se moverunt donec armati transirent;
10 postquam primos superasse angustias viderunt,
postremos [1] nondum appropinquantes, impedimenta
et sarcinas invadunt, caesisque custodibus partim
ea quae in plaustris erant diripere, partim sub oneri-
11 bus iumenta abstrahere. Unde postquam clamor
primum ad eos, qui iam ingressi saltum sequebantur,
deinde etiam ad primum agmen est perlatus, utrimque in medium concurritur, et inordinatum pluribus
12 simul locis proelium conseritur. Thraecas praeda
ipsa impeditos oneribus et plerosque, ut ad rapiendum
vacuas manus haberent, inermes ad caedem praebet; [2]
Romanos iniquitas locorum barbaris per calles notas

[1] postremos ς: supremos *B*.
[2] praebet ς: praebent *B*.

---

[1] It was the Thracian plan to let the van go through, block the road so that the van could not get back, and then attack the baggage.

a road awaited him, for about ten miles wooded, narrow, rough, and by reason of the difficulty of this route he divided the army into two sections, and, having ordered one to go ahead and the other to bring up the rear at a great distance, he placed the baggage between them; there were carts loaded with public money and other valuable booty. As they were marching in this order through the defile, not more than ten thousand Thracians, of four tribes, the Astii and the Caeni and the Maduateni and the Coreli, blocked the road at the narrow point.[1] It was generally believed that this did not happen without treachery on the part of Philip, king of the Macedonians; he knew that the Romans would return by no other route than through Thrace, and he knew how much money they would bring with them. The commander was with the van, being concerned about the unfavourable character of the terrain. The Thracians did not move until the armed troops were past; when they saw that the van was out of the defile and that the rear was not yet at hand, they fell upon the trains and the baggage, and having killed the guards some of them carried off what was in the wagons, others drove off the pack-animals, loads and all. When the uproar reached first those who were following and just entering the defile and then came to the head of the column, there was a rush from both directions towards the centre, and a disorderly battle began in several places at once. The Thracians were exposed to slaughter, hampered as they were by the burden of the booty itself, while many of them were without arms, in order that they might keep their hands free to plunder; the Romans were betrayed by the unfavourable ground, since the barbarians B.C. 188

A.U.C. 566 occursantibus et latentibus interdum per[1] cavas
13 valles prodebat. Ipsa etiam onera plaustraque,
ut fors tulit, his aut illis incommode obiecta pugnantibus impedimento sunt. Alibi praedo alibi praedae
14 vindex cadit. Prout locus iniquus aequusve[2] his
aut illis, prout animus pugnantium est, prout numerus
—alii enim pluribus, quam ipsi erant, alii paucioribus occurrerant—varia fortuna pugnae est; multi
15 utrimque cadunt. Iam nox appetebat, cum proelio
excedunt Thraeces, non fuga vulnerum aut mortis,
sed quia satis praedae habebant.

XLI. Romanorum primum agmen extra saltum
circa templum Bendidium castra loco aperto posuit;
pars altera ad custodiam impedimentorum medio in
2 saltu, duplici circumdato vallo, mansit. Postero die
prius explorato saltu quam moverent primis se con-
3 iungunt. In eo proelio cum et impedimentorum et
calonum pars et[3] milites aliquot, cum passim toto
prope saltu pugnaretur, cecidissent, plurimum[4]
Q. Minucii Thermi morte damni[5] est acceptum,
4 fortis ac strenui viri. Eo die ad Hebrum flumen
perventum est. Inde Aeniorum fines praeter
Apollinis Zerynthium quem vocant incolae templum
5 superant. Aliae angustiae circa Tempyra excipiunt
—hoc loco nomen est—nec minus confragosae
quam priores; sed, quia nihil silvestre circa est, ne

[1] per ς : et *B*.
[2] aequusue ς : aequusque *B*.
[3] et ς : *om. B*.
[4] plurimum ς : *om. B*.
[5] damni *ed. Frobeniana* 1535 : amissum *B*ς.

---

[1] Livy does not commit himself with regard to this battle. For the contradictory accounts of it, cf. xlvii. 6–9 with xlix. 7–12 below.

[2] A native divinity identified with Artemis or with Cybele.

charged them over familiar paths and sometimes laid ambushes for them in low-lying valleys. Even the loads and the wagons, inconveniently placed for one side or the other, as chance determined, hindered the fighters. Here the plunderer fell, there the defender of the plunder. Just as the terrain was unfavourable or favourable for one party or the other, just as the spirits of the fighters varied, just as their numbers—for some met parties larger than their own and others smaller—just so the fortune of the battle changed; many fell on both sides. Night was now at hand when the Thracians retired from the fight, not to avoid wounds or death, but because they had enough of spoils.[1] B.C. 188

XLI. The head of the Roman column encamped outside the defile near the temple of Bendis [2] on open ground; the rest remained within the defile to guard the trains, sheltered by a double rampart. The following day, having reconnoitred the defile before they moved, they joined the van. In this battle there was a loss both of baggage and of camp-followers and a considerable number of soldiers had fallen, since there was fighting everywhere along the whole defile, but the most serious blow received was the death of Quintus Minucius Thermus, a man of courage and energy.[3] That day they reached the Hebrus river. Then they crossed the frontiers of the Aenians near the temple of Apollo, whom the natives call Zerynthius. Another pass confronted them near Tempyra—this is the name of the place—not less rough than the former; but, because there is no wooded country around it, it does not furnish

[3] He had been consul in 193 B.C. and was one of the ten commissioners.

A.U.C. 566

6 latebras quidem ad insidiandum praebent. Huc[1]
ad eandem spem praedae Thrausi, gens et ipsa
Thraecum, convenere; sed, quia nudae valles procul
ut[2] conspicerentur angustias obsidentes efficiebant,
minus terroris tumultusque fuit apud Romanos;
quippe etsi iniquo loco, proelio tamen iusto, acie
7 aperta, signis collatis dimicandum erat. Conferti
subeunt et cum clamore impetu facto primum
expulere loco hostes, deinde avertere; fuga inde
caedesque suis ipsos impedientibus angustiis fieri
8 coepta est. Romani victores ad vicum Maronitarum—Salen appellant—posuerunt castra.[3] Postero die patenti itinere Priaticus campus eos
excepit, triduumque ibi frumentum accipientes
manserunt, partem ex agris Maronitarum, confe-
rentibus ipsis, partem ex navibus suis, quae cum
9 omnis generis commeatu sequebantur. Ab stativis
10 diei via Apolloniam fuit. Hinc per Abderitarum
agrum Neapolim perventum est. Hoc omne per
Graecorum colonias pacatum iter fuit; reliquum
inde per medios Thraecas dies noctesque, etsi non
infestum, tamen suspectum, donec in Macedoniam
11 pervenerunt. Mitiores Thraecas idem exercitus,
cum a Scipione eadem via duceretur, habuerat,
nullam ob aliam causam quam quod praedae minus
12 quod peteretur fuerat; quamquam tunc quoque
Claudius auctor est ad quindecim milia Thraecum

[1] huc ς : hoc *B*.
[2] ut ς : *om. B*.
[3] posuerunt castra ς : *om. B*.

---

[1] The modern Cavalla.
[2] Philip received the credit for this in XXXVII. vii. 16.

even hiding-places for ambuscades. The Thrausi, B.C. 188
these too being Thracians, assembled here with the same hope of plunder; but, since the exposed valleys brought it about that those who blocked the pass could be seen from afar, there was less consternation and confusion among the Romans; indeed, although on uneven ground, there was none the less a pitched battle to be fought, a regular engagement with battle-lines open to view. They moved forward in close array, and charging with a shout they first dislodged the enemy and then broke their line; then flight and slaughter began to take place, since the enemy were entangled in the narrow pass which they had themselves selected. The victorious Romans encamped near a village of the Maroneans—they call it Salê. The next day, marching in open country, the Priatic plain received them, and they spent three days there collecting grain, partly from the fields of the Maroneans, brought in by the people themselves, partly from their own ships, which were following with all manner of supplies. From this station it was a day's march to Apollonia. Thence they came through the country of the Abderites to Neapolis.[1] All this journey was peaceful, amid the colonies of Greeks; the rest from there on, through the midst of the Thracians, while not dangerous, yet required vigilance by day and night until they arrived in Macedonia. The same army, led over the same route by Scipio, had found the Thracians more peacefully inclined, for no other reason than that there was less of booty to be sought;[2] and yet Claudius[3] asserts that even then about fifteen thousand Thracians en-

[3] Perhaps Livy had not read the account of Claudius when he wrote XXXVII. vii. 16 and xxxiii.

A.U.C. 566

praecedenti ad exploranda loca agmen Muttini Numidae occurrisse. Quadringentos equites fuisse
13 Numidas, paucos elephantos; Muttinis filium per medios hostes cum centum quinquaginta [1] delectis equitibus [2] perrupisse; eundem mox, cum iam Muttines in medio elephantis locatis, in cornua equitibus dispositis manum cum hoste conseruisset,
14 terrorem ab tergo praebuisse, atque inde turbatos equestri velut procella hostes ad peditum agmen non
15 accessisse. Cn. Manlius per Macedoniam in Thessaliam exercitum traduxit. Inde per Epirum Apolloniam cum pervenisset, nondum adeo hiberno contempto mari ut traicere auderet, Apolloniae hibernavit.

XLII. Exitu prope anni M. Valerius consul ex Liguribus ad magistratus subrogandos Romam venit nulla memorabili in provincia gesta re, ut ea probabilis morae causa esset quod solito serius ad comitia
2 venisset. Comitia consulibus rogandis fuerunt a. d.[3] XII. Kal. Martias; creati M. Aemilius Lepidus C.
3 Flaminius. Postero die praetores facti Ap. Claudius
4 Pulcher Ser. Sulpicius Galba Q. Terentius Culleo L. Terentius Massiliota Q. Fulvius Flaccus M.
5 Furius Crassipes. Comitiis perfectis [4] quas provincias praetoribus esse placeret retulit ad senatum consul. Decreverunt duas Romae iuris dicendi

[1] quinquaginta ς: *om. B.*
[2] equitibus *edd. vett.*: peditibus *B*ς.
[3] diem ς: *om. B.*
[4] perfectis ς: persecutis *B.*

countered Muttines the Numidian who was preceding the column to reconnoitre. He says that there were four hundred Numidian cavalry with a few elephants; that the son of Muttines with a hundred and fifty picked troopers broke through the centre of the enemy; and that a little later, when Muttines, having placed the elephants in the centre and stationed the cavalry on the flanks, had closed with the enemy, this same son had caused panic by an attack in the rear, and that the enemy, thrown into confusion by this cavalry-storm, so to speak, had not reached the column of the infantry. Gnaeus Manlius led the army through Macedonia into Thrace. When he had proceeded from there through Epirus to Apollonia, not yet holding the wintry sea in such light esteem that he dared to cross it, he passed the winter in Apollonia. B.C. 188

XLII. At almost the end of this year the consul Marcus Valerius came from the Ligurians to Rome to hold the elections of magistrates, having done nothing in the province so worthy of note that it could be a plausible reason for delay, to cause him to arrive later than usual for the elections. The election of consuls took place on the twelfth day before the Kalends of March; the successful candidates were Marcus Aemilius Lepidus and Gaius Flaminius. The next day the praetors were chosen, Appius Claudius Pulcher, Servius Sulpicius Galba, Quintus Terentius Culleo, Lucius Terentius Massiliota, Quintus Fulvius Flaccus, Marcus Furius Crassipes. Having finished the elections, the consul referred to the senate the question as to which provinces they desired to assign to the praetors. They decreed that two should be stationed in Rome to

A.U.C. 566 causa, duas extra Italiam, Siciliam ac Sardiniam, duas
6 in Italia, Tarentum et Galliam; et extemplo, priusquam inirent magistratum, sortiri iussi. Ser. Sulpicius urbanam, Q. Terentius peregrinam est sortitus,
L. Terentius Siciliam, Q. Fulvius Sardiniam, Ap.
Claudius Tarentum, M. Furius Galliam.

7 Eo anno L. Minucius Myrtilus et L. Manlius,
quod legatos Carthaginienses pulsasse dicebantur,
iussu M. Claudii praetoris urbani[1] per fetiales
traditi sunt legatis et Carthaginem avecti.

A.U.C. 567 8 In Liguribus magni belli et gliscentis in dies
magis fama erat. Itaque consulibus novis, quo die
de provinciis et de re publica retulerunt, senatus
9 utrisque Ligures provinciam decrevit. Huic senatus
consulto Lepidus consul intercedebat, indignum esse
praedicans consules ambos in valles Ligurum includi,
10 M. Fulvium et Cn. Manlium biennium iam, alterum
in Europa, alterum in Asia, velut pro Philippo atque
Antiocho substitutos regnare. Si exercitus in his
terris esse placeat, consules iis potius quam privatos
11 praeesse oportere. Vagari eos cum belli terrore per
nationes, quibus bellum indictum non sit, pacem

[1] urbani ς : urbis *B*.

---

[1] The whole procedure is irregular, probably because the elections were held less than a month before the inauguration.

[2] Claudius probably acted under instructions from the senate. Valerius Maximus (VI. vi. 3), who cites this incident as an example of *publica fides*, dates it a year later.

[3] Lepidus raises an important constitutional question, not to be easily answered, whether a magistrate could hold his *imperium* indefinitely, *i.e.* until he was relieved. The *imperium* of Fulvius and Manlius had been prorogued for one year (xxxv. 3 above), and this period was now at an end. Another question which he raises is whether a proconsul

administer justice, two outside Italy, in Sicily and Sardinia, and two in Italy, at Tarentum and in Gaul;[1] and they were ordered to cast lots at once, before they were inaugurated. Servius Sulpicius received the civil jurisdiction, Quintus Terentius that between citizens and aliens, Lucius Terentius Sicily, Quintus Fulvius Sardinia, Appius Claudius Tarentum, Marcus Furius Gaul. B.C. 188

In that year Lucius Minucius Myrtilus and Lucius Manlius, because they were said to have beaten Carthaginian ambassadors, by order of Marcus Claudius, the city praetor, were delivered by the fetials to ambassadors and taken to Carthage.[2]

There was the rumour of a great war, growing more dangerous every day, among the Ligurians. So, on the day when the new consuls laid before the senate the question of the provinces and the general policy, the senate decreed to both consuls the Ligurians as their province. To this decree of the senate the consul Lepidus objected, declaring that it was improper that both the consuls should be shut up in the valleys of the Ligurians while Marcus Fulvius and Gnaeus Manlius for two years now, the one in Europe, the other in Asia, were lording it as if they were the successors to Philip and Antiochus. If it were the senate's pleasure that there should be armies in those lands, consuls rather than private citizens[3] should command them. These men were wandering about, carrying the threat of war to nations upon whom no war had been declared, selling peace for a B.C. 187

was technically a *privatus* in the sense that Scipio, for example, was *privatus cum imperio* in Spain. Unfortunately, Lepidus is too much influenced by his feud with Fulvius to be a good witness on either point.

A.U.C. 567 pretio venditantes. Si eas provincias exercitibus obtinere opus esset, sicut M'. Acilio L. Scipio consul, L. Scipioni M. Fulvius et Cn. Manlius successissent
12 consules, ita Fulvio Manlioque C. Livium et M. Valerium consules debuisse succedere. Nunc certe, perfecto Aetolico bello, recepta ab Antiocho Asia, devictis Gallis, aut consules ad exercitus consulares mitti aut reportari legiones inde reddique tandem rei
13 publicae debere. Senatus his auditis in sententia perseveravit ut consulibus ambobus Ligures provincia esset; Manlium Fulviumque decedere de provinciis et exercitus inde deducere[1] ac redire Romam placuit.

XLIII. Inimicitiae inter M. Fulvium et M. Aemilium consulem erant, et super cetera Aemilius serius biennio se consulem factum M. Fulvii opera
2 ducebat. Itaque ad invidiam ei faciendam legatos Ambracienses in senatum subornatos criminibus introduxit, qui sibi, cum in pace essent imperataque prioribus consulibus fecissent et eadem oboedienter
3 praestare M. Fulvio parati essent, bellum illatum questi, agros primum[2] depopulatos, terrorem direp-

[1] de—deducere ς : *om. B.* [2] primum ς : *om. B.*

[1] Manlius, rather than Fulvius, was guilty of this conduct, and the narrative of the Galatian campaign (xii–xxvii above; see also the notes, *passim*) gives altogether too much support to these charges. They were elaborated by Furius and Aemilius Paulus in chaps. xlv–xlvi below.

[2] Fulvius had presided at the election of his own colleague in the peculiar election for 189 B.C. (XXXVII. xlvii. 7) and at the election for 188 B.C. (xxxv. 1 above), and on both

price.[1] If it was necessary, he continued, to hold these provinces with troops, just as the consul Lucius Scipio had succeeded Manius Acilius and had in turn been superseded by the consuls Marcus Fulvius and Gnaeus Manlius, so Fulvius and Manlius should have been replaced by the consuls Gaius Livius and Marcus Valerius. Now, at any rate, when the Aetolian war was finished, when Asia was rescued from Antiochus, when the Gauls were conquered, either consuls should be sent to command consular armies or the legions should be recalled from there and at length restored to the state. After hearing this the senate persisted in its decision that both consuls should have the Ligurians as their province; it was voted that Manlius and Fulvius should retire from their provinces and withdraw their armies from them and return to Rome. B.C. 187

XLIII. There was a feud between Marcus Fulvius and the consul Marcus Aemilius, and, in addition to everything else, Aemilius considered that it was due to the efforts of Marcus Fulvius that he himself had reached the consulship two years late.[2] Therefore, with a view to making Fulvius unpopular, he introduced to the senate ambassadors of the Ambraciots, previously coached as to their charges, who were to complain that, while they were at peace and had performed the orders of the previous consuls and were ready to render the same obedience to Marcus Fulvius, war had been declared on them, and first their fields had been laid waste and fear of plunder

occasions Aemilius was defeated. He had then some reason for blaming Fulvius particularly for his failures. However, the interval between his praetorship (191 B.C.) and his consulship was not unusually long for this period.

A.U.C. 567 tionis et caedis urbi iniectum, ut eo metu claudere
4 cogerentur portas; obsessos deinde et oppugnatos se
et omnia exempla belli edita [1] in se caedibus incendiis
ruinis direptione urbis, coniuges liberos in servitium
5 abstractos, bona adempta, et, quod se ante omnia
moveat, templa tota urbe spoliata ornamentis; simu-
lacra deum, deos immo ipsos, convulsos ex sedibus suis
ablatos esse; parietes postesque nudatos quos ado-
rent, ad quos precentur et supplicent, Ambraciensi-
6 bus superesse: haec querentes interrogando criminose
ex composito consul ad plura velut non sua sponte
7 dicenda eliciebat. Motis patribus alter consul C.
Flaminius M. Fulvii causam excepit, qui veterem
8 viam et obsoletam ingressos Ambracienses dixit; sic
M. Marcellum ab Syracusanis, sic Q. Fulvium a
Campanis accusatos. Quin eadem opera T. Quinctium a Philippo rege, M'. Acilium et L. Scipionem
ab Antiocho, Cn. Manlium a Gallis, ipsum M.
Fulvium ab Aetolis et Cephallaniae populis accusari
9 paterentur? "Ambraciam oppugnatam et captam et signa inde ornamentaque ablata et cetera
facta quae captis urbibus soleant, negaturum aut
me pro M. Fulvio aut ipsum M. Fulvium censetis,
10 patres conscripti, qui ob has res gestas [2] triumphum

[1] edita *ed. Parisina* 1513: habita *B*ς.
[2] res gestas ς: gestas res *B*.

---

[1] Cf. XXVI. xxx. 12.

and slaughter held before the city, so that they were B.C. 187
compelled by that fear to close their gates; that then they were beleaguered and besieged and that every form of war had been waged against them—slaughter, fires, destruction, plunder of the city; that their wives and children had been carried off into slavery, their property taken from them, and, what disturbed them most of all, the temples throughout the city had been stripped of their ornaments; the images of the gods, or rather the gods themselves, had been torn from their seats and carried away; bare walls and door-posts, they said, had been left to the Ambracians to adore, to pray to, and to supplicate: as they made these complaints the consul, asking leading questions as they had agreed, drew them on, as if against their will, to say even more. When the Fathers were aroused, the other consul, Gaius Flaminius, took up the cause of Marcus Fulvius, saying that the Ambraciots were following an old and long-abandoned path; thus Marcus Marcellus had been accused by the Syracusans, thus Quintus Fulvius by the Campanians.[1] Nay, would they permit similar accusations to be brought against Titus Quinctius by King Philip, against Manius Acilius and Lucius Scipio by Antiochus, against Gnaeus Manlius by the Gauls and even against Marcus Fulvius by the Aetolians and the peoples of Cephallania? "That Ambracia was besieged and captured and that its statues and works of art were removed from there and that other things were done which are usually done when cities are captured, do you think that either I on behalf of Marcus Fulvius or Marcus Fulvius on his own behalf will deny, conscript Fathers, since for these achievements he will

A.U.C. 567

a vobis postulaturus sit,[1] Ambraciam captam signaque
quae ablata criminantur, et cetera spolia eius urbis
ante currum laturus et fixurus in postibus suis?
11 Nihil est quod se ab Aetolis separent; eadem Ambra-
12 ciensium et Aetolorum causa est. Itaque collega
meus vel in alia causa inimicitias exerceat vel, si in
hac utique [2] mavult, retineat Ambracienses suos in
13 adventum M. Fulvii; ego nec de Ambraciensibus [3]
nec de Aetolis decerni quicquam absente M. Fulvio
patiar."

XLIV. Cum Aemilius callidam malitiam inimici
velut notam omnibus insimularet et tempus eum
morando extracturum diceret, ne consule inimico
Romam veniret, certamine consulum biduum ab-
2 sumptum [4] est; nec praesente Flaminio decerni quic-
3 quam videbatur posse. Captata occasio est, cum
aeger forte Flaminius abesset, et referente Aemilio
4 senatus consultum factum est ut Ambraciensibus
suae res omnes redderentur; in libertate essent ac
legibus suis uterentur; portoria quae [5] vellent terra
marique caperent, dum eorum immunes Romani
5 ac socii nominis Latini essent; signa aliaque ornamenta, quae quererentur ex aedibus sacris sublata
esse, de iis, cum M. Fulvius Romam revertisset, placere ad collegium pontificum referri, et quod ii cen-
6 suissent fieri. Neque his contentus consul fuit, sed

[1] postulaturus sit ς: postulet *B*.
[2] utique ς: *om. B*.
[3] ambraciensibus ς: ambracienses *B*.
[4] absumptum ς: assumptum *B*.
[5] portoria quae *ed. Parisina* 1513: portari ea quae *B*ς.

---

[1] *i.e.* a representation of the captured city.

claim from you a triumph, the captured Ambracia[1] B.C. 187
and the statues which they accuse him of removing and the other spoils of that city will be carried before his chariot and fixed to his door-posts? There is no respect in which they can separate themselves from the Aetolians; the situation of Ambraciots and Aetolians is identical. Let my colleague, then, either expend his malice in some other case or, if he prefers to do so in this matter especially, let him keep his Ambraciots here until the arrival of Marcus Fulvius; I shall permit no decree to be passed concerning either the Ambraciots or the Aetolians in the absence of Marcus Fulvius."

XLIV. While Aemilius was thus assailing the shrewd hostility of his enemy as if known to all, and was claiming that Fulvius would drag out the time by delaying, that he might not come to Rome while his foe was consul, two days were wasted by the bickering of the consuls; and it seemed that no decree could be passed while Flaminius was present. Aemilius took advantage of an opportunity when Flaminius was kept away by illness, and on his motion the senate passed a decree that the Ambraciots should recover all their property; that they should be free and should enjoy their own laws; that they should collect port duties at their pleasure, by land and sea, provided that the Romans and the allies of the Latin confederacy should be exempt from paying them; that as to the statues and other works of art which they complained had been taken from their sacred shrines, when Marcus Fulvius had returned to Rome, the question concerning them should be referred to the college of pontiffs, and that whatever they should have ordered should be done. The consul was not

A.U.C. 567 postea per infrequentiam adiecit senatus consultum,
Ambraciam vi captam esse non videri.
7 Supplicatio inde ex decemvirorum decreto pro
valetudine populi per triduum fuit, quia gravis pesti-
8 lentia urbem atque agros vastabat. Latinae inde
fuerunt. Quibus religionibus liberati consules et di-
lectu perfecto—novis enim uterque maluit uti militibus—in provinciam profecti sunt, veteresque omnes
dimiserunt.
9 Post consulum profectionem Cn. Manlius proconsul Romam venit; cui cum ab Ser. Sulpicio prae-
10 tore senatus ad aedem Bellonae datus esset, et ipse
commemoratis rebus ab se gestis postulasset ut ob
eas diis immortalibus honos haberetur sibique tri-
11 umphanti urbem invehi liceret, contradixerunt pars
maior decem legatorum qui cum eo fuerant, et ante
alios L. Furius Purpurio et L. Aemilius Paulus.

XLV. Legatos sese Cn. Manlio datos pacis cum
Antiocho faciendae causa foederisque legum quae
cum L. Scipione inchoatae fuissent perficiendarum.
2 Cn. Manlium summa ope tetendisse ut eam pacem
turbaret, et Antiochum, si sui potestatem fecisset,
insidiis exciperet; sed illum cognita fraude consulis,
cum saepe colloquiis petitis captatus esset, non

---

[1] This last charge has some substantiation (cf. ix. 9 above), and one wonders why it was not pressed. Cato emphasized it in his attacks on Fulvius (Gellius, V. vi. 25; Meyer, pp. 52–53). If it was true, the action of Fulvius was illegal.

[2] The commissioners could have had relations with Manlius only because he had succeeded to the tasks left unfinished by Scipio. According to xxxvii. 11 above they did not reach Asia until after the Galatian campaign was concluded, and they could have had no military duties as *legati* except on the return, although Manlius speaks of them as eye-witnesses of his victory (xlvii. 4 below).

satisfied with this, but later, in a sparsely attended meeting, added a decree of the senate, to the effect that it did not appear that Ambracia had been captured by force.[1] B.C. 187

Then a three-day period of prayer was proclaimed in accordance with a decree of the decemvirs for the health of the people, because a severe pestilence was wasting the City and the country districts. Next the Latin Festival was held. The consuls, released from these ceremonies and having finished the levy—for each of them preferred to employ new soldiers—departed to the province and discharged all the veterans.

After the departure of the consuls, Gnaeus Manlius the proconsul arrived in Rome; when an audience before the senate in the temple of Bellona had been granted him by the praetor Servius Sulpicius and he, after relating his exploits, had demanded that on account of them honour should be paid to the immortal gods and that he should be permitted to ride into the City in triumph, the majority of the ten commissioners who had been with him opposed it, and, beyond the rest, Lucius Furius Purpurio and Lucius Aemilius Paulus.

XLV. They said that the commissioners had been assigned to Gnaeus Manlius[2] for the purpose of making peace with Antiochus and of putting into final form the terms of the treaty which had been initiated by Lucius Scipio. Gnaeus Manlius, they said, had striven with all his might to break the peace and to take Antiochus by treachery, if the king should have given him any opportunity to do so; but he, being aware of the deceitfulness of the consul, although often approached with requests for conferences, had

A.U.C. 567

congressum modo sed conspectum etiam eius
3 vitasse. Cupientem transire Taurum aegre omnium
legatorum precibus, ne carminibus Sibyllae prae-
dictam superantibus terminos fatales cladem experiri
vellet, retentum admosse tamen exercitum et prope
in ipsis [1] iugis ad divortia aquarum castra posuisse.
4 Cum ibi nullam belli causam inveniret quiescentibus
regiis, circumegisse [2] exercitum ad Gallograecos;
5 cui nationi non ex senatus auctoritate, non populi
iussu [3] bellum illatum. Quod quem umquam de sua
sententia facere [4] ausum? Antiochi Philippi Hanni-
6 balis et Poenorum recentissima bella esse; de omnibus his consultum senatum, populum iussisse,[5] per [6]
legatos ante res repetitas, postremo qui bellum indi-
7 cerent, missos. "Quid [7] eorum, Cn. Manli, factum est,
ut istud publicum populi Romani bellum et non tuum
8 privatum latrocinium ducamus? At eo [8] ipso contentus fuisti, recto itinere exercitum duxisti ad eos, quos
9 tibi hostes desumpseras; an per omnes amfractus
viarum, cum ad bivia [9] consisteres ut, quo flexisset

[1] in ipsis *Madvig*: ipsis *B*ς.
[2] circumegisse ς: circumiecisse *B*.
[3] iussu ς: iussum *B*.
[4] facere ς: *om. B*.
[5] iussisse ς: fuisse *B*.
[6] per *Madvig*: saepe *B*ς.
[7] quid ς: quod *B*.
[8] at eo *ed. Frobeniana* 1535: adeo *B*ς.
[9] ad bivia *ed. Frobeniana* 1535: auia *B*: uia ς.

---

[1] There seems to be no basis for either charge in the preceding narrative of Livy, but this may be due to his selection of sources.

[2] This may explain the rather aimless invasion of Pamphylia mentioned in xv. 5–6 above.

avoided, not merely a meeting with him, but even the sight of him.[1] Manlius, they said, when he desired to cross the Taurus,[2] had with difficulty been held back by the pleas of all his lieutenants from trying to test the prediction of ruin found in the verses of the Sibyl[3] for those who crossed the fateful boundaries, but, none the less, had moved up the army and encamped near by on the very crest at the parting of the waters. Finding no pretext for war there, the king's forces remaining passive, he led the army around against the Galatians, a people against whom war had not been declared by the authority of the senate or the vote of the assembly.[4] Who, they asked, had ever ventured to do this on his own motion? The most recent wars were those with Antiochus, Philip, Hannibal and the Carthaginians; in all these cases the senate had passed decrees, the assembly had voted, restitution had previously been demanded by ambassadors, finally, delegates had been sent to declare war.[5] "Which of these things was done, Gnaeus Manlius, so that we can consider this a public war of the Roman people and not a private piratical expedition of your own? Were you even content with that and did you lead your army directly against those whom you had picked out to be your enemies? Or, moving by all the roundabout ways, stopping at B.C. 187

[3] There seems to be no other allusion to this prophecy, but there may have been many such oracles in independent circulation and attributed to the Sibyl to increase their authority.

[4] The senate had foreseen the probability of a war with the Gauls (XXXVII. li. 10), but there is no record of a formal declaration of war or of the performance of the ceremonial acts mentioned in sect. 6 below.

[5] The speaker is describing the formal fetial procedure.

A.U.C. 567 agmen Attalus, Eumenis frater, eo consul mercennarius cum exercitu Romano sequereris, Pisidiae Lycaoniaeque et Phrygiae recessus omnes atque angulos peragrasti, stipem ab tyrannis castellanisque deviis colligens? Quid enim tibi cum Oroandis? Quid cum aliis aeque innoxiis populis?

10 "Bellum autem ipsum, cuius nomine triumphum petis, quo modo gessisti? Loco aequo, tempore tuo
11 pugnasti? Tu vero recte ut diis immortalibus honos habeatur postulas, primum quod pro temeritate imperatoris, nullo gentium iure bellum inferentis, poenas luere exercitum noluerunt; deinde quod beluas, non hostes nobis obiecerunt.

XLVI. "Nolite nomen tantum existimare mixtum [1] esse Gallograecorum; multo ante et corpora
2 et animi mixti ac vitiati sunt. An si illi Galli essent, cum [2] quibus miliens vario eventu in Italia pugnatum est, quantum in imperatore nostro fuit,
3 nuntius illinc [3] redisset? [4] Bis cum iis pugnatum est, bis loco iniquo subiit, in valle inferiore pedibus paene hostium aciem subiecit. Ut non tela ex superiore loco mitterent, sed corpora sua nuda
4 inicerent, obruere nos [5] potuerunt. Quid igitur incidit? [6] Magna fortuna populi Romani est, magnum et terribile nomen. Recenti ruina Hannibalis

[1] mixtum ς: *om. B.*
[2] cum ς: *om. B.*
[3] nuntius illinc ς: *om., spat. rel., B.*
[4] redisset ς: credidisset *B.*
[5] nos ς: non *B.*
[6] incidit ς: inci (*sic*) *B, post quod uocabulum subsidio huius codicis omnino caremus.*

every cross-road, that, wherever Attalus, the brother B.C. 187 of Eumenes, turned his course, there you, a money-seeking consul, might follow with a Roman army, did you travel over all the nooks and corners of Pisidia and Lycaonia and Phrygia, exacting tribute from tyrants and commanders of out-of-the-way fortresses? What business did *you* have with the people of Oroanda? What with other equally innocent peoples?

"But the war proper, on account of which you ask a triumph, how did you conduct it? Did you fight on favourable ground, at a time selected by you? Rightly in truth do you demand that honour be paid to the immortal gods, first, because they refused to exact the penalty from the army for the rashness of the commander, who was waging war under no law of nations; second, because they confronted us with dumb animals, not enemies.

XLVI. "Do not think that only the name of the Gallogrecians is a mixture; long since both their bodies and their minds have been mixed and corrupted. Or if they were Gauls, with whom we have fought a thousand times in Italy with varying results, so far as the issue depended on our commander, would even a messenger have come back from there? Twice he engaged in battle with them, twice he attacked over unfavourable ground and placed his battle-line in a valley below the enemy and almost at their feet. Without hurling a weapon from their higher position, and merely flinging their naked bodies down, they could have overwhelmed us. What happened then? Great is the fortune of the Roman people, great and terrible is its name. By the recent overthrow of Hannibal, Philip, Antiochus,

A.U.C. 567 Philippi Antiochi prope attoniti[1] erant. Tantae
corporum moles fundis sagittisque in fugam con-
sternatae sunt; gladius in acie cruentatus non est
5 Gallico bello; velut avium examina ad crepitum
6 primum missilium avolavere. At hercule iidem
nos—monente fortuna quid, si hostem habuissemus,
casurum fuisset—cum redeuntes in latrunculos
Thraecas incidissemus, caesi, fugati, exuti impedi-
7 mentis sumus. Q. Minucius Thermus, in quo haud
paulo plus damni factum est quam si Cn. Manlius,
cuius temeritate ea clades inciderat, perisset, cum
8 multis viris fortibus cecidit; exercitus spolia regis
Antiochi referens trifariam dissipatus, alibi primum,
alibi postremum agmen, alibi impedimenta, inter
vepres in latebris ferarum noctem unam delituit.
9 Pro his triumphus petitur? Si nihil in Thraecia cladis
ignominiaeque foret acceptum, de quibus hostibus
triumphum peteres? De iis, ut opinor, quos tibi
10 hostes senatus aut populus Romanus dedisset. Sic
huic L. Scipioni, sic illi M'. Acilio de rege Antiocho,
sic paulo ante T. Quinctio de rege Philippo, sic P.
Africano de Hannibale et Poenis et Syphace triumphus
11 datus. Et minima illa, cum iam senatus censuisset
bellum,[2] quaesita tamen sunt, quibus nuntiandum
esset: ipsis utique regibus nuntiaretur, an satis
esset ad praesidium aliquod nuntiari? Vultis ergo

[1] attoniti ς : attonitae *M*.
[2] bellum *ed. Frobeniana* 1535 : bella ς.

---

[1] The speaker contrasts the scrupulous care devoted to the fetial ritual, even in recent times (cf. XXXVI. iii. 9), with the omission thereof in this instance, since there had been no formal declaration of war.

they were well-nigh thunderstruck. Bodies of such huge size were thrown into panic by sling-bullets and arrows; no sword was made bloody in combat in the Gallic war; like flocks of birds they flew away at the first whizzing of the missiles. But, by Hercules, we, the same Romans—Fortune reminding us what would have happened if we had had an enemy—when on our return we had fallen in with the Thracian brigands, were slaughtered, put to flight, robbed of our baggage. Quintus Minucius Thermus, in whose death we suffered a far greater loss than if Gnaeus Manlius, through whose rashness this defeat had come about, had fallen, was killed along with many brave men; the army which was bringing back the spoils of King Antiochus, scattered in three sections, the van in one place, the rear in another, the trains in a third, spent one night skulking in the lairs of beasts among the thickets. For such deeds is a triumph sought? If there had been no calamity and disgrace suffered in Thrace, over what foes would you seek a triumph? Over those, I suppose, whom the senate or the Roman people had assigned to you as enemies. This is how triumphs were granted to Lucius Scipio here and Manius Acilius yonder over King Antiochus, to Titus Quinctius not long ago over King Philip, to Publius Africanus over Hannibal and the Carthaginians and Syphax. And even after the senate had already voted for the war, the most unimportant matters none the less were inquired into to determine to whom it should be announced: should the declaration be given in any case to the kings themselves, or was it sufficient that the declaration be delivered at some military post?[1] Do you wish all these formalities to be violated and B.C. 187

A.U.C. 567 haec omnia pollui et confundi, tolli fetialia iura,
12 nullos esse fetiales? Fiat, pace deum dixerim, iactura religionis; oblivio deorum capiat pectora vestra; num senatum quoque de bello consuli non
13 placet? Non ad populum ferri velint iubeantne cum
14 Gallis bellum geri? Modo certe consules Graeciam atque Asiam volebant; tamen perseverantibus vobis Ligures provinciam decernere dicto audientes
15 fuerunt. Merito ergo a vobis prospere bello gesto triumphum petent, quibus auctoribus gesserunt."

XLVII. Talis oratio Furii et Aemilii fuit. Manlium in hunc maxime modum respondisse accepi: "Tribuni plebis antea solebant triumphum postu-
2 lantibus adversari, patres conscripti; quibus ego gratiam habeo quod seu mihi seu magnitudini rerum gestarum hoc dederunt, ut non solum silentio comprobarent honorem meum, sed referre etiam si opus
3 esset viderentur parati esse;[1] ex decem legatis, si diis placet, quod consilium dispensandae cohonestandaeque[2] victoriae imperatoribus maiores dederunt
4 nostri, adversarios habeo. L. Furius et L. Aemilius currum triumphalem me conscendere prohibent, coronam insignem capiti detrahunt, quos ego, si tribuni triumphare me prohiberent, testes citaturus
5 fui rerum a me gestarum. Nullius equidem invideo honori, patres conscripti;[3] vos[4] tribunos plebei

[1] esset vid. par. esse *ed. Frobeniana* 1535: esse uid. par. essent ς.
[2] cohonestandaeque *edd. vett.*: honestandaeque ς.
[3] patres conscripti (p. c.) *ed. Frobeniana* 1535: *om.* ς.
[4] uos ς: post *M*.

---

[1] Livy may have used a speech by one or the other of the two—there is no way to determine which—as the basis for his version of the dispute.

thrown into confusion, the fetial laws to be done away with and the fetials themselves abolished? Let there be (may I speak without offence to the gods) neglect of religious observances, let forgetfulness of the gods take possession of your hearts—is it your will that the senate should not be consulted about war? Or the motion put to the people whether they 'wish and order' war to be waged with the Gauls? Not long ago the consuls certainly wished for Greece and Asia; yet when you persisted in decreeing them the Ligurians as their province they obeyed. Justly, therefore, when they have waged successful war, will they ask a triumph from you by whose authority they have waged it." B.C. 187

XLVII. Such was the argument of Furius and Aemilius.[1] Manlius, I have heard, replied in about the following manner: "It was formerly the custom, conscript Fathers, that tribunes of the people should oppose candidates for triumphs; in this case I am grateful to them because they have conceded this much, whether to me or to the greatness of my achievements—that they do not merely by their silence approve my distinction but even seem ready to propose it if necessary; it is among the ten commissioners (heaven help us!), a council which our ancestors created for awarding victory and its honours to commanders, that I find my opponents. Lucius Furius and Lucius Aemilius forbid me to mount the triumphal car, they strip the garland of victory from my head, these men whom, if the tribunes were obstructing my triumph, I should have summoned as witnesses to what I have done. For my part, conscript Fathers, I grudge no man his distinction; when the tribunes of the people, brave

A.U.C. 567 nuper, viros fortes ac strenuos, impedientes Q.
Fabii Labeonis triumphum auctoritate vestra deter-
ruistis; triumphavit, quem non bellum iniustum
6 gessisse, sed hostem omnino non vidisse inimici
iactabant; ego, qui cum centum milibus ferocis-
simorum hostium signis collatis totiens pugnavi, qui
plus quadraginta milia hominum cepi aut occidi, qui
bina castra eorum expugnavi, qui citra iuga Tauri
omnia pacatiora quam terra Italia est reliqui, non
7 triumpho modo fraudor, sed causam apud vos, patres
conscripti, accusantibus meis ipse legatis dico.
8 Duplex eorum, ut animadvertistis, patres conscripti,
accusatio fuit: nam nec gerendum mihi fuisse bellum
cum Gallis, et gestum temere atque imprudenter
dixerunt. 'Non erant Galli hostes, sed tu eos pa-
9 catos imperata facientes violasti.' Non sum postulaturus a vobis, patres conscripti, ut quae communiter de immanitate gentis Gallorum, de infestis-
simo odio in nomen Romanum scitis, ea de illis
quoque qui Asiam incolunt existimetis Gallis;
10 remota universae gentis infamia atque invidia per se
ipsos aestimate. Utinam rex Eumenes, utinam
Asiae omnes civitates adessent, et illos potius
11 querentes quam me accusantem audiretis. Mittite
agedum legatos circa omnes Asiae [1] urbes et quaerite,
utra graviori servitute, Antiocho ultra Tauri iuga

[1] omnes Asiae *ed. Frobeniana* 1535 : asiam ad omnes ς.

---

[1] In XXXVII. lx. 6 Livy quoted Valerius Antias as the authority for this triumph and seemed to have no other information about it.

and energetic men, not long ago were opposing the triumph of Quintus Fabius Labeo,[1] you checked them by your authority; he triumphed, although his enemies circulated the story, not that he had waged an illegal war, but that he had not set eyes on an enemy at all;[2] I who have so often fought with a hundred thousand of the fiercest enemies, who captured or killed more than forty thousand men, who took two of their camps, who left everything on this side of the ridges of Taurus more peaceful than is the land of Italy, am not only cheated out of my triumph but am pleading my case before you, conscript Fathers, with my own lieutenants as my accusers! Their charge, as you have observed, conscript Fathers, is twofold: for they said that I should not have waged war with the Gauls and that the war was conducted rashly and heedlessly. 'The Gauls,' they say, 'were not enemies, but you attacked them while they were peaceful and obedient to our orders.' I shall not ask you, conscript Fathers, to believe about those Gauls also who dwell in Asia what you know in general about the barbarous character of the people of the Gauls and their most deadly hatred of the name of Rome; setting aside the ill repute and ill fame of the race as a whole, judge them by themselves. Would that King Eumenes were here, would that all the cities of Asia were here, and that you could hear them complaining of rather than me accusing the Gauls. Come, send ambassadors around all the cities of Asia and ask them whether they were freed from a more grievous slavery when Antiochus was expelled beyond the B.C. 187

[2] In XL. xxxviii. 9 the consuls of 181 B.C. are said to have been the first to triumph without having done any fighting.

A.U.C. 567
12 emoto[1] an Gallis subactis, liberati sint. Quotiens
agri eorum vastati sint, quotiens praedae abactae,
referant,[2] cum vix redimendi captivos copia esset,
et mactatas humanas hostias immolatosque liberos
13 suos audirent. Stipendium scitote pependisse socios
vestros Gallis et nunc, liberatos per vos regio imperio,
fuisse pensuros, si a me foret cessatum.

XLVIII. "Quo longius Antiochus emotus esset,
hoc impotentius in Asia Galli dominarentur et,
quidquid est terrarum citra Tauri iuga, Gallorum
2 imperio, non vestro adiecissetis. At enim sunt
haec ista vera; sed[3] etiam Delphos quondam, com-
mune humani generis oraculum, umbilicum orbis
terrarum, Galli spoliaverunt, nec ideo populus
3 Romanus his bellum indixit aut intulit. Equidem
aliquid interesse rebar inter id tempus, quo nondum
in iure ac dicione vestra Graecia atque Asia erat, ad
4 curandum animadvertendumque quid in his terris
fieret, et hoc quo finem imperii Romani Taurum
montem statuistis, quo libertatem, immunitatem
civitatibus datis, quo aliis fines adicitis, alias agro
multatis, aliis[4] vectigal imponitis, regna augetis
minuitis donatis adimitis, curae vestrae censetis
5 esse, ut pacem terra marique habeant. An nisi

[1] emoto *ed. Frobeniana* 1535 : moto ς.
[2] referant *edd. vett.* : referam ς.
[3] sed *Madvig* : *om.* ς.
[4] aliis *ed. Frobeniana* 1535 : *om.* ς.

---

[1] Manlius contrasts his own realistic and his opponents' legalistic points of view. He then renders the latter absurd by putting into the mouths of his opponents the argument

ridges of Taurus or when the Gauls were subdued. B.C. 187
Let them tell you how often their fields were devastated, how often plunder was carried away, when they had barely the wealth to ransom their captives and kept hearing of human victims slain and their own children sacrificed. Know that your own allies had been paying tribute to the Gauls and even now, when liberated by you from the king's control, would still have been paying it if I had failed them.

XLVIII. "The farther Antiochus should be removed, the more uncontrollable would be the rule of the Gauls in Asia, and all the lands on this side of the ridges of Taurus you would have added to Gallic territory, not to your own. Grant, if you will, that what my opponents say is true; but even on one occasion,[1] Delphi, the common oracle of the human race, the navel of the world, the Gauls despoiled, and the Romans did not on that account declare or wage a war upon them. For my part, I thought that there was some difference between that time, when Greece and Asia were not yet under your control and sway, as regards your interest and concern in what was happening in those lands, and this time, when you have fixed the Taurus mountain as the boundary of the Roman empire, when you bestow liberty and immunity upon cities, increase the territory of some, deprive others of their lands, impose tribute upon others, enlarge, diminish, give, take away kingdoms, and deem it your responsibility that they shall have peace on land and sea. Or,

that Rome did not even intervene to protect Delphi in 279 B.C. (*sed etiam* introduces a special case illustrating the general line of argument in *ista*). He refutes this imaginary argument by pointing out Rome's new position in the world.

A.U.C. 567 praesidia deduxisset Antiochus, quae quieta in suis arcibus [1] erant, non putaretis liberatam Asiam; si Gallorum exercitus effusi vagarentur, rata dona vestra, quae dedistis, regi Eumeni, rata libertas
6 civitatibus esset? Sed quid ego haec ita argumentor, tamquam non acceperim, sed fecerim hostes Gallos?
7 Te, L. Scipio, appello, cuius ego mihi, succedens in vicem imperii tui, virtutem felicitatemque pariter non frustra ab diis immortalibus precatus sum, te, P. Scipio, qui legati ius, collegae maiestatem et apud fratrem consulem et apud exercitum habuisti, sciatisne in exercitu Antiochi Gallorum legiones
8 fuisse, videritis in acie eos, in cornu utroque—id enim roboris esse videbatur—locatos, pugnaveritis ut cum hostibus iustis, cecideritis, spolia eorum retu-
9 leritis. Atqui cum Antiocho, non cum Gallis bellum et [2] senatus decreverat et populus iusserat. Sed simul, ut opinor, cum his decreverant iusserantque
10 qui intra praesidia eius fuissent; ex quibus praeter Antiochum, cum quo pacem pepigerat Scipio, et cum quo nominatim foedus ut fieret mandaveratis, omnes hostes erant, qui pro Antiocho arma adversus
11 nos tulerunt. In qua causa cum Galli ante omnes

[1] arcibus *ed. Frobeniana* 1535 : partibus ς.
[2] et ς : *om. M.*

---

[1] Manlius omits, as damaging to his argument, the fact that some, at least, of these Gauls were mercenaries (XXXVII. xviii. 7).

[2] The phrase is curiously used. In XXXVII. xl. 3 the phalanx is called the strongest part of the army, and the meaning here may be simply that the Gauls were more valuable on the flanks than in the centre.

[3] The line of argument, not entirely free from fallacy, is briefly this: Rome had declared war on Antiochus and would have included his allies had she known in advance who they

supposing that Antiochus had not withdrawn his garrisons, which remained peacefully in their citadels, would you consider that Asia had not been set free; but, on the other hand, should the armies of the Gauls be wandering at will, would these gifts which you have presented to King Eumenes have been assured, would liberty have been assured to the cities? But why do I argue as if I had made the Gauls our enemies, not found them so? I appeal to you, Lucius Scipio (and when I succeeded to your authority I prayed to the immortal gods, and not in vain, for your valour and good fortune), to you, Publius Scipio, who had the rank of lieutenant but the authority of a colleague both with your brother the consul and with the army, to say whether you know that in the army of Antiochus there were legions of Gauls,[1] whether you saw them in the line of battle, stationed on both flanks—for this was their strength, as it seemed[2]—whether you fought with them as with lawful enemies, slew them, and carried off their spoils. But yet, they say, it was with Antiochus and not with the Gauls that both the senate had decreed and the assembly had ordered war. But at the same time, in my judgment, they had decreed and ordered war with those who were within his ranks; of those, with the exception of Antiochus, with whom Scipio had contracted a peace and with whom you had expressly ordered that a treaty be made, all were enemies who bore arms against us in the cause of Antiochus.[3] Although the Gauls B.C. 187

would be; peace had been made with Antiochus but not with the allies, upon whom war had not been formally declared; Manlius, on succeeding Scipio, had inherited any unfinished business and therefore needed no new or specific declaration of war upon such allies.

A.U.C. 567 fuissent et reguli quidam et tyranni, ego tamen et cum aliis, pro dignitate imperii vestri coactis luere peccata sua, pacem pepigi, et Gallorum animos si
12 possent mitigari a feritate insita temptavi et, postquam indomitos atque implacabiles cernebam, tum demum vi atque armis coercendos ratus sum.
13 "Nunc, quoniam suscepti belli purgatum est crimen, gesti reddenda est ratio. In quo confiderem equidem causae meae, etiam si non apud Romanum sed apud Carthaginiensem senatum agerem, ubi in crucem tolli imperatores dicuntur, si prospero eventu,
14 pravo consilio rem gesserunt; sed ego in ea civitate, quae ideo omnibus rebus incipiendis gerendisque deos adhibet, quia nullius [1] calumniae subicit ea quae dii comprobaverunt, et in sollemnibus verbis habet, cum supplicationem aut triumphum de-
15 cernit, 'quod bene ac feliciter rem publicam administrarit,' si nollem, si grave ac superbum existimarem virtute gloriari, si pro [2] felicitate mea exercitusque mei, quod tantam nationem sine ulla
16 militum iactura devicimus, postularem ut diis immortalibus honos haberetur et ipse triumphans in Capitolium ascenderem, unde votis rite nuncupatis

[1] nullius ς : nullus *M*.
[2] si pro *Crévier* : pro ς.

---

[1] Livy's narrative does not support this. The statement is broad enough and vague enough to permit Manlius to say that all the persons from whom he collected money came under this category.

[2] It suffices to compare *luendamque pecunia noxam* (xxxvii. 3 above).

before all were in this class and certain chiefs and tyrants,[1] nevertheless I both negotiated for peace with the others, compelling them, in keeping with the dignity of your empire, to atone for their sins,[2] and tried the sentiments of the Gauls, in the hope that perhaps their native fierceness could be softened, and, after I saw that they were untamed and intractable, then at length I decided that I must restrain them by force of arms. B.C. 187

"Now, since I have answered the charge that I initiated the war, I must render account for its conduct. In this I for my part should trust my own cause even if I were pleading, not before the Roman, but before the Carthaginian senate, where commanders are said to be crucified if they have conducted a campaign with successful result but defective policy;[3] but in this state, which, in initiating and carrying out every action, calls upon the gods, for the reason that it exposes to the criticism of no man those actions which the gods have sanctioned, and which includes among its formal phrases, when it decrees a thanksgiving or a triumph, 'because he has conducted the affairs of the state well and successfully,' if I should be unwilling to speak, if I considered it overbearing and presumptuous to exult in our valour, if in recognition of the good fortune of myself and my army, in that we overthrew so great a nation with no loss of soldiers, I demanded that honour should be paid to the immortal gods and that I myself might in triumph mount to the Capitoline, whence I set out after duly announcing

[3] Cf. Valerius Maximus II. vii. ext. 1. Extant cases seem to illustrate only crucifixion after defeat (*e.g. Per.* XVII).

A.U.C. 567

profectus sum, negaretis hoc mihi cum diis immortalibus?

XLIX. "Iniquo enim loco dimicavi. Dic igitur, quo aequiore potuerim dimicare. Cum hostes montem cepissent, loco se munito tenerent, nempe eundum ad hostes erat, si vincere vellem. Quid?
2 Si urbem eo loco haberent et moenibus se tenerent? Nempe oppugnandi erant. Quid? Ad Thermopylas aequone loco M'. Acilius cum rege Antiocho pug-
3 navit? Quid? Philippum non eodem modo super Aoum[1] amnem iuga tenentem montium T. Quinctius deiecit? Equidem adhuc qualem aut sibi fingant aut vobis videri velint hostem fuisse non invenio.
4 Si degenerem et emollitum amoenitate Asiae, quid periculi vel iniquo loco subeuntibus fuit? Si timendum et feritate animorum et robore corporum,
5 huicine tantae victoriae triumphum negatis? Caeca invidia est, patres conscripti, nec quicquam aliud scit quam detractare virtutes, corrumpere honores
6 ac praemia earum.[2] Mihi quaeso ita ignoscatis, patres conscripti, si longiorem orationem non cupiditas gloriandi de me, sed necessaria criminum
7 defensio fecit. An etiam per Thraciam saltus patentes qui angusti erant et plana ex arduis et culta ex silvestribus facere potui et praestare, necubi notis

[1] super Aoum *edd. vett.*: superatum ς.
[2] earum *ed. Frobeniana* 1535: eorum ς.

---

[1] Neither the grammar nor (possibly) the logic of this cumbersome sentence is impeccable, but I have not tried to improve either.

my vows, would you refuse this to me as well as to the immortal gods?[1] B.C. 187

XLIX. " 'Yes,' you say, for I fought on unfavourable ground. Tell me, then, in what more favourable place I could have fought. Since the enemy had occupied the mountain and were keeping themselves within a fortified place, naturally I had to go to the enemy if I wished to defeat them. What if they had had a city in that place and were holding themselves within the walls? Naturally a siege would be necessary. Well, did Manius Acilius at Thermopylae fight with King Antiochus on favourable ground? Well, was not Philip in the same fashion, when he held the crest of the mountains above the Aous, dislodged by Titus Quinctius? For my part, I still do not discover what sort of enemy they are picturing to themselves, or what they want him to seem to you. If he was an enemy degenerate and made effeminate by the pleasant life of Asia, what danger was there if we attacked even over unfavourable ground? If he was an enemy to be feared because of both fierceness of temper and strength of body, why do you refuse a triumph to so great a victory as this? It is blind jealousy, conscript Fathers, and it knows nothing except how to belittle deeds of valour and to spoil the distinctions and rewards they earn. I beg that you will pardon me, conscript Fathers, on this ground, if my speech is made over-long, not by my desire to boast about myself, but by the need to defend myself against their accusations. Again, could I make the passes in Thrace wide when they were narrow, level ground instead of steep, neat groves instead of wild forests, and could I guarantee that there should be no

A.U.C. 567

8 sibi latebris delitescerent latrones Thraces, ne quid
carcinarum raperetur, ne quod iumentum ex tanto
agmine abstraheretur, ne quis vulneraretur, ne ex
vulnere vir fortis ac strenuus Q. Minucius moreretur?
9 In hoc casu, quo [1] infeliciter incidit ut talem civem
10 amitteremus, haerent; quod saltu iniquo, loco alieno
cum adortus nos hostis esset, duae simul acies primi
et novissimi agminis haerentem ad impedimenta
nostra exercitum barbarorum circumvenerunt, quod
11 multa milia illo ipso [2] die, plura multo post dies
paucos ceciderunt et ceperunt, hoc, si ipsi tacuerint,
vos scituros, cum testis orationis meae totus exercitus
12 sit, non credunt? Si gladium in Asia non strinxissem,
si hostem non vidissem, tamen [3] triumphum in Thracia
duobus proeliis merueram. Sed iam dictum satis
13 est; quin pro eo, quod pluribus verbis vos quam
vellem fatigavi, veniam a vobis petitam impetratamque velim, patres conscripti."

L. Plus crimina eo die quam defensio valuisset, ni altercationem in serum perduxissent. Dimittitur senatus in ea opinione ut negaturus triumphum fuisse

[1] casu quo *ed. Aldina*: casu *et* hoc casu *et* iniquo casu ϛ.

[2] illo ipso *Weissenborn*: ipso ϛ.

[3] tamen *Weissenborn*: tamen per ϛ: tamen proconsul *ed. Frobeniana* 1535.

---

[1] Livy said nothing of this vengeance in his account of the battle (xl–xli above), and his whole picture of the episode differs greatly from that of Manlius. It is impossible to judge their relative accuracy.

[2] This pair of speeches, taken with the narrative which covers the ground of both, may furnish a test for the historical accuracy of both the speeches and the narrative. It will be observed that both speeches contain statements of historical facts which are not mentioned in the narrative. Polybius gives us no help, but the account of the return journey given

Thracian brigands lurking in ambushes known to B.C. 187 them, that there should be no loss of baggage, that no pack-animal from so long a train should be driven off, that no one should be wounded, that that brave and energetic man Quintus Minucius should not die from his wound? They dwell on this misfortune, because it happened to our sorrow that we lost such a citizen; the fact that, when the enemy attacked us in a defile hard to pass through, on unfavourable ground, the two divisions of our army, the van and the rear, at the same time surrounded the army of the barbarians which was lingering around our trains, that they killed and captured many thousands on that same day and many more a few days later,[1] if they keep silent about all this, do they think that you will not learn of it, since the whole army is here to bear witness to what I say? If I had not drawn sword in Asia, if I had seen no enemy, I should still have earned a triumph in Thrace by these two battles. But enough has already been said; rather, I should wish, conscript Fathers, that pardon be asked and granted for my wearying you with a longer speech than I should have wished to make."[2]

L. The accusations would have had more weight that day than the defence had they not prolonged the debate to a late hour. The senate adjourned, having given the impression that the triumph would

by Appian (*Syr.* 43) is even more hostile than the speech of Furius Aemilius. One is inclined to conclude that the speeches are better rhetoric than history, and that the narrative would have been improved if some items in the speeches (cf. the preceding note) had been critically examined. The tone of the narrative makes it impossible to believe that Livy followed Claudius at this point (cf. xxiii. 8 and the note), but there is no other clue to the source.

A.U.C. 567

2 videretur. Postero die et cognati amicique Cn.
Manlii summis opibus adnisi sunt, et auctoritas
3 seniorum valuit, negantium exemplum proditum
memoriae esse, ut imperator, qui devictis perduellibus, confecta provincia exercitum reportasset, sine curru et laurea privatus inhonoratusque urbem iniret. Hic pudor malignitatem vicit, triumphumque frequentes decreverunt.

4 Oppressit deinde mentionem memoriamque omnem
contentionis huius maius et cum maiore et clariore
5 viro certamen ortum. P. Scipioni Africano, ut Valerius Antias auctor est, duo Q. Petillii diem dixerunt.
Id prout cuiusque ingenium erat interpretabantur.
6 Alii non tribunos plebis, sed universam civitatem
7 quae id pati posset incusabant: duas maximas orbis
terrarum urbes ingratas uno prope tempore in principes inventas, Romam ingratiorem, si quidem victa Carthago victum Hannibalem in exilium expulisset,
8 Roma victrix victorem Africanum expellat. Alii,
neminem unum civem tantum eminere [1] debere ut legibus interrogari non possit; nihil tam aequandae libertatis esse quam potentissimum quemque posse
9 dicere causam. Quid autem tuto cuiquam, nedum
summam rem publicam, permitti, si ratio non sit reddenda? Qui ius aequum pati non possit, in eum

[1] un. civ. tan. em. *ed. Frobeniana* 1535 : un. tan. em. ciu. ς.

---

[1] A survey of the triumphs awarded during this period shows that the literal accuracy of this statement cannot be maintained, but that to a steadily increasing degree actual achievement was less important than influence with the senate. The senate is ingenious in finding reasons why triumphs should be awarded to its favourites and denied to men in disfavour.

be refused. The next day the relatives and friends of Manlius exerted all their efforts and the elder senators also prevailed by their influence, saying that no precedent had been handed down in tradition that a commander who, after decisively defeating the enemy and accomplishing the task assigned him as his province, had brought home his army, should enter the City without the car and laurel, a private citizen and without honour.[1] Respect for this tradition prevailed over ill-will and a full session voted the triumph. B.C. 187

Then all talk and thought of this debate were put into the background by a struggle greater and originating with a greater and more famous man. Publius Scipio Africanus, as Valerius Antias asserts, was prosecuted by two men, each named Quintus Petillius. This action each man interpreted according to his own inclinations. Some reproached, not the tribunes of the people, but the whole state, for being able to allow this—the two greatest cities in the world, they said, were at about the same time found ungrateful towards their foremost citizens, but Rome was more ungrateful, because conquered Carthage had driven the conquered Hannibal into exile, while victorious Rome was driving out the victorious Scipio. Others argued that no single citizen should attain such eminence that he could not be questioned under the laws; that nothing was so essential to equally distributed liberty as that every man, however powerful, should plead his cause. What now—not to mention supreme position in the state—could be safely entrusted to any man if no accounting could be asked? Against a man, they said, who cannot brook equitable law, no violence

A.U.C. 567 10 vim haud iniustam esse. Haec agitata sermonibus,
donec dies causae dicendae venit. Nec alius antea
quisquam nec ille ipse Scipio consul censorve maiore
omnis generis hominum frequentia quam reus illo
11 die in forum est deductus. Iussus dicere causam
sine ulla criminum mentione orationem adeo mag-
nificam de rebus ab se gestis est exorsus ut satis
constaret neminem umquam neque melius neque
12 verius laudatum esse. Dicebantur enim ab eo
eodem [1] animo ingenioque quo [2] gesta erant, et
aurium fastidium aberat, quia pro periculo non in
gloriam referebantur.

LI. Tribuni vetera luxuriae crimina Syracusa-
norum hibernorum et Locris Pleminianum tumultum
cum ad fidem praesentium criminum retulissent,
suspicionibus magis quam argumentis pecuniae captae
2 reum accusarunt: filium captum sine pretio redditum,
omnibusque aliis rebus Scipionem, tamquam in eius
unius manu pax Romana bellumque esset, ab An-
3 tiocho cultum; dictatorem eum consuli, non legatum
in provincia fuisse; nec ad aliam rem eo profectum
quam ut, id quod Hispaniae Galliae Siciliae Africae
iam pridem persuasum esset, hoc Graeciae Asiaeque
et omnibus ad orientem versis regibus gentibusque
4 appareret, unum hominem caput columenque imperii

[1] eo eodem *P. Burman*: eodem ς.
[2] quo *P. Burman*: a quo ς.

---

[1] Cf. XXIX. xix. 12, etc.
[2] Cf. XXIX. viii. 6 ff., etc.
[3] The actual charges against Scipio, as well as the specifications which supported them, are variously stated by the sources. Polybius, who should have known, is nowhere explicit as to the trial. In their most serious form, as reported, *e.g.*, by Gellius (IV. xviii. 7), the major charge could easily

is illegal. Such was the current of talk until the day B.C. 187 of the trial came. No other man before him, not even this same Scipio, when consul or censor, was ever escorted to the Forum by a greater crowd of men of every rank than was Scipio that day when he was the defendant. Being bidden to plead his cause, he began so magnificent a speech about his achievements that it was very clear that no man had ever been better eulogized or more truthfully. For he spoke of his deeds in the same temper and spirit in which he performed them, and there was no resentment among his hearers, since he was speaking to ward off peril and not to boast.

LI. When the tribunes revived the old charges of luxury in his winter-quarters at Syracuse [1] and the disturbances caused by Pleminius at Locri,[2] to make their present charges more credible, on the basis of suspicions rather than of evidence they charged him with having accepted bribes:[3] that his captured son had been restored without a ransom and that in all other respects Antiochus had paid court to Scipio as if in his hands alone lay peace and war with Rome; he had been, they alleged, a dictator, not a lieutenant, in relation to the consul in the province; he had gone there for no other reason than that which Spain, Gaul, Sicily and Africa had long since come to believe should be manifest to Greece and Asia and all the kings and tribes that lie towards the east, namely, that one man was the source and stay of

have been treason. One admits that some of Scipio's messages to Antiochus (*e.g.* XXXVII. xxxvii. 8) may easily be interpreted as lending aid and comfort to the enemy, when removed from their contexts. Yet the statements of Livy and the conduct of the trial indicate that the charges were less grave.

A.U.C. 567
Romani esse, sub umbra Scipionis civitatem dominam
orbis terrarum latere, nutum eius pro decretis patrum,
pro populi iussis esse. Infamia intactum invidia qua
5 possunt urgent. Orationibus in noctem perductis
6 prodicta dies est. Ubi ea venit, tribuni in Rostris
prima luce consederunt; citatus reus magno agmine
amicorum clientiumque per mediam contionem ad
7 Rostra subiit silentioque facto "hoc" inquit "die,
tribuni plebis vosque, Quirites, cum Hannibale et
Carthaginiensibus signis collatis in Africa bene ac
8 feliciter pugnavi. Itaque, cum hodie litibus et
iurgiis supersederi aequum sit, ego hinc extemplo in
Capitolium ad Iovem optimum maximum Iunonem-
que et Minervam ceterosque deos qui Capitolio
9 atque arci praesident salutandos ibo, hisque gratias
agam, quod mihi et hoc ipso die et saepe alias
egregie gerendae rei publicae mentem facultatemque
10 dederunt. Vestrum quoque quibus commodum est,
Quirites, ite mecum et orate deos ut mei similes
11 principes habeatis, ita, si ab annis septemdecim ad
senectutem semper vos aetatem meam honoribus
vestris anteistis, ego vestros honores rebus gerendis
12 praecessi." Ab Rostris in Capitolium ascendit.
Simul se universa contio avertit et secuta Scipionem
est, adeo ut postremo scribae viatoresque tribunos
relinquerent, nec cum iis praeter servilem comitatum

---

[1] That is, this was the anniversary of Zama and should be a day of thanksgiving and rejoicing.

[2] Scipio's youth had not prevented his election to offices for which he was technically ineligible, but he reminds the people that he had, before these elections, demonstrated his capacity.

[3] The various literary versions of this speech differ a good deal in form but not in their essential character. The same is true of other incidents of the trial.

Roman power, that under the shadow of Scipio the City which was the mistress of the world lay sheltered, that his nod was weighty as decrees of the senate and enactments of the assembly. A man untouched by ill repute they loaded with innuendo in every possible way. The speeches having continued until nightfall, the matter was adjourned. When the appointed day came, the tribunes took their seats on the Rostra at dawn; the defendant when summoned came with a great throng of friends and clients through the midst of the meeting to the Rostra, and, when silence ensued, he spoke as follows: "On this day,[1] tribunes of the people, and you, citizens, I fought well and successfully in pitched battle with Hannibal and the Carthaginians in Africa. Therefore, since it is meet on this day to refrain from trials and quarrels, I shall proceed at once from here to the Capitoline to offer homage to Jupiter Optimus Maximus and Juno and Minerva and the other gods who preside over the Capitoline and the citadel, and I shall give thanks to them because both on this same day and on many other occasions they have given me the purpose and the capacity to render conspicuous service to the state. Let all of you too, citizens, for whom it is convenient, come with me and pray to the gods that you may have leaders like me, but on this condition, that, if from my seventeenth year to my old age you have always gone ahead of my years in bestowing honours upon me,[2] I have anticipated your honours by my deeds."[3] From the Rostra he went up to the Capitoline. At the same time the whole meeting withdrew and followed Scipio, so that finally even the clerks and messengers left the tribunes, nor did anyone remain with them B.C. 187

A.U.C. 567
et praeconem qui reum ex Rostris citabat quisquam
13 esset. Scipio non in Capitolio modo, sed per totam urbem omnia templa deum cum populo Romano
14 circumiit. Celebratior is prope dies favore hominum et aestimatione vera[1] magnitudinis eius fuit quam quo triumphans de Syphace rege et Carthaginiensibus urbem est invectus.

LII. Hic speciosus ultimus dies P. Scipioni illuxit. Post quem cum invidiam et certamina cum tribunis prospiceret, die longiore prodicta[2] in Literninum concessit certo consilio ne ad causam dicendam ades-
2 set. Maior animus et natura erat ac maiori fortunae adsuetus quam ut reus esse sciret et summittere se
3 in humilitatem causam dicentium. Ubi dies venit citarique absens est coeptus, L. Scipio morbum
4 causae esse cur abesset excusabat. Quam excusationem cum tribuni qui diem dixerant non acciperent, et ab eadem superbia non venire ad causam dicendam arguerent qua iudicium et tribunos plebis et con-
5 tionem reliquisset et, quibus ius sententiae de se dicendae et libertatem ademisset, his comitatus, velut captos trahens, triumphum de populo Romano egisset secessionemque eo die in Capitolium a tribunis plebis fecisset: "Habetis ergo temeritatis illius
6 mercedem; quo duce et auctore nos reliquistis, ab

[1] vera *Perizonius*: uerae ς.
[2] prodicta *J. F. Gronovius*: producta ς.

---

[1] Cf. XXX. xlv. 2–7.
[2] Liternum was a colony, and Scipio's retirement thereto was not, technically, exile. See, however, the *Periocha* of this Book.
[3] That is, at the third and final day of the trial.

except their retinue of slaves and the herald who from the Rostra summoned the defendant. Scipio visited all the temples of the gods, not only on the Capitoline but through the whole City, with the Roman people in attendance upon him. This day was rendered almost more famous by the general applause of men and by the true estimate of his greatness than that on which he rode into the City in triumph over King Syphax and the Carthaginians.[1] B.C. 187

LII. This was the last day of glory to shine on Publius Scipio. Since in future he foresaw unpopularity and quarrels with the tribunes, obtaining a longer adjournment he retired to his country place at Liternum,[2] with the definite intention of not being present to plead his cause.[3] His soul and character were too lofty, and too much accustomed to a greater fortune, to know how to be a defendant and to come down to the lowly position of men who must plead their cause. When the day arrived and the summons for the absent defendant began to be proclaimed, Lucius Scipio gave illness as the reason for his absence. When the tribunes who had accused him refused to accept this plea and maintained that he had not come to plead his cause because of the same arrogance as that with which he had deserted the trial and the tribunes of the people and the assembly, and with which, attended by those whom he had robbed of their right to express their opinion of him and of their liberty, leading them captive, as it were, he had celebrated a triumph over the Roman people and had brought about a secession that day from the tribunes of the people to the Capitoline: "You have, therefore," they said, "your reward for that rash conduct; under his leadership and

A.U.C. 567

7 eo ipsi relicti estis, et tantum animorum in dies nobis decrescit ut, ad quem ante annos septemdecim[1] exercitum et classem habentem tribunos plebis aedilemque mittere in Siciliam ausi sumus, qui prenderent eum et Romam reducerent, ad eum privatum ex villa sua extrahendum ad causam dicen-
8 dam mittere non audeamus";[2] tribuni plebis appellati ab L. Scipione ita decreverunt: si[3] morbi causa excusaretur, sibi placere accipi eam causam
9 diemque a collegis prodici.[4] Tribunus plebis eo tempore Ti. Sempronius Gracchus erat, cui inimicitiae cum P. Scipione intercedebant. Is, cum vetuisset nomen suum decreto collegarum adscribi, tristioremque omnes sententiam expectarent, ita
10 decrevit: cum L. Scipio excusasset morbum esse causae fratri, satis id sibi videri; se P. Scipionem priusquam Romam redisset accusari non passurum; tum quoque, si se appellet, auxilio ei futurum ne
11 causam dicat: ad id fastigium rebus gestis, honoribus populi Romani P. Scipionem deorum hominumque consensu pervenisse, ut sub Rostris reum stare et

[1] ante annos septendecim *Crévier*: antea ς: ante annos quindecim *M*.
[2] audeamus *ed. Frobeniana* 1535: audemus ς.
[3] si *ed. Frobeniana* 1531: ut si ς.
[4] prodici *Gronovius*: produci ς.

---

[1] Cf. XXIX. xx. 6; this was in connection with the affair of Pleminius.
[2] This appeal was taken to the college of tribunes as a whole against the refusal of the Petillii to accept the plea of illness.

sanction you abandoned us and by him you are yourselves abandoned, and so far has our spirit declined day by day that a man for whom seventeen years ago,[1] when he commanded an army and a fleet, we dared to send tribunes of the people and an aedile, to arrest him and bring him back to Rome—to that man, when a private citizen, we do not dare to send messengers to hale him forth from his country place to plead his cause"; the tribunes of the people, when appealed to[2] by Lucius Scipio, thus decreed: that, if the plea of illness were submitted, it was their pleasure that this plea should be accepted and the case adjourned by their colleagues. One of the tribunes of the people at this time was Tiberius Sempronius Gracchus,[3] between whom and Publius Scipio there was a feud. When he had forbidden his name to be signed to the decree of his colleagues, and all men were anticipating a harsher proposal, he thus decreed: that, since Lucius Scipio had given illness as the excuse for his brother, this seemed to him sufficient; that he would not permit Publius Scipio to be prosecuted before he returned to Rome; that even then, if he were appealed to, he would come to Scipio's aid, to save him from pleading his cause:[4] such heights had Publius Scipio reached, as a result of his own deeds and of the honours conferred by the Roman people, with the approbation of gods and men, that to compel him to stand as a defendant before the Rostra and listen to the insults B.C. 187

[3] Cf. XXXVII. vii. 11; he plays an important part in the following chapters.

[4] Gracchus would prevent, by the use of his tribunicial powers, a condemnation in Scipio's absence and, on request, any further prosecution.

A.U.C. 567 praebere aures adolescentium conviciis populo Romano magis deforme quam ipsi sit.

LIII. Adiecit decreto indignationem: "Sub pedibus vestris stabit, tribuni, domitor ille Africae
2 Scipio? Ideo quattuor nobilissimos duces Poenorum in Hispania, quattuor exercitus fudit fugavitque; ideo Syphacem cepit, Hannibalem devicit, Cartha-
3 ginem vectigalem nobis fecit, Antiochum—recipit [1] enim fratrem consortem huius gloriae L. Scipio—ultra iuga Tauri emovit, ut duobus Petilliis succum-
4 beret? Vos de P. Africano palmam peti feretis? [2] Nullisne meritis suis, nullis vestris honoribus umquam [3] in arcem tutam et velut sanctam clari viri pervenient ubi, si non venerabilis, inviolata saltem
5 senectus eorum considat?" Movit et decretum et adiecta oratio non ceteros modo sed ipsos etiam accusatores, et deliberaturos se quid iuris sui et
6 officii esset dixerunt. Senatus deinde concilio plebis dimisso haberi est coeptus. Ibi gratiae ingentes ab universo ordine, praecipue a consularibus senioribusque, Ti. Graccho actae sunt, quod rem publicam
7 privatis simultatibus potiorem habuisset, et Petillii vexati sunt probris, quod splendere aliena invidia voluissent et spolia ex Africani triumpho peterent.
8 Silentium deinde de Africano fuit. Vitam Literni

[1] recipit *Madvig*: recepit ς.
[2] peti feretis *Madvig*: peteritis *M*: peteretis ς.
[3] umquam *ed. Frobeniana* 1531: cum qua *M*: *om.* ς.

---

[1] In later times at least, if not at this time, the prosecution of some prominent person was a means of self-advertisement much sought after by ambitious young men: the careers of Cicero and Caesar illustrate.

of young men[1] would be a greater disgrace to the Roman people than to Scipio himself. B.C. 187

LIII. He supplemented his decree with an indignant speech: "Are your feet, tribunes, to trample down Scipio, that conqueror of Africa? Was it for this that he repulsed and routed four of the most noted generals of the Carthaginians in Spain, and four armies? Was it for this that he captured Syphax, overthrew Hannibal, made Carthage tributary to us, drove Antiochus—for Lucius Scipio admits his brother to a share in this glory—beyond the ridges of Taurus, that he should fall a victim to the two Petillii? Will you allow a victory over Publius Africanus to be sought? Shall distinguished men by no services of their own, by no honours of your bestowal, ever reach a safe and, as it were, sacred citadel where their old age, if not respected, at least secure, may find rest?" Both the decree and the supplementary speech touched not only the tribunes but even the prosecutors themselves, and the latter said that they would take counsel as to what their right and duty required. After that, when the assembly of the people had been adjourned, a meeting of the senate began. There boundless gratitude was expressed by the whole order and especially by the senators of consular rank and greater age, because Tiberius Gracchus had shown greater regard for the public interest than for his personal quarrels, and the Petillii were assailed with abuse because they had tried to become conspicuous by darkening another's reputation and were seeking spoils from a triumph over Africanus. Thenceforth there was silence regarding Africanus. He spent his life at Liternum, with no desire to

A.U.C. 567 egit sine desiderio urbis; morientem rure eo ipso loco sepeliri se iussisse ferunt monumentumque ibi aedi-
9 ficari, ne funus sibi in ingrata patria fieret. Vir memorabilis, bellicis tamen quam pacis artibus memorabilior. Nobilior [1] prima pars vitae quam postrema fuit, quia in iuventa bella adsidue gesta, cum senecta res quoque defloruere, nec praebita est
10 materia ingenio. Quid ad [2] primum consulatum secundus, etiam si censuram adicias? Quid Asiatica legatio, et valetudine adversa inutilis et filii casu deformata et post reditum necessitate aut subeundi
11 iudicii aut simul cum patria deserendi? Punici tamen belli perpetrati, quo nullum neque maius neque [3] periculosius Romani gessere, unus [4] praecipuam gloriam tulit.

LIV. Morte Africani crevere inimicorum animi, quorum princeps fuit M. Porcius Cato, qui vivo quoque eo adlatrare [5] magnitudinem eius solitus erat.
2 Hoc auctore existimantur Petillii et vivo Africano rem
3 ingressi et mortuo rogationem promulgasse. Fuit autem rogatio talis: "Velitis iubeatis, Quirites,[6]

[1] Nobilior *Weissenborn* : *om.* ς.

[2] Quid ad *ed. Frobeniana* 1535: quoad *M* : quoad *et* qui ad ς.

[3] neque maius neque *edd. vett.* : neque *aut* maius ς.

[4] unus *ed. Frobeniana* 1535 : unam ς.

[5] adlatrare *edd. vett.*: lacerare ς.

[6] Quirites *Brissonius* : quaeratur ς.

---

[1] One infers from this and from liv. 1 below that the death of Scipio soon followed, but in XXXIX. lii. 1 his death is said to have occurred in 183 B.C. The same uncertainty prevailed regarding his burial-place and the circumstances of his death, on which Livy declines to express an opinion. He gives, however, in chap. lvi. below, some interesting

return to the City; when dying[1] they say that he gave orders that he should be buried in that same place in the country and that his tomb should be erected there, that his funeral might not be held in an ungrateful home-land. He was a man to be remembered, although more to be remembered for his achievements in war than for his deeds in peace. The first part of his life was more distinguished than the last, since in his youth he was continually waging wars, while with old age his deeds too faded, nor was any opportunity afforded to display his talent. What was his second consulship compared to the first, even if you add the censorship? What was gained by his lieutenancy in Asia, rendered unprofitable as it was by his illness and disfigured by the misfortune[2] of his son and, after his return, by the necessity of either standing trial or leaving the trial and his country at the same time? Nevertheless, since he brought to an end the Punic War, than which there was waged none greater nor more dangerous by the Romans, he has secured a singular pre-eminence of fame. B.C. 187

LIV. On the death of Africanus the spirits of his adversaries rose, the first of them being Marcus Porcius Cato, who even during his life had been accustomed to snarl at his greatness. It was with his backing, it is thought, that the Petillii initiated the prosecution of Africanus while he lived and after his death introduced a motion. The motion was to this effect: "Do you wish and order,[3] citizens, with

historical criticism which contrasts strangely with his dogmatic statements elsewhere (but note *ferunt* in this section).

[2] Cf. XXXVII. xxxiii. 4–7.

[3] The formula retains the subjunctive even in direct quotation.

A.U.C. 567 quae pecunia capta ablata coacta ab rege Antiocho est quique sub imperio eius fuerunt, quod eius in
4 publicum relatum non est, uti de ea re Ser. Sulpicius praetor urbanus ad senatum referat quem eam rem velit senatus quaerere de iis qui praetores nunc sunt?"
5 Huic rogationi primo Q. et L. Mummii[1] intercedebant, senatum quaerere de pecunia non relata in publicum, ita ut antea semper factum esset, aequum
6 censebant. Petillii nobilitatem et regnum in senatu Scipionum accusabant. L. Furius Purpurio con-
7 sularis, qui in decem legatis in Asia fuerat, latius rogandum censebat, non quae ab Antiocho modo pecuniae captae forent, sed quae ab aliis regibus
8 gentibusque, Cn. Manlium inimicum incessens. Et L. Scipio, quem magis pro se quam adversus legem dicturum apparebat, dissuasor processit. Is morte P. Africani fratris, viri omnium fortissimi clarissimique, eam exortam rogationem est conquestus;

[1] Mummii *Sigonius*: numini *et al.* ϛ.

---

[1] There was no systematic or effective method of verifying a general's returns of the booty he had collected; one device, of uncertain validity, was seen in the case of Glabrio (XXXVII. lvii. 13–14). The episode of Scipio Nasica (XXXVI. xxxvi. 1–2 and the note) suggests that the senate was either unable to secure accurate information or tolerant of plausible irregularities in the accounts of a general and his quaestor. Yet the fears of Manlius and the investigation which follows of the accounts of the Scipios show that some method existed, although one wonders how the Petillii knew that there were discrepancies in the present instance.

respect to the money which was captured from, B.C. 187
taken from, levied upon King Antiochus and those who were under his rule, and what of this money has not been accounted for to the state,[1] that regarding this matter Servius Sulpicius the city praetor shall refer to the senate the question, whom, of those who are now praetors, the senate wishes to investigate this matter?" This proposal was at first vetoed by Quintus and Lucius Mummius; they deemed it proper that the senate should inquire regarding money which had not been turned in to the treasury in the manner in which it had always been done before.[2] The Petillii kept assailing the influential position and tyrannical power of the Scipios in the senate. Lucius Furius Purpurio, a man of consular rank, who had been one of the ten commissioners in Asia, proposed to extend the field of the investigation to include moneys which had been taken, not only from Antiochus, but from other kings and peoples as well, striking at his enemy Gnaeus Manlius.[3] Lucius Scipio also, who was evidently about to speak for himself rather than against the bill, came forward to oppose it. He complained that only after the death of his brother Publius Africanus, a man conspicuous above all for courage and fame, this proposal had originated; for it was not

[2] The protest is not against the auditing of the accounts but at the method, which, to judge from similar incidents in Roman history, was designed to increase the probability of a conviction. The Romans were generally intuitively distrustful of special procedures invented for particular situations.

[3] It is clear from XXXIX. vi. 4 that Manlius was afraid of such an inquiry, although he could say that missing property had been carried off by the Thracians.

A.U.C. 567

9 parum enim fuisse non laudari pro Rostris P. Afri-
10 canum post mortem, nisi etiam accusaretur; et Carthaginienses exilio Hannibalis contentos esse, populum Romanum ne morte quidem P. Scipionis exsatiari, nisi et ipsius fama sepulti laceretur et
11 frater insuper, accessio invidiae, mactetur. M. Cato suasit rogationem—exstat et oratio eius de pecunia regis Antiochi—et Mummios tribunos auctoritate
12 deterruit ne adversarentur rogationi. Remittentibus ergo his intercessionem omnes tribus uti rogassent iusserunt.

LV. Ser. Sulpicio deinde referente, quem rogatione Petillia quaerere vellent, Q. Terentium Culleonem
2 patres iusserunt. Ad hunc praetorem, adeo amicum Corneliae familiae ut, qui Romae mortuum elatumque P. Scipionem—est enim ea quoque fama—tradunt, pilleatum, sicut in triumpho ierat, in funere quoque ante lectum isse memoriae prodiderint, et ad Portam Capenam mulsum prosecutis funus dedisse, quod ab eo inter alios captivos in Africa ex
3 hostibus receptus esset, aut adeo inimicum eundem, ut propter insignem simultatem ab ea factione quae adversa Scipionibus erat, delectus sit potissimum ad
4 quaestionem exercendam; ceterum ad hunc nimis

---

[1] The habit of pronouncing public *laudationes* over distinguished men was very old (II. xlvii. 11, etc.). It would appear from liii. 8 above that Africanus had not wanted such a eulogy.

[2] The alternative formula "*uti rogas*" is also employed: cf. XXXIII. xxv. 7.

[3] Cf. XXX. xlv. 5. The *pilleus* was the conical cap worn by newly-manumitted slaves.

[4] Cf. lvi. 4 below. The tomb of the Scipios, still to be seen, is close to this gate.

enough that no eulogy had been pronounced before the Rostra over Publius Africanus after his death[1] without also bringing charges against him; even the Carthaginians had been satisfied with the exile of Hannibal, the Roman people was not content even with the death of Publius Scipio without also tearing to shreds his reputation as he lay in the tomb, and, besides, sacrificing his brother as an additional victim to their jealousy. Marcus Cato supported the bill—and a speech of his on the money of King Antiochus is extant—and by his influence deterred the tribunes, the Mummii, from further opposing the measure. With their veto withdrawn, therefore, all the tribes voted "aye."[2] B.C. 187

LV. Servius Sulpicius then brought up the question of what praetor they wished to have conduct the investigation under the Petillian law, and the Fathers selected Quintus Terentius Culleo. Before this praetor, either so friendly to the Cornelian family that those who say that Publius Scipio died and was buried at Rome—for this too is reported—have put it on record that, wearing the cap of freedom, just as he had marched in the triumphal procession,[3] he walked also before the bier at the funeral, and at the Porta Capena[4] served wine and honey to those who attended the funeral, because he had been rescued from the enemy by Scipio, along with the other prisoners in Africa, or, on the other hand, so hostile that on account of his well-known unfriendliness the faction which was opposed to the Scipios chose him in preference to anyone else to conduct the investigation; at any rate,[5] before this praetor, too well or

[5] Livy becomes so involved in his discussion of the partisanship of Culleo that he has to make a fresh start in his sentence.

A.U.C. 567

aequum aut iniquum praetorem reus extemplo factus
L. Scipio. Simul et delata et recepta nomina lega-
5 torum eius, A. et L. Hostiliorum Catonum, et C.
Furii Aculeonis [1] quaestoris et, ut omnia contacta
societate peculatus viderentur, scribae quoque duo
et accensus. L. Hostilius et scribae et accensus,
priusquam de Scipione iudicium fieret, absoluti sunt,
Scipio et A. Hostilius legatus et C. Furius damnati:
6 quo commodior pax Antiocho daretur, Scipionem sex
milia pondo auri, quadringenta octoginta argenti plus
7 accepisse quam in aerarium retulerit, A. Hostilium
octoginta pondo auri et argenti quadringenta tria,
Furium quaestorem auri pondo centum triginta,
8 argenti ducenta. Has ego summas auri et argenti
relatas apud Antiatem inveni. In L. Scipione malim
equidem librarii mendum quam mendacium scrip-
9 toris esse in summa auri atque argenti; similius
enim veri est argenti quam auri maius pondus fuisse,
et potius quadragiens quam ducentiens quadragiens
10 litem aestimatam, eo magis quod tantae summae

[1] Furii Aculeonis *ed. Frobeniana* 1535: furii culleonis *M*: furiacii leonis ς.

---

[1] They have not been mentioned before as *legati* of Scipio.

[2] They were discharged for lack of evidence by the praetor at the preliminary hearing; there seemed to be a *prima facie* case against the others.

[3] Livy is more charitable than on other occasions towards the vagaries of Antias; it is not quite clear what the annalist said about the fine.

[4] Reckoning one pound of gold as 4,000 sesterces and one pound of silver as 336 sesterces, 6,000 pounds of gold, leaving the silver out of account, would be 24,000,000 sesterces; reversing the figures, 480 pounds of gold (1,920,000 sesterces) plus 6,000 pounds of silver (2,016,000 sesterces) would produce approximately 4,000,000 sesterces to be recovered by the

too ill disposed, Lucius Scipio was immediately arraigned. At the same time the names of two of his lieutenants, Aulus and Lucius Hostilius Cato,[1] were both brought forward and accepted, and that of his quaestor, Gaius Furius Aculeo, and, that everything might seem infected by a conspiracy for peculation, also those of two clerks and an orderly. Lucius Hostilius and the clerks and the orderly were acquitted[2] before the trial of Scipio took place; Scipio and his lieutenant Aulus Hostilius and Gaius Furius were convicted: the charge was that, in order to secure more favourable terms of peace for Antiochus, Scipio had received six thousand pounds of gold, and four hundred and eighty pounds of silver more than he turned in to the treasury, Aulus Hostilius eighty pounds of gold and four hundred and three of silver, the quaestor Furius one hundred and thirty pounds of gold, two hundred of silver. These amounts of gold and silver I have found recorded in the writings of Antias. In the case of Lucius Scipio, I should myself prefer to see an error of the scribe rather than a falsification of the historian[3] in the amounts of gold and silver; for it is more probable that the greater weight would have been of silver and not of gold and that the fine assessed would have been four million sesterces rather than twenty-four million,[4] the more so because there is a tradition[5] that an accounting for just this B.C. 187

fine. (I have borrowed these calculations from Weissenborn-Müller, from Mommsen and Hultsch.)

[5] This other tradition (Polybius or another annalist) may be the actual source of this criticism of Antias. At any rate, Livy appears at this point to abandon Antias, whom he has followed from l. 5 above, in favour of another authority. He appears also to go back to Antias at chap. lviii. below.

A.U.C. 567 rationem etiam ab ipso P. Scipione requisitam esse
11 in senatu tradunt librumque rationis eius cum Lucium fratrem adferre iussisset, inspectante senatu suis ipsum manibus concerpsisse[1] indignantem
12 quod, cum bis milliens in aerarium intulisset, quad-
13 ragiens ratio ab se posceretur. Ab eadem fiducia animi, cum quaestores pecuniam ex aerario contra legem promere non auderent, poposcisse claves et se aperturum aerarium dixisse, qui ut clauderetur effecisset.

LVI. Multa alia in Scipionis exitu maxime vitae dieque dicta, morte, funere, sepulcro, in diversum trahunt, ut cui famae, quibus scriptis adsentiar non
2 habeam. Non de accusatore convenit: alii M. Naevium, alii Petillios diem dixisse scribunt, non de tempore quo dicta dies sit, non de anno quo mortuus
3 sit, non ubi mortuus aut elatus sit; alii Romae, alii Literni et mortuum et sepultum. Utrobique monumenta ostenduntur et statuae; nam et Literni monumentum monumentoque statua superimposita fuit,

[1] concerpsisse *Sabellicus* : compressisse ς.

---

[1] That is, 4,000,000 sesterces.

[2] This anecdote is told also by Polybius (XXIV. ix; he has also the following story), Gellius (IV. xviii. 7–12), *Auct. De Vir. Ill.* (49. 17), all with small variations. Polybius alone mentions definite sums, substituting 3,000 talents and 15,000 talents for those given by Livy. Under the circumstances it seems useless to try to determine whether Polybius or an annalist, probably Claudius, is Livy's source. The following chapter well illustrates the uncertainty which still exists regarding these events.

[3] No pre-Livian source for this anecdote is known except Polybius; he makes it clear that this episode had nothing to do with the preceding. The impossibility of equating the sums given by Polybius (see the preceding note) with

sum[1] was also demanded in the senate from Publius Scipio himself, and that, when he had directed his brother Lucius to bring the account-book, he had himself, with his own hands, torn it up, being angry that after he had brought two hundred millions into the treasury he should be asked to account for four millions.[2] With the same self-confidence, they say, when the quaestors did not dare to take money from the treasury[3] contrary to the law, he demanded the keys and said that he would open the treasury who had brought it to pass that it was closed. B.C. 187

LVI. Much else is said, especially about the end of Scipio's life, his trial, his death, his funeral, his tomb, all so contradictory that I find no tradition, no written documents, which I can accept. There is no unanimity as to his accuser: some say that Marcus Naevius[4] accused him, others the Petillii; there is no agreement as to the time when he was prosecuted nor as to the year when he died[5] nor as to where he died or was buried; some say that both death and burial took place at Rome, others at Liternum. In both places tombs and statues are shown; for at Liternum[6] there is a tomb and a statue placed upon

those of Livy leaves it doubtful still whether Polybius is the source for both anecdotes. The second means, of course, that it was due to Scipio that there was any money to be guarded in the treasury.

[4] Naevius was tribune in 184 B.C. (XXXIX. lii. 4 below).

[5] Livy returns to this question in dealing with the year 183 B.C. (XXXIX. lii.).

[6] Seneca, writing to Lucilius from Scipio's villa at Liternum, says . . . *ara quam sepulchrum esse tanti viri suspicor* (*Ep.* LXXXVI. 1). Strabo (p. 243) also mentions the tomb, but there seems to be no other reference to the statue of which Livy speaks.

A.U.C. 567

4 quam tempestate disiectam nuper vidimus ipsi, et Romae extra Portam Capenam in Scipionum monumento tres statuae sunt, quarum duae P. et L. Scipionum dicuntur esse, tertia poetae Q. Ennii.
5 Nec inter scriptores rerum discrepat solum, sed orationes quoque, si modo ipsorum sunt quae feruntur,
6 P. Scipionis et Ti. Gracchi abhorrent inter se. Index orationis P. Scipionis nomen M. Naevii tribuni plebis habet, ipsa oratio sine nomine est accusatoris; modo
7 nebulonem, modo nugatorem appellat. Ne Gracchi quidem oratio aut Petilliorum accusatorum Africani aut
8 diei dictae Africano ullam mentionem habet. Alia tota serenda fabula est Gracchi orationi conveniens, et illi auctores sequendi sunt qui, cum L. Scipio et accusatus et damnatus sit pecuniae captae ab rege legatum in
9 Etruria fuisse Africanum tradunt; qua post famam de casu fratris adlatam relicta legatione cucurrisse eum Romam et, cum a porta recta ad forum se contulisset, quod in vincula duci fratrem dictum erat, reppulisse a corpore eius viatorem, et tribunis retinentibus magis

---

[1] No inscriptions to Publius or Lucius Scipio and no identifiable statue of either has been found in the Scipio tomb. The bust which some suppose to be that of Ennius exists in the Vatican Museum.

[2] Cicero (*Brutus* 77) had few specimens of Scipio's style, but he quotes a punning fragment from a speech against Naevius (*quid hoc Naevio ignavius*: *De Or.* II. 249). But Livy (sect. 6 below) says that Naevius was not mentioned in the speech itself. There is a slight indication that Livy and Gellius (*l.c.*) read the same speech, since Livy says that Scipio called his accuser *nebulonem*, and this word occurs in the direct quotation given by Gellius.

[3] This speech is otherwise unknown.

the tomb, which I myself saw recently, shattered by a storm, and at Rome, outside the Porta Capena, in the tomb of the Scipios, there are three statues, two of which are said to represent Publius and Lucius Scipio, the third the poet Quintus Ennius.[1] Not only is there disagreement among historians, but the speeches also (if indeed those which are in circulation are genuine works of these men) of Publius Scipio[2] and Tiberius Gracchus[3] are inconsistent with one another. The *index*[4] of the speech of Publius Scipio contains the name of Marcus Naevius, tribune of the people; the speech itself lacks the name of the accuser; it calls him now "a ne'er-do-well," now "a no-good." Nor does the speech of Gracchus make any mention at all either of the Petillii as accusers of Africanus or of the prosecution of Africanus. Another entirely different story must be put together, consistent with the oration of Gracchus, and those writers must be followed who say that, when Lucius Scipio was both accused and convicted of receiving money from the king, Africanus was serving on a commission in Etruria;[5] that, leaving this post after receiving the news of his brother's downfall, he hastened to Rome, and when he had gone from the gate straight to the Forum, because it was said that his brother was being put in chains, that he drove the messenger from him, and that when the tribunes tried to stop him he attacked them, with more B.C. 187

[4] The *index* was a tag fastened to the projecting end of the rod on which the roll was wound, containing the title of the work contained in that roll.

[5] Nothing further is known of this commission, although Gellius (VI. (VII.) xix) tells the rest of the story, with greater detail.

A.U.C. 567

10 pie quam civiliter vim fecisse. Haec enim ipsa Ti.
Gracchus queritur dissolutam esse a privato tribuniciam potestatem, et ad postremum, cum auxilium L. Scipioni pollicetur, adicit tolerabilioris
exempli esse a tribuno plebis potius quam a privato
victam videri et tribuniciam potestatem et rem
11 publicam esse. Sed ita hanc unam impotentem eius
iniuriam invidia onerat ut increpando, quod degenerarit[1] tantum a se ipse, cumulatas ei[2] veteres
laudes moderationis et temperantiae pro reprehen-
12 sione praesenti reddat; castigatum enim quondam
ab eo populum ait, quod eum perpetuum consulem et
dictatorem vellet facere; prohibuisse statuas sibi in
comitio, in Rostris, in curia, in Capitolio, in cella
13 Iovis poni; prohibuisse ne decerneretur ut imago sua
triumphali ornatu e templo Iovis optimi maximi
exiret.

LVII. Haec vel in laudatione posita ingentem magnitudinem animi moderantis ad civilem[3] habitum
honoribus significarent, quae exprobrando inimicus
2 fatetur. Huic Graccho minorem ex duabus filiis—
nam maior P. Cornelio Nasicae haud dubie a patre

[1] degenerarit *ed. Frobeniana* 1535: generauit *et* generauerit ς.

[2] ei *ed. Frobeniana* 1531: et ς.

[3] moderantis ad civilem *Drakenborch*: moderantis uilem *M*: moderandis ad ciuilem ς.

---

[1] The presumable situation was this: L. Scipio had been condemned by a tribune to pay a fine; in default of bond he would be imprisoned and could be released only by another tribune; Gracchus finally assumed the responsibility of freeing him after Africanus had committed his assault.

[2] Valerius Maximus (IV. i. 6) tells a similar story, but the occasion of the rebuke is unknown. It seems probable that Livy uses *perpetuus* in the sense of "for a considerable con-

affection for his brother than respect for the laws. B.C. 187
For it is just this conduct that Tiberius Gracchus complains of—that the tribunicial power had been infringed by a private citizen, and at the end, when he promised his official assistance to Lucius Scipio, he added that it seemed to be a more endurable precedent that a tribune of the people rather than a private citizen should have overthrown both the tribunicial power and the state.[1] But this one act of uncontrolled violence on Scipio's part he loaded with reproaches in such a way that, taunting him because he had fallen so far below his own standards, he paid him, as compensation for his criticism of the moment, lasting and accumulated praises for his integrity and self-command; for he said that the people had once been rebuked by Scipio because they wished to make him perpetual[2] consul and dictator; that he forbade statues to himself to be erected in the Comitium, on the Rostra, in the Curia, on the Capitoline, in the cell of Jupiter; that he prevented also a decree that his image in triumphal dress should appear to be coming out of the temple of Jupiter Optimus Maximus.[3]

LVII. Such statements, even if included in a eulogy, would indicate the unusual greatness of a soul which restricted distinctions to conformity with a democratic constitution, and they were made by an enemy and accompanied by censure. To this Gracchus the younger of Scipio's two daughters—for the elder was betrothed to Publius Cornelius Nasica

tinuous period," contrasting it with *in annum*: cf. XXIV. viii. 7.

[3] Appian (*Iber.* 23) reports that this was done despite the protests of Scipio.

A.U.C. 567 3 collocata erat—nuptam fuisse convenit. Illud
parum constat, utrum post mortem patris et desponsa
sit et nupserit, an verae illae opiniones sint, Gracchum, cum L. Scipio in vincula duceretur, nec quis-
4 quam collegarum auxilio esset, iurasse sibi inimicitias
cum Scipionibus quae fuissent manere, nec se gratiae
quaerendae causa quicquam facere, sed, in quem
carcerem reges et imperatores hostium ducentem
vidisset P. Africanum, in eum se fratrem eius duci
5 non passurum. Senatum eo die forte in Capitolio
cenantem consurrexisse et petisse, ut inter epulas
6 Graccho filiam Africanus desponderet. Quibus ita
inter [1] publicum sollemne sponsalibus rite factis cum
se domum recepisset, Scipionem Aemiliae uxori
7 dixisse filiam se minorem despondisse. Cum illa,
muliebriter indignabunda nihil de communi filia
secum consultatum, adiecisset non si Ti. Graccho
daret expertem consilii debuisse matrem esse,
8 laetum Scipionem tam concordi iudicio ei [2] ipsi
desponsam respondisse. Haec de tanto viro quam
et opinionibus et monumentis litterarum variarent,
proponenda erant.

LVIII. Iudiciis a Q. Terentio praetore perfectis, Hostilius et Furius damnati praedes eodem die quaes-

[1] inter *ed. Frobeniana* 1535 : in ς.   [2] ei *Walch* : et ς.

---

[1] They were the parents of the famous tribunes.

[2] Probably in connection with some religious festival.

[3] Whether this is anything more than a pleasant story which Livy had picked up somewhere or not, it is probably characteristic of the conduct of the Roman aristocracy at this period.

[4] With this anecdote Livy concludes his parenthetical miscellany and returns to the narrative based on Valerius Antias: cf. the note to lv. 10 above.

and beyond doubt by her father—was married, as all B.C. 187
agree.[1] What is not certain is whether she was both betrothed and married after the death of her father, or whether the opinions are true, that Gracchus, when Lucius Scipio was being taken to prison and no one of his colleagues was coming to his assistance, swore that his feud with the Scipios continued as before and that he was doing nothing to curry favour, but that he would not permit the brother of Africanus to be put into that prison into which he had seen Publius Africanus thrusting kings and generals of the enemy. The story goes on that the senate, which chanced to dine that day on the Capitoline,[2] had risen up and begged that during the banquet Africanus should betroth his daughter to Gracchus. When the contract had been duly made at this public ceremony and Scipio had returned home, he told his wife Aemilia that he had arranged a marriage for their younger daughter. When she, being irritated, as a woman would naturally be, that he had not consulted with her about the daughter of both of them, had added that not even if he were promising her to Tiberius Gracchus should the mother have been excluded from the deliberation, Scipio, they say, rejoicing at their harmony of opinion, replied that it was to Gracchus that he had betrothed her.[3] However much at variance are these accounts of so great a man, they have seemed worthy of presentation.[4]

LVIII. When the trials [5] had been completed by Quintus Terentius the praetor, Hostilius and Furius, who were convicted, gave bond the same day to the

[5] Livy seems to be technically correct in his terminology. The *iudicium* was the trial proper, as distinguished from the preliminary hearing: cf. lv. 5 above and the note.

A.U.C. 567

2 toribus urbanis dederunt; Scipio cum contenderet omnem quam accepisset pecuniam in aerario esse, nec se quicquam publici habere, in vincula duci est coeptus.
3 P. Scipio Nasica tribunos appellavit orationemque habuit plenam veris decoribus non communiter modo Corneliae gentis, sed proprie familiae suae.
4 Parentes suos et P. Africani ac L. Scipionis, qui in carcerem duceretur, fuisse Cn. et P. Scipiones,
5 clarissimos viros. Eos, cum per aliquot annos in terra Hispania adversus multos Poenorum Hispanorumque et duces et exercitus nominis Romani famam
6 auxissent non bello solum, sed quod Romanae temperantiae fideique specimen illis gentibus dedissent, ad extremum ambo pro republica mortem[1] occu-
7 buisse. Cum illorum gloriam tueri posteris satis esset, P. Africanum tantum paternas superiecisse laudes ut fidem fecerit non sanguine humano sed
8 stirpe divina satum se esse. L. Scipionem, de quo agatur, ut quae in Hispania, quae in Africa, cum legatus fratris esset, gessisset, praetereantur, consulem et ab senatu dignum habitum[2] cui extra sortem Asia provincia et bellum cum Antiocho rege decerneretur, et a fratre cui post duos consulatus censu-
9 ramque et triumphum legatus in Asiam iret. Ibi ne magnitudo et splendor legati laudibus consulis officeret, forte ita incidisse ut, quo die ad Magnesiam

[1] mortem *edd. vett.*: morte ς.
[2] habitum *Weissenborn*: uisum ς.

[1] Execution of judgment on the person of the condemned was permitted when he had or claimed to have no property and did not furnish bond.

City quaestors; when Scipio protested that all the money which he had received was in the treasury and that he had no public property, they proceeded to put him in prison.[1] Publius Scipio Nasica appealed to the tribunes and delivered a speech full of deserved tributes, not only to the Cornelian *gens* as a whole, but specifically to his own family. The fathers, he said, both of himself and of Publius Africanus and the Lucius Scipio who was being imprisoned, were Gnaeus and Publius Scipio, men of the highest distinction. After they had, through many years in the land of Spain, against many generals and armies alike of Carthaginians and Spaniards, increased the fame of the Roman name, not only in war but because they had given those peoples an example of Roman self-control and devotion, both had in the end met death for their fatherland. While it would have been enough, he continued, to maintain for posterity their standard of glory, Publius Africanus had so far surpassed his father's praises that he had given reason to believe that he was born, not of human blood, but of divine stock. Lucius Scipio, whose fate was now in question, not to mention what he had done in Spain, in Africa, while serving as his brother's lieutenant, had, as consul, been deemed by the senate worthy to have decreed to him, without recourse to the lot, the province of Asia and the war with King Antiochus, and had been deemed by his brother worthy to be attended to Asia by that brother as his lieutenant, after he had been twice consul and censor and had celebrated a triumph.[2] There, that the greatness and glory of the lieutenant might not obscure the consul's fame, it happened that, on the day when B.C. 187

[2] Cf. XXXVII. i. 9.

A.U.C. 567 signis collatis L. Scipio Antiochum devicisset, aeger
10 P. Scipio Elaeae dierum aliquot abesset via. Non
fuisse minorem eum exercitum quam Hannibalis, cum
quo in Africa esset pugnatum; Hannibalem eundem
fuisse inter multos alios regios duces, qui imperator
Punici belli fuerit. Et bellum quidem ita gestum
esse ut ne fortunam quidem quisquam criminari
11 possit; in pace crimen quaeri; eam dici venisse. Hic
decem legatos simul argui,[1] quorum ex consilio data
12 pax esset; quamquam exstitissent [2] ex decem legatis,
qui Cn. Manlium accusarent, tamen non modo ad
criminis fidem, sed ne ad moram quidem triumphi
eam accusationem valuisse.

LIX. At hercule in Scipione leges ipsas pacis, ut
nimium accommodatas Antiocho, suspectas esse;
integrum enim ei regnum relictum; omnia possidere
2 eum victum, quae ante bellum eius fuerint; auri et
argenti cum vim magnam habuisset, nihil in publicum
3 relatum, omne in privatum versum; an praeter
omnium oculos tantum auri argentique in triumpho
L. Scipionis quantum non decem aliis triumphis, si
4 omne in unum conferatur, latum?[1] Nam quid de fini-

[1] argui *ed. Frobeniana* 1535: arguique *et* argui quoque ς.
[2] quamquam exstitissent *Drakenborch*: quamquam exstitisse *M*: quam (*aut* quem) exstitisse ς.

---

[1] Cf. XXXVII. xli. 1 and the note.
[2] This is one of the minor mysteries in this affair: Livy's narrative shows that their dealings had been entirely with Manlius, who, as a matter of fact, had far more opportunity to convert tribute and booty to his own use than Scipio had

Lucius Scipio defeated Antiochus in pitched battle at Magnesia, Publius Scipio was sick at Elaea, some days' journey away. That army, he went on, was no smaller than that of Hannibal, with which they had fought in Africa; that same Hannibal,[1] who had been commander in the Punic War, was there among many other generals of the king. And the war indeed had been so conducted that no one could find fault even with fortune; it was in the peace that ground for accusation was sought; the peace, they said, had been sold. On this point, he maintained, the ten commissioners were likewise accused, by whose advice the peace had been concluded;[2] although some of the ten commissioners had come forward to accuse Gnaeus Manlius, this charge had failed, not only to win belief in his guilt, but even to delay his triumph. B.C. 187

LIX. But, by Hercules, they say in the case of Scipio that the very terms of peace were suspicious, as too favourable to Antiochus; for it was implied that his kingdom had been left undiminished; that after his defeat he possessed everything he had owned before the war; that, although he had had a great quantity of gold and silver, none of it had been turned in to the treasury, all of it converted to private use; but (as to the last charge) had not so much gold and silver been displayed before the eyes of all in the triumph of Lucius Scipio as had not been carried in ten other triumphs if they were combined into one? 3 For what (returning to their first charge) shall I say

had. The following sentence is almost conclusive proof that the Scipios were victims of political animus, regardless of their actual guilt or innocence.

[3] Cf. XXXVII. lix. 2–5.

A.U.C. 567

bus regni dicam? Asiam omnem et proxima Euro-
5 pae tenuisse Antiochum. Ea quanta regio orbis terrarum sit, a Tauro monte in Aegaeum usque prominens mare, quot non urbes modo sed gentes
6 amplectatur, omnes scire. Hanc regionem dierum plus triginta iter in [2] longitudinem, decem inter duo maria in latitudinem patentem usque ad Tauri
7 montis iuga Antiocho ademptam, expulso in ultimum angulum orbis terrarum. Quid si gratuita pax esset plus adimi ei potuisse? Philippo victo Macedoniam, Nabidi Lacedaemonem relictam, nec Quinctio crimen quaesitum; non enim habuisse eum Africanum fratrem; cuius cum [3] gloria prodesse L. Scipioni
8 debuisset, invidiam nocuisse. Tantum auri argentique iudicatum esse in domum L. Scipionis illatum quantum venditis omnibus bonis redigi non posset. Ubi [4] ergo esse regium aurum, ubi tot hereditates
9 acceptas? In domo quam sumptus non exhauserint, exstare debuisse novae fortunae cumulum. At enim, quod ex bonis redigi non possit, ex corpore et tergo per vexationem et contumelias L. Scipionis
10 petituros inimicos, ut in carcere inter fures nocturnos et latrones vir clarissimus includatur et in robore et tenebris exspiret, deinde nudus ante carcerem
11 proiciatur. Non id Corneliae magis familiae quam urbi Romanae fore erubescendum.

[1] latum *Crévier*: sit latum ϛ.
[2] iter in *Weissenborn*: in *M*: *om.* ϛ.
[3] cuius cum *ed. Frobeniana* 1535: *om.* ϛ.
[4] ubi *ed. Frobeniana* 1535: id ubi ϛ.

about the boundaries of the kingdom of Antiochus? B.C. 187
He had held, as we know, all Asia and the adjacent parts of Europe. How great this section of the earth is, extending from the Taurus mountain clear to the Aegean Sea, how many cities and even nations it contains, all men know. This region, extending in length more than thirty days' march and ten in width between the two seas, as far as the crest of the Taurus mountain, had been taken from Antiochus, who had been driven back into the farthest corner of the earth. What more could have been taken from him by a peace granted without a bribe? Macedonia, he reminded them, had been left to Philip after his defeat, Lacedaemon to Nabis, nor had Quinctius been the victim of a trumped-up charge; he, of course, had not had Africanus as a brother; although his fame should have aided Lucius Scipio, his unpopularity had done him harm. Judgment had been given that so much gold and silver had been conveyed into the house of Lucius Scipio as the sale of all his property could not produce. Where, then, he asked, was the royal gold, where all the legacies he had received? In a house which extravagance had not drained, this heap of new wealth should be apparent. But, of course, what cannot be obtained from his property the foes of Lucius Scipio will seek from his body and from his back, by means of persecution and insults, so that this most distinguished man may be shut up in prison among thieves of the night and brigands and may die in the darkness of a cell and then be cast out naked before the prison. And it was not, he concluded, to the Cornelian family so much as to the City of Rome that this would bring the blush of shame.

A.U.C. 567

LX. Adversus ea Terentius praetor rogationem Petilliam et senatus consultum[1] et iudicium de L.
2 Scipione factum recitavit; se, ni referatur pecunia in publicum, quae iudicata sit, nihil habere quod faciat nisi ut prendi damnatum et in vincula duci iubeat.
3 Tribuni cum in consilium secessissent, paulo post C. Fannius ex sua collegarumque aliorum, praeter Gracchum, sententia pronuntiavit praetori non intercedere
4 tribunos quo minus sua potestate utatur. Ti. Gracchus ita decrevit, quo minus ex bonis L. Scipionis quod iudicatum sit redigatur, se non intercedere
5 praetori; L. Scipionem, qui regem opulentissimum orbis terrarum devicerit, imperium populi Romani
6 propagaverit in ultimos terrarum fines, regem Eumenem, Rhodios, alias tot Asiae urbes devinxerit populi Romani beneficiis, plurimos duces hostium in triumpho ductos carcere incluserit, non passurum inter hostes populi Romani in carcere et vinculis
7 esse, mittique eum se iubere. Tanto adsensu auditum est decretum, adeo dimissum Scipionem laeti homines viderunt ut vix in eadem civitate videretur
8 factum iudicium. In bona deinde L. Scipionis possessum publice quaestores praetor misit. Neque in iis non modo vestigium ullum comparuit pecuniae regiae, sed nequaquam tantum redactum est quantae
9 summae damnatus fuerat. Collata ea pecunia a cognatis amicisque et clientibus est L. Scipioni ut, si

[1] et senatus consultum *ed. Frobeniana* 1535: ex senatus consulto ς.

LX. In reply to this the praetor Terentius read the Petillian law and the decree of the senate and the sentence which had been passed on Lucius Scipio; unless the fine which was imposed was paid to the treasury there was nothing which he could do except to order the convicted man to be arrested and taken to prison. When the tribunes had withdrawn for consultation, a little later Gaius Fannius announced that, in accordance with the decision of himself and his colleagues except Gracchus, the tribunes would not interfere with the praetor so as to prevent his exercise of his authority. Tiberius Gracchus thus decreed: that he would not prevent the praetor from collecting, out of the property of Lucius Scipio, the fine that had been imposed; Lucius Scipio himself, who had conquered the richest king in the world, extended the empire of the Roman people to the most distant limits of the earth, bound King Eumenes, the Rhodians, and so many cities of Asia by obligations to the Roman people, had led in his triumph and thrown into prison so many leaders of the enemy, he would not permit to lie in prison and in chains among the enemies of the Roman people, and he ordered him to be released. This decree was listened to with such applause and with such joy did men see Scipio released that it scarcely seemed that the trial had taken place in the same state. Then the praetor sent the quaestors to take possession, on behalf of the state, of the property of Lucius Scipio. Not only was there no trace of the king's wealth discovered, but by no means was there as much property found as would equal the amount of the fine. Such a sum was raised for Lucius Scipio by his relatives and friends and clients that if he had

B.C. 187

A.U.C. 567

acciperet eam, locupletior aliquanto esset quam ante
10 calamitatem fuerat. Nihil accepit; quae necessaria
ad cultum erant, redempta ei a proximis cognatis
sunt; verteratque Scipionum invidia in praetorem
et consilium eius et accusatores.

received it he would have been a great deal richer B.C. 187
than he had been before his downfall. He accepted none of it; what was necessary for a decent existence was redeemed for him by his nearest relatives; and the ill-will against the Scipios ended by recoiling upon the heads of the praetor and his advisers and the accusers.[1]

[1] It has seemed unwise to attempt any further reconstruction of these scenes in the drama of the Scipios. Livy is unusually conscious of the contradictions and difficulties of the story without being able to solve the problems they create. Excessive space would be required to discuss these problems adequately, and the results would be incommensurate with the effort required.

LIBRI XXXVIII PERIOCHA

M. Fulvius cos. in Epiro Ambracienses obsessos in deditionem accepit, Cephallaniam subegit, Aetolis perdomitis pacem dedit. Cn. Manlius cos., collega eius, Gallograecos, Tolostobogios et Tectosagos et Trocmos,[1] qui Brenno duce in Asiam transierant, cum soli citra Taurum montem non apparerent, vicit. Eorum origo et quo modo[2] ea loca quae tenent occupaverint refertur. Exemplum quoque virtutis et pudicitiae in femina traditur. Quae cum regis Gallograecorum uxor fuisset, capta centurionem qui ei vim intulerat occidit. Lustrum a censoribus conditum est. Censa sunt civium capita $\overline{\text{CCLVIII}}$ CCCX.[3] Cum Ariarathe, Cappadociae rege, amicitia iuncta est. Cn. Manlius, contradicentibus X legatis ex quorum consilio foedus cum Antiocho conscripserat, de Gallograecis acta pro se in senatu causa triumphavit. Scipio Africanus die ei dicta, ut quidam tradunt, a Q.[4] Petillio tr. pl., ut quidam, a Naevio, quod praeda ex Antiocho capta aerarium fraudasset, postquam is dies venit, evocatus in rostra: "Hac die" inquit "Quirites, Carthaginem vici," et prosequente populo Capitolium escendit. Inde ne amplius tribuniciis iniuriis vexaretur, in voluntarium exilium Liternum[5] concessit. Incertum ibi an Romae defunctus sit; nam monumentum

[1] *These names, much confused in the MSS., are corrected from the Livy text.*

[2] quo modo *Jahn*: quoniam *N P*.

[3] *The number is left as it is found in the MSS., although it disagrees with that given by Livy in xxxvi.* 10 *above.*

[4] Q. *Sigonius ex vet. lib.*: p. *codd.*

[5] Liternum *edd.*: *om. codd.*

SUMMARY OF BOOK XXXVIII

The consul Marcus Fulvius besieged the Ambraciots in Epirus and received their surrender, subdued Cephallania, and granted peace to the conquered Aetolians. Gnaeus Manlius his colleague defeated the Gallogrecians, that is, the Tolostobogii, the Tectosagi and the Trocmi, who had crossed into Asia under the leadership of Brennus, when they alone of the peoples on this side of the Taurus mountain did not offer submission. Their origin and the manner in which they gained control of the districts which they hold are recorded. An example also of virtue and chastity in a woman is reported. She, being the wife of the king of the Gallogrecians, and being a prisoner, slew a centurion who had violated her. The *lustrum* was closed by the censors. The number of citizens rated was two hundred and fifty-eight thousand three hundred and ten. A treaty of friendship was concluded with Ariarathes, king of Cappadocia. Gnaeus Manlius, despite the opposition of the ten commissioners by whose advice he had put into form the treaty with Antiochus, having pleaded his cause in person before the senate, triumphed over the Gallogrecians. Scipio Africanus, having been accused, as some say, by Quintus Petillius the tribune of the people, as others say, by Naevius, on the ground that he had cheated the treasury of booty taken from Antiochus, when the day came and he was summoned to the Rostra, said: "On this day, citizens, I conquered Carthage," and with the people attending him ascended the Capitoline. Then, to avoid being further annoyed by the attacks of the tribunes, he withdrew to Liternum in voluntary exile. It is uncertain whether he died there or in Rome;

eius utrobique fuit. L. Scipio Asiaticus, frater Africani, eodem crimine peculatus accusatus damnatusque cum in vincula et carcerem duceretur, Ti. Sempronius Gracchus tr. pl., qui antea Scipionibus inimicus fuerat, intercessit et ob id beneficium Africani filiam duxit. Cum quaestores in bona eius publice possidenda missi essent,[1] non modo in his ullum vestigium pecuniae regiae apparuit, sed nequaquam tantum redactum quantae summae erat damnatus. Collatam a cognatis et amicis innumerabilem pecuniam accipere noluit; quae necessaria ei erant ad cultum redempta.

[1] missi essent *J. F. Gronovius*: misissent *codd.*

for there was a tomb to him in each place. Lucius Scipio Asiaticus, the brother of Africanus, was accused and convicted on the same charge of embezzlement, and, when he was being led to chains and prison, Tiberius Sempronius Gracchus, tribune of the people, who had formerly been an enemy of the Scipios, intervened for him, and in return for that act of kindness was given the daughter of Africanus in marriage. When the quaestors had been sent to take possession, on behalf of the state, of the property of Scipio, not only was there no trace of the king's wealth discovered, but by no means was there as much found as would equal the amount of the fine. A countless amount of money collected by his relatives and friends he refused to accept; what was necessary for a decent existence for him was redeemed.

BOOK XXXIX

LIBER XXXIX

A.U.C. 567

I. Dum haec, si modo hoc anno acta sunt, Romae
aguntur, consules ambo in Liguribus gerebant bellum.
2 Is hostis velut natus ad continendam inter magnorum
intervalla bellorum Romanis militarem disciplinam
erat; nec alia provincia militem magis ad virtutem
3 acuebat. Nam Asia et amoenitate urbium et copia
terrestrium maritimarumque rerum et mollitia hostium regiisque opibus ditiores quam fortiores exerci-
4 tus faciebat. Praecipue sub imperio Cn. Manlii
solute ac neglegenter habiti sunt. Itaque asperius
paulo iter in Thracia et exercitatior hostis magna
5 clade eos castigavit. In Liguribus omnia erant quae
militem excitarent, loca montana et aspera, quae et
ipsis capere labor erat et ex praeoccupatis deicere
6 hostem; et itinera ardua angusta infesta insidiis;
hostis levis et velox et repentinus, qui nullum usquam
tempus,[1] nullum locum quietum aut securum esse

[1] nullum usquam tempus *Heraeus*: usquam tempus nullus ς.

---

[1] The allusion is to the uncertainty as to the date of the trial of the Scipios: cf. XXXVIII. lvi. 2 above.

[2] The assignment of Liguria to the consuls was reported at XXXVIII. xliii. 8 above.

[3] This charge was not made in the speech of Furius Aemilius (XXXVIII. xlv.–xlvi. above), but is brought up again in

BOOK XXXIX

I. WHILE these things were going on at Rome, if indeed they did happen that year,[1] both consuls were waging war against the Ligurians.[2] This enemy was born, as it were, to keep alive the military discipline of the Romans during the intervals between their great wars; nor did any province do more to put an edge to the soldier's courage. For Asia, on account of the pleasantness of its cities and the abundance of its treasures of land and sea and the feebleness of the enemy and the wealth of its kings, made armies richer rather than braver. Especially under the command of Gnaeus Manlius was discipline slackly and indifferently enforced;[3] and so a somewhat more difficult advance in Thrace and a rather more effective enemy had taught them a lesson with great slaughter. Among the Ligurians there was everything to keep an army alert—hilly and rough ground, which was difficult both for the men themselves to occupy and to dislodge the enemy who had already occupied it, and roads difficult, narrow, dangerous by reason of ambuscades; an enemy lightly equipped, mobile and unexpected in his movements, who permitted no time or place whatever to be quiet or B.C. 187

vi. 5 and vii. 3 below. Its presence here, in contrast with its absence from the preceding Book, may indicate a change of source.

A.U.C. 567

sineret; oppugnatio necessaria munitorum castellorum, laboriosa simul periculosaque; inops regio, quae parsimonia astringeret milites, praedae haud
7 multum praeberet. Itaque non lixa sequebatur, non iumentorum longus ordo agmen extendebat. Nihil praeter arma et viros omnem spem in armis
8 habentes erat. Nec deerat umquam cum iis vel materia belli vel causa, quia propter domesticam inopiam vicinos agros incursabant. Nec tamen in discrimen summae rerum pugnabatur.

II. C. Flaminius consul, cum Friniatibus [1] Liguribus in agro eorum pluribus proeliis secundis factis,
2 in deditionem gentem accepit et arma ademit. Ea quia non sincera fide tradebant, cum castigarentur, relictis vicis in montem Auginum profugerunt.
3 Confestim secutus est consul. Ceterum effusi rursus, et pars maxima inermes, per invia et rupes deruptas praecipitantes fugerunt, qua sequi hostis non posset. Ita trans Appenninum abierunt. Qui castris se
4 tenuerant, circumsessi et expugnati sunt. Inde trans Appenninum ductae legiones. Ibi montis quem ceperant altitudine paulisper se tutati mox in deditionem concesserunt. Tum conquisita cum in-
5 tentiore cura arma et omnia adempta. Translatum deinde ad Apuanos Ligures bellum, qui in agrum

[1] cum Friniatibus *ed. Frobeniana* 1535: confirmatis ϛ.

---

[1] This reflection seems to be fully warranted by Livy's narrative, and raises doubts as to the legitimacy of some of the Ligurian triumphs, which were still notorious in Cicero's day (*Brutus* 255).

[2] The Friniates lived mainly south of the Apennines.

[3] The Apuani lived west of the Apennines. A raid covering

safe; the besieging of fortified points was necessary B.C. 187
and at the same time toilsome and dangerous; the district was poor, which constrained the soldiers to simple living and offered them little plunder. Accordingly, no civilian camp-follower went along, no long train of pack-animals stretched out the column. There was nothing except arms and men who placed all their trust in their arms. Nor was there ever wanting either the occasion or the cause for war with them, because on account of their poverty at home they were constantly raiding their neighbours' lands. And yet the fighting never brought about the final settlement of a campaign.[1]

II. The consul Gaius Flaminius, having fought several successful battles with the Ligurian Friniates [2] on their own soil, received the tribe in surrender and disarmed them. When they were reproved because they did not surrender the arms in good faith, they abandoned their villages and fled to the Auginus mountain. The consul followed in haste. But they scattered again, the largest part being unarmed, and fled at full speed through pathless country and over steep cliffs where the enemy could not pursue. So they departed across the Apennines. Those who remained in camp were surrounded and captured. Thence the legions were led across the Apennines. There the enemy defended themselves for a while by virtue of the height of the mountain which they had occupied, but presently yielded in surrender. At this time the arms were sought out with greater diligence, and all were taken from them. The war was then transferred to the Ligurian Apuani,[3] who

all the country between Pisa and Bologna was an ambitious undertaking.

A.U.C. 567 Pisanum Bononiensemque ita incursaverant ut coli
6 non possent. His quoque perdomitis consul pacem
dedit finitimis. Et quia a bello quieta ut esset provincia effecerat, ne in otio militem haberet, viam a
7 Bononia perduxit Arretium. M. Aemilius alter consul agros Ligurum vicosque, qui in campis aut vallibus
erant, ipsis montes duos Ballistam [1] Suismontiumque
8 tenentibus, deussit depopulatusque est. Deinde eos
qui in montibus erant adortus primo levibus proeliis
fatigavit, postremo coactos in aciem descendere
iusto proelio devicit, in quo et aedem Dianae vovit.
9 Subactis cis Appenninum omnibus, tum transmontanos
adortus—in his et Friniates [2] Ligures erant, quos non
adierat C. Flaminius—omnes Aemilius subegit armaque ademit et de montibus in campos multitudinem
10 deduxit. Pacatis Liguribus exercitum in agrum
Gallicum duxit viamque a Placentia ut Flaminiae
11 committeret Ariminum perduxit. Proelio ultimo,
quo cum Liguribus signis collatis conflixit, aedem
Iunoni reginae vovit. Haec in Liguribus eo anno
gesta.

III. In Gallia M. Furius praetor insontibus Cenomanis, in pace speciem belli quaerens, ademerat

[1] Ballistam *edd. vett.* : uallis tamen *et similia* ς.
[2] Friniates ς : erisinates *M*.

---

[1] If, as seems probable, there was already a road from Arezzo to Rome, the new road provided a route to Gaul shorter than the Via Flaminia (built in 220 B.C. by the father of the present consul) and the Via Aemilia (see sect. 10 below), by way of Ariminum.

[2] In XL. lii. 1–3, Aemilius, as censor in 179 B.C., received

had raided the lands of Pisa and Bologna to such B.C. 187 effect that they could not be cultivated. Having subdued them too, the consul granted peace to their neighbours. And, because he had brought it to pass that the province was free from war, that he might not leave his army idle, he built a road from Bologna to Arezzo.[1] The other consul, Marcus Aemilius, burned and ravaged the farms and villages of the Ligurians which were in the plains or valleys, the people themselves holding the two mountains Ballista and Suismontium. Then, attacking the men who were on the mountains, he first wore them out with small skirmishes, then forced them to come down to face his battle-line and defeated them in a regular battle, in the course of which he vowed a temple to Diana.[2] Having subdued all the tribes on this side of the Apennines, Aemilius then attacked those beyond the mountains—among whom there were those Ligurian Friniates also whom Gaius Flaminius had not visited—and subdued them all, took away their arms and transferred the population from the hills to the plains. Leaving the Ligurians pacified, he led his army into Gallic territory, and built a road from Placentia to Ariminum, in order to make a junction with the Via Flaminia. In the final encounter in which he engaged the Ligurians in a pitched battle, he vowed a temple to Juno Regina. Such were the events of that year among the Ligurians.

III. In Gaul the praetor Marcus Furius, seeking in peace the appearance of war, had disarmed the

an appropriation for games in connection with the dedication of temples to Diana and Juno Regina (sect. 11 below). Both were near the Circus Flaminius.

A.U.C. 567 2 arma. Id[1] Cenomani questi Romae apud senatum
reiectique ad consulem Aemilium, cui ut cognosceret
statueretque senatus permiserat, magno certamine
3 cum praetore habito obtinuerunt causam. Arma
reddere Cenomanis, decedere provincia praetor
iussus.

4 Legatis deinde sociorum Latini nominis, qui toto
undique ex Latio frequentes convenerant, senatus
datus est. His querentibus magnam multitudinem
civium suorum Romam commigrasse et ibi censos esse,
5 Q. Terentio Culleoni praetori negotium datum est ut
eos conquireret, et quem C. Claudio M. Livio[2] censoribus postve eos censores ipsum parentemve eius
apud se censum esse probassent socii, ut redire eo
6 cogeret, ubi censi essent. Hac conquisitione duodecim milia Latinorum domos redierunt, iam tum
multitudine alienigenarum urbem onerante.

IV. Priusquam consules redirent Romam, M. Ful-
2 vius proconsul ex Aetolia redit; isque ad aedem
Apollinis in senatu cum de rebus in Aetolia Cephalla-
niaque ab se gestis disseruisset, petit a patribus ut,

[1] id *Gelenius* : inde et *M* : inde *aut* in ς.
[2] Liuio ς : iulio *M*.

---

[1] The Cenomani had been quiet since their defeat by Cethegus in 197 B.C. (XXXIII. xxiii. 4).

[2] The allied cities and the Latin colonies, whose status was similar, were under obligations to Rome, in accordance with their several treaties and constitutions. The migration of their citizens to Rome increased the burden on those who remained at home; the status of the migrants is uncertain: they seem not to have acquired Roman citizenship and yet to have been assessed by the censors.

Cenomani,[1] who had given no provocation: they in B.C. 187
consequence laid a complaint about this before the senate at Rome, and were referred to the consul Aemilius, whom the senate had authorized to investigate and decide, and after engaging in great contention with the praetor won their case. The praetor was ordered to restore their arms to the Cenomani and to leave the province.

Then ambassadors from the allies of the Latin confederacy, who had assembled from all Latium in great numbers from every side, were granted an audience by the senate. When they complained that a great number of their citizens had migrated to Rome and had been assessed there,[2] Quintus Terentius Culleo the praetor was instructed to search them out, and, on receiving from the allies proof that any person or the father of such person[3] had been assessed among the allies in the censorship of Gaius Claudius and Marcus Livius[4] or after that censorship, to compel such persons to return to the places where they had been registered. As a consequence of this investigation twelve thousand of the Latins returned home, for even at that time a multitude of aliens was burdening the city.

IV. Before the consuls returned to Rome, the proconsul Marcus Fulvius returned from Aetolia; and when the senate, in the temple of Apollo, had heard him describe his exploits in Aetolia and Cephallania, he asked the Fathers, if they deemed it proper, by

[3] Since only heads of families were listed, the omission of this provision would have opened the door to persons who moved to Rome in the lifetimes of their fathers.

[4] They were censors in 204 B.C. The date chosen was probably arbitrary and the result of compromise.

A.U.C. 567 si[1] aequum censerent, ob rem publicam bene ac feliciter gestam et diis immortalibus honorem haberi
3 iuberent et sibi triumphum decernerent. M. Aburius tribunus plebis si quid de ea re ante M. Aemilii consulis adventum decerneretur intercessurum se
4 ostendit: eum contra dicere velle, proficiscentemque in provinciam ita sibi mandasse ut ea disceptatio integra in adventum suum servaretur. Fulvium temporis iacturam facere: senatum etiam praesente
5 consule[2] quod vellet decreturum. Tum[3] Fulvius: si aut simultas M. Aemilii secum ignota hominibus esset, aut quam is eas inimicitias impotenti ac prope
6 regia ira exerceret, tamen non fuisse ferendum absentem consulem et deorum immortalium honori obstare et meritum debitumque triumphum morari,
7 imperatorem rebus egregie gestis victoremque exercitum cum praeda et captivis ante portas stare, donec consuli ob hoc ipsum moranti redire Romam libitum
8 esset. Verum enimvero cum sint notissimae sibi cum consule inimicitiae, quid ab eo quemquam posse aequi exspectare, qui per infrequentiam furtim sena-
9 tus consultum factum ad aerarium detulerit, Ambraciam non videri vi captam, quae aggere ac vineis oppugnata sit, ubi incensis operibus alia de integro

[1] ut si *Madvig*: ut ς. [2] pr. con. ς: con. pr. *M.*
[3] tum *Muretus*: *om.* ς.

reason of his successful and fortunate conduct of the business of the state, both to order that honour should be paid to the immortal gods and to decree a triumph to him. Marcus Aburius, tribune of the people, announced that, if any decree on that subject were passed prior to the arrival of Marcus Aemilius, he would veto it: Aemilius, he said, wished to speak against it, and on his departure to his province had given instructions to him, the tribune, that this whole discussion should be reserved for his return. Fulvius, he said, was suffering the loss of time only: even with the consul present the senate would decree what he wished. Then Fulvius replied: if either the quarrel between him and Marcus Aemilius was unknown to men, or if it was unknown with what uncontrollable and almost tyrannical passion Aemilius carried on the feud, even then it would have been unendurable that the absent consul should both stand in the way of the honour due to the immortal gods and delay an earned and merited triumph, and that a general after a brilliant campaign and a victorious army with its booty and prisoners should stand before the gates until it suited the fancy of a consul (who stayed away for just that reason) to return to Rome. But as a matter of fact, he went on, since his quarrel with the consul was very well known, what justice could be expected from a man who had deposited in the treasury a decree of the senate passed stealthily and in a poorly attended meeting, to the effect that Ambracia did not appear to have been taken by force, although it had been besieged with a mound and sheds, where other works were built anew when the first were burned, where the battle had raged B.C. 187

A.U.C. 567 facta sint, ubi circa muros supra subterque terram
10 per dies quindecim pugnatum, ubi a prima luce, cum
iam transcendisset muros miles, usque ad noctem diu
anceps proelium tenuerit, ubi plus tria milia hostium
11 sint caesa. Iam de deorum immortalium templis
spoliatis in capta urbe qualem calumniam . . .[1] ad
12 pontifices attulerit? Nisi Syracusarum ceterarumque
captarum civitatium ornamentis urbem exornari fas
fuerit, in Ambracia una capta non valuerit belli ius.
13 Se et patres conscriptos orare et ab tribuno petere,
ne se superbissimo inimico ludibrio esse sinant.

V. Undique omnes alii deprecari tribunum, alii
castigare. Ti. Gracchi collegae plurimum oratio
2 movit. Ne suas quidem simultates pro magistratu
exercere boni exempli esse: alienarum vero simulta-
tum tribunum plebis cognitorem fieri turpe et indignum collegii eius potestate et sacratis legibus
3 esse. Suo quemque iudicio et homines odisse aut
diligere et res probare aut improbare debere, non
pendere ex alterius vultu ac nutu nec alieni momentis
animi circumagi, adstipularique irato consuli tribunum
4 plebei; et quid privatim M. Aemilius mandaverit

[1] *lacunam susp. Madvig.*

---

[1] I have filled out the suspected lacuna in what seems the simplest way consistent with grammar and sense. Madvig takes the passage to mean that spoils captured by Fulvius would bestow fame upon the pontiffs when they used them in the decoration of temples. The action referred to is the decree reported in XXXVIII. xliv. 5 above.

[2] *Adstipulari* is at least semi-technical, implying giving support to a legal proceeding.

[3] The consul had no right to issue official orders of this sort to the tribune.

around the walls for fifteen days, above and below the ground, where from daylight, after the soldiers had already scaled the walls, until nightfall the battle had been maintained with uncertain issue, and where more than three thousand of the enemy had perished? Then, too, as to the plundering of the temples of the immortal gods in the captured city, what kind of insult was it that he had turned the booty over to the pontiffs?[1] Unless it had been lawful to adorn the City with the trophies of Syracuse and other captured towns, but that in the case of captured Ambracia alone the law of war did not hold good! He begged the conscript Fathers and he requested of the tribune that they should not permit him to be made a laughing-stock by this most insolent personal enemy. B.C. 187

V. Everybody from all sides began to address the tribune, some with entreaties, some with reproaches. The argument of his colleague Tiberius Gracchus impressed him most. He said that it was not a good precedent to follow up even one's own contentions while holding a magistracy; but it was disgraceful for a tribune of the people to take sides in the contentions of others, and unworthy of the authority of that college and of its sacred laws. Each man, he said, in accordance with his own judgment should both hate or love men and approve or disapprove measures, should not depend upon another's expression and nod or be led this way or that under the pressure of another's will, nor should a tribune of the people be a second[2] to an angry consul; he should not remember any commission which Marcus Aemilius had privately[3] entrusted to him, and forget the office of tribune which had been

A.U.C. 567

meminisse, tribunatum sibi a populo Romano mandatum oblivisci, et mandatum pro auxilio ac libertate
5 privatorum, non pro consulari regno. Ne hoc quidem
cernere eum, fore ut memoriae ac posteritati mande-
tur eiusdem collegii alterum ex duobus tribunis plebis
suas inimicitias remisisse rei publicae, alterum alienas
6 et mandatas exercuisse. His victus castigationibus
tribunus cum templo excessisset, referente Ser.
Sulpicio praetore triumphus M. Fulvio est decretus.
7 Is cum gratias patribus conscriptis egisset, adiecit
ludos magnos se Iovi optimo maximo eo die quo
Ambraciam cepisset vovisse; in eam rem sibi centum
8 pondo auri a civitatibus collatum; petere ut ex ea
pecunia quam in triumpho latam [1] in aerario positurus
9 esset id aurum secerni iuberent. Senatus pontificum
collegium consuli iussit, num omne id aurum in ludos
10 consumi necesse esset. Cum pontifices negassent
ad religionem pertinere quanta impensa in ludos
fieret, senatus Fulvio quantum impenderet permisit,
11 dum ne summam octoginta milium excederet. Triumphare mense Ianuario statuerat: sed cum audisset
consulem M. Aemilium, litteris M. Aburii tribuni
12 plebis acceptis de remissa intercessione, ipsum ad

[1] latam ς : delatam *M*.

---

[1] The first tribune is, of course, Gracchus himself.

[2] Neither the vow nor the contribution has been mentioned before. The celebration of the games is reported at xxii. 1 below.

[3] The denomination of the coins is omitted. If the allowance was 80,000 sesterces, as is probable, only twenty pounds of gold would be used; 80,000 *denarii* would amount to eighty pounds. In either case, one wonders what became of the balance. The senate's decree probably did not forbid the expenditure of private funds in addition.

entrusted to him by the Roman people, and entrusted for the purpose of rendering assistance to and protecting the liberty of private citizens, not of bolstering up the consular authority. Aburius, he said, did not even see that the result would be that tradition and posterity would have the story how in the same college one of two tribunes of the people had laid aside his own enmities for the sake of the state, the other had assumed and carried on those of another because they had been entrusted to him.[1] When the tribune, overcome by this criticism, had left the temple, after the question was raised by Serv. Sulpicius, praetor, the triumph was voted to Marcus Fulvius. When he had thanked the conscript Fathers, he went on to say that he had vowed the Great Games to Jupiter Optimus Maximus on the day when he had captured Ambracia, that for this purpose a hundred pounds of gold had been contributed by the cities;[2] he requested that, from this money which he had planned to display in his triumph and then deposit in the treasury, this particular sum should, by their order, be kept separate. The senate ordered the college of pontiffs to be consulted whether it was necessary to spend this entire sum on the games. When the pontiffs had replied that from the point of view of religion it was immaterial how much should be spent on the games, the senate granted permission to Fulvius for whatever amount he should spend, provided that he did not exceed a total of eighty thousand sesterces.[3] He had decided to triumph in the month of January; but when he had heard that the consul Marcus Aemilius, having received a letter from Marcus Aburius about the withdrawal of the veto, was himself coming to Rome B.C. 187

A.U.C. 567 impediendum triumphum Romam venientem aegrum
in via substitisse, ne plus in triumpho certaminum
quam in bello haberet, praetulit triumphi diem.
13 Triumphavit ante diem decimum Kal. Ianuarias de
14 Aetolis et de Cephallania. Aureae coronae centum
duodecim pondo ante currum latae[1] sunt; argenti
pondo milia octoginta tria, auri pondo ducenta quad-
15 raginta tria, tetrachma Attica centum octodecim
milia, Philippei nummi duodecim milia trecenti[2]
viginti duo, signa aenea septingenta octoginta
quinque, signa marmorea ducenta triginta, arma tela
16 cetera spolia hostium, magnus numerus, ad hoc cata-
pultae, ballistae, tormenta omnis generis; duces aut
Aetoli et Cephallanes aut regii ab Antiocho ibi relicti
17 ad viginti septem. Multos eo die priusquam in urbem
inveheretur in circo Flaminio tribunos praefectos
equites centuriones, Romanos sociosque, donis militaribus donavit. Militibus ex praeda vicenos quinos[3]
denarios divisit, duplex centurioni, triplex equiti.

VI. Iam consularium comitiorum appetebat tempus; quibus quia M. Aemilius, cuius sortis ea cura

[1] latae ς: delatae *M*.
[2] trecenti *Madvig*: trecenta *M*: quadringenti ς.
[3] vicenos quinos *ed. Aldina*: uiginti quinque *M*: quinos vicenos ς.

---

[1] It is always uncertain whether *pondo* should be read in such passages, and I have followed in each case what seems to be the most trustworthy reading of the MSS. The additional complication exists in this instance, that Livy has already recorded (XXXVIII. ix. 13 above) the gift of a single crown weighing 150 pounds, but we do not know that this was to be carried in the procession, nor whether the gift for the games should be included. See also the note to the passage just quoted.

to hinder the triumph, but had been detained on the way by illness, he advanced the date, lest he have more strife in the triumph than in the war. He triumphed the tenth day before the Kalends of January over the Aetolians and over Cephallania. Golden crowns of one hundred and twelve pounds[1] in weight were carried before his car; he displayed also eighty-three thousand pounds of silver, two hundred and forty-three pounds of gold, one hundred and eighteen thousand Attic four-drachma pieces, twelve thousand three hundred and twenty-two coins called "Philippei,"[2] bronze statues to the number of seven hundred and eighty-five and two hundred and thirty of marble, weapons, javelins and other spoils taken from the enemy, in great quantities, besides catapults, ballistae and every variety of artillery; there marched also generals, whether Aetolians and Cephallanians or commanders of the king left there by Antiochus, to the number of twenty-seven. On that day, before he rode into the City, in the Circus Flaminius,[3] he presented many tribunes, prefects, cavalrymen and centurions, Romans and allies, with military decorations.[4] To the soldiers, out of the booty, he gave twenty-five *denarii* each, twice that amount to each centurion, and thrice to each cavalryman. B.C. 187

VI. The time for the consular elections was now at hand; for these, since Marcus Aemilius, to whom

[2] Cf. XXXVII. lix. 4 and the note.

[3] This circus was probably the only enclosure of suitable size which lay outside the *pomerium*.

[4] The generosity of Fulvius in this respect was severely criticized by Cato (Gellius V. vi. 24–25, where a fragment of a speech is preserved).

A.U.C. 567 erat, occurrere non potuit, C. Flaminius Romam
venit. Ab eo creati [1] consules Sp. Postumius Albinus
2 Q. Marcius Philippus. Praetores inde facti T.
Maenius P. Cornelius Sulla C. Calpurnius Piso M.
Licinius Lucullus C. Aurelius Scaurus L. Quinctius
Crispinus.

3 Extremo anni, magistratibus iam creatis, ante diem
tertium nonas Martias Cn. Manlius Volso de Gallis
4 qui Asiam incolunt triumphavit. Serius ei tri-
umphandi causa fuit, ne Q. Terentio Culleone praetore causam lege Petillia diceret et incendio alieni
5 iudicii quo L. Scipio damnatus erat conflagraret, eo
infensioribus in se quam in illum iudicibus quod
disciplinam militarem severe ab eo conservatam
successorem ipsum omni genere licentiae corrupisse
6 fama attulerat. Neque ea sola infamiae erant, quae
in provincia procul ab oculis facta narrabantur, sed
ea etiam magis quae in militibus eius cotidie aspicie-
7 bantur. Luxuriae enim peregrinae origo ab exercitu
Asiatico invecta in urbem est. Ii primum [2] lectos
aeratos, vestem stragulam pretiosam, plagulas et alia
textilia, et quae tum magnificae supellectilis habe-
bantur, monopodia et abacos Romam advexerunt.

[1] creati ς : decreti *M*.
[2] ii primum *Gelenius* : inde primum ς.

---

[1] It may be accidental that so many of the names on this list are relatively unfamiliar; it may also be true that conditions had made the Romans somewhat distrustful of the families that had been exercising political and military leadership and had encouraged them to look elsewhere for talent.

[2] Manlius probably had good reason to fear prosecution, especially before Culleo, who had displayed his inflexibility in the trial of Scipio. Until his triumph Manlius was outside the City and exempt from prosecution by virtue of his proconsulship; in the brief interval between the triumph and

this responsibility had fallen by lot, was unable to come, Gaius Flaminius came to Rome. He announced the choice of Spurius Postumius Albinus and Quintus Marcius Philippus as consuls. Then the praetors were elected, Titus Maenius, Publius Cornelius Sulla, Gaius Calpurnius Piso, Marcus Licinius Lucullus, Gaius Aurelius Scaurus, Lucius Quinctius Crispinus.[1] B.C. 187

At the end of the year, when the new magistrates had already been elected, on the third day before the Nones of March, Gnaeus Manlius Volso triumphed over the Gauls who inhabit Asia. His purpose in delaying so long to celebrate his triumph was to avoid pleading his cause under the Petillian law before the praetor Quintus Terentius Culleo and being himself consumed in the flames of another's trial, in which Lucius Scipio had been condemned,[2] seeing that the jurors were far more hostile to him than to Scipio because it was rumoured that he, when he succeeded Scipio, had ruined the military discipline, strictly maintained by his predecessor, by permitting every kind of licence. Nor was this only a matter of unfavourable report of what was said to have happened in the province, far from their eyes, but still more of what was apparent every day among his soldiers. For the beginnings of foreign luxury were introduced into the City by the army from Asia. They for the first time imported into Rome couches of bronze, valuable robes for coverlets, tapestries and other products of the loom, and what at that time was considered luxurious furniture—tables with one

the Ides (when a new praetor would succeed Culleo) a trial could not be completed. See the notes to XXXVIII. liv. 3; 7; lviii. 12 above.

A.U.C. 567

8 Tunc psaltriae sambucistriaeque et convivalia alia ludorum oblectamenta addita epulis; epulae quoque ipsae et cura et sumptu maiore apparari coeptae.
9 Tum coquus, vilissimum antiquis mancipium et aestimatione et usu, in pretio esse, et quod ministerium fuerat, ars haberi coepta. Vix tamen illa, quae tum conspiciebantur, semina erant futurae luxuriae.

VII. In triumpho tulit Cn. Manlius coronas aureas ducentas duodecim,[1] argenti pondo ducenta viginti milia, auri[2] pondo duo milia centum tria, tetrachmum[3] Atticum centum viginti septem milia, cistophori ducenta quinquaginta, Philippeorum[4] aureorum
2 nummorum sedecim milia trecentos viginti; et arma spoliaque multa Gallica carpentis travecta, duces hostium duo et quinquaginta ducti ante currum. Militibus quadragenos binos denarios divisit, duplex centurioni, triplex in equites, et stipendium duplex
3 dedit;[5] multi omnium ordinum donati militaribus donis currum secuti sunt. Carminaque a militibus ea in imperatorem dicta, ut facile appareret in ducem indulgentem ambitiosumque ea dici, triumphum esse

[1] ducentas duodecim *Lentz*: ducentas duodecim pondo *M*: decem duas ς: CC decem pondo duas *edd. vett.*

[2] auri *Gelenius*: argenti ς.

[3] tetrachmum *Bekker*: tetracinum *et similia* ς.

[4] Philippeorum *edd. vett.*: philipporum ς.

[5] dedit *Madvig*: in pedites dedit ς.

---

[1] Pliny (XXXIV. 14) derives from the annalist Piso a similar list of articles of luxury first imported at this time. It does not necessarily follow that Piso was Livy's source also.

[2] He probably includes dancing-girls, buffoons, and the like.

pedestal and sideboards.[1] Then female players of the lute and the harp and other festal delights of entertainments[2] were made adjuncts to banquets; the banquets themselves, moreover, began to be planned with both greater care and greater expense. At that time the cook, to the ancient Romans the most worthless of slaves, both in their judgment of values and in the use they made of him, began to have value, and what had been merely a necessary service came to be regarded as an art. Yet those things which were then looked upon as remarkable were hardly even the germs of the luxury to come. B.C. 187

VII. In his triumph Gnaeus Manlius carried two hundred and twelve golden crowns, two hundred and twenty thousand pounds of silver, two thousand one hundred and three pounds of gold, of Attic four-drachma pieces one hundred and twenty-seven thousand, of *cistophori*[3] two hundred and fifty thousand, of gold *Philippei* sixteen thousand three hundred and twenty; there were also arms and many Gallic spoils transported in carts, and fifty-two leaders of the enemy led before his car. To the soldiers he gave forty-two *denarii* each, twice that amount to each centurion and thrice to each cavalryman, and he gave them also double pay;[4] many of all ranks, presented with military decorations, followed his car. Such songs were sung by the soldiers about their commander that it was easily seen that they were sung about an indulgent leader who sought popularity, and that the triumph was

[3] Cf. XXXVII. xlvi. 3.

[4] The grammar of the sentence is peculiar and there is corruption in the text. I have given what seems to be the most reasonable translation.

A.U.C. 567 4 militari magis favore quam populari celebrem. Sed
ad populi quoque gratiam conciliandam amici Manlii
5 valuerunt; quibus adnitentibus senatus consultum
factum est ut, ex pecunia quae in triumpho translata
esset, stipendium collatum a populo in publicum quod
eius solutum antea non esset solveretur. Vicenos
quinos et semisses in milia aeris quaestores urbani
cum fide et cura solverunt.

6 Per idem tempus tribuni militum duo ex duabus
Hispaniis cum litteris C. Atinii et L.[1] Manlii qui eas
7 provincias obtinebant venerunt. Ex iis litteris cognitum est Celtiberos Lusitanosque in armis esse et sociorum agros populari. De ea re consultationem integram senatus ad novos magistratus reiecit.

8 Ludis Romanis eo anno, quos [2] P. Cornelius Cethegus A. Postumius Albinus faciebant, malus in circo
instabilis in signum Pollentiae procidit atque id
9 deiecit. Ea religione moti patres et diem unum
adiciendum ludorum censuerunt et signa duo pro
10 uno reponenda et novum auratum faciendum. Et
plebeii ludi ab aedilibus C. Sempronio Blaeso et M.
Furio Lusco diem unum instaurati sunt.

[1] L. *ed. Frobeniana* 1535 : cn. ς.
[2] quos *edd. vett.* : quo ς.

---

[1] This *stipendium* may have been some extraordinary tax, paid in an emergency and regarded as a loan to the treasury, analogous to the contribution mentioned in XXVI. xxxvi. 8 (cf. XXIX. xvi. 1; XXXI. xiii. 2–9; XXXIII. xlii. 2). Nothing further is known of it, and no translation can be more than a guess.

[2] It is not clear whether this is a final payment, a payment on account, or a favourable composition with creditors.

marked more by the applause of the military than of the civil population. But the friends of Manlius were able to curry favour with the people as well; at their instance a decree of the senate was passed that, with regard to the tax[1] which had been paid by the people into the treasury, whatever portion of this was in arrears should be paid out of the money which had been carried in the triumph. The city quaestors, displaying fidelity and diligence, paid twenty-five and one-half *asses* each per thousand *asses*.[2] B.C. 187

About the same time two tribunes of the soldiers arrived from the two Spains, bringing dispatches from Gaius Atinius and Lucius Manlius, who were holding those provinces.[3] From these letters it was learned that the Celtiberians and Lusitanians were in arms and were ravaging the lands of the allies. The decision regarding the whole question was left to the new magistrates by the senate.

At the Roman Games that year, which Publius Cornelius Cethegus and Aulus Postumius Albinus gave, a badly-fixed mast[4] in the Circus fell on the statue of Pollentia and shattered it. The Fathers, disturbed by this omen, voted, first, that one day should be added to the Games, and, second, that two statues should be set up in place of one and the new one gilded. The Plebeian Games too were repeated, to the extent of one day, by the plebeian aediles Gaius Sempronius Blaesus and Marcus Furius Luscus.

[3] Cf. XXXVIII. xxxv. 10 above for their assignment.

[4] Probably this was a permanent mast set up on the *spina*; less probably it was one of the spars which supported the awnings.

A.U.C. 568

VIII. Insequens annus Sp. Postumium Albinum et Q. Marcium Philippum consules ab exercitu bellorumque et provinciarum cura ad intestinae coniura-
2 tionis vindictam avertit. Praetores provincias sortiti sunt, T. Maenius urbanam, M. Licinius Lucullus inter cives et peregrinos, C. Aurelius Scaurus Sardiniam, P. Cornelius Sulla Siciliam, L. Quinctius Crispinus Hispaniam citeriorem, C. Calpurnius Piso
3 Hispaniam ulteriorem. Consulibus ambobus quaestio de clandestinis coniurationibus decreta est. Graecus ignobilis in Etruriam primum venit nulla cum arte earum, quas multas ad animorum corporumque cultum nobis eruditissima omnium gens invexit, sacri-
4 ficulus et vates; nec is qui aperta religione, propalam et quaestum et disciplinam profitendo, animos errore imbueret, sed occultorum et nocturnorum antistes
5 sacrorum. Initia erant quae primo paucis tradita sunt deinde vulgari coepta sunt per viros mulieresque. Additae voluptates religioni vini et epularum, quo
6 plurium animi illicerentur. Cum vinum animos incendisset,[1] et nox et mixti feminis mares, aetatis tenerae maioribus, discrimen omne pudoris exstinxissent, corruptelae primum omnis generis fieri coeptae, cum ad id quisque, quo natura pronioris libidinis
7 esset, paratam voluptatem haberet. Nec unum genus noxae, stupra promiscua ingenuorum feminarumque erant, sed falsi testes, falsa signa testamen-
8 taque [2] et indicia ex eadem officina exibant: venena

[1] animos incendisset *Madvig*: *om.* ς.
[2] testamentaque *Roever*: testimoniaque ς.

---

[1] Rome's treatment of the Christians illustrates her general attitude towards meetings conducted with any degree of concealment.

VIII. The following year diverted the consuls Spurius Postumius Albinus and Quintus Marcius Philippus from the army and the administration of wars and provinces to the suppression of an internal conspiracy. The praetors drew lots for their provinces, Titus Maenius receiving the city jurisdiction, Marcus Licinius Lucullus that between citizens and aliens, Gaius Aurelius Scaurus Sardinia, Publius Cornelius Sulla Sicily, Lucius Quinctius Crispinus Nearer Spain, Gaius Calpurnius Piso Farther Spain. To both consuls the investigation of secret conspiracies was decreed. A nameless Greek came first to Etruria, possessed of none of those many arts which the Greek people, supreme as it is in learning, brought to us in numbers for the cultivation of mind and body, but a dabbler in sacrifices and a fortune-teller; nor was he one who, by frankly disclosing his creed and publicly proclaiming both his profession and his system, filled minds with error, but a priest of secret rites performed by night.[1] There were initiatory rites which at first were imparted to a few, then began to be generally known among men and women. To the religious element in them were added the delights of wine and feasts, that the minds of a larger number might be attracted. When wine had inflamed their minds, and night and the mingling of males with females, youth with age, had destroyed every sentiment of modesty, all varieties of corruption first began to be practised, since each one had at hand the pleasure answering to that to which his nature was more inclined. There was not one form of vice alone, the promiscuous matings of free men and women, but perjured witnesses, forged seals and wills and evidence, all issued from this same B.C. 186

A.U.C. 568

indidem intestinaeque caedes, ita ut ne corpora quidem interdum ad sepulturam exstarent. Multa dolo, pleraque per vim audebantur. Occulebat vim quod prae ululatibus tympanorumque et cymbalorum strepitu nulla vox quiritantium inter stupra et caedes exaudiri poterat.

IX. Huius mali labes ex Etruria Romam veluti
contagione morbi penetravit. Primo urbis magnitudo capacior patientiorque talium malorum ea cela-
vit: tandem indicium hoc maxime modo ad Postu-
2 mium consulem pervenit. P. Aebutius, cuius pater
publico equo stipendia fecerat, pupillus relictus,
mortuis deinde tutoribus sub tutela Duroniae matris
3 et vitrici T. Sempronii Rutili educatus fuerat. Et
mater dedita viro erat et vitricus, quia tutelam ita
gesserat ut rationem reddere non posset, aut tolli
pupillum aut obnoxium sibi vinculo aliquo fieri cupie-
4 bat. Via una corruptelae Bacchanalia erant. Mater
adulescentem [1] appellat: se pro aegro eo vovisse ubi
primum convaluisset, Bacchis eum se initiaturam;
damnatam voti benignitate deum exsolvere id velle.
Decem dierum castimonia opus esse: decimo die
cenatum, deinde pure lautum in sacrarium deductu-

[1] adolescentem ς: adulescentulum *M*.

---

[1] He was an *eques equo publico*, receiving an annual allowance for the purchase and upkeep of his mounts.

[2] A *tutor* rendered to the court which appointed him an account of his administration of the property, at least when the ward came of age.

[3] A vow, to a Roman, created a quasi-contractual obligation, which was as effective as the sentence of a court: hence *damnatam voti*.

workshop: likewise poisonings and secret murders, so that at times not even the bodies were found for burial. Much was ventured by craft, more by violence. This violence was concealed because amid the howlings and the crash of drums and cymbals no cry of the sufferers could be heard as the debauchery and murders proceeded.

IX. The destructive power of this evil spread from Etruria to Rome like the contagion of a pestilence. At first the size of the City, with abundant room and tolerance for such evils, concealed it: at length information came to the consul Postumius in about this manner. Publius Aebutius, whose father had performed his military service with a horse supplied by the state,[1] was left a ward, and later, on the death of his guardians, was brought under the tutelage of his mother Duronia and his stepfather Titus Sempronius Rutilus. His mother was devoted to her husband, and his stepfather, who had so administered his guardianship that he could not render an accounting,[2] desired that the ward should either be done away with or be made dependent upon them by some tie. The one method of corrupting him was through the Bacchanalia. The mother addressed the young man: while he was sick, she said, she had vowed for him that as soon as he had recovered she would initiate him into the Bacchic rites; being compelled, by the kindness of the gods, to pay her vow,[3] she wished to fulfil it. For ten days, she continued, he must practise continence: on the tenth day she would conduct him to the banquet and then, after ritual purification,[4] to the shrine. There was a well-

[4] Paulus Diaconus (p. 248) defines *pure lautum* as *aqua pura lautum*.

A.U.C. 568
5 ram. Scortum nobile libertina Hispala Faecenia, non
digna quaestu cui ancillula adsuerat, etiam postquam
6 manumissa erat, eodem se genere tuebatur. Huic
consuetudo iuxta vicinitatem cum Aebutio fuit,
minime adulescentis aut[1] rei aut famae damnosa:
ultro enim amatus appetitusque erat et maligne
omnia praebentibus suis meretriculae munificentia
7 sustinebatur. Quin eo processerat consuetudine
capta ut post patroni mortem, quia in nullius manu
erat, tutore ab tribunis et praetore petito, cum testa-
mentum faceret, unum Aebutium institueret heredem.

X. Haec amoris pignora cum essent, nec quicquam
secretum alter ab altero haberent, per iocum adulescens vetat eam mirari, si per aliquot noctes secu-
2 buisset: religionis se causa ut voto pro valetudine
sua facto liberetur, Bacchis initiari velle. Id ubi
mulier audivit, perturbata "dii meliora!" inquit:
mori et sibi et illi satius esse quam id faceret; et in
caput eorum detestari minas periculaque, qui id
3 suasissent. Admiratus cum verba tum perturbatio-
nem tantam adulescens parcere exsecrationibus iubet:
4 matrem id sibi adsentiente vitrico imperasse. "Vi-

[1] aut *ed. Frobeniana* 1535 : *om. Mς*.

---

[1] *i.e.*, worthy of something better.

[2] A freedwoman was subject to the *manus* of her patron, who was often her former owner. Faecenia had no patron and no relative who would naturally assume the responsibilities of guardianship, and could therefore petition the praetor and the tribunes jointly for the appointment of a *tutor*, whose approval was necessary to the performance of any legal act, such as making a will.

known courtesan, a freedwoman named Hispala Faecenia, not worthy[1] of the occupation to which, while still a mere slave, she had accustomed herself, and even after she had been manumitted she maintained herself in the same way. Between her and Aebutius, since they were neighbours, an intimacy developed, not at all damaging either to the young man's fortune or to his reputation; for he had been loved and sought out without any effort on his part, and, since his own relatives made provision for all his needs on a very small scale, he was maintained by the generosity of the courtesan. More than that, she had gone so far, under the influence of their intimacy, that, after the death of her patron, since she was under the legal control of no one, having petitioned the tribunes and the praetor for a guardian, when she made her will she had instituted Aebutius as her sole heir.[2] B.C. 186

X. Since there were these bonds of affection between them, and neither had any secrets from the other, the young man jestingly told her not to be surprised if he were away from her for several nights: as a matter of religious duty, he said, to free himself from a vow made for the sake of his health, he intended to be initiated in the Bacchic rites. When the woman heard this she exclaimed in great distress, "The gods forbid!" She said that it would be much better both for him and for her to die rather than do that; and she called down curses and vengeance upon the heads of those persons who had given him this counsel. Wondering both at her language and at her so manifest distress, the young man bade her spare her curses: it was his mother, he said, with the approval of his stepfather, who had ordered it.

A.U.C. 568 tricus ergo" inquit "tuus—matrem enim insimulare forsitan fas non sit—pudicitiam famam spem vitamque tuam perditum ire hoc facto properat."
5 Eo magis mirabundo quaerentique quid rei esset, pacem veniamque precata deorum dearumque, si coacta caritate eius silenda enuntiasset, ancillam se ait dominae comitem id sacrarium intrasse, liberam
6 numquam eo accessisse. Scire corruptelarum omnis generis eam officinam esse; et iam biennio constare
7 neminem initiatum ibi maiorem annis viginti. Ut quisque introductus sit, velut victimam tradi sacerdotibus. Eos deducere in locum, qui circumsonet ululatibus cantuque symphoniae et cymbalorum et tympanorum pulsu, ne vox quiritantis,[1] cum per vim
8 stuprum inferatur, exaudiri possit. Orare inde atque obsecrare ut eam rem quocumque modo discuteret nec se eo praecipitaret, ubi omnia infanda patienda
9 primum, deinde facienda essent. Neque ante dimisit eum quam fidem dedit adulescens ab his sacris se temperaturum.

XI. Postquam domum venit, et mater mentionem intulit, quid eo die, quid deinceps ceteris, quae ad sacra pertinerent, faciendum esset, negat eorum se quicquam facturum nec initiari sibi in animo esse.
2 Aderat sermoni vitricus. Confestim mulier exclamat Hispalae concubitu carere eum decem noctes non

[1] quiritantis *ed. Parisina* 1513: quaeritantis ς.

"Your stepfather, then," she replied, "is making haste—for perhaps it is not right to accuse your mother—to destroy in this way your virtue, your reputation and your life." As he marvelled the more and asked her what she meant, beseeching gods and goddesses for peace and forgiveness if, compelled by her love for him, she had declared what should be concealed, she told him that while she was a slave she had attended her mistress to that shrine, but that as a free woman she had never visited it. She knew, she said, that it was the factory of all sorts of corruptions; and it was known that for two years now no one had been initiated who had passed the age of twenty years. As each was introduced, he became a sort of victim for the priests. They, she continued, would lead him to a place which would ring with howls and the song of a choir and the beating of cymbals and drums, that the voice of the sufferer, when his virtue was violently attacked, might not be heard. Then she begged and besought him to put an end to this matter in any way he could and not to plunge into a situation where all disgraceful practices would have first to be endured and then performed. Nor would she let him go until the young man gave her his promise that he would have nothing to do with those mysteries. B.C. 186

XI. When he came home and his mother began to tell him what he had to do that day and on the following days in connection with the rites, he informed her that he would do none of them and that it was not his intention to be initiated. His stepfather was present at the interview. Straightway the woman exclaimed that he could not do without his mistress Hispala for ten nights; infected with the

A.U.C. 568 posse; illius excetrae[1] delenimentis et venenis imbutum nec parentis nec vitrici nec deorum verecundiam habere. Iurgantes hinc mater, hinc vitricus
3 cum quattuor eum servis domo exegerunt. Adulescens inde ad Aebutiam se amitam contulit, causamque ei, cur esset a matre eiectus, narravit, deinde ex auctoritate eius postero die ad consulem Postu-
4 mium arbitris remotis rem detulit. Consul post diem tertium redire ad se iussum dimisit; ipse Sulpiciam gravem feminam, socrum suam, percunctatus est,
5 ecquam anum Aebutiam ex Aventino nosset. Cum ea nosse probam et antiqui moris feminam respondisset, opus esse sibi ea conventa dixit: mitteret nun-
6 tium ad eam, ut veniret. Aebutia accita ad Sulpiciam venit et consul paulo post, velut forte intervenisset, sermonem de Aebutio fratris eius filio infert.
7 Lacrimae mulieri obortae et miserari casum adulescentis coepit, qui spoliatus fortunis, a quibus minime oporteret, apud se tunc esset, eiectus a matre, quod probus adulescens—dii propitii essent—obscenis, ut fama esset, sacris initiari nollet.

XII. Satis exploratum de Aebutio ratus consul non vanum auctorem esse, Aebutia dimissa socrum rogat ut Hispalam indidem ex Aventino libertinam, non ignotam viciniae, arcesseret ad sese: eam quoque
2 esse quae[2] percunctari vellet. Ad cuius nuntium

[1] excetrae *ed. Frobeniana* 1531 : exterae ς.
[2] quae *ed. Frobeniana* 1531 : quam ς.

---

[1] The prayer is due to the fear that the compliment might provoke the jealousy of the gods.

enchantments and poisons of that vampire, he had no respect for his mother or his stepfather or yet the gods. Berating him thus, his mother on one side, his stepfather with four slaves on the other, drove him from the house. The young man thereupon went to his aunt Aebutia and explained to her the reason why his mother had driven him out, and on her recommendation the following day reported the affair to the consul Postumius with no witnesses present. The consul sent him away with instructions to return the third day; he himself asked his mother-in-law Sulpicia, a woman of high character, whether she was acquainted with an elderly woman, Aebutia, from the Aventine. When she replied that she knew that she was a virtuous woman of the old style, he said that he felt the need of an interview with her: Sulpicia should send her a message to come. Aebutia, summoned by Sulpicia, came, and a little later the consul, as if he had come in by chance, brought in an allusion to Aebutius, the son of her brother. Tears flowed from the woman's eyes, and she began to bewail the fate of the young man who was robbed of his estate by those who should least of all have treated him thus, and who was then at her house, driven from home by his mother because the virtuous youth—might the gods be gracious [1]—refused to be initiated into rites which, if reports were to be believed, were full of lewdness. B.C. 186

XII. The consul, thinking that he had learned enough about Aebutius to trust his story, sent Aebutia away and asked his mother-in-law to summon to her Hispala, also from the Aventine, a freedwoman and no stranger in the neighbourhood: he wished to ask her also certain questions. Hispala,

A.U.C. 568

perturbata Hispala, quod ad tam nobilem et gravem
feminam ignara causae arcesseretur, postquam lic-
tores in vestibulo turbamque consularem et consulem
3 ipsum conspexit, prope exanimata est. In interiorem partem aedium abductam socru adhibita consul,
si vera dicere inducere in animum posset, negat
perturbari debere; fidem vel a Sulpicia, tali femina,
4 vel ab se acciperet; expromeret sibi, quae in luco
Stimulae [1] Bacchanalibus in sacro nocturno solerent
5 fieri. Hoc ubi audivit, tantus pavor tremorque
omnium membrorum mulierem cepit, ut diu hiscere
6 non posset. Tandem confirmata puellam admodum
se ancillam initiatam cum domina ait: aliquot annis,
7 ex quo manumissa sit, nihil quid ibi fiat scire. Iam
id ipsum consul laudare, quod initiatam se non in-
fitiaretur: sed et cetera eadem fide expromeret.
8 Neganti ultra quicquam scire, non eandem dicere, si
coarguatur ab alio, ac per se [2] fatenti veniam aut
gratiam fore; eum sibi omnia exposuisse, qui ab illa
audisset.

XIII. Mulier haud dubie, id quod erat, Aebutium
indicem arcani rata esse, ad pedes Sulpiciae procidit,
2 et eam primo orare coepit, ne mulieris libertinae cum
amatore sermonem in rem non seriam modo sed capi-

[1] Stimulae *Gronovius*: simili *et* simulae *et* simul ς.
[2] per se *ed. Moguntina*: *om.* ς.

---

[1] Stimula is identified with Semele, the mother of Bacchus. The name is obviously appropriate. The grove was near the Tiber and the Aventine.

alarmed by her message, because without knowing the reason she was summoned to so important and respected a woman, when she saw the lictors in the vestibule and the consul's retinue and the consul himself, almost swooned. Conducting her into the inner part of the house, with his mother-in-law present, the consul told her that if she could bring herself to tell the truth she had no cause to feel alarmed; she would receive a pledge either from Sulpicia, a woman of such standing, or from himself; she should state to them what rites were usually performed in the nocturnal orgies at the Bacchanalia in the grove of Stimula.[1] When she heard this, such fear and trembling seized the woman in all her limbs that for a long time she could not open her mouth. Being at length restored, she said that when quite young and a slave she had been initiated with her mistress; that for many years after her manumission she had known nothing of what went on there. Then the consul praised her on this ground, that she had not denied that she had been initiated; but she was to tell, under the same pledge, the rest as well. When she insisted that she knew nothing more, he told her that she would not receive the same forgiveness or consideration if she were convicted by the evidence of someone else as if she had confessed of her own accord; the man, he added, who had heard it from her had told him the whole story. B.C. 186

XIII. The woman, thinking without a doubt, as was indeed the fact, that Aebutius had revealed the secret, threw herself at the feet of Sulpicia, and at first began to plead with her not to try to turn the chatter of a freedwoman with her lover into something that was not merely serious but even fatal:

A.U.C. 568
talem etiam verti vellet: se terrendi eius causa, non
3 quod sciret quicquam, ea locutam esse. Hic Postumius accensus ira tum quoque ait eam cum Aebutio
se amatore cavillari credere, non in domo gravissimae
feminae et cum consule loqui. Et Sulpicia attollere
paventem, simul illam [1] adhortari, simul iram generi
4 lenire. Tandem confirmata, multum incusata per-
fidia Aebutii, qui optime de ipso [2] meritae talem
5 gratiam rettulisset, magnum sibi metum deorum,
quorum occulta initia enuntiaret, maiorem multo
dixit hominum esse, qui se indicem manibus suis
6 discerpturi essent. Itaque hoc se Sulpiciam, hoc
consulem orare, ut se extra Italiam aliquo ablegarent,[3] ubi reliquum vitae degere tuto posset.
7 Bono animo esse iubere eam consul et sibi curae fore
8 dicere ut Romae tuto habitaret. Tum Hispala
originem sacrorum expromit. Primo sacrarium id
feminarum fuisse, nec quemquam eo virum admitti
solitum. Tres in anno statos [4] dies habuisse, quibus
interdiu Bacchis initiarentur; sacerdotes in vicem
9 matronas creari solitas. Pacullam Anniam Cam-
panam sacerdotem omnia, tamquam deum monitu,
immutasse: nam et viros eam primam filios suos
initiasse, Minium et Herennium Cerrinios; et nocturnum sacrum ex diurno, et pro tribus in anno
diebus quinos singulis mensibus dies initiorum fecisse.

[1] illam ς: etiam *M*.
[2] de ipso *Madvig*: in eo ipso ς.
[3] ablegarent ς: amandarent *M*.
[4] statos *Gelenius*: statutos ς.

---

[1] One thinks of the *Bacchae* of Euripides.

she had spoken thus for the purpose of frightening him, not because she knew anything. At this point Postumius, inflamed with wrath, said that she believed even then that she was jesting with her lover Aebutius, and not speaking in the house of a most respectable matron and in the presence of a consul. Sulpicia too lifted up the terror-stricken woman, and at the same time encouraged her and mollified the anger of her son-in-law. At length regaining her self-control, and complaining much of the treachery of Aebutius, who had returned such gratitude to one who deserved so well of him, she declared that she feared greatly the wrath of the gods whose hidden mysteries she was to reveal, but far more the wrath of the men who would, if she informed against them, with their own hands tear her limb from limb. Accordingly she begged Sulpicia and the consul that they would banish her somewhere outside Italy, where she could pass the rest of her life in safety. The consul bade her be of good cheer and assured her that it would be his responsibility to see that she could safely live in Rome. Then Hispala set forth the origin of the mysteries. At first, she said, it was a ritual for women,[1] and it was the custom that no man should be admitted to it. There had been three days appointed each year on which they held initiations into the Bacchic rites by day; it was the rule to choose the matrons in turn as priestesses. Paculla Annia, a Campanian, she said, when priestess, had changed all this as if by the advice of the gods; for she had been the first to initiate men, her sons, Minius and Herennius Cerrinius; she had held the rites by night and not by day, and instead of a mere three days a year she had established five days of initiation in every month. B.C. 186

A.U.C. 568 10 Ex quo in promiscuo sacra sint et permixti viri
feminis, et noctis licentia accesserit, nihil ibi facinoris,
nihil flagitii praetermissum. Plura virorum inter sese
11 quam feminarum esse stupra. Si qui minus patientes
dedecoris sint et pigriores ad facinus, pro victimis
immolari. Nihil nefas ducere, hanc summam inter
12 eos religionem esse. Viros, velut mente capta, cum
iactatione fanatica corporis vaticinari; matronas
Baccharum habitu crinibus sparsis cum ardentibus
facibus decurrere ad Tiberim, demissasque in aquam
faces, quia vivum sulpur cum calce insit, integra
13 flamma efferre. Raptos a diis homines dici, quos
machinae illigatos ex conspectu in abditos specus
abripiant: eos esse, qui aut coniurare aut sociari
14 facinoribus aut stuprum pati noluerint. Multitudinem ingentem, alterum iam prope populum esse;
in his nobiles quosdam viros feminasque. Biennio
proximo institutum esse, ne quis maior viginti annis
initiaretur: captari aetates et erroris et stupri
patientes.

XIV. Peracto indicio advoluta rursus genibus pre-
2 ces easdem, ut se ablegaret, repetivit. Consul rogat
socrum ut aliquam partem aedium vacuam faceret

---

[1] The torches probably contained the elements mentioned in the form of a mixture of free sulphur and calcium sulphate, which is still to be found in Italy. A torch of this composition, if burning well, would not be extinguished by a brief or partial immersion in water, so that the Bacchanals could perform the feat mentioned if they were reasonably swift in their movements. Calcium sulphate will not burn; free elementary sulphur burns, and we should probably translate *vivum* as "free" or "elementary" and therefore "burnable." But it is rather remarkable that Livy, who was not a scientist, should have approached scientific fact so closely. I am indebted for this information to Dr. E. Ward Tillotson,

From the time that the rites were performed in common, men mingling with women and the freedom of darkness added, no form of crime, no sort of wrongdoing, was left untried. There were more lustful practices among men with one another than among women. If any of them were disinclined to endure abuse or reluctant to commit crime, they were sacrificed as victims. To consider nothing wrong, she continued, was the highest form of religious devotion among them. Men, as if insane, with fanatical tossings of their bodies, would utter prophecies. Matrons in the dress of Bacchantes, with dishevelled hair and carrying blazing torches, would run down to the Tiber, and plunging their torches in the water (because they contained live sulphur mixed with calcium) would bring them out still burning.[1] Men were alleged to have been carried off by the gods who had been bound to a machine and borne away out of sight to hidden caves: they were those who had refused either to conspire or to join in the crimes or to suffer abuse. Their number, she said, was very great, almost constituting a second state; among them were certain men and women of high rank. Within the last two years it had been ordained that no one beyond the age of twenty years should be initiated: boys of such age were sought for as admitted both vice and corruption. B.C. 186

XIV. Having finished her testimony, again falling at their feet, she repeated the same prayers that they should banish her. The consul asked his mother-in-law to vacate some part of the house into

Assistant Director, and Dr. W. W. Duecker, Senior Industrial Fellow, both of the Mellon Institute of Industrial Research of the University of Pittsburgh.

A.U.C. 568 quo Hispala immigraret. Cenaculum super aedes datum est, scalis ferentibus in publicum obseratis,
3 aditu in aedes verso. Res omnes Faeceniae extemplo translatae et familia arcessita, et Aebutius migrare ad consulis clientem iussus.

Ita cum indices ambo in potestate essent, rem ad senatum Postumius defert, omnibus ordine expositis, quae delata primo, quae deinde ab se inquisita forent.
4 Patres pavor ingens cepit, cum publico nomine, ne quid[1] eae coniurationes coetusque nocturni fraudis occultae aut periculi importarent, tum privatim suorum cuiusque[2] vicem, ne quis adfinis ei noxae esset.
5 Censuit autem senatus gratias consuli agendas quod eam rem et cum singulari cura et sine ullo tumultu
6 investigasset. Quaestionem deinde de Bacchanalibus sacrisque nocturnis extra ordinem consulibus mandant; indicibus Aebutio ac Faeceniae ne fraudi ea res sit curare et alios indices praemiis invitare
7 iubent;[3] sacerdotes eorum sacrorum, seu viri seu feminae essent, non Romae modo sed per omnia fora et conciliabula conquiri, ut in consulum potestate essent; edici praeterea in urbe Roma et per totam
8 Italiam edicta mitti, ne quis qui Bacchis initiatus esset coisse aut convenisse sacrorum causa velit, neu quid talis rei divinae fecisse. Ante omnia ut quaestio

[1] ne quid *Gelenius*: quid ς.
[2] cuiusque *Doering*: quisque ς.
[3] iubent ς: iubet *M*.

[1] The *cenaculum* was an apartment on an upper floor, with its own stairway to the street. In this house there was also a stairway to the inside of the house.

which Hispala might move. An apartment above the house[1] was assigned to her, the stairs leading to the street being closed up and an approach to the house arranged. All the household goods of Faecenia were at once moved and her slaves summoned, and Aebutius was directed to move to the house of a client of the consul. B.C. 186

When both witnesses were thus available, Postumius laid the matter before the senate, everything being set forth in detail; first what had been reported, then what he had himself discovered. Great panic seized the Fathers, both on the public account, lest these conspiracies and gatherings by night might produce something of hidden treachery or danger, and privately, each for himself, lest anyone might be involved in the mischief. The senate, moreover, decreed that the consul should be thanked because he had investigated the affair both with great industry and without creating any confusion. Then the investigation of the Bacchanals and their nocturnal orgies they referred to the consuls, not as a part of their regular duties; they directed the consuls to see to it that the witnesses Aebutius and Faecenia did not suffer harm and to attract other informers by rewards; the priests of these rites, whether men or women, should be sought out, not only at Rome but through all the villages and communities, that they might be at the disposal of the consuls; that it should be proclaimed in addition in the city of Rome and that edicts should be sent through all Italy, that no one who had been initiated in the Bacchic rites should presume to assemble or come together for the purpose of celebrating those rites or to perform any such ritual. Before all, it

A.U.C. 568 de iis habeatur, qui coierint coniuraverintve, quo
9 stuprum flagitiumve inferretur. Haec senatus decrevit. Consules aedilibus curulibus imperarunt ut
sacerdotes eius sacri omnes conquirerent, compre-
hensosque libero conclavi ad quaestionem servarent;
aediles plebis viderent[1] ne qua sacra in operto fierent.
10 Triumviris capitalibus mandatum est ut vigilias dis-
ponerent per urbem servarentque ne qui nocturni
coetus fierent, utque ab incendiis caveretur; adiutores triumviris quinqueviri uls cis[2] Tiberim suae
quisque regionis aedificiis praeessent.

XV. Ad haec officia dimissis magistratibus consules
in rostra escenderunt, et contione advocata cum sollemne carmen precationis, quod praefari, priusquam
populum adloquantur, magistratus solent, peregisset
2 consul, ita coepit. "Nulli umquam contioni, Quirites,
tam non[3] solum apta sed etiam necessaria haec
sollemnis deorum comprecatio fuit, quae vos admo-
neret hos esse deos, quos colere venerari precarique
3 maiores vestri instituissent, non illos, qui pravis et
externis religionibus captas mentes velut furialibus
stimulis ad omne scelus et ad omnem libidinem
4 agerent. Equidem nec quid taceam nec quatenus

[1] viderent *Gronovius*: uidere ς.
[2] uls cis *Heusinger*: uti cis *et similia* ς.
[3] tam non ς: non *M*.

---

[1] They were minor magistrates charged with assisting in the maintenance of order.

[2] It is not known whether these two boards of five, one operating on the left bank (*cis*) of the river, the other on the right bank (*uls*), were regular magistrates or posses of civilians, organized in case of emergency. The form of the title, especially the ante-classical *uls* (standing for *ultra* much as *cis* is used for *citra*), suggests an early origin.

was decreed that an inquiry should be conducted regarding those persons who had come together or conspired for the commission of any immorality or crime. Such was the decree of the senate. The consuls ordered the curule aediles to search out all the priests of this cult and to keep them under surveillance, in free custody for the investigation; the plebeian aediles were to see to it that no celebration of the rites should be held in secret. The task was entrusted to the *triumviri capitales*[1] of placing guards through the City, of seeing that no night meetings were held, and of making provision against fire; as assistants to the *triumviri*, the *quinqueviri uls cis Tiberim*[2] were to stand guard each over the buildings of his own district. B.C. 186

XV. When the magistrates had been dispatched to these posts, the consuls mounted the Rostra and called an informal meeting[3] of the people, and, when the consul had finished the regular formula of prayer which magistrates are accustomed to pronounce before they address the people, he thus began: "Never for any assembly, citizens, has this formal prayer to the gods been not only so suitable but even so necessary, a prayer which reminds us that these are the gods whom our forefathers had appointed to be worshipped, to be venerated, to receive our prayers, not those gods who would drive our enthralled minds with vile and alien rites, as by the scourges of the Furies, to every crime and every lust. For my part, I do not discover what I should refrain from telling or how far I should speak out. If you

[3] Cf. XXXI. vii. 1 and the note. This meeting was called simply to hear the news about the conspiracy and the measures taken to suppress it.

A.U.C. 568

proloquar invenio. Si aliquid ignorabitis, ne locum
neglegentiae dem, si omnia nudavero, ne nimium
5 terroris offundam vobis vereor. Quidquid dixero,
minus quam pro atrocitate et magnitudine rei dictum
scitote esse: ut ad cavendum satis sit, dabitur opera
6 a nobis. Bacchanalia tota iam pridem Italia et nunc
per urbem etiam multis locis esse, non fama solum
accepisse vos sed crepitibus etiam ululatibusque nocturnis, qui personant tota urbe, certum habeo,
7 ceterum quae ea res sit, ignorare: alios deorum
aliquem cultum, alios concessum ludum et lasciviam
credere esse, et, qualecumque sit, ad paucos pertinere.
8 Quod ad multitudinem eorum attinet, si dixero multa
milia hominum esse, ilico necesse est exterreamini,
9 nisi adiunxero qui qualesque sint. Primum igitur
mulierum magna pars est, et is fons mali huiusce
fuit; deinde simillimi feminis mares, stuprati et
constupratores, fanatici, vigiliis,[1] vino, strepitibus
10 clamoribusque nocturnis attoniti. Nullas adhuc vires
coniuratio, ceterum incrementum ingens virium ha-
11 bet, quod in dies plures fiunt. Maiores vestri ne vos
quidem, nisi cum aut vexillo in arce posito comitiorum causa exercitus eductus[2] esset, aut plebi
concilium tribuni edixissent, aut aliquis ex magistratibus ad contionem vocasset, forte temere coire
voluerunt; et ubicumque multitudo esset, ibi et

[1] vigiliis *Crévier*: uigiles ς.
[2] eductus *Gruter*: edictus ς.

---

[1] For the military character of the *comitia centuriata*, of which the speaker is thinking, cf. XXXI. v. 9 and the note.

[2] In the *concilium plebis*; Livy generally seems not to distinguish between this and the *comitia tributa*, but the problem is too complicated for discussion here.

are left ignorant of anything, I fear that I shall leave room for carelessness; if I lay bare everything, that I shall scatter abroad an excess of terror. Whatever I shall have said, be sure that my words are less than the dreadfulness and the gravity of the situation: to take sufficient precautions will be our task. As to the Bacchanalia, I am assured that you have learned that they have long been celebrated all over Italy and now even within the City in many places, and that you have learned this not only from rumour but also from their din and cries at night, which echo throughout the City, but I feel sure that you do not know what this thing is: some believe that it is a form of worship of the gods, others that it is an allowable play and pastime, and, whatever it is, that it concerns only a few. As regards their number, if I shall say that there are many thousands of them, it cannot but be that you are terrified, unless I shall at once add to that who and of what sort they are. First, then, a great part of them are women, and they are the source of this mischief; then there are men very like the women, debauched and debauchers, fanatical, with senses dulled by wakefulness, wine, noise and shouts at night. The conspiracy thus far has no strength, but it has an immense source of strength in that they grow more numerous day by day. Your ancestors did not wish that even you should assemble casually and without reason, except when the standard was displayed on the citadel and the army was assembled for an election,[1] or the tribunes had announced a meeting of the plebeians,[2] or some of the magistrates had called you to an informal gathering; and wherever there was a crowd collected they thought that there should also be a

B.C. 186

A.U.C. 568

legitimum rectorem multitudinis censebant esse de-
12 bere. Quales primum nocturnos coetus, deinde pro-
13 miscuos mulierum ac virorum esse creditis? Si quibus aetatibus initientur mares sciatis, non misereat
vos eorum solum, sed etiam pudeat. Hoc sacra-
mento initiatos iuvenes milites faciendos censetis,
14 Quirites? His [1] ex obsceno sacrario eductis arma
committenda? Hi cooperti stupris suis alienisque
pro pudicitia coniugum ac liberorum vestrorum ferro
decernent?

XVI. "Minus tamen esset si flagitiis tantum
effeminati forent—ipsorum id magna ex parte
dedecus erat—a facinoribus manus, mentem a
2 fraudibus abstinuissent: numquam tantum malum
in re publica fuit, nec ad plures nec ad plura per-
tinens. Quidquid his annis libidine, quidquid fraude,
quidquid scelere peccatum est, ex illo uno sacrario
3 scitote ortum esse. Necdum [2] omnia in quae coniu-
rarunt edita facinora habent. Adhuc privatis noxiis,
quia nondum ad rem publicam [3] opprimendam satis
virium est, coniuratio sese impia tenet. Crescit et
serpit cotidie malum. Iam maius est quam ut [4]
capere id privata fortuna possit: ad summam rem
4 publicam spectat. Nisi praecavetis, Quirites, iam
huic diurnae, legitime ab consule vocatae, par
nocturna contio esse poterit. Nunc illi vos singuli
universos contionantes timent: iam ubi vos dilapsi
domos et in rura vestra eritis, illi coierint, consulta-

[1] his *edd. vett.*: iis ς.
[2] necdum *ed. Frobeniana* 1535: nec ς.
[3] rem publicam ς: po. romanum (*sic*) *M*.
[4] quam ut *Gelenius*: quam ς.

[1] One thinks of the caustic remarks of Cato on the participation of women in public affairs (XXXIV. ii.–iv. *passim*).

legal leader of the crowd. Of what sort do you think are, first, gatherings held by night, second, meetings of men and women in common?[1] If you knew at what ages males were initiated, you would feel not only pity for them but also shame. Do you think, citizens, that youths initiated by this oath should be made soldiers? That arms should be entrusted to men mustered from this foul shrine? Will men debased by their own debauchery and that of others fight to the death on behalf of the chastity of your wives and children? B.C. 186

XVI. "Yet it would be less serious if their wrongdoing had merely made them effeminate—that was in great measure their personal dishonour—and if they had kept their hands from crime and their thoughts from evil designs: never has there been so much evil in the state nor affecting so many people in so many ways. Whatever villainy there has been in recent years due to lust, whatever to fraud, whatever to crime, I tell you, has arisen from this one cult. Not yet have they revealed all the crimes to which they have conspired. Their impious compact still limits itself to private crimes, since as yet it does not have strength enough to crush the state. Daily the evil grows and creeps abroad. It is already too great to be purely a private matter: its objective is the control of the state. Unless you are on guard betimes, citizens, as we hold this meeting in the day-time, summoned by a consul, in accordance with law, so there can be one held at night. Now, as single individuals, they stand in fear of you, gathered here all together in this assembly: presently, when you have scattered to your homes and farms, they will have come together and they will take measures

A.U.C. 568

bunt de sua salute simul ac vestra pernicie: tum
5 singulis vobis universi timendi erunt. Optare igitur
unusquisque vestrum debet ut bona mens suis
omnibus fuerit. Si quem libido, si furor in illum
gurgitem abripuit, illorum eum, cum quibus in omne
flagitium et facinus coniuravit, non suum iudicet esse.
6 Ne quis etiam errore labatur vestrum, Quirites,[1]
non sum securus. Nihil enim in speciem fallacius
7 est quam prava religio. Ubi deorum numen prae-
tenditur sceleribus, subit animum timor, ne fraudibus
humanis vindicandis divini iuris aliquid immixtum
violemus. Hac vos religione innumerabilia decreta
pontificum, senatus consulta, haruspicum denique
8 responsa liberant. Quotiens hoc patrum avorumque
aetate negotium est magistratibus datum uti sacra
externa fieri vetarent, sacrificulos vatesque foro circo
urbe prohiberent, vaticinos[2] libros conquirerent
comburerentque, omnem disciplinam sacrificandi
9 praeterquam more Romano abolerent. Iudicabant
enim prudentissimi viri omnis divini humanique iuris
nihil aeque dissolvendae religionis esse, quam ubi
10 non patrio sed externo ritu sacrificaretur. Haec
vobis praedicenda ratus sum, ne qua superstitio
agitaret animos vestros, cum demolientes nos
Bacchanalia discutientesque nefarios coetus cer-

[1] Quirites *Weissenborn*: quidem *et* quod ς.
[2] vaticinos *ed. Frobeniana* 1531: uaticinios *M*: etacinios *et al.* ς.

for their own safety and at the same time for your destruction: then you, as isolated individuals, will have to fear them as a united body. Therefore each one of you should hope that all your friends have been endowed with sound minds. If lust, if madness has carried off anyone into that whirlpool, let each consider that such a person belongs, not to himself, but to those with whom he has conspired to every wickedness and wrong. I am not free of anxiety lest some even of you, citizens, may go astray through error. Nothing is more deceptive in appearance than a false religion. When the authority of the gods is put forward as a defence for crime, there steals upon the mind a fear lest in punishing human misdeeds we may violate something of divine law which became mixed up with them. From this scruple innumerable edicts of the pontiffs, decrees of the senate, and finally responses of the *haruspices* free you. How often, in the times of our fathers and our grandfathers, has the task been assigned to the magistrates of forbidding the introduction of foreign cults, of excluding dabblers in sacrifices and fortune-tellers from the Forum, the Circus, and the City, of searching out and burning books of prophecies, and of annulling every system of sacrifice except that performed in the Roman way. For men wisest in all divine and human law used to judge that nothing was so potent in destroying religion as where sacrifices were performed, not by native, but by foreign, ritual. I have thought that this warning should be given you, that no religious fear may disturb your minds when you see us suppressing the Bacchanalia and breaking up these nightly meetings. All these things, if the B.C. 186

A.U.C. 568

11 neretis. Omnia diis propitiis volentibusque faciemus;[1] qui quia suum numen sceleribus libidinibusque contaminari indigne ferebant, ex occultis ea tenebris in lucem extraxerunt, nec patefieri, ut impunita essent, sed ut vindicarentur et oppri-
12 merentur, voluerunt. Senatus quaestionem extra ordinem de ea re mihi collegaeque meo mandavit. Nos quae ipsis nobis agenda sunt impigre exsequemur; vigiliarum nocturnarum curam per urbem
13 minoribus magistratibus mandavimus. Vos quoque aequum est, quae vestra munia sunt, quo quisque loco positus erit, quod imperabitur, impigre praestare, et dare operam, ne quid fraude noxiorum periculi aut tumultus oriatur."

XVII. Recitari deinde senatus consulta iusserunt indicique praemium proposuerunt si quis quem ad
2 se deduxisset nomenve absentis detulisset. Qui nominatus profugisset, diem certam se finituros, ad quam nisi citatus respondisset, absens damnaretur. Si quis eorum, qui tum extra terram Italiam essent, nominaretur, ei laxiorem diem daturos, si venire ad
3 causam dicendam vellet. Edixerunt deinde ne quis quid fugae causa vendidisse neve emisse vellet; ne quis reciperet celaret ope ulla iuvaret fugientes.

4 Contione dimissa terror magnus urbe tota fuit, nec moenibus se tantum urbis aut finibus Romanis con-

[1] faciemus *Bauer*: ea faciemus ς.

gods are favourable and willing, we shall do; they, because they were indignant that their own divinity was being polluted by acts of crime and lust, have dragged these matters from darkness into the light, nor have they willed that they should be discovered in order that they might be unpunished, but that they might be coerced and suppressed. The senate has entrusted the investigation of this affair, by extraordinary assignment, to my colleague and myself. We shall zealously carry through what has to be done by ourselves; the responsibility of keeping watch through the City we have entrusted to the minor magistrates. For you too it is proper, whatever duties are assigned you, in whatever place each one is posted, to obey zealously and to see to it that no danger or confusion may arise from the treachery of criminals." B.C. 186

XVII. Then they ordered the decrees of the senate to be read and announced the reward to be paid the informer if anyone had brought any person before them or had reported the name of anyone who was absent. If anyone was named and had escaped, for him they would designate a fixed day, and, if he did not respond when summoned on that day, he would be condemned in his absence. If anyone was named of those who were at that time outside the land of Italy, they would fix a more elastic date if he wished to come to plead his cause. They next proclaimed that no one should venture to sell or buy anything for the purpose of flight; that no one should harbour, conceal, or in any wise aid the fugitives.

When the meeting was dismissed there was great panic in the whole City, nor was this confined only to the walls or the boundaries of Rome; but gradually

A.U.C. 568

tinuit, sed passim per totam Italiam, litteris hos-
pitum de senatus consulto et contione et edicto
5 consulum acceptis, trepidari coeptum est. Multi ea
nocte, quae diem insecuta est quo in contione res
palam facta est, custodiis circa portas positis fugientes
a triumviris comprehensi et reducti sunt: multorum
delata nomina. Quidam ex iis viri feminaeque
6 mortem sibi consciverunt. Coniurasse supra septem
milia virorum ac mulierum dicebantur. Capita autem
coniurationis constabat esse M. et C. Atinios[1] de
plebe Romana et Faliscum L. Opicernium et Minium
7 Cerrinium Campanum: ab his omnia facinora et
flagitia orta, eos maximos sacerdotes conditoresque
eius sacri esse. Data opera, ut primo quoque tempore comprehenderentur. Adducti ad consules
fassique de se nullam moram iudicio fecerunt.

XVIII. Ceterum tanta fuga ex urbe facta erat ut,
quia multis actiones[2] et res peribant, cogerentur
praetores T. Maenius et M. Licinius per senatum
res in diem tricesimum differre, donec quaestiones a
2 consulibus perficerentur. Eadem solitudo, quia
Romae non respondebant nec inveniebantur, quorum
nomina delata erant, coegit consules circa fora
3 proficisci ibique quaerere et iudicia exercere. Qui
tantum initiati erant et ex carmine sacro, praeeunte
verba sacerdote, precationes fecerant, quibus[3]

[1] M. et C. Atinios *Sigonius*: m. et l. catinios *M* m. catinium *et similia* ς.
[2] multis actiones *Gelenius*: multae santiones ς.
[3] quibus *H. J. Mueller*: in quibus ς.

---

[1] Cases could not be tried because of the absence of one or both parties to suits. The remedy adopted was the proclamation of a *iustitium* for thirty days: this suspended all ordinary public and private business.

through all Italy, as letters were received from their B.C. 186 friends concerning the decree of the senate, concerning the assembly and the edict of the consuls, the terror began to spread. Many during the night after the day when the revelation was made in the meeting were caught trying to escape and brought back by the guards whom the *triumviri* had posted at the gates: the names of many were reported. Certain of these, men and women, committed suicide. In the conspiracy, it was said, more than seven thousand men and women were involved. But the heads of the conspiracy, it was clear, were Marcus and Gaius Atinius of the Roman *plebs*, and the Faliscan Lucius Opicernius and the Campanian Minius Cerrinius: they were the source of all wickedness and wrongdoing, the story went, and they were the supreme priests and the founders of the cult. It was seen to that at the first opportunity they were arrested. They were brought before the consuls, confessed, and asked for no delay in standing trial.

XVIII. But so numerous were the persons who had fled from the City that, since in many instances legal proceedings and causes were falling through,[1] the praetors Titus Maenius and Marcus Licinius were compelled, through the intervention of the senate, to adjourn court for thirty days, until the investigations should be finished by the consuls. The same depopulation, because at Rome men whose names had been given in did not respond or were not found, compelled the consuls to make the rounds of the villages and there investigate and conduct trials. Those who had merely been initiated and had made their prayers in accordance with the ritual formula,

A.U.C. 568

nefanda coniuratio in omne facinus ac libidinem
continebatur, nec earum rerum ullam,[1] in quas
iureiurando obligati erant, in se aut alios admiserant,
4 eos in vinculis relinquebant; qui stupris aut caedibus
violati erant, qui falsis testimoniis, signis adulterinis,
subiectione testamentorum, fraudibus aliis con-
5 taminati, eos capitali poena adficiebant. Plures
necati quam in vincula coniecti sunt. Magna vis in
6 utraque causa virorum mulierumque fuit. Mulieres
damnatas cognatis, aut in quorum manu essent,
tradebant, ut ipsi in privato animadverterent in eas:
si nemo erat idoneus supplicii exactor, in publico
7 animadvertebatur. Datum deinde consulibus negotium est ut omnia Bacchanalia Romae primum, deinde
per totam Italiam diruerent, extra quam si qua ibi
8 vetusta ara aut signum consecratum esset. In
reliquum deinde senatus consulto cautum est ne
qua Bacchanalia Romae neve in Italia essent. Si
quis tale sacrum sollemne et necessarium duceret,[2]
nec sine religione et piaculo se id omittere [3] posse,
apud praetorem urbanum profiteretur, praetor
9 senatum consuleret. Si ei permissum esset, cum in
senatu centum non minus essent, ita id sacrum
faceret, dum ne plus quinque sacrificio interessent,

[1] ullam ς: ulla res *M*.
[2] duceret *ed. Parisina* 1513: duceret et ς.
[3] id omittere *Gelenius*: id dimittere *M*: dimittere ς.

---

[1] Such punishments were inflicted by virtue of *patria potestas*.
[2] Their antiquity was their guarantee that they antedated

the priest dictating the words, in which the wicked conspiracy to all vice and lust was contained, but had committed none of the acts to which they were bound by the oath against either themselves or others, they left in chains; upon those who had permitted themselves to be defiled by debauchery or murder, who had polluted themselves by false testimony, forged seals, substitution of wills or other frauds, they inflicted capital punishment. More were killed than were thrown into prison. There was a large number of men and women in both classes. Convicted women were turned over to their relatives or to those who had authority over them, that they might be punished in private:[1] if there was no suitable person to exact it, the penalty was inflicted by the state. Then the task was entrusted to the consuls of destroying all forms of Bacchic worship, first at Rome and then throughout Italy, except in cases where an ancient altar or image had been consecrated.[2] For the future it was then provided by decree of the senate that there should be no Bacchanalia in Rome or Italy. If any person considered such worship to be ordained by tradition or to be necessary, and believed that he could not omit it without sin and atonement, he was to make a declaration before the city praetor, and the latter would consult the senate. If permission were granted to him, at a meeting where not fewer than one hundred were in attendance, he should offer the sacrifice, provided that not more than five people should take part in the rite, and that there B.C. 186

the abuse of the Bacchus worship and were free from its bad features. In any case the Romans were inclined to respect venerable age.

A.U.C. 568 neu qua pecunia communis neu quis magister sacrorum aut sacerdos esset.

XIX. Aliud deinde huic coniunctum referente Q. Marcio consule senatus consultum factum est, ut de iis quos pro indicibus consules habuissent integra res ad senatum referretur, cum Sp. Postumius
2 quaestionibus perfectis Romam redisset. Minium Cerrinium Campanum Ardeam in vincula mittendum censuerunt, magistratibusque Ardeatium praedicendum ut intentiore eum custodia adservarent, non solum ne effugeret, sed ne mortis consciscendae
3 locum haberet. Sp. Postumius aliquanto post Romam venit: eo referente de P. Aebutii et Hispalae Faeceniae praemio, quod eorum opera indicata
4 Bacchanalia essent, senatus consultum factum est, uti singulis his centena milia aeris quaestores urbani ex aerario darent; utique consul cum tribunis plebis ageret, ut ad plebem primo quoque tempore ferrent, ut P. Aebutio emerita stipendia essent, ne invitus

---

[1] The last clauses prevent a definite organization of the cult. The decree, however, legalizes traditional rites in honour of Bacchus and necessary individual acts of worship.

We are fortunate in possessing an inscription (CIL. I. 196), containing, in the form of a letter addressed to the Teurani, a federated state of Bruttium, the substance of the senate's decisions (the celebrated *Senatus Consultum de Bacchanalibus*). In general the statements of Livy agree with the inscription, although the evidence of language gives no indication that Livy saw the inscription.

[2] The ultimate fate of Cerrinius is not recorded.

should be no common purse or master of sacrifices or priest.[1] B.C. 186

XIX. Then another decree of the senate, allied to this, was passed on the motion of the consul Quintus Marcius, that the entire question of those whose services as informers the consuls had enjoyed should be referred to the senate when Spurius Postumius should have returned to Rome after completing the investigations. Minius Cerrinius the Campanian they voted should be sent to Ardea for imprisonment, advance notice being given to the magistrates of the Ardeans that they should keep especially close guard over him, not only to prevent his escape but also to allow him no opportunity to commit suicide.[2] Spurius Postumius returned to Rome a considerable time later: on his motion with reference to the rewards for Publius Aebutius and Hispala Faecenia, because it was through their information that the Bacchanalia had been discovered, a decree of the senate was passed that to each of them one hundred thousand *asses*[3] should be paid by the city quaestors out of the treasury; and that the consuls should take up with the tribunes of the people the matter of their presenting to the assembly at the earliest possible moment proposals that Publius Aebutius should be rated as having performed his military service,[4] that he should not serve in the

[3] This was the sum required for assignment to the first census-class.

[4] The proposal to exempt Aebutius from his military obligations is genuine, so far as one can see, but nevertheless odd at this period, when military service was still a recognized part of the citizen's duty. It cannot be determined whether the exemption carried with it immediate eligibility to office, since Aebutius had no political ambitions.

A.U.C. 568

militaret neve censor ei invito[1] equum publicum
5 assignaret; utique Faeceniae Hispalae datio, deminutio, gentis enuptio, tutoris optio item esset, quasi ei vir testamento dedisset; utique ei ingenuo nubere liceret, neu quid ei qui eam duxisset ob id
6 fraudi ignominiaeve esset; utique consules praetoresque, qui nunc essent quive postea futuri essent, curarent ne quid ei mulieri iniuriae fieret, utique tuto esset. Id senatum velle et aequum censere ut
7 ita fieret. Ea omnia lata ad plebem factaque sunt ex senatus consulto; de ceterorum indicum impunitate praemiisque consulibus permissum est.

XX. Et iam[2] Q. Marcius quaestionibus suae regionis perfectis in Ligures provinciam proficisci parabat, tribus milibus peditum Romanorum, centum quinquaginta equitibus, et quinque milibus Latini nominis peditum, ducentis equitibus in supplementum
2 acceptis. Eadem provincia, idem numerus peditum

[1] censor ei invito *Mommsen*: censor licinius *M* : censores ς.
[2] et iam ς : ita *M*.

---

[1] The assignment of an *equus publicus* (cf. xlii. 6 and xliv. 1 below and the notes) would make Aebutius liable to service and so cancel the exemption just granted. Service as a volunteer would be performed in the capacity of an *eques equo publico*.

[2] The interests of a *patronus* in the property of his *libertus* were well protected by Roman law. Although the *patronus* of Faecenia was dead his interests survived, descending in this case to his *gens*, and the senate therefore bestows upon her the right to give away or otherwise alienate her property irrespective of gentile rights (*datio* may be synonymous with *alienatio*, the term employed by later jurists). The proposal of some scholars to understand *capitis* with *deminutio*, which would grant her the right to accept inferior civic status, seems to be self-contradictory. But it is not certain that Livy understood what he wrote.

army except by his own act, that the censor should not assign him a public horse without his consent;[1] that Hispala Faecenia should have the rights of bestowing and alienating property,[2] of marriage outside her *gens*,[3] and choice of a *tutor* just as if her husband had given it to her by his will;[4] that she should be permitted to marry a man of free birth, nor should any fraud or disgrace on this account attach to a man who should have married her; that the consuls and praetors who were at this time in office and those who should follow them should have a care that no injury should be done to this woman and that she should be secure. The senate, they were to say, wished and judged it proper that this should be done. All these motions were presented to the assembly and passed in accordance with the decree of the senate; with respect to the impunity and rewards of the rest of the informers discretion was left to the consuls. B.C. 186

XX. And by this time Quintus Marcius, having completed the investigation in his district, was preparing to set out against the Ligurians, who composed his province, having received three thousand Roman infantry and one hundred and fifty cavalry and five thousand infantry and two hundred cavalry of the allies of the Latin confederacy as reinforcements. The same province and the same numbers

[3] The conditions surrounding *gentis enuptio* are only vaguely known. It is clear, however, that Faecenia is to have the maximum of privilege allowed to women.

[4] A wife *in manu* might be granted this privilege by her husband's will. By the bestowal of these four rights Faecenia acquired a legal status at least not inferior to that of free women generally.

A.U.C. 568

equitumque et collegae decretus erat. Exercitus
acceperunt quos priore anno C. Flaminius et M.
3 Aemilius consules habuerant.[1] Duas praeterea legiones novas ex senatus consulto scribere iussi sunt,
et viginti milia peditum sociis et nomini Latino
imperarunt et equites octingentos[2] et tria milia
4 peditum Romanorum, ducentos equites. Totum
hunc exercitum praeter legiones in supplementum
Hispaniensis exercitus duci placebat. Itaque consules, dum ipsi quaestionibus impediebantur, T.
5 Maenium dilectui habendo praefecerunt. Perfectis
quaestionibus prior Q. Marcius in Ligures Apuanos
6 est profectus. Dum penitus in abditos saltus, quae
latebrae receptaculaque illis semper fuerant, perse-
quitur, in praeoccupatis angustiis loco iniquo est
7 circumventus. Quattuor milia militum amissa, et
legionis secundae signa tria, undecim[3] vexilla
socium Latini nominis in potestatem hostium
venerunt, et arma multa, quae, quia impedimento
fugientibus per silvestres semitas erant, passim
8 iactabantur. Prius[4] sequendi Ligures finem quam
9 fugae Romani fecerunt. Consul ubi primum ex
hostium agro evasit, ne quantum deminutae copiae
forent appareret, in locis pacatis exercitum dimisit.
10 Non tamen obliterare famam rei male gestae potuit:

[1] habuerant *Madvig*: habuerunt ϛ.
[2] octingentos ϛ: mille trecentos *M*.
[3] undecim ϛ: quadraginta *M*, XL *pro* XI *fortasse interpretans*.
[4] prius ϛ: nec prius *M*.

---

[1] Unless the last clause of the sentence depends upon *scribere* above, despite the intervening clause, a verb has dropped out, which I have supplied in the translation.

[2] The term *vexilla* is used for variety only: it is more

of infantry and cavalry had been decreed to his colleague as well. They received the armies which Gaius Flaminius and Marcus Aemilius had commanded as consuls the preceding year. Besides, they were directed, under the decree of the senate, to enlist two new legions, and they called upon the allies of the Latin confederacy for twenty thousand infantry and eight hundred cavalry, and they enlisted three thousand Roman infantry and two hundred cavalry.[1] All this army, except the legions, it was resolved to send to reinforce the army in Spain. Accordingly the consuls, while they were themselves busy with the investigations, placed Titus Maenius in charge of conducting the levy. When the investigations were completed, Quintus Marcius set out before his colleague against the Ligurian Apuani. While he was following them into a retired glade, which had always been their secret retreat and hiding-place, he was surrounded on unfavourable ground in a narrow pass which had been occupied in advance. Four thousand soldiers were lost and three standards of the second legion and eleven ensigns[2] of the allies of the Latin confederacy fell into the hands of the enemy, as well as many weapons which were thrown away everywhere because they hindered the flight along the paths in the forest. The Ligurians desisted from their pursuit before the Romans stopped their flight. As soon as the consul got free of the enemy's country, that it might not be seen how great was the loss, he disbanded the army in a peaceful region. He could not, however, erase the record of his defeat; for the glade from B.C. 186

regularly used for the guidons of cavalry, while both Roman and allied infantry carried *signa*.

A.U.C. 586 nam saltus, unde eum Ligures fugaverant, Marcius est appellatus.

XXI. Sub hunc nuntium ex Ligustinis vulgatum litterae ex Hispania mixtam gaudio tristitiam ad-
2 ferentes recitatae sunt.[1] C. Atinius,[2] qui biennio ante praetor in eam provinciam profectus erat, cum Lusitanis in agro Hastensi signis collatis pugnavit: ad sex milia hostium sunt caesa, ceteri fusi et fugati
3 castrisque exuti. Ad oppidum deinde Hastam oppugnandum legiones ducit: id quoque haud multo maiore certamine cepit quam castra; sed dum incautius subit muros, ictus ex vulnere post dies
4 paucos moritur. Litteris de morte propraetoris recitatis senatus censuit mittendum, qui ad Lunae portum C. Calpurnium praetorem consequeretur, nuntiaretque senatum aequum censere ne sine imperio provincia esset maturare eum proficisci.
5 Quarto die qui missus erat Lunam venit: paucis ante
6 diebus Calpurnius profectus erat. Et in citeriore Hispania L. Manlius Acidinus, qui eodem tempore, quo C. Atinius in provinciam ierat,[3] cum Celtiberis
7 acie conflixit. Incerta victoria discessum est, nisi quod Celtiberi castra inde nocte proxima moverunt, Romanis et suos sepeliendi et spolia legendi ex
8 hostibus potestas facta est. Paucos post dies maiore coacto exercitu Celtiberi ad Calagurrim oppidum
9 ultro lacessiverunt proelio Romanos. Nihil traditur,

[1] recitatae sunt ς : uenerunt *M*.
[2] C. Atinius *Sigonius* : c. catinius ς.
[3] provinciam ierat *Gelenius* : prouincia erat ς.

---

[1] Its position is unknown.

which the Ligurians had driven him was called "Marcius."[1] B.C. 186

XXI. About the time the news from the Ligurians was published, dispatches from Spain were read, bringing sorrow mingled with joy. Gaius Atinius, who as praetor two years before had set out to that province, had engaged in pitched battle with the Lusitanians in the territory of Hasta: about six thousand of the enemy fell and the rest were repulsed and routed and stripped of their camp. He then led the legions to assault the town of Hasta: this too he took without much more of a fight than the camp; but while he was too carelessly approaching the walls he was hit and a few days later died from his wound. When the letter regarding the death of the propraetor was read, the senate decreed that a messenger should be sent to overtake the praetor Gaius Calpurnius at the harbour of Luna and announce to him that the senate deemed it proper that he should hasten his departure, that the province might not be left without a governor. The messenger who was sent arrived at Luna on the fourth day: Calpurnius had departed a few days before. And in Nearer Spain Lucius Manlius Acidinus, who had gone to the province at the same time as Gaius Atinius, engaged in a battle with the Celtiberians. Both sides withdrew with the result indecisive, except that the Celtiberians moved their camp from there the next night and gave the Romans the chance both to bury their dead and collect the spoils from the enemy. A few days later, having collected a larger army, the Celtiberians spontaneously challenged the Romans to battle near the town of Calagurris. It is not explained what made

A.U.C. 568 quae causa numero aucto infirmiores eos[1] fecerit. Superati proelio sunt: ad duodecim milia hominum caesa, plus duo capta et castris Romanus potitur.
10 Et nisi successor adventu suo inhibuisset impetum victoris, subacti Celtiberi forent. Novi praetores ambo in hiberna exercitus deduxerunt.

XXII. Per eos dies, quibus haec ex Hispania nuntiata sunt, ludi Taurii per biduum facti religionis causa. Decem deinde dies magno apparatu[2] ludos
2 M. Fulvius, quos voverat Aetolico bello, fecit. Multi artifices ex Graecia venerunt honoris eius causa. Athletarum quoque certamen tum primo Romanis spectaculo fuit, et venatio data leonum et pantherarum, et prope huius saeculi copia ac varietate
3 ludicrum celebratum est. Novemdiale deinde sacrum tenuit, quod in Piceno per triduum lapidibus pluerat, ignesque caelestes multifariam orti adussisse complurium levi adflatu vestimenta maxime dicebantur.
4 Addita et unum diem supplicatio est ex decreto pontificum, quod aedis Opis in Capitolio de caelo tacta erat. Hostiis maioribus consules procurarunt
5 urbemque lustraverunt. Sub idem tempus et ex

[1] infirmiores eos *edd. vett.*: firmiores eos *aut* firmiores eos non ς.

[2] decem deinde dies magno apparatu *Novák*: decem apparatos deinde ς.

---

[1] These games, instituted under the monarchy, were in honour of the gods of the lower world.

[2] While the expression is vague, it would seem that there was some special reason for celebrating these games at this time.

them weaker after their numbers were increased. B.C. 186 They were defeated in the battle: about twelve thousand men were killed and two thousand captured and the Romans gained possession of the camp. And, if the arrival of his successor had not prevented the victor from exploiting his success, the Celtiberians might have been subdued. Both new praetors led their armies into winter quarters.

XXII. About the time that these reports were brought from Spain, the Taurian Games[1] were performed for two days for religious reasons.[2] Then for ten days, with great magnificence, Marcus Fulvius gave the games which he had vowed during the Aetolian war.[3] Many actors too came from Greece to do him honour. Also a contest of athletes[4] was then for the first time made a spectacle for the Romans and a hunt of lions and panthers was given, and the games, in number and variety, were celebrated in a manner almost like that of the present time.[5] Then a nine-day feast took place because in Picenum through three days there had been showers of stones, and especially because flames shining in the sky in many places were said to have set fire to the garments of many when a light breeze blew upon them. A one-day period of prayer was also added by decree of the pontiffs because the temple of Ops on the Capitoline had been struck by lightning. The consuls atoned for this with full-grown victims and purified the City. About the same time

[3] Cf. v. 7–10 above. If the emendation here adopted is correct, Fulvius probably exceeded his appropriation of 80,000 sesterces there mentioned.

[4] They were probably boxers or wrestlers.

[5] The Greek features of the games were marks of the Greek culture of Fulvius.

A.U.C. 563 Umbria nuntiatum est semimarem duodecim ferme
annos natum inventum. Id prodigium abominantes
arceri Romano agro necarique quam primum
iusserunt.
6 Eodem anno Galli Transalpini transgressi in Vene-
tiam sine populatione aut bello haud procul inde, ubi
nunc Aquileia est, locum oppido condendo ceperunt.
7 Legatis Romanis de ea re trans Alpes missis responsum est neque profectos ex auctoritate gentis eos,
nec quid in Italia facerent sese scire.
8 L. Scipio ludos eo tempore, quos bello Antiochi
vovisse sese dicebat, ex collata ad id pecunia ab regi-
9 bus civitatibusque per dies decem fecit. Legatum
eum post damnationem et bona vendita missum in
Asiam ad dirimenda inter Antiochum et Eumenem
10 reges certamina Valerius Antias est auctor: tum
collatas ei pecunias congregatosque per Asiam artifices, et quorum ludorum post bellum, in quo votos
diceret, mentionem non fecisset, de iis post legationem
demum in senatu actum.

XXIII. Cum iam in exitu annus esset, Q. Marcius
absens magistratu abiturus erat, Sp. Postumius
quaestionibus cum summa fide curaque perfectis
2 comitia habuit. Creati consules sunt Ap. Claudius
Pulcher M. Sempronius Tuditanus. Postero die

---

[1] Cf. the treatment of a similar creature reported at XXXI. xii. 8.

[2] This is the first invasion of Italy over the eastern passes of the Alps. Possibly these invaders were not Gauls, but came from farther east.

[3] Neither the vow nor the embassy is mentioned elsewhere by Livy.

it was reported too from Umbria that a hermaphrodite about twelve years old had been discovered. In their fear and awe of this portent they ordered the prodigy to be removed from Roman soil and killed as soon as possible.[1] B.C. 186

In the same year Transalpine Gauls, crossing into Venetia without any devastation or war, took possession of a site for founding a town not far from where Aquileia now stands. Roman ambassadors sent across the Alps to inquire into the matter received the reply that this party had not set out with the authority of the state, nor did they know what they were doing in Italy.[2]

Lucius Scipio at this time celebrated for ten days the games which he said he had vowed during the war with Antiochus, with money contributed for the purpose by the kings and cities. Valerius Antias is the authority for the statement that after his condemnation and the sale of his property he had been sent as an ambassador to Asia to resolve the disputes between the two kings, Antiochus and Eumenes: he adds that at that time the money was contributed to him and artists collected throughout Asia, and that finally, after his embassy, action was taken in the senate about these games, of which he had made no mention after the war in which he said that they had been vowed.[3]

XXIII. When the year was now coming to its end, Quintus Marcius was about to retire from office while absent from Rome and Spurius Postumius, having conducted the investigations with the greatest faithfulness and energy, held the elections. The consuls elected were Appius Claudius Pulcher and Marcus Sempronius Tuditanus. Next day the

A.U.C. 568 praetores facti P. Cornelius Cethegus A. Postumius Albinus C. Afranius[1] Stellio C. Atilius Serranus L. Postumius Tempsanus M. Claudius Marcellinus.
3 Extremo anni, quia Sp. Postumius consul renuntiaverat peragrantem se propter quaestiones utrumque litus Italiae desertas colonias Sipontum supero,
4 Buxentum infero mari invenisse, triumviri ad colonos eo scribendos ex senatus consulto ab T.[2] Maenio praetore urbano creati sunt L. Scribonius Libo M. Tuccius Cn. Baebius Tamphilus.

A.U.C. 569
5 Cum Perseo rege et Macedonibus bellum quod imminebat, non unde plerique opinantur, nec ab ipso Perseo causas cepit: inchoata initia a Philippo sunt; et is ipse, si diutius vixisset, id bellum gessisset.
6 Una eum res, cum victo leges imponerentur, maxime angebat, quod qui Macedonum ab se defecerant in bello, in eos ius saeviendi ademptum ei ab senatu
7 erat, cum, quia rem integram Quinctius in condicionibus pacis distulerat, non desperasset impetrari
8 posse. Antiocho rege deinde bello superato ad Thermopylas, divisis partibus, cum per eosdem dies

[1] C. Afranius *ed. Frobeniana* 1531 : c. arranius ς.
[2] T. *ed. Moguntina* : l. ς.

---

[1] Livy omits to record the inauguration of the new magistrates and the assignment of provinces and armies.

[2] Livy here makes an abrupt transition from Rome to Macedonia. His chronology, however, is uncertain, as is inevitable in a transitional passage designed to sum up the causes of the war with Perseus, who, incidentally, was not yet king. Livy has said little about Greek affairs since he described the Achaean–Lacedaemonian difficulties in XXXVIII. xxx.–xxxiv., where the chronology is also obscure.

[3] The allusion must be to such states as the Orestae (XXXIII. xxxiv. 6), although Livy has mentioned no such prohibition as that of which Philip complained, and, indeed,

praetors were chosen, Publius Cornelius Cethegus, B.C. 186
Aulus Postumius Albinus, Gaius Afranius Stellio, Gaius Atilius Serranus, Lucius Postumius Tempsanus, Marcus Claudius Marcellinus. At the end of the year, because the consul Spurius Postumius had reported that on his journeys in the prosecution of the investigations on both coasts of Italy he had found colonies abandoned, Sipontum on the upper sea, Buxentum on the lower, three commissioners to enroll colonists for them were elected in accordance with a decree of the senate and under the presidency of the praetor Titus Maenius. The commissioners were Lucius Scribonius Libo, Marcus Tuccius, Gnaeus Baebius Tamphilus.[1]

The war[2] with King Perseus and the Mace- B.C. 185
donians which was threatening did not arise from the causes which most people assign to it, nor from Perseus himself: the beginnings had been made by Philip; and Philip himself, had he lived longer, would have waged that war. One thing, when terms of peace were dictated to him after his defeat, especially offended him—that the right of punishing those of the Macedonians who had revolted from him during the war had been taken from him by the senate, although, since Quinctius, in their negotiations for peace, had postponed the whole question, he had not despaired of obtaining it.[3] Then, when King Antiochus had been defeated at Thermopylae, the tasks had been divided,[4] and at the same time

has said nothing at all of the treatment of revolted Macedonian cities except in the instance mentioned.

[4] For the phrase, cf. XXXVII. xxi. 8, where, as here, it refers to co-ordinated action of commanders. The joint campaign referred to was described by Livy in XXXVI. xxxv.

A.U.C. 569 consul Acilius Heracleam, Philippus Lamiam oppug-
9 nasset, capta Heraclea quia iussus abscedere a
moenibus Lamiae erat Romanisque oppidum de-
10 ditum est, aegre eam rem tulerat. Permulsit iram
eius consul, quod ad Naupactum ipse festinans, quo
se ex fuga Aetoli contulerant, Philippo permisit
Athamaniae et Amynandro bellum inferret, et[1]
urbes, quas Thessalis Aetoli ademerant, regno ad-
11 iceret. Haud magno certamine et Amynandrum
Athamania expulerat et urbes receperat aliquot.
12 Demetriadem quoque, urbem validam et ad omnia
opportunam, et Magnetum gentem[2] suae dicionis
13 fecit. Inde et in Thracia quasdam urbes, novae
atque insuetae libertatis vitio seditionibus principum
turbatas, partibus, quae domestico certamine vin-
cerentur, adiungendo sese cepit.

XXIV. His sedata in praesentia regis ira in
Romanos est. Numquam tamen remisit animum a
colligendis in pace viribus, quibus, quandoque data
2 fortuna esset, ad bellum uteretur. Vectigalia regni
non fructibus tantum agrorum portoriisque maritimis
auxit sed metalla etiam et vetera intermissa recoluit

[1] et *ed. Aldina* : *om.* ς.
[2] gentem *ed. Frobeniana* 1535 : gentes ς.

---

[1] The sequence of events here described does not quite agree with that found in Book XXXVI *passim*. The passages agree in general as to the extent of Philip's gains, which had awakened the suspicions of Flamininus (XXXVI. xxxv. 9–10).

[2] The occupation of Aenus and Maronea had taken place after the other events related, and has not been previously mentioned by Livy. These towns had been at various times under Ptolemaic, Macedonian and finally Seleucid rule before they were liberated by the Romans after the defeat of Antiochus (XXXVII. lx. 7).

the consul Acilius had laid siege to Heraclea, Philip to Lamia; but when Heraclea was taken Philip had felt aggrieved because he had been ordered to retire from the walls of Lamia and the town had been surrendered to the Romans. The consul soothed his wrath, because, when he was himself in haste to move towards Naupactus, whither the Aetolians had gone from their flight, he had permitted Philip to make war on Athamania and Amynander and to add to his kingdom the cities which the Aetolians had taken from the Thessalians. Without great effort he had both driven Amynander from Athamania and recovered a considerable number of towns. Demetrias also, a powerful city, opportunely situated in every respect, and the tribes of the Magnesians he had brought under his control.[1] After that he had also gained certain cities in Thrace, amid the disorder caused by the quarrels of their leading citizens—the fault of new and unwonted liberty—by joining himself to the parties which were being worsted in this internal rivalry.[2] B.C. 185

XXIV. By these means the anger of the king against the Romans was temporarily assuaged. Never, however, did he relax his attention to the assembling in time of peace of strength which, whenever the chance should be given, he could use in time of war.[3] He not only increased the revenues of his kingdom from the farm crops and the harbour duties, but also reopened old mines long

[3] The true story of the alienation of Philip after the reconciliation during the war with Antiochus would be interesting and revealing. We cannot, however, expect to find it in Livy, and the narrative of Polybius is too fragmentary to be very helpful.

A.U.C. 569

3 et nova multis locis instituit. Ut vero antiquam
multitudinem hominum quae belli cladibus amissa
erat restitueret, non subolem tantum stirpis parabat
cogendis omnibus procreare atque educare liberos,
4 sed Thracum etiam magnam multitudinem in Macedoniam traduxerat, quietusque aliquamdiu a bellis
omni cura in augendas regni opes intentus fuerat.
5 Rediere deinde causae, quae de integro iram move-
6 rent in Romanos. Thessalorum et Perrhaeborum
querellae de urbibus suis ab eo possessis, et legatorum
Eumenis regis de Thraciis oppidis per vim occupatis
traductaque in Macedoniam multitudine, ita auditae
7 erant ut eas non neglegi satis appareret. Maxime
moverat senatum, quod iam Aeni et Maroneae
affectari possessionem audierant;[1] minus Thessalos
8 curabant. Athamanes quoque venerant legati, non
partis amissae, non finium iacturam querentes, sed
totam Athamaniam sub ius iudiciumque regis
9 venisse; et Maronitarum exsules venerant,[2] pulsi,
quia libertatis causam defendissent ab regio praesidio: ii non Maroneam modo sed etiam Aenum in

[1] iam A. et M. affectari p. audierant *Gelenius*: eum a. et m. affectare p. audieret *M*: iam eum et maroniae affectari p. auαierant (-at) ς.

[2] venerant *Crévier*: erant ς.

---

[1] The dangers attending Rome's policy in the east are here manifest. The adversity of one eastern power inevitably meant the prosperity of another, and constant vigilance on Rome's part was necessary to ensure the maintenance of any equilibrium. The fact that there was now no considerable Greek power made the "liberation" of the Greeks more and

disused and began operations on new ones in many places. But that he might restore the ancient population, which had been lost in the calamities of war, he did not merely look to the natural increase of the people, by requiring all to beget and rear children, but he had transferred a great number of Thracians to Macedonia as well, being for some time free from wars and devoting all his thought to increasing the resources of his kingdom. Then causes recurred which aroused anew his anger against the Romans. The complaints of the Thessalians and the Perrhaebians with regard to their cities which were in his hands and those of the envoys of King Eumenes with regard to his violent occupation of the Thracian towns and the transfer of the population to Macedonia had been so received that it was plainly evident that they would not be ignored.[1] The senate had been especially moved by the fact that they had heard that he now coveted the possession of Aenus and Maronea; they were less concerned about the Thessalians. Athamanian ambassadors had also arrived, complaining, not of the occupation of part of their kingdom or of the loss of territory, but that all Athamania had come under the sovereignty and sway of the king;[2] exiles of the Maroneans had also come, expelled because they had defended the cause of liberty against the king's garrison: they brought the news that not only Maronea but also Aenus was in the B.C. 185

more a farce and prevented the Romans from developing a Greek state which could check Philip in Europe as Eumenes checked Antiochus in Asia.

[2] This embassy must have antedated the recovery of Athamania by Amynander (XXXVIII. i. 1–iii. 2), unless Philip had again expelled him, and of this there is no record.

A.U.C. 569

10 potestate narrabant esse Philippi. Venerant et a
Philippo legati ad purganda ea, qui nihil nisi permissu
11 Romanorum imperatorum factum affirmabant: civitates Thessalorum et Perrhaeborum et Magnetum et
cum Amynandro Athamanum gentem in eadem causa
12 qua Aetolos fuisse; Antiocho rege pulso occupatum
oppugnandis Aetolicis urbibus consulem ad recipien-
das eas civitates Philippum misisse; armis subactos
13 parere. Senatus, ne quid absente rege statueret,
legatos ad eas controversias disceptandas misit Q.
Caecilium Metellum M. Baebium Tamphilum Ti.
14 Sempronium. Quorum sub adventum [1] ad Thessalica
Tempe omnibus iis civitatibus, quibus cum rege
disceptatio erat, concilium indictum est.

XXV. Ibi cum Romani legati disceptatorum loco,
Thessali Perrhaebique et Athamanes haud dubii
accusatores, Philippus ad audienda crimina tamquam
2 reus consedissent, pro ingenio quisque eorum, qui
principes legationum erant, et gratia cum Philippo
3 aut odio acerbius leniusve egerunt. In contro-
versiam autem veniebant Philippopolis Tricca Pha-

[1] adventum *ed. Frobeniana* 1535: aduentu ς.

---

[1] The various events which inspired these complaints had extended over a considerable period of time, but may have been forced upon Rome's attention simultaneously. One can picture the bewilderment of the senate, forced to listen to contradictory arguments and decide claims on the basis of justice plus diplomatic policy, and being, probably, none too familiar with the Greek language.

[2] The negotiations between the Roman commanders Baebius and Acilius and the king had been conducted in haste, under the pressure of war-time conditions, and had probably never been given definiteness by statement in written form. It is by no means impossible that a liberal interpretation

power of Philip.[1] Ambassadors too from Philip had B.C. 185 come to clear him on these counts, and they asserted that he had done nothing except with the consent of the Roman generals: [2] the cities of the Thessalians and Perrhaebians and Magnesians and the people of the Athamanians, including Amynander, had been in the same situation as the Aetolians; after the defeat of King Antiochus the consul, kept busy with besieging the Aetolian cities, had sent Philip to recover the above-mentioned places; subdued by arms, they now obeyed him. The senate, in order not to reach any decision in the absence of the king, sent as commissioners to settle these disputes Quintus Caecilius Metellus, Marcus Baebius Tamphilus, Tiberius Sempronius.[3] On their arrival at Thessalian Tempe all the states which had matters of dispute with the king were summoned to a council.

XXV. There, when they had taken their places, the Roman commissioners in the position of arbitrators, the Thessalians, Perrhaebians and Athamanians as unquestionably accusers, and Philip to hear the charges almost as a criminal, each one of the men who were chiefs of embassies, in accordance with his own inclinations, whether towards sympathy for Philip or towards hatred, made more harsh or more lenient proposals. But the principal grounds for controversy were Philippopolis, Tricca, Phaloria,

justified Philip in keeping what he had gained and that the Roman problem at this time was how to take away, while avoiding making Philip an enemy, what their generals had so generously and thoughtlessly given.

[3] Metellus is probably the consul of 206 B.C., Baebius the praetor of 192 B.C. who had co-operated with Philip in the early campaigns against Antiochus, Sempronius probably the tribune of 187 B.C.

A.U.C. 569

loria et Eurymenae[1] et cetera circa eas oppida,
4 utrum, Thessalorum iuris cum essent,[2] vi ademptae
possessaeque ab Aetolis forent—nam Philippum
Aetolis ademisse eas[3] constabat—an Aetolica anti-
5 quitus ea oppida fuissent: ita enim Acilium regi
concessisse, si Aetolorum fuissent, et[4] si voluntate,
non si vi atque armis coacti cum Aetolis essent.
6 Eiusdem formulae disceptatio de Perrhaeborum
Magnetumque oppidis fuit: omnium enim iura possi-
7 dendo per occasiones Aetoli miscuerant. Ad haec
quae disceptationis erant, querellae Thessalorum
adiectae, quod ea oppida, si iam redderentur sibi,
8 spoliata ac deserta redditurus esset: nam praeter
belli casibus amissos quingentos principes iuventutis in
Macedoniam abduxisse, et opera eorum in servilibus
abuti ministeriis; et quae reddiderit coactus Thes-
9 salis, inutilia ut redderet curasse. Thebas Phthias

[1] *haec nomina, multimodis in codd. corrupta, corr. Gelenius.*

[2] essent *Madvig* : *om.* ς.

[3] Aetolis ademisse eas *Gelenius* : odisse ac dimisisse ea *M* : ademisse eas ς.

[4] et *ed. Frobeniana* 1535 : *om.* ς.

---

[1] Tricca and Phaloria, as well as Malloea and Ericinium in sect. 16 below, but not Philippopolis and Eurymenae, are on the list of towns recovered from the Athamanians by Baebius and Philip (XXXVI. xiii. 6).

[2] This is inconsistent with the narrative quoted in the preceding note.

[3] The text of this passage seems to be corrupt in so many places that the real meaning remains obscure and uncertain, and no combination of emendations possesses both palaeographical and intrinsic probability. It is clear, however, that the general question involved is the priority of Thessalian and Aetolian claims to these towns. Two details make the answer particularly difficult: first, the uncertainty as to the

Eurymenae[1] and other cities near them, whether, at a time when they were under Thessalian control, they had been forcibly seized and occupied by the Aetolians—for it was agreed that Philip had taken them from the Aetolians[2]—or whether these towns had been Aetolian in earlier times; for Acilius had given them to the king subject to the condition that they had belonged to the Aetolians and, furthermore, that they had joined with the Aetolians voluntarily, not under compulsion of armed force.[3] Under the same procedure the dispute was conducted as to the cities of the Perrhaebians and Magnesians; for the Aetolians had confused all claims by seizing them as opportunity offered.[4] Besides these questions, which were matters for legal adjudication, there were the complaints of the Thessalians that if these cities should be restored to them he would give them back after they had been despoiled and abandoned; for in addition to those who had been lost in the hardships of war he had taken five hundred of the leaders of the youth away to Macedonia and was misusing their services on tasks fit only for slaves; and what he had restored to the Thessalians, under compulsion, he had taken care to return unusable. Phthian Thebes, they said, had once been B.C. 185

meaning of the word *antiquitus*, since Aetolian expansion seems to have begun only after the Macedonian conquest; second, the fact that the condition said here to have been imposed by Acilius has not been mentioned before. Both text and translation, it must be admitted, are a patch-work.

[4] The incessant shifting of military control rendered impossible any purely legal adjudication of such questions which could be regarded as final. Rome's decisions were certain to offend some party and were likely to offend all parties, even if they were purely impersonal and equitable.

A.U.C. 569 unum maritimum emporium fuisse quondam Thessalis
quaestuosum et frugiferum: ibi navibus onerariis
comparatis regem, quae praeter Thebas Demetriadem cursum derigerent, negotiationem mari-
10 timam omnem eo[1] avertisse. Iam ne a legatis
quidem, qui iure gentium sancti sint, violandis
abstinere: insidias positas euntibus ad T. Quinc-
11 tium. Itaque ergo in tantum metum omnes Thessalos coniectos, ut non in civitatibus suis, non in
communibus gentis conciliis quisquam hiscere audeat.
Procul enim abesse libertatis auctores Romanos:
lateri adhaerere gravem dominum, prohibentem uti
beneficiis populi Romani. Quid autem, si vox libera
12 non sit, liberum esse? Nunc se fiducia et praesidio
legatorum ingemiscere magis quam loqui. Nisi
provideant aliquid Romani, quo et Graecis Macedoniam accolentibus metus et audacia Philippo
minuatur, nequiquam et illum victum et se liberatos
13 esse. Ut equum tenacem, non parentem frenis
14 asperioribus castigandum esse. Haec acerbe pos-
tremi, cum priores leniter permulsissent iram eius
15 petentes ut ignosceret pro libertate loquentibus et
ut deposita domini acerbitate adsuesceret socium
atque amicum sese praestare, et imitaretur populum
Romanum, qui caritate quam metu adiungere sibi
16 socios mallet. Thessalis auditis Perrhaebi Gonno-

[1] eo *edd. vett.*: in eo ς.

[1] This incident has not been mentioned.

the one maritime market of the Thessalians which B.C. 185
was profitable and productive of revenue: by assembling there cargo-boats which would steer past Thebes to Demetrias, the king had diverted thither all the sea-trade. At last not even ambassadors, who were inviolable under the law of nations, had he refrained from attacking: he had laid an ambush for them while they were on their way to Titus Quinctius.[1] As a result, then, they said, all Thessalians had been thrown into such a panic that no one dared to open his mouth either in his own city or in the common councils of the people. The Romans, the source of their liberty, were far away: close beside them was a threatening master, forbidding them to take advantage of the kindnesses of the Roman people. What, pray, was free if there was no free speech? Even now, with the confidence and under the safeguards of ambassadors, they were lamenting rather than stating their case. Unless the Romans found some device by which both the fear of the Greeks who were neighbours of Macedonia and the aggressiveness of Philip could be diminished, both his defeat and their liberation would be in vain. Like a stubborn horse which would not obey, more cruel reins must be employed to control him. These remarks the last speakers made in bitterness, although previous speakers had gently soothed his wrath, begging that he would pardon their pleas for liberty, that he would lay aside the harshness of a tyrant and train himself to act as an ally and friend, and that he would imitate the Roman people, which preferred to win for itself allies by affection rather than by fear. When the Thessalians had been heard, the Perrhaebians argued

A.U.C. 569 condylum, quod Philippus Olympiadem appellaverat,
Perrhaebiae fuisse, et ut sibi restitueretur, agebant;
et de Malloea et Ericinio eadem postulatio erat.
17 Athamanes libertatem repetebant et castella Athenaeum et Poetneum.

XXVI. Philippus, ut accusatoris potius quam rei
speciem haberet, et ipse a querellis orsus Mene-
laidem in Dolopia, quae regni sui fuisset, Thessalos
vi atque armis expugnasse questus est; item Petram
in Pieria[1] ab iisdem Thessalis Perrhaebisque captam.
2 Xynias quidem, haud dubie Aetolicum oppidum, sibi
contribuisse eos; et Paracheloida, quae sub Athamania esset, nullo iure Thessalorum formulae
3 factam. Nam quae sibi crimina obiciantur de
insidiis legatorum et maritimis portubus frequentatis
4 aut desertis, alterum ridiculum[2] esse, se reddere
rationem, quos portus mercatores aut nautici petant,
5 alterum mores respuere suos.[3] Tot annos esse per
quos numquam cessaverint legati nunc ad imperatores Romanos nunc Romam ad senatum crimina de
se deferre: quem umquam verbo violatum esse?
6 Semel euntibus ad Quinctium insidias dici factas:
sed quid iis acciderit, non adici. Quaerentium quod
falso obiciant, cum veri nihil habeant, ea crimina

[1] Petram in Pieria *ed. Frobeniana* 1531: petram imperiam ς.

[2] ridiculum ς: deridiculum *M*.

[3] mores respuere suos *Gronovius*: mores pueros uos ς.

---

[1] This demand is inconsistent with Livy's previous narrative. Poetneum is otherwise unknown. For Athenaeum cf. XXXVIII. i. 11.

that Gonnocondylum, which Philip had named Olympias, belonged to Perrhaebia and should be restored to them; the same demand was also made for Malloea and Ericinium. The Athamanians sought liberty and the forts of Athenaeum and Poetneum.[1] B.C. 185

XXVI. Philip, so as to assume the pose of the accuser rather than the accused, himself began with complaints, alleging that the Thessalians had seized by force of arms Menelaïs in Dolopia, which had belonged to his kingdom; similarly, Petra in Pieria had been taken by the same Thessalians and the Perrhaebians. Xyniae indeed, which was certainly an Aetolian town, they had annexed as their own; and Paracheloïs, which was under Athamania, had been made Thessalian under no rule of law. Now as to the charges which they had made against him regarding the ambushing of ambassadors and the frequenting or deserting of maritime harbours, the one, he said, was nonsense, that he should be accountable for what harbours merchants or sailors would seek, the other was inconsistent with his character. It was so many years now that ambassadors had never stopped going now to Roman commanders, now to the senate in Rome, carrying charges against him: who of these, he asked, had ever been harmed even by word? They said that once ambassadors going to Quinctius had been ambushed; but what had happened to them they did not add. These were the allegations of men seeking some false charge to make, since they had nothing true to say.

[1] The discrepancies between these chapters and Livy's account in Book XXXVI suggest that Livy here follows a different source. The real facts become, in consequence, less attainable.

A.U.C. 569
7 esse. Insolenter et immodice abuti Thessalos indulgentia populi Romani, velut ex diutina siti nimis
8 avide meram haurientes libertatem: ita[1] servorum
modo praeter spem repente manumissorum licentiam
vocis et linguae experiri et iactare sese insectatione
9 et conviciis dominorum. Elatus deinde ira adiecit
nondum omnium dierum solem occidisse. Id mina-
citer dictum non Thessali modo in sese, sed etiam
10 Romani acceperunt. Et cum fremitus post eam
vocem ortus et tandem sedatus esset, Perrhaeborum
inde Athamanumque legatis respondit eandem, de
11 quibus illi agant, civitatium causam esse. Consulem Acilium et Romanos sibi dedisse eas, cum
12 hostium essent. Si suum munus qui dedissent
adimere velint, scire cedendum esse: sed meliori
et fideliori amico in gratiam levium et inutilium
13 sociorum iniuriam eos facturos. Nec enim ullius
rei minus diuturnam esse gratiam quam libertatis,
praesertim apud eos, qui male utendo eam corrupturi
14 sint. Causa cognita pronuntiarunt legati placere
deduci praesidia Macedonum ex iis urbibus, et
antiquis Macedoniae terminis regnum finiri. De
iniuriis quas ultro citroque illatas querantur[2] quo
modo inter eas gentes et Macedonas disceptetur,
formulam iuris exsequendi constituendam esse.

[1] ita *ed. Frobeniana* 1535 : itaque ς.
[2] querantur *ed. Frobeniana* 1535 : querebantur ς.

---

[1] The expression has a proverbial sound; Philip's last day had not come.

[2] What boundaries are meant is uncertain: the treaty of 196 B.C. (XXXIII. xxx.) fixed them only vaguely and only on the south. Roman decisions at this period frequently and perhaps deliberately err in the direction of being too sententious and consequently ambiguous.

Arrogantly and excessively did the Thessalians misuse the indulgence of the Roman people, as if after a long thirst they drank too greedily a draught of pure freedom: thus, like slaves suddenly set free contrary to their expectations, they were trying out their freedom of voice and tongue and were making a show of themselves by attacking and insulting their masters. Carried away by anger, he added that the sun of all his days had not yet set.[1] This remark not only the Thessalians took as a threat against them, but the Romans also. And when after this speech a roar of protest began and was finally quieted, he replied next to the Perrhaebians and the Athamanians, that the status of the cities about which they were arguing was the same. He claimed that the consul Acilius and the Romans had given them to him because they were on the side of the enemy. If they who had given them wished to take away their gift, he was aware, he said, that he would have to yield; but they would be doing an injury to a better and more loyal friend to gratify fickle and useless allies. For nothing was gratitude less enduring than for liberty, especially when bestowed upon men who are certain to spoil it by misuse. Having heard the case, the commissioners gave judgment that it was their pleasure that the Macedonian garrisons should be withdrawn from these cities and that the kingdom should be reduced to the ancient boundaries of Macedonia.[2] Regarding the injuries which they complained of as committed by both sides, they would have to determine the rule of procedure to be followed, so as to know in what manner to settle the disputes between these peoples and the Macedonians. B.C. 185

A.U.C. 569 XXVII. Inde graviter offenso rege Thessalonicen ad cognoscendum de Thraciae urbibus proficiscuntur.
2 Ibi legati Eumenis, si liberas esse Aenum et Maroneam velint Romani, nihil sui pudoris esse ultra dicere quam ut admoneant, re, non verbo eos liberos relinquant, nec suum munus intercipi ab alio patian-
3 tur. Sin autem minor cura sit civitatium in Thracia positarum, multo verius esse, quae sub Antiocho fuerint, praemia belli Eumenem quam Philippum
4 habere, vel pro patris Attali meritis bello, quod adversus Philippum ipsum gesserit populus Romanus, vel suis, quod [1] Antiochi bello terra marique laboribus
5 periculisque omnibus interfuerit. Habere eum praeterea decem legatorum in eam rem praeiudicium, qui cum Chersonesum Lysimachiamque dederint, Maroneam quoque atque Aenum profecto dedisse, quae ipsa propinquitate regionis velut appendices
6 maioris muneris essent. Nam Philippum quidem quo aut merito in populum Romanum aut iure imperii, cum tam procul a finibus Macedoniae absint, civitatibus his praesidia imposuisse? Vocari Maronitas iuberent: ab iis certiora omnia de statu civitatium earum scituros.
7 Legati Maronitarum vocati non uno tantum loco urbis praesidium regium esse, sicut in aliis civitatibus,

[1] quod *ed. Moguntina*: quo ς.

---

[1] By "another" they, of course, mean Philip. The words have a peculiar sound on the lips of Eumenes, who had profited so much from Rome's victory over Antiochus.

[2] The commissioners who had been sent to Asia to formulate the peace-treaty with Antiochus.

[3] Aenus and Maronea had apparently been in some way overlooked in the final settlement with Antiochus.

[4] Philip's claim to these cities seems weak in comparison with his rights to some of the other districts in dispute.

XXVII. Thence, having given serious offence to the king, they proceeded to Thessalonica to investigate the condition of the cities of Thrace. There ambassadors of Eumenes told them that if the Romans wished Aenus and Maronea to be free, the king's sense of propriety permitted them to say nothing more, except to suggest that they leave them free in fact and not merely in name, and not allow their own work to be a source of gain to another.[1] But if there were less concern for the cities situated in Thrace, it was far more proper that towns which had belonged to Antiochus should fall as prizes of war to Eumenes rather than to Philip, either in consideration of the services of his father Attalus in the war which the Roman people had waged against Philip himself, or of his own services, in that he had taken part, during the war with Antiochus, in all its labours and perils on land and sea. They said that Eumenes had in addition the preliminary opinion of the ten commissioners[2] on the matter, who, since they had given him the Chersonesus and Lysimachia, surely gave him Maronea and Aenus too, which, from their nearness to his country, were mere appendages to the larger gift.[3] In consequence of what service to the Roman people, they asked, or of what right to rule had Philip imposed his garrisons upon these cities when they were so far away from the boundaries of Macedonia?[4] Let the commissioners order the Maroneans to be summoned: from them they would receive all certain information about the condition of these cities. B.C. 185

The agents of the Maroneans, when called in, said that the royal garrison occupied, not merely one place in the city, as in other towns, but several at

A.U.C. 569 dixerunt, sed pluribus simul, et plenam Macedonum
8 Maroneam esse. Itaque dominari adsentatores regios: his solis loqui et in senatu et in contionibus licere; eos omnes honores et capere ipsos et dare
9 aliis. Optimum quemque, quibus libertatis, quibus legum cura sit, aut exsulare pulsos patria aut in-
10 honoratos et deterioribus obnoxios silere. De iure etiam finium pauca adiecerunt: Q. Fabium Labeonem, cum in regione ea fuisset, derexisse [1] finem Philippo veterem viam regiam, quae ad Thraciae Paroreian subeat, nusquam ad mare declinantem: Philippum novam postea deflexisse viam,[2] qua Maronitarum urbes agrosque amplectatur.

XXVIII. Ad ea Philippus longe aliam quam adversus Thessalos Perrhaebosque nuper ingressus disserendi viam "non cum Maronitis" inquit "mihi aut cum Eumene disceptatio est, sed iam vobiscum, Romani, a quibus nihil aequi me impetrare
2 iam diu animadverto. Civitates Macedonum quae a me inter indutias defecerant, reddi mihi aequum censebam, non quia magna accessio ea regni futura

[1] derexisse *H. J. Mueller*: direxisse ς.
[2] veterem . . . viam *ut hoc loco legitur Gelenius*: ueterem regiam quae thraciae paroreiam sub ea nusquam ad mare ferentem deflexisse uiam ς.

---

[1] The aristocratic party in a Greek city of this period was generally pro-Roman, and the constitutions of Flamininus (cf. XXXIV. li. 6; XXXV. xxxiv. 3 and the note) favoured this element. It is interesting to note that the commissioners feel no necessity of hearing from the opposing (democratic and pro-Macedonian) party in Maronea.

[2] The meaning seems to be that Labeo had established as a boundary between Macedonia and the territory surrendered by Antiochus an old road which perhaps followed the general course of the Roman Via Egnatia. Since the boundary was

once, and that Maronea was full of Macedonians. B.C. 185
As a result, the king's partisans were in control: they alone were permitted to speak in the senate and in the public meetings; they either held themselves or gave to others all offices. All the aristocrats, who felt some concern for liberty and the laws, were either in exile, driven from their homes, or were silent, unhonoured and at the mercy of their inferiors.[1] And as to the boundary rights, they had little new to say: only that Quintus Fabius Labeo, when he had been in that region, had fixed as the boundary for Philip the ancient royal road which leads to Paroreia in Thrace, nowhere approaching the sea: Philip had later laid out a new road which encompassed the cities and lands of the Maroneans.[2]

XXVIII. In reply to this Philip followed a very different line of argument from that recently used against the Thessalians and Perrhaebians: "With the Maroneans or with Eumenes," he said, "I have no debate, but now, Romans, the debate is with you, from whom I have for some time observed that I receive no fair treatment. The cities of the Macedonians which had revolted from me during the truce[3] I deemed it right that I should recover, not because it would be an important addition to my kingdom—for

probably described by a term as vague as "a certain road," Philip had availed himself of the vagueness by relocating the old road or building a new one which put Maronea on his side of the boundary as thus described. But corruption in the text and the lack of any other version of the affair leave the true sense in doubt. It may be added that the authority of Labeo to take such action as is here described (Livy has not mentioned it before) is more than questionable.

[3] Possibly the truce of 197 B.C. (XXXII. xxxvi. 8), but the revolt has not been mentioned before.

A.U.C. esset—sunt enim et parva oppida et in finibus ex-
569 tremis posita—sed quia multum ad reliquos Mace-
3 donas continendos exemplum pertinebat. Negatum
est mihi. Bello Aetolico Lamiam oppugnare iussus
a consule M'. Acilio cum diu fatigatus ibi operibus
proeliisque essem, transcendentem me iam muros a
capta prope urbe revocavit consul et abducere copias
4 inde coegit. Ad huius solacium iniuriae permissum
est ut Thessaliae Perrhaebiaeque et Athamanum
reciperem quaedam castella magis quam urbes.
Ea quoque ipsa vos mihi, Q. Caecili, paucos ante dies
5 ademistis. Pro non dubio paulo ante, si diis placet,
legati Eumenis sumebant, quae Antiochi fuerunt
Eumenem aequius esse quam me habere. Id ego
longe aliter iudico esse. Eumenes enim, non nisi
vicissent Romani, sed nisi bellum gessissent, manere
in regno suo non potuit. Itaque ille vestrum meri-
6 tum habet, non vos illius. Mei autem regni tantum
aberat ut ulla pars in discrimine fuerit ut tria milia
talentum et quinquaginta tectas naves et omnes
Graeciae civitates, quas antea tenuissem, pollicentem
ultro Antiochum in mercedem societatis sim asper-
7 natus; hostemque ei me esse prius etiam quam M'.
Acilius exercitum in Graeciam traiceret praetuli.
Et cum eo consule belli partem quamcumque mihi
8 delegavit gessi, et insequenti consuli L. Scipioni, cum
terra statuisset ducere exercitum ad Hellespontum,
non iter tantum per regnum nostrum dedi, sed vias

[1] Hannibal had urged that every means should be used to win over Philip (XXXVI. vii. 3 ff.), but Livy has said nothing to suggest that actual overtures were made to him by Antiochus.

they are small towns and, moreover, situated on the farthest frontiers—but because it was a valuable precedent for holding within bounds the other Macedonians. This was refused me. During the Aetolian war, ordered by the consul Manius Acilius to besiege Lamia, after I had been wearied for a long time by the siege and battles and when I was on the point of scaling the walls, I was recalled by him from the city, which was all but taken, and compelled to march my troops away. As a consolation for this injustice it was permitted to me to recover certain fortresses (such they were rather than cities) of Thessaly and Perrhaebia and the Athamanians. Even these, Quintus Caecilius, you took away from me a few days ago. Just now (heaven help us!) the ambassadors of Eumenes assumed it as not to be gainsaid that it was more just for Eumenes than for me to have what had belonged to Antiochus. I judge the matter far differently. Eumenes could not have remained in his kingdom, I do not mean if the Romans had not conquered, but if they had not undertaken the war. And so he has received favours from you, not you from him. So far from true was it that any part of my kingdom was in danger that when Antiochus voluntarily promised me three thousand talents and fifty decked ships and all the cities of Greece which I had held before, as the price of my alliance,[1] I refused; I preferred to be his enemy even before Manius Acilius brought his army across to Greece. And with that consul I conducted whatever campaign he assigned to me; and for the following consul, Lucius Scipio, when he had decided to lead his army to the Hellespont by land, I not merely gave him a right of way through our kingdom but also paved roads, built B.C. 185

A.U.C. 569

9 etiam munivi, pontes feci, commeatus praebui; nec
per Macedoniam tantum, sed per Thraciam etiam,
ubi inter cetera pax quoque praestanda a barbaris
10 erat. Pro hoc studio meo erga vos, ne dicam merito,
utrum adicere vos, Romani, aliquid et amplificare et
augere regnum meum munificentia vestra oportebat
an, quae haberem aut meo iure aut beneficio vestro
11 eripere, id quod nunc facitis? Macedonum civitates
quas regni mei fuisse fatemini non restituuntur.
Eumenes tamquam ad Antiochum spoliandum me
venit et, si diis placet, decem legatorum decretum
calumniae [1] impudentissimae praetendit, quo maxi-
12 me et refelli et coargui potest. Disertissime enim
planissimeque in eo scriptum est Chersonesum et
Lysimachiam Eumeni dari. Ubi tandem Aenus et
Maronea et Thraciae civitates adscriptae sunt?
Quod ab illis ne postulare quidem est ausus, id apud
13 vos, tamquam ab illis impetraverit, obtinebit? Quo
in numero me apud vos esse velitis, refert. Si tamquam inimicum et hostem insectari propositum est,
14 pergite ut coepistis facere: sin aliquis respectus est
mei ut socii atque amici regis, deprecor ne me tanta
iniuria dignum iudicetis."

XXIX. Movit aliquantum oratio regis legatos.
Itaque medio responso rem suspenderunt: si decem
legatorum decreto Eumeni datae civitates eae essent,
2 nihil se mutare; si Philippus bello cepisset eas,

[1] calumniae *Gelenius* : pecuniae calumniae ς

---

[1] Philip's claims here are supported by Livy's narrative. The commissioners had left his services entirely unrewarded.

[2] The silence of the commissioners receives an interpretation contradicting that of xxvii. 5 above.

bridges, furnished supplies; and this not through Macedonia alone but also through Thrace, where, along with everything else, I had to maintain peace with the barbarians. For this zeal in your behalf, not to say for these services to you, was it right, Romans, that you should add to and enlarge and increase somewhat my domains by your generosity, or that you should take away what I have, either by my own right or by your kindness, as you are doing now?[1] The cities of the Macedonians, which you admit were part of my dominion, are not restored. Eumenes has come to despoil me as if I were Antiochus, and (heaven help us!) he brings forward, for his most impudent manipulation of the facts, the decree of the ten commissioners, by which more than anything else he can be both refuted and convicted. For it was written therein most explicitly and clearly that the Chersonesus and Lysimachia were given to Eumenes. Where, pray, were Aenus and Maronea and the Thracian cities assigned to him?[2] What he did not even dare to ask of them shall he obtain from you as if he had been granted it by them? It makes a difference in what category you wish me to be with reference to you. If you have determined to harass me as a private and public enemy, continue to act as you have begun; but if some consideration is due me as an allied and friendly king, I beg you not to judge me worthy of such an injury."

B.C. 185

XXIX. The speech of the king affected the commissioners profoundly. Therefore they left the question unsettled by an indecisive answer: if by the decree of the ten commissioners these cities had been assigned to Eumenes, they were making no change; if Philip had captured them in war, he should

A.U.C. 569 praemium victoriae iure belli habiturum; si neutrum eorum foret, cognitionem placere senatui reservari et, ut omnia in integro [1] manerent, praesidia quae in iis urbibus sint deduci.

3 Hae causae maxime animum Philippi alienaverunt ab Romanis, ut non a Perseo filio eius novis causis motum, sed ob has a patre bellum relictum filio videri
4 possit. Romae nulla Macedonici belli suspicio erat. L. Manlius proconsul ex Hispania redierat; cui postulanti ab senatu in aede Bellonae triumphum rerum gestarum magnitudo impetrabilem faciebat;
5 exemplum obstabat quod ita comparatum more maiorum erat ne quis qui exercitum non deportasset triumpharet, nisi perdomitam pacatamque provinciam tradidisset successori. Medius tamen honos Manlio
6 habitus ut ovans urbem iniret. Tulit coronas aureas quinquaginta duas, auri praeterea pondo centum
7 triginta duo, argenti sedecim milia trecenta, et pronuntiavit in senatu decem milia pondo argenti et octoginta auri Q. Fabium quaestorem advehere: id quoque se in aerarium delaturum.

8 Magnus motus servilis eo anno in Apulia fuit. Tarentum provinciam L. Postumius praetor habebat.

[1] integro *Gelenius*: integrum ς.

---

[1] From Philip's standpoint this decision does not leave the affair "in its original state," and one is not surprised that it contributed to Philip's feeling that he was being mistreated. The opposite decision would have been equally unfair to the other parties in the case. It is never made clear whether the Maroneans wished to be given to Eumenes.

[2] This is a variation on the form of statement adopted in XXXVIII. i. 3; it is obvious that the senate has discovered

hold them as the prize of victory under the law of war; if neither of these was true, it was their pleasure that the decision should be reserved for the senate and, in order that everything might remain in its original state, that the garrisons which were in these cities should be withdrawn.[1] B.C. 185

These were the principal causes which had turned the thoughts of Philip away from the Romans, so that the war can appear, not as begun for new reasons by his son Perseus, but as a heritage from the father to the son. At Rome there was no suspicion of a Macedonian war. Lucius Manlius the proconsul had returned from Spain; when he demanded from the senate, meeting in the temple of Bellona, a triumph for his achievements, their importance made the request reasonable; precedent stood in the way, because it had been so arranged by the custom of their forefathers that a general who had not brought back his army should not triumph unless he had handed over to his successor a province thoroughly conquered and pacified.[2] Nevertheless, the intermediate distinction, of entering the City in ovation, was granted to Manlius. He carried in his procession fifty-two golden crowns, in addition to one hundred and thirty-two pounds of gold and sixteen thousand three hundred of silver, and he declared in the senate that his quaestor Quintus Fabius was bringing ten thousand pounds of silver and eighty of gold: this too he would put into the treasury.

There was a serious slave insurrection that year in Apulia. Lucius Postumius the praetor had Tarentum as his province. He conducted a strict investi-

the art of juggling with the conditions to suit its shifting purposes.

A.U.C. 569
9 Is de pastorum coniuratione, qui vias latrociniis
pascuaque publica infesta habuerant, quaestionem
severe exercuit. Ad septem milia hominum condemnavit: multi inde fugerunt, de multis sumptum
10 est supplicium. Consules diu retenti ad urbem
dilectibus tandem in provincias profecti sunt.

XXX. Eodem anno in Hispania praetores C. Calpurnius et L. Quinctius, cum primo vere ex hibernis
copias eductas in Baeturia iunxissent, in Carpetaniam, ubi hostium castra erant, progressi sunt, com-
2 muni animo consilioque parati rem gerere. Haud
procul Dipone et Toleto urbibus inter pabulatores
pugna orta est, quibus dum utrimque subvenitur a
castris, paulatim omnes copiae in aciem eductae sunt.
3 In eo tumultuario certamine et loca sua et genus
pugnae pro hoste fuere. Duo exercitus Romani fusi
atque in castra compulsi sunt. Non institere per-
4 culsis hostes. Praetores Romani, ne postero die
castra oppugnarentur, silentio proximae noctis tacito
5 signo exercitum abduxerunt. Luce prima Hispani
acie instructa ad vallum accesserunt, vacuaque
praeter spem castra ingressi, quae relicta[1] inter
nocturnam trepidationem erant, diripuerunt, regressique in castra sua paucos dies quieti stativis[2]
6 manserunt. Romanorum sociorumque in proelio
fugaque ad quinque milia occisa, quorum se spoliis
hostes armarunt. Inde ad Tagum flumen profecti
7 sunt. Praetores interim Romani omne id tempus

[1] relicta ς : derelicta *M*.
[2] quieti statiuis ς : quietis hi statiuis *M*.

---

[1] The order for departure was given not by voice or trumpet but by written message (*per tesseram*).

gation into a conspiracy of shepherds who had B.C. 185 endangered the highways and the public pasture-lands by their brigandage. He condemned about seven thousand men: many of them escaped, many were executed. The consuls, long delayed in the City by the levies, at length set out for their provinces.

XXX. The same year the praetors in Spain, Gaius Calpurnius and Lucius Quinctius, when in the beginning of spring they had led their troops out of winter quarters and had united in Baeturia, marched into Carpetania, where the camp of the enemy lay, and prepared to conduct the campaign with a common plan and policy. Not far from the towns of Dipo and Toletum a fight broke out between foraging parties, and as these were reinforced, each from its own camp, gradually all the troops were drawn out into the line. In this sudden engagement both the familiar ground and the nature of the fighting favoured the enemy. The two Roman armies were routed and driven back into camp. The enemy did not keep up their pressure on the defeated foe. The Roman praetors, in order that their camp might not be attacked the next day, in the quiet of the following night with silent signals[1] led the army away. At daybreak the Spaniards approached the rampart in battle-line and entering an empty camp, contrary to expectations, plundered what had been left behind in the confusion of the night, and returning to their own camp remained quietly in their quarters for a few days. About five thousand of the Romans and allies fell in the battle and rout, and with their spoils the enemy armed themselves. Then they moved away to the river Tagus. Meanwhile the Roman praetors spent all their time in collecting

A.U.C. 569 contrahendis ex civitatibus sociis Hispanorum auxiliis
et reficiendis ab terrore adversae pugnae militum
8 animis consumpserunt. Ubi satis placuere vires et
iam miles quoque ad delendam priorem ignominiam
hostem poscebat, duodecim milia passuum ab Tago
9 flumine posuerunt castra. Inde tertia vigilia sublatis
signis quadrato agmine principio lucis ad Tagi ripam
10 pervenerunt. Trans fluvium in colle hostium castra
erant. Extemplo, qua duobus locis vada nudabat
amnis, dextra parte Calpurnius, laeva Quinctius
exercitus traduxerunt quieto hoste, dum miratur
subitum adventum consultatque, qui tumultum
inicere trepidantibus in ipso transitu amnis potuisset.
11 Interim Romani, impedimentis quoque omnibus
traductis contractisque in unum locum, quia iam
moveri videbant hostem nec spatium erat castra
12 communiendi, aciem instruxerunt. In medio locatae [1]
quinta Calpurnii legio et octava Quinctii: id robur
totius exercitus erat. Campum apertum usque
ad hostium castra habebant, liberum a metu in-
sidiarum.

XXXI. Hispani postquam in citeriore ripa duo
Romanorum agmina conspexerunt, ut, priusquam se
iungere atque instruere possent, occuparent eos,
castris repente effusi cursu ad pugnam tendunt.
2 Atrox in principio proelium fuit, et Hispanis recenti
victoria inflatis et insueta ignominia milite Romano
3 accenso. Acerrime media acies, duae fortissimae

[1] locatae *ed. Frobeniana* 1535: locata ς.

auxiliaries from the allied towns of the Spaniards and in restoring the courage of the men after the panic of the defeat. When their strength was sufficient and even the soldiers were now demanding the enemy in order to wipe out the previous disgrace, they encamped twelve miles from the river Tagus. Thence, breaking camp in the third watch, they marched in a hollow square at dawn to the banks of the Tagus. Across the river on a hill was the camp of the enemy. Immediately, where the river revealed fords in two places, Calpurnius on the right, Quinctius on the left, led the army across, the enemy quietly watching while they marvelled at their sudden advance and talked about how they might have caused confusion while the Romans were disorganized in the act of crossing the river. Meanwhile the Romans, having brought over all their trains and massed them in one place, because they saw the enemy already in motion and there was no opportunity to fortify a camp, drew up their line of battle. In the centre were posted the fifth legion of Calpurnius and the eighth of Quinctius: these constituted the strength of the whole army. They had an open plain as far as the camp of the enemy, free from any danger of ambuscade. B.C. 185

XXXI. When the Spaniards saw the two Roman columns on the nearer bank, in order to catch them before they could unite and form their ranks, rushing hastily out of their camp they hastened to the conflict. There was a fierce fight at the outset, the Spaniards on the one side being puffed up by their recent victory, the Roman soldiers on the other incensed by their unaccustomed defeat. The fiercest fight was in the centre of the line, composed of the two bravest

A.U.C. 569 legiones, dimicabant. Quas cum aliter moveri loco
non posse hostis cerneret, cuneo institit pugnare;
et usque plures confertioresque medios urgebant.
4 Ibi postquam laborare aciem Calpurnius praetor vidit,
T. Quinctilium Varum et L. Iuventium Talnam legatos
ad singulas legiones adhortandas propere mittit;
5 docere et monere iubet in illis spem omnem vin-
cendi et retinendae Hispaniae esse: si illi loco
cedant, neminem eius exercitus non modo Italiam, sed
ne Tagi quidem ulteriorem ripam umquam [1] visurum.
6 Ipse cum equitibus duarum legionum paulum
circumvectus in cuneum hostium, qui mediam urge-
7 bat aciem, ab latere incurrit. Quinctius cum sociis [2]
equitibus alterum hostium latus invadit. Sed longe
acrius Calpurniani equites pugnabant, et praetor ante
8 alios: nam et primus hostem percussit et ita se
immiscuit mediis ut vix utrius partis esset nosci
9 posset; et equites praetoris eximia virtute et equitum pedites accensi sunt. Pudor movit primos centuriones, qui inter tela hostium praetorem conspexerunt. Itaque urgere signiferos pro se quisque,
iubere inferre signa et confestim militem sequi.
10 Renovatur ab omnibus clamor: impetus fit velut ex
superiore loco. Haud secus ergo quam torrentis
modo fundunt sternuntque perculsos, nec sustineri alii
11 super alios inferentes sese possunt. Fugientes in
castra equites persecuti sunt, et permixti turbae

[1] umquam *ed. Frobeniana* 1535: usquam ς.
[2] sociis *Heusinger*: suis ς.

legions. When the enemy saw that they could be dislodged in no other way, they began to attack in wedge formation; and ever more men, more closely massed, were pressing on the centre. After Calpurnius the praetor saw that the line was in distress there, he sent Titus Quinctilius Varus and Lucius Juventius Talna, the lieutenants, at full speed to encourage the single legions; he ordered them to instruct and remind the troops that in them lay all their hopes of victory and of holding Spain: if they retired from that spot, no one in that army would ever see—not to mention Italy—even the farther bank of the Tagus river. He himself with the cavalry of the two legions, making a short detour, took in flank the wedge of the enemy which was pressing on the centre. Quinctius with the allied cavalry attacked the other flank of the enemy. But the cavalry of Calpurnius fought far more furiously, and the praetor beyond the rest: for he was both the first to strike down an enemy and so threw himself into the midst that it could scarcely be told to which side he belonged; and the cavalry were inspired by the remarkable valour of the praetor and in turn inspired the infantry. Shame moved the senior centurions when they saw the praetor amid the weapons of the enemy. And so each for himself urged on the standard-bearers, ordered them to advance and the soldiers to follow at once. The shouting was renewed by all: an attack was launched as if from higher ground. And so they swept forward like a torrent and overwhelmed the panic-stricken enemy, nor as they charged wave after wave could they be resisted. The cavalry pursued the fugitives to the camp, and mingling with the throng of the enemy B.C. 185

A.U.C. 569 hostium intra vallum penetraverunt; ubi ab relictis
in praesidio castrorum proelium instauratum, coacti-
que sunt Romani equites descendere ex equis.
12 Dimicantibus iis legio quinta supervenit; deinde ut
13 quaeque potuerant, copiae adfluebant. Caeduntur
passim Hispani per tota castra; nec plus quam
quattuor milia hominum effugerunt. Inde tria milia
fere qui arma retinuerant montem propinquum
ceperunt; mille semiermes maxime per agros palati
14 sunt. Supra triginta quinque milia hostium fuerant,
ex quibus tam exigua pars pugnae superfuit. Signa
15 capta centum triginta tria.[1] Romani sociique paulo
plus sescenti et provincialium auxiliorum centum
16 quinquaginta ferme ceciderunt. Tribuni militum
quinque amissi et pauci equites Romani cruentae
maxime victoriae speciem fecerunt. In castris
hostium, quia ipsis spatium sua communiendi non
17 fuerat, manserunt. Pro contione postero die laudati
donatique a C. Calpurnio equites phaleris, pronun-
tiavitque eorum maxime opera hostes fusos, castra
18 capta et expugnata esse. Quinctius alter praetor
suos equites catellis ac fibulis[2] donavit. Donati et
centuriones ex utriusque exercitu permulti, maxime
qui mediam aciem tenuerant.[3]

XXXII. Consules dilectibus aliisque quae Romae
agendae erant peractis rebus in Ligures provinciam
2 exercitum duxerunt. Sempronius a Pisis profectus

[1] tria *ed. Moguntina*: duo ς.
[2] fibulis *ed. Moguntina*: fistulis ς.
[3] tenuerant *Madvig*: tenuerunt ς.

---

[1] The apparent meaning is that the losses of officers and knights (*i.e.* men of rank) were disproportionately heavy.

made their way inside the rampart; there the battle was renewed by the troops who had been left to guard the camp, and the Roman cavalry were forced to dismount. While they were fighting thus the fifth legion came up; then, as they could, new forces were joining the battle. Spaniards were being slaughtered everywhere through the whole camp, and not more than four thousand men escaped. About three thousand of them, who had kept their weapons, occupied a mountain near by; a thousand, most of them partially armed, straggled through the fields. There had been more than thirty-five thousand of the enemy, of whom so small a remnant survived the battle. One hundred and thirty-three standards were taken. Of the Romans and allies a few more than six hundred fell, and of the auxiliaries from the province about a hundred and fifty. The loss of five tribunes of the soldiers and of a few Roman knights particularly gave the appearance of a bloody victory.[1] They remained in the camp of the enemy because there had been no opportunity to fortify their own. Before an assembly the next day Gaius Calpurnius praised and decorated the cavalry with trappings for their horses and proclaimed publicly that the enemy had been defeated and his camp taken and captured mainly through their efforts. Quinctius, the other praetor, decorated his cavalry with chains and clasps. Also many centurions from both armies were honoured, especially those who had held the centre of the line. B.C. 185

XXXII. The consuls, having finished the levies and the other business which had to be transacted in Rome, led the army against the Ligurians, who constituted their province. Sempronius, setting out

A.U.C. 569 in Apuanos Ligures, vastando agros urendoque vicos
et castella eorum aperuit saltum usque ad Macram
3 fluvium et Lunae portum. Hostes montem, antiquam sedem maiorum suorum, ceperunt; et inde
4 superata locorum iniquitate proelio deiecti sunt. Et
Ap. Claudius felicitatem virtutemque collegae in
Liguribus Ingaunis aequavit secundis aliquot proeliis.
Sex praeterea oppida eorum expugnavit; multa milia
hominum in iis cepit; belli auctores tres et quadraginta securi percussit.

5 Iam comitiorum appetebat tempus. Prior tamen
Claudius quam Sempronius, cui sors comitia habendi
obtigerat, Romam venit, quia P. Claudius frater eius
6 consulatum petebat. Competitores habebat patricios
L. Aemilium Q. Fabium Ser. Sulpicium Galbam,
veteres candidatos, et ab repulsis eo magis debitum
7 quia primo negatus erat honorem repetentes. Etiam
quia plus quam unum ex patriciis creari non licebat,
8 artior petitio quattuor petentibus erat. Plebeii
quoque gratiosi homines petebant, L. Porcius Q.
Terentius Culleo Cn. Baebius Tamphilus, et hi
repulsi in spem impetrandi tandem aliquando honoris
9 dilati. Claudius ex omnibus unus novus [1] candidatus

[1] novus *Gelenius* : nobilis ς.

---

[1] They probably lived south-west of Genoa.

[2] For the psychology cf. XXXV. xxiv. 5.

[3] The dates of the praetorships of the candidates were: Claudius, 188; Aemilius, 191; Fabius, 189; Sulpicius, 187; Porcius, 193; Terentius, 187; Baebius, 199 (all B.C.). These dates give some indication of the possible duration of a political career at this period, and show that there were other

from Pisa against the Ligurian Apuani, devastating B.C. 185 their lands and burning the villages and forts, opened up the pass as far as the river Macra and the harbour of Luna. The enemy retired to a mountain, the ancient seat of their forefathers; even from there, the handicap of unfavourable ground having been overcome, they were dislodged by an attack. Appius Claudius too equalled the good fortune and valour of his colleague among the Ligurian Ingauni[1] in a number of victories. In addition he captured six of their towns; in them he took many thousands of men; forty-three, who had been responsible for the war, he beheaded.

The time for the elections was now approaching. But Claudius arrived in Rome earlier than Sempronius, to whom had fallen by lot the conduct of the elections, because his brother Publius Claudius was seeking the consulship. He had as patrician competitors Lucius Aemilius, Quintus Fabius, Servius Sulpicius Galba, all perennial candidates, who after defeats were again seeking an office which was due them all the more because it had been at first refused.[2] Also, because it was not lawful that more than one from the patricians should be elected, there was a closer race among the four candidates. Influential plebeians also were contending for the office, Lucius Porcius, Quintus Terentius Culleo, Gnaeus Baebius Tamphilus,[3] and these too, having suffered defeat, were put off in the hope that some day they would at last[4] win in the election. Claudius was the only new candidate of them all. In the general

hard-fought campaigns than those which Livy singles out for special mention: cf. also XL. xxxvii. 6 below

[4] The combination *tandem aliquando* is highly colloquial.

A.U.C. 569 erat. Opinione hominum haud dubie destinabantur
10 Q. Fabius Labeo et L. Porcius Licinus.[1] Sed
Claudius consul sine lictoribus cum fratre toto foro
volitando, clamitantibus adversariis et maiore parte
11 senatus, meminisse eum debere se prius consulem
populi Romani quam fratrem P. Claudii esse: quin ille
sedens pro tribunali aut arbitrum aut tacitum specta-
torem comitiorum se praeberet?—coerceri tamen ab
12 effuso studio nequit. Magnis contentionibus tribunorum quoque plebis, qui aut contra consulem aut pro
studio eius pugnabant, comitia aliquotiens turbata,
donec pervicit Appius ut deiecto Fabio fratrem trahe-
13 ret. Creatus P. Claudius Pulcher praeter spem suam
et ceterorum. Locum suum tenuit L. Porcius Licinus,
quia moderatis studiis, non vi[2] Claudiana inter ple-
14 beios certatum est. Praetorum inde comitia sunt
habita: C. Decimius Flavus P. Sempronius Longus
P. Cornelius Cethegus Q. Naevius Matho C. Sempronius Blaesus A. Terentius Varro praetores facti.
15 Haec eo anno, quo Ap. Claudius M. Sempronius
consules fuerunt, domi militiaeque gesta.

A.U.C. 570 XXXIII. Principio insequentis anni P. Claudius
L. Porcius consules, cum Q. Caecilius M. Baebius
Ti. Sempronius, qui ad disceptandum inter Philippum et Eumenem reges Thessalorumque civitates
2 missi erant, legationem renuntiassent, regum quoque
eorum civitatiumque legatos in senatum introduxe-

[1] Licinus *Sigonius*: licinius ς. [2] vi *Gelenius*: ut ς.

---

[1] The *tribunal* was a platform erected in the Campus Martius, from which the presiding magistrate conducted the election.

[2] The direct reference is to the activity of the consul in the election, with more than a hint that such impetuosity was characteristic of the *gens Claudia*.

opinion of men Quintus Fabius Labeo and Lucius Porcius Licinus were almost certain of success. But the consul Claudius, without his lictors, flitting with his brother around the whole Forum, though his adversaries and the greater part of the senate kept crying out that he should remember that he was the consul of the Roman people rather than the brother of Publius Claudius (why should he not take his seat on the tribunal[1] and act either as an umpire or else as a silent spectator of the elections?), nevertheless could not be restrained from his zealous canvass. Great contentions among the tribunes of the people, as well, who took part in the fight either against the consul or on his side, disturbed the elections several times, until Appius succeeded in bringing in his brother, Fabius being defeated. Publius Claudius Pulcher was elected contrary to his own expectations and those of others. Lucius Porcius Licinus held his place because among the plebeians the contest was conducted with moderate partisanship, not with Claudian violence.[2] Then the praetorian elections were held: Gaius Decimius Flavus, Publius Sempronius Longus, Publius Cornelius Cethegus, Quintus Naevius Matho, Gaius Sempronius Blaesus and Aulus Terentius Varro were chosen praetors. Such were the events, at home and abroad, of the consular year of Appius Claudius and Marcus Sempronius. B.C. 185

XXXIII. In the beginning of the following year, when Quintus Caecilius, Marcus Baebius and Tiberius Sempronius, who had been sent to arbitrate between the kings, Philip and Eumenes, and the cities of the Thessalians, had reported on their mission, the consuls Publius Claudius and Lucius Porcius also introduced into the senate the ambassadors of these B.C. 184

A.U.C. 570 3 runt. Eadem utrimque iterata, quae dicta apud
legatos in Graecia erant. Aliam deinde novam
legationem patres, cuius princeps Ap. Claudius fuit,
in Graeciam et Macedoniam decreverunt ad visendum,
redditaene civitates Thessalis et Perrhaebis essent.
4 Iisdem mandatum, ut ab Aeno et Maronea praesidia
deducerentur, maritimaque omnis Thraciae ora a
5 Philippo et Macedonibus liberaretur. Peloponnesum quoque adire iussi, unde prior legatio dis-
cesserat incertiore statu rerum quam si non venissent:
nam super cetera etiam sine responso dimissi, nec
6 datum petentibus erat Achaeorum concilium. De
qua re querente graviter Q. Caecilio et simul Lacedaemoniis deplorantibus moenia diruta, abductam
plebem in Achaiam et venumdatam, ademptas,
quibus ad eam diem civitas stetisset, Lycurgi leges,
7 Achaei maxime concilii negati crimen excusabant
recitando legem, quae nisi belli pacisve causa, et
cum legati ab senatu cum litteris aut scriptis mandatis
8 venirent, vetaret indici concilium. Ea ne postea
excusatio esset, ostendit senatus curae iis esse debere,
ut legatis Romanis semper adeundi concilium gentis

---

[1] In chaps. xxiv.–xxix. above, Livy said nothing about a visit to the Achaean League by the commission headed by Caecilius. In XXIII. xi. (XXII. xv.), however, Polybius gives the same account as that which Livy gives here.

[2] Cf. XXXVIII. xxxiv; the enslaved commons here are apparently the *adscripti* of that chapter.

kings and of the cities. The same arguments were repeated on both sides that had been used before the commissioners in Greece. Then the Fathers decreed another new commission, of which Appius Claudius was the chief, to go to Greece and Macedonia to see whether the cities had been restored to the Thessalians and Perrhaebians. They were also instructed that the garrisons were to be withdrawn from Aenus and Maronea and that the whole sea coast should be freed from Philip and the Macedonians. They were directed to visit the Peloponnesus also, from which the previous commission[1] had come away leaving the position of things more uncertain than if they had not gone: for in addition to everything else they had even been sent away without an answer, and the Achaean council had not been summoned as they requested. When Quintus Caecilius complained bitterly of this conduct and the Lacedaemonians at the same time lamented that their walls had been destroyed, their common people taken away to Achaia and enslaved, the laws of Lycurgus, on which their state had been based up to that time, annulled,[2] the principal reply of the Achaeans to the charge that a council had been refused was to read the law which forbade the calling of the council except when it was a question of peace or war or when ambassadors arrived from the senate with letters or written instructions.[3] That this excuse might not be given again, the senate made it plain that it was their duty to see that Roman commissioners should always have the opportunity to address the council of the people, B.C. 184

[3] It is nowhere made clear whether this was a law of the council itself (cf. XXXI. xxv. 9) or a part of the treaty between Rome and the League.

A.U.C. 570 potestas fieret, quem ad modum et illis quotiens vellent senatus daretur.

XXXIV. Dimissis iis legationibus, Philippus a suis certior factus cedendum civitatibus deducendaque praesidia esse, infensus omnibus in Maronitas iram
2 effundit. Onomasto, qui praeerat maritimae orae, mandat, ut partis adversae principes interficeret. Ille per Casandrum quendam, unum ex regiis iam diu habitantem Maroneae, nocte Thracibus intro-
3 missis velut in bello capta urbe caedem fecit. Idem[1] apud Romanos legatos querentes tam crudeliter adversus innoxios Maronitas, tam superbe adversus populum Romanum factum ut, quibus libertatem restituendam senatus censuisset, ii pro hostibus trucidarentur, abnuebat quicquam eorum ad se aut
4 quemquam suorum pertinere; seditione inter ipsos dimicatum, cum ad se alii, alii ad Eumenem civitatem
5 traherent; id facile scituros esse; percunctarentur ipsos Maronitas, haud dubius, perculsis omnibus terrore tam recentis caedis, neminem hiscere adversus
6 se ausurum. Negare Appius rem evidentem pro dubia quaerendam. Si ab se culpam removere vellet, Onomastum et Casandrum, per quos acta res diceretur, mitteret Romam, ut eos senatus percunctari
7 posset. Primo adeo perturbavit ea vox regem ut

[1] idem *M. Mueller*: id ϛ.

---

[1] The situation required a delicate adjustment between the sovereignty of the League and the quasi-protectorate of Rome.

just as to them too the senate was open as often as they wished.[1] B.C. 184

XXXIV. When these embassies had been dismissed, Philip was informed by his representatives that he was to retire from the cities and withdraw his garrisons; being angered at everyone, he vented his wrath on the Maroneans. He sent word to Onomastus, who was in command of the sea coast, to kill the leading men of the opposing party. Onomastus, through the agency of a certain Casander, one of the king's supporters who had long been a resident of Maronea, admitting the Thracians by night, caused a slaughter as if the town had been captured in war. When the Roman commissioners complained of such cruel treatment of the unoffending Maroneans and of such arrogant conduct towards the Roman people, that those men whose liberty the senate had declared was to be restored were murdered as if they were enemies, Philip in reply denied that any of this concerned himself or any one of his subjects; there had been fighting as a consequence of internal strife, since some were for transferring the city to him, others to the Romans; this fact they could easily ascertain; let them, he said, question the Maroneans themselves—not doubting that when all were smitten with the terror of so recent a massacre no one would dare to open his mouth against him. Appius replied that so clear a case needed no investigation as if it were not clear. If Philip wished to avert blame from himself he should send Onomastus and Casander, through whom it was said that the plan had been executed, to Rome, in order that the senate might question them. This speech at first so disconcerted the king that he could not control his colour or

A.U.C. 570 non color, non vultus ei constaret; deinde collecto
tandem animo Casandrum, qui Maroneae fuisset, si
8 utique vellent, se missurum dixit: ad Onomastum
quidem quid eam rem pertinere, qui non modo Maroneae, sed ne in regione quidem propinqua fuisset?
9 Et parcebat magis Onomasto, honoratiori amico, et
eundem indicem haud paulo plus timebat, quia et
ipse sermonem cum eo contulerat et multorum talium
10 ministrum et conscium habebat. Casander quoque,
missis qui per Epirum ad mare prosequerentur eum,
ne qua indicium emanaret, veneno creditur sublatus.

XXXV. Et legati a Philippi colloquio ita digressi
2 sunt, ut prae se ferrent nihil eorum sibi placere, et
Philippus minime, quin rebellandum esset, dubius.
Quia tamen [1] immaturae ad id vires erant, ad moram
interponendam Demetrium minorem filium mittere
Romam simul ad purganda [2] crimina, simul ad de-
3 precandam iram senatus statuit, satis credens ipsum
etiam iuvenem, quod Romae obses specimen indolis
4 regiae dedisset, aliquid momenti facturum. Interim
per speciem auxilii Byzantiis ferendi, re ipsa ad
terrorem regulis Thracum iniciendum profectus,
perculsis iis uno proelio et Amadoco duce capto
in Macedoniam rediit, missis ad accolas Histri fluminis
barbaros, ut in Italiam irrumperent, sollicitandos.

[1] quia tamen *ed. Moguntina*: quia dum quia *et similia* ς.
[2] purganda *ed. Frobeniana* 1531: depurganda ς.

---

[1] Polybius (XXIII. xiv.) says bluntly that he was poisoned.

[2] The earlier career of Demetrius is briefly sketched in the following. A still younger son, Philip (XLII. lii. 5), is consistently ignored in the Books contained in this volume.

[3] The barbarians referred to were probably the Bastarnae (XL. v. 10), who lived along the lower Hister (Danube) river.

expression; then, at length collecting his wits, he said that he would send Casander, who had been at Maronea, if they really wished it; but how did this affair concern Onomastus, who had not only not been at Maronea but had not even been in any district close to it? And in fact he was both careful to spare Onomastus, as a more valued friend, and was likewise much more afraid of him as an informer, because he himself had exchanged views with him and used him as an agent and accomplice in many such affairs. Casander, moreover, when men were sent to conduct him through Epirus to the sea, was believed to have been done away with by poison, lest in some way his evidence might get out.[1] B.C. 184

XXXV. And the commissioners went away from the conference with Philip in such fashion as to advertise the fact that nothing in his conduct pleased them, and Philip had no doubt at all that he would have to resort to war. Yet, since his strength was still insufficient for that, in order to cause delay, he determined to send his younger son Demetrius [2] to Rome, partly to explain away the charges against him, partly to turn aside the wrath of the senate, being well persuaded that he, even though a young man, because while he was a hostage at Rome he had shown signs of possessing a kingly nature, would have some influence. Meanwhile, setting out under the pretence of bringing aid to the Byzantines, but in reality in order to inspire the chiefs of the Thracians with fear, having defeated them in one battle and captured their leader Amadocus, he returned to Macedonia, sending agents to stir up the barbarians [3] living along the Hister river, to the end that they might invade Italy.

A.U.C. 570

5 Et in Peloponneso adventus legatorum Romanorum, qui ex Macedonia in Achaiam ire iussi erant, exspectabatur; adversus quos ut praeparata consilia
6 haberent, Lycortas praetor concilium indixit. Ibi de Lacedaemoniis actum: ex hostibus eos accusatores factos, et periculum esse ne victi magis timendi forent quam bellantes fuissent. Quippe in bello sociis Romanis Achaeos usos: nunc[1] eosdem Romanos
7 aequiores Lacedaemoniis quam Achaeis esse, ubi Areus etiam et Alcibiades, ambo exsules, suo beneficio restituti, legationem Romam[2] adversus gentem Achaeorum ita de ipsis meritam suscepissent, adeoque infesta oratione usi essunt ut pulsi patria non
8 restituti in eam viderentur. Clamor undique ortus, referret[3] nominatim de iis; et cum omnia ira non consilio gererentur, capitis damnati sunt. Paucos post dies Romani legati venerunt. His Clitore in Arcadia datum est concilium.

XXXVI. Priusquam agerent quicquam, terror Achaeis iniectus erat et cogitatio, quam non ex
2 aequo disceptatio futura esset, quod Areum et Alcibiadem capitis ab se concilio proximo damnatos cum legatis videbant; nec hiscere quisquam audebat.
3 Appius ea quae apud senatum questi erant Lacedaemonii displicere senatui ostendit: caedem primum

[1] usos: nunc *edd. vett.*: ausos tunc ς.
[2] Romam *ed. Aldina*: romanam ς.
[3] referret ς: referri *M*.

[1] They had been exiled by Nabis.

In the Peloponnesus also the coming of the Roman commissioners, who had been ordered to proceed from Macedonia to Achaia, was being awaited; and in order that they might have their arguments prepared in advance with which to confront the Romans, the praetor Lycortas called a council. There the question concerned the Lacedaemonians: from enemies they had turned accusers, and there was danger that in defeat they would prove more to be feared than they had been when at war. In the war, they reflected, the Achaeans had had the Romans as allies: now the same Romans were more favourably disposed towards the Lacedaemonians than towards the Achaeans, in a situation where even Areus and Alcibiades, both exiles,[1] restored through Achaean influence, had undertaken an embassy to Rome against the Achaean people which had deserved so well of them, and had expressed sentiments so hostile that they seemed to have been driven from their country, not restored to it. A cry went up from all sides that the praetor should offer a motion concerning them by name; and since everything was governed by passion, not deliberation, they were condemned to death. A few days later the Roman commissioners arrived. A council was called for them at Clitor in Arcadia. B.C. 184

XXXVI. Before they did anything, fear struck the Achaeans and the thought came to them on how unequal grounds the argument was likely to be conducted, because they saw Areus and Alcibiades, who had been condemned to death by them at the latest council, with the commissioners; nor did anyone dare to open his mouth. Appius stated that the conduct of which the Lacedaemonians had complained before the senate was displeasing to the senate: first, the

A.U.C. 570 ad Compasium[1] factam eorum, qui a Philopoemene
4 ad causam dicendam evocati venissent; deinde cum in homines ita saevitum esset ne[2] ulla parte crudelitas eorum cessaret, muros dirutos urbis nobilissimae esse, leges vetustissimas abrogatas, inclutamque per
5 gentes disciplinam Lycurgi sublatam. Haec cum Appius dixisset, Lycortas, et quia praetor et quia Philopoemenis, auctoris omnium quae Lacedaemone
6 acta fuerant, factionis erat, ita respondit: "Difficilior nobis, Ap. Claudi, apud vos oratio est quam
7 Romae nuper apud senatum fuit. Tunc enim Lacedaemoniis accusantibus respondendum erat: nunc a vobis ipsis accusati sumus, apud quos causa
8 est dicenda. Quam iniquitatem condicionis subimus illa spe, iudicis animo te auditurum esse, posita contentione qua paulo ante egisti. Ego certe, cum ea quae et hic antea apud Q. Caecilium[3] et postea Romae questi sunt Lacedaemonii, a te paulo ante relata sint, non tibi sed illis me apud te respondere
9 credam.[4] Caedem obicitis eorum, qui a Philopoemene praetore evocati ad causam dicendam inter-

[1] Compasium *Crévier*: conflictum ς.
[2] ne *Madvig*: nec *M*: ne in ς.
[3] Q. Caecilium ς: p. sulpitium *M*.
[4] credam *ed. Frobeniana* 1531: credebam ς.

---

[1] Cf. XXXVIII. xxxiii. The scene of the episode has not been mentioned before. Rome had apparently given no indication of its attitude towards this affair, except as it might be inferred from their general attitude towards the Achaeans.

[2] He probably means the embassy reported in xxxiii. 7 above, although it is not recorded that Lycortas himself was a member of that embassy, and Livy has not mentioned any

slaughter which took place at Compasium of those B.C 184
Lacedaemonians who had come in response to the summons of Philopoemen to plead their cause;[1] second, that after they had treated men with such violence, that they might overlook no form of cruelty, they had torn down the walls of a most illustrious city, had repealed their most ancient laws, and had done away with the discipline of Lycurgus, famed as it was throughout the world. When Appius had said this, Lycortas, both because he was praetor and because he belonged to the party of Philopoemen, who was responsible for whatever had been done in Lacedaemon, replied thus: "It is more difficult for us, Appius Claudius, to speak in your presence than it was recently in Rome before the senate.[2] For then our task was to answer the accusations of the Lacedaemonians: now we have been accused by you, before whom we must plead our cause. This disadvantage of situation we accept in the hope that you will listen in the spirit of a judge, laying aside the vehemence of a prosecutor with which you spoke a little while ago. I at any rate, when these complaints which were presented, both here previously before Quintus Caecilius[3] and in Rome later by the Lacedaemonians, were repeated by you a little while ago, shall believe that I am replying, not to you, but to them in your presence. You bring up the murder of those men who were killed when they had been summoned by the praetor Philopoemen to plead their

argument with the Lacedaemonians at that time. Lycortas was also at Rome in 189 B.C. (XXXVIII. xxxii. 5–10).

[3] There must have been unofficial conferences with the commissioners even if no meeting of the council was held: cf. xxxiii. 6 above.

A.U.C. 570 fecti sunt. Hoc ego crimen non modo a vobis, Romani,
sed ne apud vos quidem nobis obiciendum fuisse
arbitror. Quid ita? Quia in vestro foedere erat ut
10 maritimis urbibus abstinerent Lacedaemonii. Quo
tempore armis captis urbes, a quibus abstinere iussi
erant, nocturno impetu occupaverunt, si T.[1] Quinctius, si exercitus Romanus, sicut antea, in Peloponneso fuisset, eo nimirum capti et oppressi con-
11 fugissent. Cum vos procul essetis, quo alio nisi ad
nos, socios vestros, quos antea Gytheo opem ferentes,
quos Lacedaemonem vobiscum simili de causa op-
12 pugnantes viderant, confugerent? Pro vobis igitur
iustum piumque bellum suscepimus. Quod cum
alii laudent, reprehendre ne Lacedaemonii quidem
possint, dii quoque ipsi comprobaverint, qui nobis
victoriam dederunt, quonam modo ea quae belli iure
acta sunt in disceptationem veniunt? Quorum
13 tamen maxima pars nihil pertinet ad nos. Nostrum
est quod evocavimus ad causam dicendam eos, qui
ad arma multitudinem exciverant, qui expugnaverant
maritima oppida, qui diripuerant, qui caedem princi-
14 pum fecerant. Quod vero illi venientes in castra
interfecti sunt, vestrum est, Areu et Alcibiade, qui
nunc nos, si diis placet, accusatis, non nostrum.
15 Exules Lacedaemoniorum, quo ex [2] numero hi quoque duo fuerunt, et tunc nobiscum erant, et quod
domicilio sibi delegerant maritima oppida, se petitos
credentes, in eos, quorum opera patria extorres ne

[1] t. ς : ti. *F*. [2] ex *codd. Modii* : in ς.

---

[1] Cf. XXXVIII. xxx.–xxxi. and the note to xxx. 6.

cause. This charge, in my opinion, should not only B.C. 184 not have been made against us by you, Romans, but not even by them before you. Why so? Because it was stated in your treaty that the Lacedaemonians should keep their hands off the towns on the coast. At the time when they took up arms and seized, by a night attack, those cities which they had been ordered to let alone, if Titus Quinctius, if a Roman army, as before, had been in the Peloponnesus, the captured and oppressed would doubtless have fled to them.[1] Since you were far away, where else could they flee except to us, whom they had previously seen bringing aid to Gytheum and besieging Lacedaemon in common cause with you? On your behalf, then, we undertook a legal and righteous war. Since others applaud it, since not even the Lacedaemonians can criticize it, and since the very gods themselves, by giving us the victory, have approved it, how can those things which took place under the law of war come into dispute? Yet the greatest part of those things have nothing to do with us. It is our affair that we summoned to plead their cause those who had called the multitude to arms, who had captured the coast towns, who had plundered them, who had caused the murder of the leading men. But as to the fact that they were killed while they were coming to our camp, that is your affair, Areus and Alcibiades—who now (heaven help us!) are accusing us—not ours. The exiles of the Lacedaemonians, to which number even these two belonged, were indeed at that time with us, and because they had chosen as their places of residence the towns on the coast believing that they were being sought out, they made an attack on those men thanks to whose efforts they

A.U.C. 570 in tuto quidem exsilio posse consenescere se indigna-
16 bantur, impetum fecerunt. Lacedaemonii igitur Lacedaemonios, non Achaei interfecerunt; nec iure an iniuria caesi sint, argumentari refert.

XXXVII. "At enim illa certe vestra sunt, Achaei, quod leges disciplinamque vetustissimam Lycurgi
2 sustulistis, quod muros diruistis. Quae utraque ab iisdem obici qui possunt, cum muri Lacedaemonis non ab Lycurgo, sed paucos ante annos ad dissolven-
3 dam Lycurgi disciplinam exstructi sint? Tyranni enim nuper eos arcem et munimentum sibi, non civitati paraverunt; et si exsistat hodie ab inferis Lycurgus, gaudeat ruinis eorum, et nunc se patriam
4 et Spartam antiquam agnoscere dicat. Non Philopoemenem exspectare nec Achaeos, sed vos ipsi, Lacedaemonii, vestris manibus amoliri et diruere
5 omnia vestigia tyrannidis debuistis. Vestrae enim illae deformes veluti notae [1] servitutis erant, et cum sine muris per octingentos prope annos liberi, aliquando etiam principes Graeciae fuissetis, muris velut compedibus circumdatis vincti per centum annos
6 servistis. Quod ad leges ademptas attinet, ego antiquas Lacedaemoniis [2] leges tyrannos ademisse

[1] veluti notae *Weissenborn*: notae *F* ς: ueluti cicatrices *M*.
[2] lacedaemoniis ς: lacedaemonis *F*.

---

[1] Lycortas overlooks the fact that on the day after the riot 63 Lacedaemonians were put to death after a sort of trial, apparently before the Achaeans (XXXVIII. xxxiii. 11). The responsibility of the exiles can extend, then, only to the 17 who were killed in the rioting.

It may be remarked that the Achaeans show no sympathy for the victims of Nabis on the ground of their aristocratic tendencies, and are interested in them, so far as one can judge, solely because they provided a means of creating internal discord in Lacedaemon.

saw with indignation that they, exiles from home, could not grow old even in a safe place of exile. Lacedaemonians, then, were killed by Lacedaemonians, not by Achaeans; whether they were killed justly or unjustly it is not important to inquire.[1] B.C. 184

XXXVII. " But, you say, those other actions were at any rate your acts, Achaeans—the abolition of the laws and the most ancient discipline of Lycurgus, and the destruction of the walls. But how can both these criticisms be made by the same persons, since the walls of Lacedaemon were not built by Lycurgus, but were constructed a few years ago to overthrow the system of Lycurgus? For the tyrants recently erected them, a citadel and protection for themselves, not for the city; and if Lycurgus should rise from the dead to-day he would rejoice in their destruction and would say that now he recognized his home and the ancient Sparta. You yourselves, Lacedaemonians, should not have waited for Philopoemen and the Achaeans, but should with your own hands have torn down and destroyed all traces of the tyranny. For they were yours—those disfiguring scars of servitude, if I may so call them, and while, without walls, you had been free for eight hundred years and for a considerable period even the first state in Greece, when the walls were thrown around you like shackles you were bound in slavery for a hundred years.[2] As far as the abolition of the laws is concerned, I consider that the tyrants took away their ancient laws from the Lacedaemonians; that we did not

[2] The method of calculation throughout is obscure. For the eight centuries under the laws of Lycurgus, cf. XXXVIII. xxxiv. 9. There is no agreement as to the date of the construction of the walls (XXXIV. xxxviii. 2 and the note).

A.U.C. 570 arbitror; nos non suas iis ademisse, quas non habe-
7 bant, sed nostras leges dedisse; nec male consuluisse
civitati, cum concilii nostri eam fecerimus et nobis
miscuerimus, ut corpus unum et concilium[1] totius
8 Peloponnesi esset. Tunc, ut opinor, si aliis ipsi legibus viveremus, alias istis iniunxissemus, queri se
iniquo iure esse et indignari possent.
9 "Scio ego, Ap. Claudi, hanc orationem qua sum
adhuc usus neque sociorum apud socios neque
liberae gentis esse, sed vere servorum disceptantium
10 apud dominos. Nam si non vana illa vox praeconis
fuit, qua liberos esse omnium primos Achaeos iussistis,
si foedus ratum est, si societas et amicitia ex aequo
observatur, cur ego, quid Capua capta feceritis
Romani, non quaero, vos rationem reposcitis, quid
11 Achaei Lacedaemoniis bello victis fecerimus? Interfecti aliqui sunt, finge, a nobis: quid? Vos senatores
12 Campanos securi non percussistis? At muros[2]
diruimus: vos non muros tantum sed urbem agros
13 ademistis. Specie, inquis, aequum est foedus: re
apud Achaeos precaria libertas, apud Romanos etiam
14 imperium est. Sentio, Appi, et, si non oportet, non

[1] et concilium ς: ut consilium *F*.
[2] at muros *Drakenborch*: muros *F*ς.

[1] The decree of 196 B.C. (XXXIII. xxxii. 5; Polybius XVIII. xlvi.) named no Peloponnesian state except Corinth, the others being omitted, presumably, because they were already free. The speaker is therefore inexact in his quotation, although *omnium primos* is exact to the extent that Corinth was the first state mentioned in the decree.

[2] The case of Capua was frequently brought up by Greek critics of Rome: cf., *e.g.*, XXXI. xxix. 11.

[3] This must be regarded as a fair statement of the situation, even if the Greeks themselves were mainly to blame. Lycortas appears to mean by the last clause that such liberty as the

take from them what they did not possess, but gave them our own laws; I believe, too, that the measures we took were not for the disadvantage of the Lacedaemonian state, since we made it part of our League and united it with us, so that there was one body and one council for the whole Peloponnesus. Then and then only, in my judgment, if we ourselves lived under one code and imposed another upon them, would they be able to complain and feel indignant that their status was unfair. B.C. 184

"I know, Appius Claudius, that the speech that I have thus far delivered is neither that of allies in the presence of allies nor that of a free people, but in reality that of slaves arguing before their masters. For if those words of the herald, with which you Romans ordered the Achaeans first of all to be free,[1] were not a mere sham, if the treaty was in fact valid, if the alliance and friendship are being impartially observed, why do I not ask what you Romans did when you took Capua, as you demand an explanation of what we Achaeans did when the Lacedaemonians were conquered in war?[2] Some of them, let us assume, were killed by us: what of it? Did you not behead Campanian senators? But, you say, we tore down their walls: you destroyed, not the walls alone, but the city, the farm lands. The treaty, you say, looks as if it were between equals: in fact, among the Achaeans liberty is a thing bestowed as a favour, among the Romans it amounts even to sovereignty.[3] I know this, Appius, and if I should

Achaeans possess under a treaty that was nominally *aequum* is the gift of the Romans (*precaria*), but that the Romans by virtue of their *imperium* could take away their gift as easily as they could make it. The reply of Claudius confirms this.

A.U.C. 570

indignor: sed oro vos, quantumlibet intersit inter
Romanos et Achaeos, modo ne in aequo hostes vestri
nostrique apud vos sint ac nos socii, immo ne meliore
15 iure sint. Nam ut in aequo essent nos fecimus, cum
leges iis nostras dedimus, cum, ut Achaici [1] concilii
essent, effecimus. Parum est victis, quod victoribus
satis est; plus postulant hostes quam socii habent.
16 Quae iureiurando, quae monumentis litterarum in
lapide insculptis in aeternam memoriam sancta atque
sacrata sunt, ea cum periurio nostro tollere parant.
17 Veremur quidem vos, Romani, et si ita vultis, etiam
timemus: sed plus et [2] veremur et timemus deos
18 immortales." Cum adsensu maximae partis est
auditus, et locutum omnes pro maiestate magistratus
censebant, ut facile appareret molliter agendo dig-
19 nitatem suam tenere Romanos non posse. Tum
Appius suadere se magnopere Achaeis dixit ut, dum
liceret voluntate sua facere, gratiam inirent, ne mox
20 inviti et coacti facerent. Haec vox audita quidem
cum omnium gemitu est, sed metum iniecit [3] im-

[1] Achaici *Gronovius*: achaei *F*ς.
[2] et *ed. Frobeniana* 1535: *om.* ς.
[3] metum iniecit *Gelenius*: metu iniecto ς.

---

[1] A copy of the decree by which Lacedaemon was taken into the League would doubtless be set up in the temple at Aegium.

[2] For the thought cf. sect. 21 below and the note. Lycortas was the father of Polybius, and therefore, even if any corresponding speech in Polybius were preserved, we should find it impossible to judge how much of the version of Livy was genuine. Its sophistry is evident, and it is difficult to see how even a supporter of Philopoemen could have honestly maintained that Lacedaemon had equal rights in the League. But, genuine or imaginary, the speech seems to

not I do not object; but at any rate I beg you, no B.C. 184 matter how great the difference may be between the Romans and the Achaeans, not to permit your enemies and ours to be on an equal footing before you with us, your allies, or rather on a better footing. For we brought it about that they were equal when we gave them our laws, when we made them members of the Achaean League. That is too little for the conquered which is sufficient for the conquerors; enemies demand more than allies possess! Those things which were made sanctified and sacred by oath, by written records[1] carved on stone for eternal preservation, they are trying, by making us perjurers, to destroy. Indeed we respect you, Romans, and, if you wish it so, we even fear you; but still more do we both respect and fear the immortal gods."[2] Lycortas was heard with applause on the part of the majority, and all said that he had spoken in a manner consistent with the dignity of his office, so that it was readily apparent that by a soft answer the Romans could not maintain their position. Then Appius said that he earnestly advised the Achaeans to come to terms while it was still possible to do so of their own free will, lest presently they be forced to take the same action against their will and under compulsion. This speech was received with a general groan, but it made the Achaeans fear to refuse what

picture fairly the actual situation that existed in Greece, and its accuracy suggests that Livy had some evidential basis for his composition. For an excellent and well-documented discussion of this question, see Larsen, "Was Greece Free between 196 and 146 B.C.?" in *Classical Philology* 30, 1935, 193–214. Larsen's findings agree in general with the point of view of this note, although he does not use this speech as evidence.

A.U.C. 570

21 perata recusandi. Id modo petierunt ut Romani, quae viderentur, de Lacedaemoniis mutarent nec Achaeos religione obstringerent irrita ea, quae iureiurando sanxissent, faciendi. Damnatio tantum Arei et Alcibiadis, quae nuper facta erat, sublata est.

XXXVIII. Romae principio eius anni, cum de provinciis consulum et praetorum actum est, consulibus Ligures, quia bellum nusquam alibi erat, decreti.
2 Praetores C. Decimius Flavus[1] urbanam, P. Cornelius
3 Cethegus inter cives et peregrinos sortiti sunt, C. Sempronius Blaesus Siciliam, Q. Naevius Matho Sardiniam et ut idem quaereret de veneficiis, A. Terentius Varro Hispaniam citeriorem, P. Sempro-
4 nius Longus Hispaniam ulteriorem. De iis duabus provinciis legati per id fere tempus L. Iuventius Talna
5 et T. Quinctilius Varus venerunt, qui quantum bellum iam profligatum in Hispania esset senatu edocto postularunt simul, ut pro rebus tam prospere gestis diis immortalibus haberetur honos et ut praetoribus
6 exercitum deportare liceret. Supplicatio in biduum decreta est: de legionibus deportandis, cum de consulum praetorumque exercitibus ageretur, rem integ-
7 ram referri iusserunt. Paucos post dies consulibus in Ligures binae legiones, quas Ap. Claudius et M.
8 Sempronius habuerant, decretae sunt. De Hispaniensibus exercitibus magna contentio fuit inter

[1] Decimius Flavus *ed. Frobeniana* 1535 : decimus flauius ς

---

[1] The Achaeans, recognizing the inevitability of changes, ask that these changes be enforced upon them by Rome, to spare them the humiliation of breaking their oaths by repealing laws which they had sworn to obey.

[2] The praetors were clearly warned by the experience of Acidinus (xxix. 4–5 above and the note), and tried to avoid giving the senate an excuse to refuse their triumphs.

was ordered. They requested only this, that the B.C. 184
Romans should make such changes as seemed proper to them regarding the Lacedaemonians and should not involve the Achaeans in the religious difficulty of making void what they had ratified by oath.[1] Only the vote of condemnation which had recently been passed on Areus and Alcibiades was repealed.

XXXVIII. At Rome, in the beginning of this year, when the question of the provinces for the consuls and praetors came up, the Ligurians were decreed to the consuls, since there was war nowhere else. Of the praetors, Gaius Decimius Flavus received the civil jurisdiction, Publius Cornelius Cethegus that between citizens and aliens, Gaius Sempronius Blaesus Sicily, Quintus Naevius Matho Sardinia and the additional task of investigating cases of poisoning, Aulus Terentius Varro Nearer Spain, Publius Sempronius Longus Farther Spain. From these two provinces at about the same time came the lieutenants, Lucius Juventius Talna and Titus Quinctilius Varus, who, after informing the senate how great a war had now been finished in Spain, asked at the same time that by reason of such victories honour should be paid to the immortal gods and that the praetors should be permitted to bring home their armies.[2] A thanksgiving for two days was decreed: as to bringing back the legions, they ordered that the question should be brought up anew when the matter of troops for the consuls and praetors was discussed. A few days later the consuls were assigned, for service against the Ligurians, two legions each, which had been under the command of Appius Claudius and Marcus Sempronius. With respect to the Spanish armies, great strife arose between the new praetors and the

A.U.C. 570 novos praetores et amicos absentium, Calpurnii
9 Quinctiique. Utraque causa tribunos plebis, utraque
consulem habebat. Hi se intercessuros senatus consulto, si deportandos censerent exercitus, denuntia-
bant: illi, si haec intercessio fieret, nullam rem aliam
10 se decerni passuros. Victa postremo absentium
gratia est et senatus consultum factum ut praetores
quattuor milia peditum Romanorum scriberent,
trecentos equites, et quinque milia peditum sociorum
Latini nominis, quingentos equites, quos secum in
11 Hispaniam portarent. Cum ea quattuor milia in
legiones discripsissent,[1] quo [2] plus quam quina milia
peditum, treceni equites in singulis legionibus esset,[3]
dimitterent, eos primum, qui emerita stipendia
12 haberent, deinde ut cuiusque fortissima opera Calpurnius et Quinctius in proelio usi essent.

XXXIX. Hac sedata contentione alia subinde C.
2 Decimii praetoris morte exorta est. Cn. Sicinius et
L. Pupius, qui aediles proximo anno fuerant, et C.
Valerius flamen Dialis et Q. Fulvius Flaccus—is quia
aedilis curulis designatus erat, sine toga candida, sed
3 maxima ex omnibus contentione—petebant; certa-
menque ei cum flamine [4] erat. Et postquam primo

[1] ea quattuor milia in legiones discripsissent *M. Mueller*: ea legiones quattuor descripsissent ς.

[2] quo *Madvig*: quod ς.

[3] esset *ed. Aldina*: essent ς.

[4] flamine *ed. Frobeniana* 1535: flamine diale ς.

---

[1] Since the negative always prevailed in such circumstances, a complete deadlock and suspension of public business were threatened.

[2] Livy has confused the story. If Fulvius was aedile-elect only, there could have been no objection to his wearing the *toga candida* (a curule magistrate wore the *toga praetexta*), and no question of holding two offices at once could have arisen,

friends of the absent, Calpurnius and Quinctius. B.C. 184
Each side had tribunes of the people, each a consul. The one side threatened that they would veto a decree of the senate if they should vote that the armies should be brought home: the others, that if this veto should be used they would permit no other decree to be passed.[1] In the end the influence of the absent praetors proved unavailing, and a decree of the senate was passed that the praetors should enlist four thousand Roman infantry, three hundred cavalry, and of the allies of the Latin confederacy five thousand infantry and five hundred cavalry, whom they should take with them to Spain. When they had assigned these four thousand to the legions, in proportion as they numbered more than five thousand infantry and three hundred cavalry per legion, they should discharge the surplus; first, those who had completed their terms of service, second, those individuals whose conspicuous services Calpurnius and Quinctius had enjoyed in the battle.

XXXIX. When this strife had calmed down, another straightway arose as a consequence of the death of Gaius Decimius the praetor. Gnaeus Sicinius and Lucius Pupius, who had been aediles the preceding year, and Gaius Valerius the *flamen Dialis* and Quintus Fulvius Flaccus—he, because he was curule aedile elect,[2] did not wear the *toga candida*, but was canvassing more energetically than the rest—were the candidates. The race was between Fulvius and the *flamen*. And when Fulvius

since his partial term as praetor would expire when his term as aedile began (cf. VII. xlii. 2 for the law forbidding two offices at the same time). We must therefore conclude with Mommsen (*St. R.* I. 513, n. 3) that Fulvius was aedile, not aedile-elect.

A.U.C. 570 aequare, mox superare etiam est visus, pars tribunorum plebis negare rationem eius habendam esse,
4 quod duos simul unus magistratus, praesertim curules, neque capere posset nec gerere; pars legibus eum solvi aequum censere, ut quem vellet praetorem
5 creandi populo potestas fieret. L. Porcius consul primo in ea sententia esse ne nomen eius acciperet;
6 deinde, ut ex auctoritate senatus idem faceret, convocatis patribus referre se ad eos dixit, quod nec iure ullo nec exemplo tolerabili liberae civitati aedilis curulis designatus praeturam peteret; sibi, nisi quid aliud iis videretur, in animo esse e lege comitia habere.
7 Patres censuerunt, uti L. Porcius consul cum Q. Fulvio ageret ne impedimento esset quo minus comitia praetoris in locum C. Decimii subrogandi e lege
8 haberentur. Agenti consuli ex senatus consulto respondit Flaccus nihil quod se[1] indignum esset facturum. Medio responso spem ad voluntatem interpretantibus fecerat cessurum patrum auctoritati esse.
9 Comitiis acrius etiam quam ante petebat criminando, extorqueri sibi a consule et senatu populi Romani beneficium, et invidiam fieri geminati honoris, tamquam non appareret, ubi designatus praetor esset,

[1] quod se *edd. vett.*: quidem se quod ς.

---

[1] The presiding magistrate had wide discretion in accepting or rejecting candidacies.

[2] The doctrine here expressed had been most recently invoked for the benefit of Flamininus in 199 B.C. (XXXII. vii. 11).

[3] One expects *renuntiatus* rather than *designatus*, but there is no authority for it in the MSS.

seemed at first to be on equal terms with Valerius B.C. 184 and then even to be passing him, part of the tribunes of the people declared that his candidacy ought not to be accepted [1] because one man could not seek or hold two offices simultaneously, especially curule offices; part thought that he should be exempted from the operation of the laws, so that the people might have the opportunity of electing whomsoever they wished to the praetorship.[2] Lucius Porcius the consul was at first of the opinion that he should not accept his name; then, that he might take this action with the authorization of the senate, calling together the Fathers, he said that he was referring the matter to them because there was neither any law nor any precedent, acceptable in a free state, that a curule aedile elect might seek the praetorship; unless something else seemed best to them, it was his intention to hold the election in accordance with the law. The Fathers voted that the consul Lucius Porcius should appeal to Quintus Fulvius not to stand in the way of the election of a praetor, as a successor to Gaius Decimius, being held in accordance with the law. When the consul made this appeal in accordance with the decree of the senate, Flaccus replied that he would do nothing which was unworthy of himself. By this ambiguous answer he had created, in the minds of men who interpreted it to suit their own desires, the hope that he would yield to the authority of the Fathers. At the election he continued his canvassing even more actively than before, charging that the consul and the senate were wresting from him the gift of the Roman people and were arousing hostility to him by their talk of duplicated offices, as if it were not evident that when he should be elected [3]

A.U.C. 570

10 extemplo aedilitate se abdicaturum. Consul cum
et pertinaciam petentis crescere et favorem populi
magis magisque in eum inclinari cerneret, dimissis
comitiis senatum vocavit. Censuerunt frequentes,
quoniam Flaccum auctoritas patrum nihil movisset,
11 ad populum cum Flacco agendum. Contione advocata
cum egisset consul, ne tum quidem de sententia motus
gratias populo Romano egit, quod tanto studio,
quotienscumque declarandae voluntatis potestas
12 facta esset, praetorem se voluisset facere: ea sibi
studia civium suorum destituere non esse in animo.
Haec vero tam obstinata vox tantum ei favorem
accendit ut haud dubius praetor esset, si consul
13 accipere nomen vellet. Ingens certamen tribunis
et inter se ipsos et cum consule fuit, donec senatus a
14 consule est habitus decretumque: quoniam praetoris
subrogandi comitia ne legibus fierent, pertinacia Q.
Flacci et prava studia hominum impedirent, senatum
15 censere satis praetorum esse; P. Cornelius utramque
in urbe iurisdictionem haberet, Apollinique ludos
faceret.

XL. His comitiis prudentia et virtute senatus sublatis, alia maioris certaminis, quo et maiore de re et
2 inter plures potentioresque viros, sunt exorta. Cen-

---

[1] The first appeal had been made privately, although the reply of Flaccus had at once been made known.

[2] Their ardour cooled later, and Flaccus did not become praetor until two years after this (lvi. 5 below).

[3] Cf. the similar contest at the preceding election of 189 B.C. (XXXVII. lvii. 9–lviii. 2).

praetor he would immediately resign the aedileship. B.C. 184
When the consul saw both that the stubbornness of the candidate increased and that the favour of the people was turning more and more to him, he adjourned the assembly and summoned the senate. A full meeting declared that, since the authority of the Fathers had had no influence with Flaccus, the appeal to Flaccus should be made before the assembly.[1] When the consul had called an informal meeting and presented his plea, Flaccus, not even then moved from his position, expressed his gratitude to the Roman people because with such enthusiasm, as often as the opportunity to declare their desires had been granted to them, they had wished to make him praetor: it was not his intention to disappoint these desires of his fellow-citizens. This speech, obstinate though it was, aroused so much enthusiasm for him that he would be praetor beyond a doubt if the consul would accept his candidacy.[2] Then the tribunes had a great argument, both among themselves and with the consul, until the senate was convoked by the consul and passed this decree: that since the stubbornness of Quintus Flaccus and the base desires of men prevented the holding, in accordance with the laws, of the election to fill a vacancy among the praetors, the senate decreed that there were enough praetors; Publius Cornelius should hold both jurisdictions in the City and should preside at the games to Apollo.

XL. When this election had been avoided by the wisdom and courage of the senate, another followed,[3] involving a greater contest, as it was both for a more important prize and participated in by more and more powerful men. The censorship was sought with

A.U.C. 570 suram summa contentione petebant L. Valerius Flaccus P. et L. Scipiones Cn. Manlius Volso L. Furius
3 Purpurio patricii, plebeii autem M. Porcius Cato M. Fulvius Nobilior Ti. et M. Sempronii, Longus et Tuditanus. Sed omnes patricios plebeiosque nobilis-
4 simarum familiarum M. Porcius longe anteibat. In hoc viro tanta vis animi ingeniique fuit ut quocumque loco natus esset, fortunam sibi ipse facturus fuisse videretur. Nulla ars neque privatae neque publicae rei gerendae ei defuit; urbanas rusticasque res pari-
5 ter callebat. Ad summos honores alios scientia iuris, alios eloquentia, alios gloria militaris provexit: huic versatile [1] ingenium sic pariter ad omnia fuit ut natum
6 ad id unum diceres, quodcumque ageret: in bello manu fortissimus multisque insignibus clarus pugnis, idem postquam ad magnos honores pervenit, summus imperator, idem in pace, si ius consuleres, peritissi-
7 mus, si causa oranda esset, eloquentissimus, nec is tantum, cuius lingua vivo eo viguerit,[2] monumentum eloquentiae nullum exstet: vivit immo vigetque
8 eloquentia eius sacrata scriptis omnis generis. Orationes et pro se multae et pro aliis et in alios: nam non solum accusando sed etiam causam dicendo
9 fatigavit inimicos. Simultates nimio plures et

[1] versatile *edd. vett.*: uersabile ς.
[2] viguerit *edd. vett.*: uiguit ς.

---

[1] All the candidates were ex-consuls, as usual. Publius Scipio is Nasica, Lucius Scipio was striving for rehabilitation after his trial, but the outcome of the election suggests that the glory of the Scipios had, at least for a time, departed.

[2] That is, battles in which he took part as a private.

the most intense rivalry by Lucius Valerius Flaccus, Publius and Lucius Scipio, Gnaeus Manlius Volso and Lucius Furius Purpurio, patricians, as well as by the plebeians Marcus Porcius Cato, Marcus Fulvius Nobilior, Tiberius Sempronius Longus and Marcus Sempronius Tuditanus.[1] But among all the patricians and plebeians of the most illustrious houses, Marcus Porcius Cato stood out most conspicuously. In this man there was such force of mind and character that in whatever station he had been born it seemed that he would have made his fortune for himself. No art of conducting either private or public business was lacking to him; he was equally skilled in affairs of the city and of the farm. Some men were advanced to the highest offices by knowledge of the law, others by eloquence, others by military reputation: his comprehensive genius was so adapted to everything alike that you would say that whatever he was doing was the one thing for which he was born: in war he was the bravest of fighters and was famous for many remarkable battles,[2] and after he attained to the highest offices, he was likewise a consummate commander; the same man in peace was, if you asked advice on law, most skilled therein, if there was a case to be pleaded, most eloquent, nor was he merely one whose tongue was potent while he lived but left no record of his eloquence: rather, he lives and flourishes by his eloquence, enshrined in books of every kind. There are many orations, both for himself and for and against others; for he wore down his enemies not only by accusing them but also by pleading his own cause.[3] Feuds in excessive numbers pursued him B.C. 184

[3] Plutarch (*Cato Major*, xv.) says that Cato was put on trial about fifty times.

A.U.C. 570 exercuerunt eum et ipse exercuit eas; nec facile
dixeris, utrum magis presserit eum nobilitas, an ille
10 agitaverit nobilitatem. Asperi procul dubio animi et
linguae acerbae et immodice liberae fuit, sed invicti
a cupiditatibus animi, rigidae innocentiae, con-
11 temptor gratiae, divitiarum. In parsimonia, in
patientia laboris periculique [1] ferrei prope corporis
animique, quem ne senectus quidem quae solvit
12 omnia fregerit, qui sextum et octogesimum annum
agens causam dixerit, ipse pro se oraverit scrip-
seritque, nonagesimo anno Ser. Galbam ad populi
adduxerit iudicium.

XLI. Hunc, sicut omni vita, tum petentem preme-
bat nobilitas; coierantque praeter [2] L. Flaccum, qui
collega in consulatu fuerat, candidati omnes ad
2 deiciendum honore, non solum ut ipsi potius adi-
piscerentur, nec quia indignabantur novum hominem
censorem videre, sed etiam quod tristem censuram
periculosamque multorum famae et ab laeso a
3 plerisque et laedendi cupido exspectabant. Etenim
tum quoque minitabundus petebat, refragari sibi, qui

[1] periculique *ed. Parisina* 1513: periculi *aut* et p. ς.
[2] praeter *ed. Frobeniana* 1535: apud praetorem ς.

---

[1] The play on the verb is so clumsy that it may have been preserved from Livy's source.

[2] According to *Per.* XLIX, L. Scribonius and not Cato prosecuted Galba for his treacherous treatment of the Lusitanians. Cato, however, spoke against him (Cicero *de oratore* I. 227; *Brutus* 89, etc.).

This characterization raises once more the question of a special source dealing with Cato which Livy used (cf. XXXIV. xxi. 8; XXXVI. xxi. 4–6 and the notes). I see no reason—least of all the play on words mentioned in the preceding note—

and he himself pursued them;[1] nor could you easily say whether the nobility worked harder to suppress him or he to irritate the nobility. Without question he had a stern temper, a bitter tongue and one immoderately free, but he had a soul unconquerable by appetites, an unwavering integrity, and a contempt for influence and wealth. In his economy, in his endurance of toil and danger, he was of almost iron-like body and mind, and his mind not even old age, which weakens everything, could break down, since at the age of eighty-six he pleaded a case, spoke and wrote in his own defence, and in his ninetieth year brought Servius Galba to trial before the assembly.[2] B.C. 184

XLI. Against him as a candidate on this occasion the nobility, as throughout his life, used their influence; and all the candidates except Lucius Flaccus, who had been his colleague in the consulship, had formed a combination to keep him from the office,[3] not only that they themselves might rather win it nor because they objected to seeing a "new man"[4] chosen censor, but also because they anticipated a stern censorship dangerous to the reputation of many, from a man who had both been injured by many and was eager to do injury. For even then he was canvassing by means of threats, charging that

why this passage and the account of the censorship in the following chapters should not have been derived from the same source. There seems to be nothing in this passage which Cato would not have regarded as a compliment and would not have been willing to say about himself.

[3] Formal *coitiones* were illegal, but informal combinations could not be prevented. The other candidates were all more or less closely allied with the Scipionic party.

[4] Cf. XXXVII. lvii. 2 and the note.

A.U.C. 570

liberam et fortem censuram timerent, criminando.
4 Et simul L. Valerio suffragabatur: illo uno collega castigare se nova flagitia et priscos revocare mores posse. His accensi homines, adversa nobilitate, non M. Porcium modo censorem fecerunt, sed collegam ei L. Valerium Flaccum adiecerunt.

5 Secundum comitia censorum consules praetoresque in provincias profecti praeter Q. Naevium, quem quattuor non minus menses, priusquam in Sardiniam iret, quaestiones veneficii, quarum magnam partem extra urbem per municipia conciliabulaque habuit, quia ita
6 aptius visum erat, tenuerunt. Si Antiati Valerio credere libet, ad duo milia hominum damnavit. Et L. Postumius praetor, cui Tarentum provincia evenerat, magnas pastorum coniurationes vindicavit, et reliquias Bacchanalium quaestionis cum cura exsecutus
7 est. Multos, qui aut citati non adfuerant aut vades deseruerant, in ea regione Italiae latentes partim noxios iudicavit, partim comprehensos Romam ad senatum misit. In carcerem omnes a P. Cornelio coniecti sunt.

XLII. In Hispania ulteriore fractis proximo bello Lusitanis quietae res fuerunt: in[1] citeriore A. Terentius in Suessetanis oppidum Corbionem vineis et operibus expugnavit, captivos vendidit: quieta
2 deinde hiberna et citerior provincia habuit. Veteres praetores C. Calpurnius Piso et L. Quinctius Romam

[1] fuerunt: in *ed. Frobeniana* 1535: fuerant et in ς.

---

[1] Cf. xxix. 8–9 above, which seems to be duplicated by this item.

he was being opposed by men who feared a free and courageous censorship. At the same time he canvassed for Lucius Valerius also: with him alone as his colleague could he chastise the new vices and revive the ancient character. Aroused by such arguments and against the opposition of the nobility, the citizens not only chose Marcus Porcius as censor, but also gave him Lucius Flaccus as his colleague. B.C. 184

After the election of the censors the consuls and praetors departed for their provinces, with the exception of Quintus Naevius, who was detained for not less than four months before he could set out for Sardinia by the investigation of poisonings, a great part of which he conducted outside the City, in the municipalities and rural communities, because this method seemed more convenient. If one wishes to trust Valerius Antias, he condemned about two thousand persons. And Lucius Postumius the praetor, to whom the province of Tarentum had fallen, broke up large conspiracies of shepherds[1] and diligently prosecuted what was left of the Bacchanalian investigation. Many who either had not appeared when summoned or had abandoned their sureties, hiding in that part of Italy, he pronounced guilty in some cases, and in others he arrested them and sent them to the senate in Rome. All were thrown into prison by Publius Cornelius.

XLII. In Farther Spain, the Lusitanians having been broken in the last campaign, things were quiet; in Nearer Spain Aulus Terentius among the Suessetani took the town of Corbio with sheds and siege-works and sold the captives: after that the nearer province too had a quiet winter. The former praetors Gaius Calpurnius Piso and Lucius Quinctius

A.U.C. 570 redierunt. Utrique magno patrum consensu
3 triumphus est decretus. Prior C. Calpurnius de
Lusitanis et Celtiberis triumphavit: coronas aureas
tulit octoginta tres et duodecim milia pondo argenti.
4 Paucos post dies L. Quinctius Crispinus ex iisdem
Lusitanis et Celtiberis triumphavit: tantundem auri
atque argenti in eo triumpho praelatum.
5 Censores M. Porcius et L. Valerius metu mixta expectatione senatum legerunt; septem moverunt senatu, ex quibus unum insignem et nobilitate et honoribus, L. Quinctium Flamininum consularem.
6 Patrum memoria institutum fertur ut censores motis
senatu adscriberent notas. Catonis et aliae quidem
acerbae orationes exstant in eos quos aut senatorio
7 loco movit aut quibus equos ademit, longe gravissima
in L. Quinctium oratio, qua si accusator ante notam,
non censor post notam usus esset, retinere L.
Quinctium in senatu ne frater quidem T. Quinctius,
8 si tum censor esset, potuisset. Inter cetera obiecit
ei Philippum Poenum, carum ac nobile scortum, ab
Roma in Galliam provinciam spe ingentium donorum
9 perductum. Eum puerum, per[1] lasciviam cum
cavillaretur, exprobrare consuli saepe[2] solitum, quod
sub ipsum spectaculum gladiatorium abductus ab

[1] per *ed. Parisina* 1513 : *om.* ϛ (*vid. inf.*).
[2] saepe *Heraeus* : persaepe ϛ (*vid. sup.*).

---

[1] Though older than his brother Titus, he had served under him against Philip and had reached the consulship in 192 B.C.

[2] H. Meyer (*Oratorum Romanorum Fragmenta*) listed twenty-six censorial speeches of Cato (nos. 24–49 incl.), although not all are directed at individuals and the dates of some are uncertain. Other scholars compile different lists, but it is at least clear that Cato's censorship was active and that his decisions were vigorously contested.

[3] This constituted removal from the list of *equites*.

returned to Rome. To each of them a triumph was decreed by the general consent of the Fathers. First Gaius Calpurnius triumphed over the Lusitanians and Celtiberians: he displayed eighty-three golden crowns and twelve thousand pounds of silver. A few days later Lucius Quinctius Crispinus triumphed over the same Lusitanians and Celtiberians: the same amount of gold and silver was carried in this triumph. B.C. 184

The censors Marcus Porcius and Lucius Valerius chose the senate amid suspense mingled with fear; they expelled seven from the senate, one of whom was distinguished by both high birth and political success, Lucius Quinctius Flamininus, a man of consular rank.[1] Within the memory of our fathers the custom is said to have arisen that the censors should affix the *nota* to the names of those who are expelled from the senate. But in this case there are speeches of Cato [2] and indeed other bitter orations against those who were either expelled from the senate or whose horses were taken from them,[3] by far the most vehement being that against Lucius Quinctius, and if he had made this speech as an accuser before the branding rather than as censor after the branding, Lucius Quinctius could not have been kept in the senate even by his brother Titus Quinctius, had he been censor at the time. Among other things he reproached him regarding Philippus, a Carthaginian, a notorius prostitute whom he loved and whom he had attracted from Rome to his province of Gaul by the promise of great gifts. This boy, says Cato, in the course of his playful jesting, used frequently to reproach the consul because just on the eve of the gladiatorial games he had been

A.U.C. 570 Roma esset, ut obsequium amatori venditaret.[1]
10 Forte epulantibus iis, cum iam vino incaluissent, nuntiatum in convivio esse nobilem Boium cum liberis transfugam venisse; convenire consulem velle
11 ut ab eo fidem praesens acciperet. Introductum in tabernaculum per interpretem adloqui consulem coepisse. Inter cuius sermonem Quinctius scorto "vis tu," inquit, "quoniam gladiatorium spectaculum reliquisti, iam hunc Gallum morientem videre?"
12 Et cum is vixdum serio adnuisset, ad nutum scorti consulem stricto gladio, qui super caput pendebat, loquenti Gallo caput primum percussisse, deinde, fugienti fidemque populi Romani atque eorum, qui aderant, imploranti latus transfodisse.

XLIII. Valerius Antias, ut qui nec orationem Catonis legisset et fabulae tantum sine auctore editae credidisset, aliud argumentum, simile tamen et
2 libidine et crudelitate[2] peragit. Placentiae famosam mulierem, cuius amore deperiret,[3] in convivium arcessitam scribit. Ibi iactantem sese scorto inter cetera rettulisse quam acriter quaestiones exercuisset et quam multos capitis damnatos in vinculis
3 haberet, quos securi percussurus esset. Tum illam infra eum accubantem negasse umquam vidisse quemquam securi ferientem, et pervelle id videre. Hic indulgentem amatorem unum ex illis miseris[4] attrahi

[1] amatori venditaret *Lipsius* "*ex meo cod.*": amatori iactaret *M*: amator ei uenditaret ς.

[2] libidine et crudelitate ς: libidini et crudelitati *M*.

[3] deperiret ς: deperierat *M*.

[4] illis miseris *Gelenius*: damnatis ς.

---

[1] This form of the story was followed by Valerius Maximus (II. ix. 3) and possibly by Cicero (*Cato maior* 42).

[2] The phrase is conventional in erotic literature.

carried off from Rome, that he might sell his favours to his lover. By chance, when they were dining and were by now heated with wine, it was announced in the dining-room that a noble Boian, accompanied by his sons, had come as a deserter; he wished, they said, to meet the consul, that he might obtain a safeguard from him personally. Having been introduced into the tent, Cato continued, he began to address the consul through an interpreter. While he was speaking, Quinctius said to the boy, "Do you wish, since you missed the gladiatorial show, to see now this Gaul dying?" And when he nodded, although not really in earnest, the consul, at the boy's nod, seized the sword that was hanging above his head and first struck the head of the Gaul while he was speaking, and then, as the Gaul was fleeing and calling for the protection of the Roman people and of those who were present, he stabbed him through the side. B.C. 184

XLIII. Valerius Antias, as one who had never read the speech of Cato and had accepted the story as if it were nothing but a story anonymously circulated, gives another version,[1] similar, however, in its lust and cruelty. He writes that at Placentia a notorious woman, with whom Flamininus was desperately in love,[2] had been invited to dinner. There he was boasting to the courtesan, among other things, about his severity in the prosecution of cases and how many persons he had in chains, under sentence of death, whom he intended to behead. Then the woman, reclining below him, said that she had never seen a person beheaded and was very anxious to behold the sight. Hereupon, he says, the generous lover, ordering one of the wretches to be brought to him,

A.U.C. 570 4 iussum securi percussisse. Facinus sive eo modo quo
censor obiecit, sive, ut Valerius tradit, commissum est,
saevum atque atrox: inter pocula atque epulas, ubi
libare diis dapes, ubi bene precari mos esset, ad
spectaculum scorti procacis, in sinu consulis recuban-
tis, mactatam humanam victimam esse et cruore men-
5 sam respersam! In extrema oratione Catonis con-
dicio Quinctio fertur ut si id factum negaret ceteraque,
quae obiecisset, sponsione defenderet sese: sin [1]
fateretur, ignominiane sua quemquam doliturum
censeret, cum ipse vino et venere amens sanguine
hominis in convivio lusisset?

XLIV. In equitatu recognoscendo L. Scipioni
Asiatico ademptus equus. In censibus quoque acci-
piendis tristis et aspera in omnes ordines censura fuit.
2 Ornamenta et vestem muliebrem et vehicula, quae
pluris quam quindecim milium aeris essent, deciens
tanto pluris quam quanti essent [2] in censum referre
3 iuratores iussi; [3] item mancipia minora annis viginti,
quae post proximum lustrum decem milibus aeris
aut pluris eo venissent, uti ea quoque deciens [4] tanto
pluris quam quanti essent aestimarentur, et his rebus

[1] sine *ed. Veneta* 1495: qui ς.
[2] deciens tanto pluris quam quanti essent *Wesenberg*: *om.* ς.
[3] iussi *ed. Frobeniana* 1535: iussit ς.
[4] deciens *Sigonius*: decem ς.

---

[1] Although mentioned also by Plutarch (*Cato* 17), the procedure is obscure. The *sponsio* (a sort of judicial wager) was a recognized feature of legal procedure, but it may be less technically used here. Plutarch represents this challenge as given and accepted before the assembly: this could be true only in case of a conviction and an appeal. Titus seems, in Plutarch, to be a party also.

cut off his head with his sword. This deed, whether B.C. 184 it was performed in the manner for which the censor rebuked him, or as Valerius reports it, was savage and cruel: in the midst of drinking and feasting, where it is the custom to pour libations to the gods and to pray for blessings, as a spectacle for a shameless harlot, reclining in the bosom of a consul, a human victim sacrificed and bespattering the table with his blood! At the end of the speech a challenge of Cato to Quinctius is reported: if he would deny this act and the other things which Cato had charged, he should defend himself by legal methods,[1] but if he confessed it, would he think that anyone would grieve at his disgrace, since he himself, mad with drink and desire, had played with a man's blood at a feast?

XLIV. In reviewing the *equites* Cato deprived Lucius Scipio Asiaticus of his horse. Also in accepting assessments [2] his censorship was stern and harsh towards all ranks. Jewels and women's dresses and vehicles which were worth more than fifteen thousand *asses* he directed the assessors to list at ten times more than their actual value; [3] likewise slaves less than twenty years old, who had been bought since the previous *lustrum* for ten thousand *asses* or more, he directed to be assessed at ten times more than their actual cost, and he ordered that on all these

[2] The citizens appeared in person before the censors and declared their property. The censors could revise or refuse their declarations.

[3] The emendation (see the critical note) seems to be warranted by the appearance of the same words in sect. 3 below, with reference to other articles of luxury. Perhaps these measures are Cato's revenge for his defeat in the debate over the Oppian law (XXXIV. i.–viii.).

A.U.C. 570

4 omnibus terni[1] in milia aeris attribuerentur. Aquam
publicam omnem in privatum aedificium aut agrum
fluentem ademerunt; et quae in loca publica inaedificata
immolitave privati habebant, intra dies triginta
5 demoliti sunt. Opera deinde facienda ex decreta
in eam rem pecunia, lacus sternendos lapide, detergendasque,[2]
qua opus esset, cloacas, in Aventino et
in aliis partibus, qua nondum erant, faciendas
6 locaverunt. Et separatim Flaccus molem ad Neptunias
aquas, ut iter populo esset, et viam per For-
7 mianum montem, Cato atria duo, Maenium et
Titium, in lautumiis, et quattuor tabernas in publicum
emit basilicamque ibi fecit, quae Porcia appellata est.
Et vectigalia summis pretiis, ultro tributa infimis loca-
8 verunt. Quas locationes cum senatus precibus et
lacrimis victus publicanorum induci et de integro
locari iussisset, censores, edicto summotis ab hasta
qui ludificati priorem locationem erant, omnia eadem
9 paulum imminutis pretiis locaverunt. Nobilis censura
fuit simultatiumque plena, quae M. Porcium,
cui acerbitas ea assignabatur, per omnem vitam
exercuerunt.

10 Eodem anno coloniae duae, Potentia in Picenum,

[1] terni *edd. vett.*: terna *et* trina *et* tria ς.
[2] detergendasque *Gelenius*: tegendasque (-osque) ς.

---

[1] If the ordinary tax rate was one *as* per thousand (XXIV. xv. 9, etc.), this heavier tax on a much higher evaluation must have been, and was probably designed to be, almost confiscatory.

[2] It may be accidental that the number of the verb here shifts to the plural. This particular act prevented the piping into private property of water from the aqueducts.

[3] Their position is unknown.

[4] Cicero (*de lege agraria* I. 7) seems to speak of them as auction-rooms.

articles a tax of three *asses* per thousand should be imposed.[1] All public water [2] flowing into a private dwelling or lot they shut off; and what private persons had built or erected on public property they tore down on thirty days' notice. Then they let contracts for the public works to be constructed from funds appropriated for that purpose, the paving of fountain basins with stone, the cleaning of sewers wherever that was necessary, and the construction of new sewers on the Aventine and elsewhere where none had yet been built. And Flaccus separately built a dike at the Neptunian waters [3] that the people might have a footpath there, and a road over the hill at Formiae, and Cato built two markets,[4] the *Maenium* and the *Titium*, in the region of the Lautumiae,[5] and bought four shops for the state and erected there the basilica [6] which is called Porcia. The revenues also they farmed at the highest rates and contracted for voluntary services at the lowest. When the senate, moved by the prayers and tears of the *publicani*, had ordered these contracts to be cancelled and new ones made, the censors, removing by edict from the place of auction [7] those bidders who had evaded the original contracts, let all the same contracts at slightly lowered figures. It was a remarkable censorship and full of quarrels, which occupied Marcus Porcius, to whom the severity was attributed, through his whole life. B.C. 184

In the same year two colonies, Potentia in the

[5] Cf. XXXII. xvi. 7 and the note.

[6] This building, used for the law-courts, stood between the comitium and the north end of the Capitoline.

[7] Literally, "from the spear." The *hasta* or spear was a conventional sign set up to indicate a place where bidding was going on.

A.U.C. 570 Pisaurum in Gallicum agrum, deductae sunt. Sena
iugera in singulos data. Diviserunt agrum colonias-
que deduxerunt iidem tresviri, Q. Fabius Labeo, et
11 M. et Q. Fulvii, Flaccus et Nobilior. Consules eius
anni nec domi nec militiae memorabile quicquam
egerunt.

XLV. In insequentem annum crearunt consules
M. Claudium Marcellum Q. Fabium Labeonem.

A.U.C. 571 M. Claudius Q. Fabius idibus Martiis, quo die consulatum inierunt, de provinciis suis praetorumque
2 rettulerunt. Praetores creati erant C. Valerius
flamen Dialis, qui et priore anno petierat, et Sp.
Postumius Albinus et P. Cornelius Sisenna L. Pupius
3 L. Iulius Cn. Sicinius.[1] Consulibus Ligures cum
iisdem exercitibus, quos P. Claudius et L. Porcius
4 habuerant, provincia decreta est. Hispaniae extra
sortem prioris anni praetoribus cum suis exercitibus
servatae. Praetores ita sortiri iussi uti flamini Diali
utique altera iuris dicendi Romae provincia esset:
5 peregrinam est sortitus. Sisennae Cornelio urbana,
Sp. Postumio Sicilia, L. Pupio Apulia, L. Iulio Gallia,
Cn. Sicinio Sardinia evenit. L. Iulius maturare est

[1] Sicinius *ed. Frobeniana* 1535 : sulpitius ς.

---

[1] I have given the names as they stand in the text. It is not impossible that the *praenomina* of the Fulvii have been interchanged.

[2] It seems strange that Livy should have separated the praetorian election from the consular in this fashion, and the use of conjunctions in this sentence is unusual. Yet the MSS. show no signs of dislocation, and the tense of *creati erant* shows that the sentence was meant to be here, unless it was emended by some very early scribe after the dislocation had occurred.

[3] He was not permitted, by virtue of his priesthood, to be away from Rome overnight (V. lii. 13). Livy says nothing

Picene territory, Pisaurum in the Gallic, were founded. Six *iugera* were given to each colonist. The division of the land and the organization of the colonies were the work of the same commissioners, Quintus Fabius Labeo, Marcus Fulvius Flaccus and Quintus Fulvius Nobilior.[1] The consuls of this year did nothing noteworthy either at home or in the field. B.C. 184

XLV. For the following year they announced the election of Marcus Claudius Marcellus and Quintus Fabius Labeo as consuls.

Marcus Claudius and Quintus Fabius, on the Ides of March, the day on which they were inaugurated, brought up the question of provinces for themselves and the praetors. The praetors who had been elected were Gaius Valerius, the *flamen Dialis*, who had been a candidate the preceding year also, and Spurius Postumius Albinus and Publius Cornelius Sisenna, Lucius Pupius, Lucius Julius, Gnaeus Sicinius.[2] To the consuls the Ligurians were decreed as their province, with the same armies which Publius Claudius and Lucius Porcius had had. The Spains, excluded from the lot, were reserved for the praetors of the previous year, along with their armies. The praetors were ordered to draw lots with the provision that the province of the *flamen Dialis* should be one of the jurisdictions in Rome:[3] the praetorship which he drew dealt with cases between citizens and aliens. The civil jurisdiction fell to Cornelius Sisenna, Sicily to Spurius Postumius, Apulia to Lucius Pupius, Gaul to Lucius Julius, Sardinia to Gnaeus Sicinius. Lucius Julius was directed to B.C. 183

about the arrangement about his oath, which he had to take by proxy when he held the office of aedile (XXXI. i. 7 and the note).

A.U.C. 571

6 iussus. Galli Transalpini per saltus ignotae antea
viae, ut ante dictum est, in Italiam transgressi
oppidum in agro, qui nunc est Aquileiensis, aedifica-
7 bant. Id eos ut prohiberet, quod eius sine bello
posset, praetori mandatum est. Si armis pro-
hibendi essent, consules certiores faceret: ex his
placere alterum adversus Gallos ducere legiones.
8 Extremo prioris anni comitia auguris creandi
habita erant in demortui Cn. Cornelii Lentuli locum;
creatus erat Sp. Postumius Albinus.

XLVI. Huius principio anni P. Licinius Crassus
pontifex maximus mortuus est, in cuius locum M.
2 Sempronius Tuditanus pontifex est cooptatus; pontifex [1] maximus est creatus C. Servilius Geminus.
P. Licinii funeris causa visceratio data,[2] et gladiatores
centum viginti pugnaverunt, et ludi funebres per
3 triduum facti, post ludos epulum. In quo cum toto
foro strata triclinia essent, tempestas cum magnis
procellis coorta coegit plerosque tabernacula statuere

[1] est cooptatus; pontifex *Gelenius*: *om.* ς.
[2] visceratio data *Gelenius*: uisceratione data ς.

---

[1] Cf. xxii. 6–7 above and the note.
[2] I have chosen the simplest course, by retaining the reading of *M* as the nearest possible approach to the true text now available. The various readings of ς differ as to the proper nouns but agree on *creatus erat*, so that *M*ς all preserve the apparent error of fact that Postumius is said to have been elected, whereas co-optation was the rule until 104 B.C. There is, then, nothing to be gained by piecemeal emendation. The question of dislocation again arises (cf. the note to sect. 2 above), and it can be argued here that the displacement was deliberate, for the sake of continuity with the following sentence, but this emphasis seems disproportion-

hasten his departure. Transalpine Gauls, as has been said before,[1] crossing into Italy by a pass hitherto unknown, were building a city in the territory which now belongs to Aquileia. The praetor was instructed to prevent them from doing this, so far as it was possible for him to do so without war. If they had to be prevented by arms, he was to inform the consuls: it was the senate's desire that one of them should lead the legions against the Gauls. B.C. 183

At the end of the preceding year an election had been held to choose an augur in the place of Gnaeus Cornelius Lentulus, who had died; Spurius Postumius Albinus had been elected.[2]

XLVI. In the beginning of this year Publius Licinius Crassus, the pontifex maximus, died, and in his stead Marcus Sempronius Tuditanus was co-opted as pontiff;[3] Gaius Servilius Geminus was elected[4] pontifex maximus. On the occasion of the funeral of Publius Licinius a public distribution of meats took place, and one hundred and twenty gladiators fought and funeral games were given for three days, and after the games a banquet. During this, when the banqueting tables had been arranged through the whole Forum, a storm coming up with great gusts of wind drove most people to set up

ate to the historical or rhetorical importance of the sentence. Again the MSS. show no signs of dislocation and the tense of the verbs must have been changed very early, if at all.

[3] Here the regular method is employed, in contrast with that recorded in the preceding sentence.

[4] One of the pontiffs was elected pontifex maximus in the usual way, by the college of pontiffs, and while Livy may at times confuse *cooptare* and *creare* he discriminates between them here.

A.U.C. 571
4 in foro: eadem paulo post, cum undique disserenasset,[1] sublata; defunctosque vulgo ferebant quod inter
fatalia vates cecinissent, necesse esse tabernacula
5 in foro statui. Hac religione levatis altera iniecta,
quod sanguine per biduum pluvisset in area Vulcani;
et per decemviros supplicatio indicta erat eius prodigii
expiandi causa.

6 Priusquam consules in provincias proficiscerentur,
legationes transmarinas in senatum introduxerunt.
Nec umquam ante tantum regionis eius hominum
7 Romae fuerat. Nam ex quo fama per gentes, quae
Macedoniam accolunt, vulgata est crimina queri-
moniasque de Philippo non neglegenter ab Romanis
8 audiri, multis operae pretium fuisse queri, pro se
quaeque civitates gentesque, singuli etiam privatim—
gravis enim accola omnibus erat—Romam aut ad
spem levandae iniuriae aut ad deflendae [2] solacium
9 venerunt. Et ab Eumene rege legatio cum fratre
eius Athenaeo venit ad querendum simul quod non
deducerentur ex Thracia praesidia, simul quod in
Bithyniam Prusiae bellum adversus Eumenem gerenti
auxilia missa forent.

XLVII. Respondendum ad omnia iuveni tum

[1] disserenasset ς: consenerasset *M*: serenasset *Gelenius*.
[2] deflendae ς: defendendae *M*.

---

[1] Pessimists would naturally expect that the tents of the prophecy would be those of the enemy who was master of the City, but the omen has now been harmlessly fulfilled.

[2] It was near the temple of Concord (lvi. 6; XL. xix. 1 below).

[3] These events should then belong to the winter of 184–183 B.C. or the early spring of the latter year. Polybius (XXIV. i. ff.) puts them after the departure of the consuls, and so some months later in 183 B.C.

[4] Cf. xxxv. 2–3 above. Demetrius was about twenty-five

tents in the Forum: these, a little later, when it had cleared up all around, were taken down; and the general talk was that the omen had been fulfilled, because the soothsayers had declared that it was among the decrees of the fates that it was destined that tents should be set up in the Forum.[1] When they were freed from this fear another came upon them, because for two days it had rained blood in the precinct of Vulcan;[2] and a period of prayer was proclaimed by the decemvirs as expiation for this prodigy. B.C. 183

Before the consuls[3] set out for their provinces, they introduced the embassies from across the seas to the senate. Never before had there been so many people from this region in Rome. For from the time that the news spread among the tribes that live near Macedonia that charges and complaints against Philip were listened to not inattentively by the Romans, and that many had found it profitable to make complaints, each city and tribe for itself and many individuals privately—for everyone found him a neighbour hard to get along with—came to Rome either in the hope of redressing their wrongs or for the consolation of lamenting them. From King Eumenes also came an embassy, including his brother Athenaeus, to complain both because the garrisons were not withdrawn from the cities in Thrace and because aid had been sent to Prusias in Bithynia, who was waging war against Eumenes.

XLVII. Demetrius,[4] who was then quite a young

years old, and, obviously, not precocious. For a recent study of the career of Demetrius, see Edson, "Perseus and Demetrius," in *Harvard Studies in Classical Philology*, 46 (1935), 191–202.

A.U.C. 571 admodum Demetrio erat. Cum haud facile esset aut ea, quae obicerentur, aut quae adversus ea dicenda
2 erant, memoria complecti—nec enim multa solum, sed etiam pleraque oppido quam parva erant, de controversia finium, de hominibus raptis pecoribusque abactis, de iure aut dicto per libidinem aut non dicto,
3 de rebus per vim aut gratiam iudicatis—nihil horum neque Demetrium docere dilucide nec se satis liquido discere ab eo senatus cum cerneret posse, simul et tirocinio et perturbatione iuvenis moveretur, quaeri iussit ab eo, ecquem de his rebus com-
4 mentarium a patre accepisset. Cum respondisset accepisse se, nihil prius nec potius visum est quam regis ipsius de singulis responsa [1] accipere. Librum extemplo poposcerunt, deinde ut ipse recitaret
5 permiserunt. Erant autem de singulis rebus in breve coactae causae, ut alia fecisse se secundum decreta legatorum diceret, alia non per se stetisse, quo minus faceret, sed per eos ipsos, qui accusarent.
6 Interposuerat et querellas de iniquitate decretorum, et quam non ex aequo disceptatum apud Caecilium foret indigneque sibi nec ullo suo merito insultatum
7 ab omnibus esset. Has notas irritati eius animi collegit senatus: ceterum alia excusanti iuveni, alia recipienti futura ita, ut maxime vellet senatus,

[1] responsa ς : responsum *M*.

---

[1] For the phrase, cf. XXXVI. xxv. 3 and the note.

man, had to answer all these complaints. Since it B.C. 183
was not easy to remember either all the charges which were made or what was to be said in reply to them—for they were not only numerous but many of them also trivial in the extreme,[1] dealing with boundary disputes, men abducted or animals driven off, justice either administered by caprice or not administered, decisions rendered as a result of violence or influence—when the senate saw that Demetrius could give no intelligent information on any of these points and that they could learn nothing explicit from him, and when they were moved by both the inexperience and the embarrassment of the young man, they ordered that the question be asked of him whether he had received any notes from his father on these matters. When he replied that he had received them, it was resolved that nothing should have preference or precedence over hearing the answers of the king himself to these several charges. They immediately demanded the book and then allowed him to read it. The arguments, however, on single items were given in a brief digest; for example, that he had done some things in accordance with the decrees of commissioners, other things he had been prevented from doing, not through his own fault, but that of the very persons who made the accusations. He had included also complaints about the injustice of the decrees and how unfair had been the discussion before Caecilius, and how he had been trampled upon by everyone unjustifiably and in no wise as he deserved. The senate took these to be indications of his irritation; but when the young man apologized for some things and undertook that in the future

A.U.C. 571

8 responderi placuit nihil patrem eius neque rectius
nec magis quod ex voluntate senatus esset fecisse,
quam quod, utcumque ea gesta essent, per Deme-
9 trium filium satisfieri voluisset Romanis. Multa et
dissimulare et oblivisci et pati praeterita senatum
10 posse, et credere etiam Demetrio.[1] Obsidem enim se
animum eius habere, etsi corpus patri reddiderit, et
scire, quantum salva in patrem pietate possit, amicum
11 eum populi Romani esse, honorisque eius causa missuros in Macedoniam legatos, ut si quid minus factum
sit quam debuerit, tum quoque sine piaculo rerum
praetermissarum fiat. Velle etiam sentire Philippum
integra omnia sibi cum populo Romano Demetrii filii
beneficio esse.

XLVIII. Haec, quae augendae amplitudinis eius causa facta erant, extemplo in invidiam, mox etiam in perniciem adulescenti verterunt.

2 Lacedaemonii deinde introducti sunt. Multae et
parvae[2] disceptationes iactabantur; sed quae
maxime rem continerent, erant utrum restituerentur
3 quos Achaei damnaverant necne; inique an iure
occidissent quos occiderant, et[3] utrum manerent in

[1] Demetrio *Madvig*: demetrio credendum esse (esset) ς.
[2] paruae ς: paruulae *M*.
[3] et *Weissenborn*: uertebatur et *aut* uertebant et ς.

---

[1] This whole episode is based on Polybius, XXIII. (XXIV.) i.–iii. but with a good deal of rearrangement and with the postponement to the next Book of several items. By so doing Livy has improved the rhetorical quality of the passage at the expense of historical accuracy.

[2] Livy has not mentioned the exile of any Lacedaemonians by the Achaeans, but it would be very strange if some had not been banished.

[3] The victims of the massacre at Compasium: cf. xxxvi. 9 above and the note. In sect. 16 of that chapter Lycortas

other things should be done as the senate specifically B.C. 183
desired, it was decided to reply that his father had done nothing more correctly or more in accordance with the senate's wishes than that, whatever his own conduct had been, he had wished to be justified in the eyes of the Romans through his son Demetrius. The senate, they said, could close its eyes to much and could forget and let the past be past and continue to trust to Demetrius. For they held his soul hostage, even though his body had been restored to his father, and they knew that, so far as his loyalty to his father would permit, he would be a friend to the Roman people, and for the sake of doing him honour they would send ambassadors to Macedonia, to say that if anything had not been done which should have been done, it might even then be done without any atonement being required for previous omissions. They said that they wished Philip to know that all things were unchanged between him and the Roman people, thanks to his son Demetrius.

XLVIII. These things, which were done in order to enhance his distinction, were immediately turned into a cause of unpopularity and presently even of ruin to the young man.[1]

Then the Lacedaemonians were brought in. Many and trivial subjects of dispute were talked about; but those which contained the real gist of the matter had to do with the question whether the men whom the Achaeans had condemned should be restored or not;[2] whether those who had been killed[3] had been killed justly or unjustly; and

ruled this question out as unimportant, but the Lacedaemonians did not agree. Apparently the Romans did not decide either way, but see sect. 4 below.

A.U.C. 571 Achaico concilio Lacedaemonii an, ut ante fuerat, secretum eius unius in Peloponneso civitatis ius
4 esset. Restitui iudiciaque facta tolli placuit,[1] Lacedaemonem manere in Achaico concilio scribique id decretum et consignari a Lacedaemoniis et Achaeis.
5 Legatus in Macedoniam Q. Marcius est missus, iussus idem in Peloponneso sociorum res aspicere. Nam ibi quoque et ex veteribus discordiis residui motus erant, et Messene desciverat[2] a concilio
6 Achaico. Cuius belli et causas et ordinem si expromere velim, immemor sim propositi, quo statui non ultra attingere externa, nisi qua Romanis cohaererent rebus.

XLIX. Eventus memorabilis est, quod, cum bello superiores essent Achaei, Philopoemen praetor eorum capitur, ad praeoccupandam Coronen, quam hostes petebant, inita valle[3] iniqua cum equitibus
2 paucis oppressus. Ipsum potuisse effugere Thracum Cretensiumque auxilio tradunt: sed pudor relinquendi equites, nobilissimos gentis, ab ipso nuper
3 lectos,[4] tenuit. Quibus dum locum ad evadendas angustias cogendo ipse agmen praebet, sustinens

[1] placuit *ed. Aldina*: placere *et* placet *et* placeret ς.
[2] Messene desciuerat ς: messenii desciuerant *M*, *fortasse rectius*.
[3] inita valle *Heraeus*, XXI. xxxv. 4 *conferens*: in ualle ς.
[4] lectos ς: electos *M*.

---

[1] Livy has condensed and simplified the account of an affair which, according to Polybius, XXIII. (XXIV.) iv. was far from simple. Neither Livy nor Polybius is clear as to whether the first clause of the decree covered the second question of the Lacedaemonians as well as the first, or what action the Romans took on the Compasium affair.
[2] He makes an exception of the Philopoemen episode.

whether the Lacedaemonians should remain in the Achaean League or, as had been the case before, their state, alone in the Peloponnesus, should have a separate constitution. It was decided that the exiles should be restored and the judgments passed against them reversed, and that Lacedaemon should remain in the Achaean League, and that this decree should be written down and signed by the Lacedaemonians and Achaeans.[1] B.C. 183

Quintus Marcius was sent as a commissioner to Macedonia, and was likewise instructed to look into the affairs of the allies in the Peloponnesus. For there were also both the troubles that were survivals from ancient discords, and Messenê had seceded from the Achaean League. If I should wish to set forth both the causes and the events of this war,[2] I should be unmindful of my purpose, according to which I have determined not to touch further upon foreign affairs except as they are inseparable from Roman history.[3]

XLIX. One event worthy of record occurred: although the Achaeans had the advantage in the war, their praetor Philopoemen was captured, who, in order to get the lead in occupying Coronê, for which the enemy was making, entered a dangerous valley, accompanied by a small guard of cavalry, and was surprised. They say that he himself could have escaped with the aid of the Thracians and Cretans; but the shame, if he should abandon the cavalry, the noblest of the people, and recently chosen by him personally, restrained him. While he was offering them a way of escape from the narrow pass by holding the rear in person, sustaining

[3] Cf. XXXV. xl. 1.

A.U.C. 571 impetus hostium, prolapso equo et suo ipse casu et
onere equi super eum ruentis haud multum afuit, quin
4 exanimaretur, septuaginta annos iam natus et diutino
morbo, ex quo tum primum reficiebatur, viribus
5 admodum attenuatis. Iacentem hostes super-
fusi oppresserunt; cognitumque primum a verecundia memoriaque meritorum haud secus quam
ducem suum attollunt reficiuntque et ex valle devia
in viam portant, vix sibimet ipsi prae necopinato
6 gaudio credentes; pars nuntios Messenen prae-
mittunt debellatum esse, Philopoemenem captum
7 adduci. Primum adeo incredibilis visa res, ut non
pro vano modo sed vix pro sano nuntius audiretur.
Deinde ut super alium alius idem omnes affirmantes
8 veniebant, tandem facta fides; et priusquam appro-
pinquare urbi satis scirent, ad spectaculum omnes
simul liberi ac servi, pueri quoque cum feminis,
effunduntur. Itaque clauserat [1] portam turba, dum
pro se quisque, nisi ipse oculis suis credidisset, vix pro
9 comperta tantam rem habiturus videtur.[2] Aegre
summoventes obvios intrare portam, qui adducebant
Philopoemenem, potuerunt. Aeque [3] conferta turba
10 iter reliquum clauserat; et cum pars maxima exclusa
a spectaculo esset, theatrum repente, quod propinquum viae erat, compleverunt et ut eo adducere-
tur in conspectum populi una voce omnes exposce-
11 bant. Magistratus et principes veriti ne quem

[1] clauserat *ed. Frobeniana* 1535: clauserant ς.
[2] videtur *Crévier*: uideretur ς.
[3] aeque *Walch*: atque ς.

the charge of the enemy, his horse fell and he himself was very near to perishing from the shock to himself and the weight of the horse which came down upon him, being now seventy years old and much weakened in strength as the result of a long illness from which he was then just recovering. The enemy, rushing past, came upon him lying there; recognizing him at once, because of their veneration for him and their recollection of his past services, they raised him up as if he were their own leader, revived him and carried him out of the retired valley to the high-road, scarcely believing their own eyes for this unexpected joy; part of them sent messengers ahead to Messenê to say that the war was over and that they were bringing Philopoemen a prisoner. At first this seemed so incredible that his words were listened to, not merely as vain, but as the words of a messenger who was scarcely sane. Then, as one after another came, all bringing the same tidings, at length they were convinced; and before they knew for certain that he was approaching the city, all alike, free and slave, children along with the women, rushed out. So the crowd had blocked the gate, while each for himself, if he had not seen it with his own eyes, would scarcely accept so great a thing as true. The men who were bringing Philopoemen were hardly able to thrust aside the bystanders and enter the gate. An equally crowded mass had blocked the rest of the way; and when the largest part had been excluded from the spectacle, they suddenly filled the theatre, which adjoined the street, and with one voice all demanded that he should be brought there to be seen by the people. The magistrates and leading citizens, fearing that pity for so great a B.C. 183

A.U.C. 571 motum misericordia praesentis tanti viri faceret,
cum alios verecundia pristinae maiestatis collatae[1]
praesenti fortunae, alios recordatio ingentium meritorum motura esset, procul in conspectu eum statue-
12 runt, deinde raptim ex oculis hominum abstraxerunt,
dicente praetore Dinocrate esse quae pertinentia ad
summam belli percunctari eum magistratus vellent.
Inde abducto eo in curiam et senatu vocato consultari
coeptum.

L. Iam invesperascebat, et non modo cetera, sed
ne in proximam quidem noctem ubi satis tuto
2 custodiretur, expediebant. Obstupuerant ad magnitudinem pristinae eius fortunae virtutisque, et neque
ipsi domum recipere custodiendum audebant, nec
3 cuiquam uni custodiam eius satis credebant. Ad-
monent deinde quidam esse thesaurum publicum sub
terra, saxo quadrato saeptum.[1] Eo vinctus demitti-
tur, et saxum ingens quo operitur machina super-
4 impositum est. Ita loco potius quam homini cuiquam credendam custodiam rati, lucem insequentem
5 exspectaverunt. Postero die multitudo quidem
integra, memor pristinorum eius in civitatem meritorum, parcendum ac per eum remedia quaerenda
6 esse praesentium malorum censebant: defectionis[2]
auctores, quorum in manu res publica erat, in secreto
consultantes omnes ad necem eius consentiebant.
Sed utrum maturarent an differrent ambigebatur.
7 Vicit pars avidior poenae, missusque qui venenum

[1] conlatae *Duker*: conlata ς.
[2] defectionis *Gelenius*: sed defectionis *M*: factionis *aut* sed factionis ς.

---

[1] It resembled the Tullianum in Rome, in design if not in use.

man, present before their eyes, might cause some disturbance, since regret at his former greatness compared with his present fortune would move some and recollection of his tremendous services others, placed him in sight but at a distance, and then speedily removed him from the eyes of men, the praetor Dinocrates saying that there were matters pertaining to the final issue of the war on which the magistrates wished to question him. Then, after taking him to the senate-house and calling the council, they began their deliberations. B.C. 183

L. It was now growing dark, and not only were all other things uncertain, but even where they could guard him with sufficient safety even for the ensuing night. They had been awed by the greatness of his former success and courage, and neither did they dare to receive him into their own homes for guarding nor were they satisfied to entrust the guardianship of him to any one man. Then someone reminded them that there was a public treasury underground, walled in by hewn stones.[1] Bound, he was let down into it and a great stone by which it was closed placed by machinery over it. So, thinking that they should trust the place, rather than any man, to keep him safe, they waited for the coming morning. The next day the whole multitude, mindful of his former services to the state, considered that he should be spared and that through him remedies should be sought out for their present troubles: the authors of the revolt, who had the administration in their hands, held a secret consultation, and all were agreed upon his death. But it was not agreed whether they should act at once or delay. The faction that was more insistent on punishment prevailed, and a

A.U.C. 571 ferret. Accepto poculo nihil aliud locutum ferunt
quam quaesisse, si incolumis Lycortas—is alter
imperator Achaeorum erat—equitesque evasissent.
8 Postquam dictum est incolumes esse, "bene habet"
inquit et poculo impavide exhausto haud ita multo
9 post exspiravit. Non diuturnum mortis eius gaudium
auctoribus crudelitatis fuit. Victa namque Messene
bello exposcentibus Achaeis dedidit noxios, ossaque
reddita Philopoemenis sunt, et sepultus ab universo
Achaico est concilio, adeo omnibus humanis congestis
10 honoribus, ut ne divinis quidem abstineretur. Ab
scriptoribus rerum Graecis Latinisque tantum huic
viro tribuitur ut a quibusdam eorum, velut ad insignem notam huius anni, memoriae mandatum sit
tres claros imperatores eo anno decessisse, Philopoe-
11 menem, Hannibalem, P. Scipionem: adeo in aequo
eum duarum[1] potentissimarum gentium summis
imperatoribus posuerunt.

LI. Ad Prusiam regem legatus T. Quinctius
Flamininus venit, quem suspectum Romanis et
receptus post fugam Antiochi Hannibal et bellum
2 adversus Eumenem motum faciebat. Ibi seu quia
a Flaminino inter cetera obiectum Prusiae erat

[1] duarum *Gelenius* : duobus ς.

---

[1] The *hipparchus* or *praefectus equitum* (XXXV. xxxiv. 9) was second in command.

[2] This revives the question of the date of Scipio's death, to which Livy had found no answer when he wrote the latter chapters of Book XXXVIII, and which he discusses again in chap. lii. below. (It remains a mystery why he did not consolidate this chapter with his earlier discussion.) Antiquity was fond of coincidences, and it was convenient, if only for

man was sent to take him the poison. Receiving the cup, he asked only if Lycortas—he was the other commander[1] of the Achaeans—was safe and if the cavalry had escaped. When he was assured that they were safe, he said "it is well," and courageously draining the cup perished no long time afterwards. The persons responsible for this act of cruelty had no great time in which to rejoice in his death. For Messenê, being conquered in the war, at the demand of the Achaeans handed over the guilty persons, and the bones of Philopoemen were given back and he was buried by the whole Achaean League, all human distinctions being heaped upon him to such a degree that they did not even refrain from divine honours. Greek and Latin historians pay such tribute to this man that some of them have put it on record, as if it were a conspicuous brand of infamy set against this year, that three famous generals died during this year—Philopoemen, Hannibal, Publius Scipio: on terms of such equality have they placed him with the greatest commanders of the two most powerful nations.[2] B.C. 183

LI. Titus Quinctius Flamininus went as an ambassador to King Prusias, whom the Romans suspected both because he had given shelter to Hannibal after the flight of Antiochus[3] and because he had begun and was carrying on war against Eumenes. There, whether Prusias was reproached by Flamininus on this ground among others, because

mnemonic reasons, to have the three greatest generals associated in death, even if only two were associated in life (Philopoemen had been compared with Flamininus rather than with Scipio: cf. XXXV. xxx. 12–13 and the note).

[3] Cf. XXXVII. xlv. 16 and the note.

A.U.C. 571 hominem omnium, qui viverent, infestissimum populo
Romano apud eum esse, qui patriae suae primum,
deinde fractis eius opibus Antiocho regi auctor belli
3 adversus populum Romanum fuisset; seu quia ipse
Prusias, ut[1] gratificaretur praesenti Flaminino
Romanisque, per se necandi aut tradendi eius in
potestatem consilium cepit; a primo colloquio
Flaminini milites extemplo ad domum Hannibalis
4 custodiendam missi sunt. Semper talem exitum
vitae suae Hannibal prospexerat animo et Romanorum
inexpiabile[2] odium in se cernens, et fidei regum nihil
sane confisus:[3] Prusiae vero levitatem etiam expertus
erat; Flaminini quoque adventum sibi velut fatalem
5 horruerat. Ad omnia undique infesta ut iter semper
aliquod praeparatum fugae haberet, septem exitus
e domo fecerat, et ex iis quosdam occultos, ne custodia
6 saepirentur. Sed grave imperium regum nihil inex-
ploratum, quod vestigari volunt, efficit. Totius cir-
cuitum domus ita custodiis complexi sunt, ut nemo
7 inde elabi posset. Hannibal, postquam est nuntiatum[4] milites regios in vestibulo esse, postico, quod
devium maxime atque occultissimi exitus erat,
8 fugere conatus, ut id quoque occursu militum
obsaeptum sensit et omnia circa clausa custodiis
dispositis esse venenum, quod multo ante praepara-
9 tum ad tales habebat casus, poposcit. "Liberemus"
inquit[5] "diuturna cura populum Romanum, quando

[1] ut *ed. Frobeniana* 1535: *om.* ς.
[2] inexpiabile *ed. Parisina* 1513: inexplicabile ς.
[3] confisus ς: fretus *M*.
[4] est nuntiatum *ed. Aldina*: nuntiatum *M*: est enuntiatum ς.
[5] inquit *edd. vett.*: *om.* ς.

of all living men the one who was most dangerous to the Roman people was at his court, the man who had first urged his own country and then, after its defeat, King Antiochus to war upon the Roman people, or whether Prusias himself, in order to do a favour to Flamininus when he came and to the Romans, formed the plan of killing him or giving him into custody; for whatever reason, immediately after the first conference with Flamininus he sent soldiers to put the house of Hannibal under guard. Hannibal had always foreseen such an end to his life, both from his knowledge of the insatiable hatred of the Romans for him and from his lack of faith in the loyalty of kings: as for Prusias, he had in fact experienced his fickleness;[1] then too the arrival of Flamininus had made him tremble as at the signal for his doom. Having regard to the dangers which were all around him, in order that he might always have some way of escape in readiness, he had made seven exits from his house, and some of these were secret, lest he might be hemmed in by guards. But the dread power of kings leaves nothing unexplored when they want it traced down. They surrounded the whole area about the house with guards, so that no one could escape from it. When the word was brought to him that the king's troops were in the vestibule, Hannibal attempted to escape by a side door which was out of the way and especially adapted to a stealthy departure, and when he found that this too was blocked by guards stationed around it, he called for the poison which he had long kept ready for such emergencies. "Let us," he said, "relieve the Roman people of their long anxiety, since they B.C. 183

[1] The meaning of the allusion is not known.

A.U.C. 571

10 mortem senis exspectare longum censent. Nec magnam nec memorabilem ex inermi proditoque Flamininus victoriam feret. Mores quidem populi Romani quantum mutaverint, vel hic dies argumento
11 erit. Horum patres Pyrrho regi, hosti armato, exercitum in Italia habenti ut a veneno caveret praedixerunt: hi legatum consularem, qui auctor esset Prusiae per scelus occidendi hospitis, miserunt."
12 Execratus deinde in caput regnumque Prusiae et hospitales deos violatae ab eo fidei testes invocans, poculum exhausit. Hic vitae exitus fuit Hannibalis.

LII. Scipionem et Polybius et Rutilius hoc anno mortuum scribunt. Ego neque his neque Valerio adsentior, his, quod censoribus M. Porcio L. Valerio L. Valerium[1] principem senatus ipsum censorem lectum invenio, cum superioribus duobus lustris
2 Africanus fuisset, quo vivo, nisi ut ille senatu moveretur, quam notam nemo memoriae prodidit, alius
3 princeps in locum eius lectus non esset. Antiatem auctorem refellit tribunus plebis M. Naevius, adversus

[1] L. Valerium *Hertz*: *post* ipsum *coll. edd. vett.*: *om.* ς.

---

[1] Nepos (*Hannibal* 13) gives his age at his death as 70, but says that different authorities place his death in 183, 182, and 181 B.C.

[2] Polybius (XXIV. ix.–ix.*a*) and Rutilius (consul 105 B.C., a member of the Scipionic circle, although much younger than the majority, and a writer of memoirs) should have had access to family records and other evidence as to the date. Yet apparently Polybius (*l.c.*; cf. Nepos, *l.c.*), despite what Livy says here, puts the date a year later. Rutilius is nowhere else quoted by Livy.

[3] Antias dated Scipio's death in 187 B.C.: XXXVIII. liii. 8.

[4] The censors of 189 B.C. gave him this rank for the third time (XXXVIII. xxviii. 2 and the note). The choice of

find it tedious to wait for the death of an old man.[1] B.C. 183
Neither magnificent nor memorable will be the victory which Flamininus will win over a man unarmed and betrayed. How much the manners of the Roman people have changed, this day in truth will prove. Their fathers sent word to King Pyrrhus, an enemy in arms, commanding an army in Italy, warning him to beware of poison: these Romans have sent an ambassador of consular rank to urge upon Prusias the crime of murdering his guest." Then, cursing the person and the kingdom of Prusias and calling upon the gods of hospitality to bear witness to his breach of faith, he drained the cup. This was the end of the life of Hannibal.

LII. Scipio also, as both Polybius and Rutilius[2] write, died this year. For my part, I agree neither with them nor with Valerius[3]—not with them, because in the censorship of Marcus Porcius and Lucius Valerius I find that the *princeps senatus* chosen was the same Lucius Valerius who was censor, whereas in the two preceding *lustra*[4] Africanus had held this distinction, and while he lived, unless he had been expelled from the senate, a disgrace which no one has recorded, another *princeps* would not have been chosen in his stead.[5] The refutation of Antias as an authority is the tribune of the people Marcus Naevius,

Valerius in 184 B.C. is not mentioned in the running account of the censorship (xliii. 5–xliv. 9 above).

[5] Livy thus concludes that Scipio was dead before the *lectio* by Cato and Flaccus. Their active term as censors extended from March 15, 184 B.C., to about mid-September 183 B.C., and the *lectio* might have been held late in the period. So far as this evidence goes, then, Scipio's death might have occurred as late as the summer of 183 B.C., and Livy's criticism is not necessarily valid.

A.U.C. 571
4 quem oratio inscripta P. Africani est. Hic Naevius
in magistratuum libris est tribunus plebis [1] P. Claudio
L. Porcio consulibus, sed iniit tribunatum Ap.
Claudio M. Sempronio consulibus ante diem quartum
5 idus Decembres. Inde tres menses ad idus Martias
sunt, quibus P. Claudius L. Porcius consulatum
6 inierunt. Ita [2] vixisse in tribunatu Naevii videtur,
diesque ei dici ab eo potuisse, decessisse autem ante
L. Valerii et M. Porcii censuram.

7 Trium clarissimorum suae cuiusque gentis virorum
non tempore magis congruente comparabilis mors
videtur esse, quam quod nemo eorum satis dignum
8 splendore vitae exitum habuit. Iam primum omnes

[1] in magistratuum libris est tribunus plebis *Gelenius*: magistratum iniit tribunus plebis ς.

[2] ita *Gelenius* : ita et ς.

---

[1] Cf. XXXVIII. lvi. 6 and the note. Livy forgets here his own remark, that the speech itself did not contain the name of Naevius.

[2] Presumably official registers containing the names of the magistrates year by year.

[3] Inauguration day for consuls at this period was March 15; for tribunes, apparently at all times, December 10. Naevius then entered upon his office December 10, 185 B.C. (Ap. Claudius M. Sempronius coss.), and his term was concurrent with that of P. Claudius and Porcius (and of Cato and Flaccus) from March 15 to December 10, 184 B.C. If Naevius was the prosecutor Scipio could not have been tried in 187 B.C. Livy does not observe that his criticism brings under suspicion his entire narrative of the trial, so far as it is based on Antias.

[4] The last sentence seems to be an attempt to reconcile conflicting testimony. Livy has rejected 183 B.C. (Polybius and Rutilius) because he believes that Scipio was dead before the censorship of Cato and Flaccus beginning March 15, 184 B.C. He has rejected 187 B.C. (Antias) because he now

against whom was directed, according to the title,[1] the speech of Publius Africanus. This Naevius, in the books of the magistrates,[2] is named as tribune of the people in the consulship of Publius Claudius and Lucius Porcius, but he entered upon the tribunate in the consulship of Appius Claudius and Marcus Sempronius, on the fourth day before the Ides of December. From that time it is three months to the Ides of March, when Publius Claudius and Lucius Porcius were inaugurated.[3] Thus it seems that he lived in the tribunate of Naevius and that he might have been accused by him, but died before the censorship of Lucius Valerius and Marcus Porcius.[4] B.C. 183

It seems that the deaths of these three men, each the most famous among his own people, are comparable not so much because of the coincidence of their times, as because no one of them met an end worthy of the brilliance of his life. In the first

believes that Naevius was the prosecutor (term beginning December 10, 185 B.C.). Since Livy thinks that death followed soon after the trial, this reasoning brackets both events as having occurred between December 10, 185 B.C., and March 15, 184 B.C., this being the portion of the term of Naevius which does not overlap that of Cato and Flaccus.

The whole is an interesting specimen of Livy's historical criticism, the more valuable because there are so few parallels. But his readiness to follow one source, almost blindly in Book XXXVIII, while professing his inability to reconcile it with other sources, his refutation of that same source in this passage, the fallacies in his own argumentation, and his ability to omit important details, do not increase our faith in his critical sense. (Of the two pieces of evidence employed here, he neglected one and rejected the other in Book XXXVIII.) One wonders how much of what he had said in Book XXXVIII. was in his active memory when he wrote Book XXXIX. and why the earlier narrative was allowed to stand after he was convinced that it was wrong.

A.U.C. 571
non in patrio [1] solo mortui nec sepulti sunt. Veneno
absumpti Hannibal et Philopoemen; exul Hannibal,
proditus ab hospite, captus Philopoemen in carcere et
9 in vinculis exspiravit; Scipio etsi non exul neque
damnatus, die tamen dicta, ad quam non adfuerat
reus, absens citatus, voluntarium non sibimet ipse
solum sed etiam funeri suo exilium indixit.

LIII. Dum ea in Peloponneso, a quibus devertit
oratio, geruntur, reditus in Macedoniam Demetrii
legatorumque aliter aliorum affecerat animos.
2 Volgus Macedonum, quos belli ab Romanis im-
minentis metus terruerat, Demetrium ut pacis
auctorem cum ingenti favore conspiciebant, simul et
spe haud dubia regnum ei post mortem patris
3 destinabant. Nam etsi minor aetate quam Perseus
esset, hunc iusta matre familiae, illum paelice ortum
esse; illum ut ex vulgato corpore genitum nullam
certi patris notam habere, hunc insignem Philippi
4 similitudinem prae se ferre. Ad hoc Romanos
Demetrium in paterno solio locaturos, Persei nullam
5 apud eos gratiam esse. Haec vulgo loquebantur.
Itaque et Persea cura angebat, ne parum pro se una
aetas valeret, cum aliis omnibus rebus frater superior
6 esset; et Philippus ipse, vix sui arbitrii fore, quem
heredem regni relinqueret credens, sibi quoque gravi-

[1] in patrio *edd. vett.* : patrio ς.

---

[1] Cf. xlviii. 6 above.

[2] Plutarch (*Aemilius*, viii.) hints that Perseus was not the son of Philip, and in XL. ix. 2 Perseus himself suggests the same possibility.

place, none of them either died or was buried in his native land. Hannibal and Philopoemen were carried off by poison; Hannibal was an exile, betrayed by his host, Philopoemen, a captive, died in prison and in chains; Scipio, although not an exile or condemned, yet, because he was absent when summoned, on the day he failed to stand trial, pronounced a sentence of voluntary exile not only upon himself but upon his funeral. B.C. 183

LIII. While these events,[1] from which my narrative turned aside, were occurring in the Peloponnesus, the return of Demetrius and the other ambassadors to Macedonia had made different impressions upon different minds. The mass of the Macedonians, terrified by the fear of the war which threatened from the Romans, looked with very great favour upon Demetrius as the author of peace, and at the same time marked him with assured hope for the throne after the death of his father. For although he was younger in years than Perseus, men recalled that Demetrius was born of a legal wife, the other of a concubine; that the elder, the offspring of a body accessible to all, bore no sure mark of his father,[2] while Demetrius displayed a notable resemblance to Philip. Besides, they said, the Romans would establish Demetrius upon his father's throne, while Perseus would have no influence with them. Such was the general talk. Accordingly Perseus, on the one hand, was anxiously afraid that his age by itself would not carry sufficient weight in his behalf, while his brother had the advantage in all other respects, and on the other, Philip himself, believing that it would hardly be in his power to decide which son he should leave as heir to his

A.U.C. 571

7 orem esse quam vellet minorem filium aiebat. Offen-
debatur interdum concursu Macedonum ad eum, et
8 alteram iam se vivo regiam esse indignabatur. Et
ipse iuvenis haud dubie inflatior redierat, subnisus
erga se iudiciis senatus, concessisque sibi, quae patri
9 negata essent; et omnis mentio Romanorum quantam
dignitatem ei apud ceteros Macedonas, tantam
invidiam non apud fratrem modo sed etiam apud
10 patrem conciliabat, utique postquam legati alii
Romani venerunt, et cogebatur decedere Thracia
praesidiaque deducere et alia aut ex decreto priorum
legatorum aut ex nova constitutione senatus facere.
11 Sed omnia maerens quidem et gemens, eo magis
quod filium frequentiorem prope cum illis quam
secum cernebat, oboedienter tamen adversus Romanos faciebat, ne quam movendi extemplo belli
12 causam praeberet. Avertendos etiam[1] animos a
suspicione talium consiliorum ratus, mediam per[2]
Thraciam exercitum in Odrysas et Dentheletos et
13 Bessos duxit: Philippopolin urbem fuga desertam
oppidanorum, qui in proxima montium iuga cum
familiis receperant sese, cepit, campestresque barbaros, depopulatus agros eorum, in deditionem
14 accepit. Relicto inde ad Philippopolin praesidio,

[1] praeberet. avertendos etiam *Gelenius*: praeberet etiam auertendos *M*: praeuertendos etiam ς.
[2] per *Heraeus*: in ς.

---

[1] Both thought and language closely parallel those of Antiochus in similar circumstances (XXXV. xv. 4).
[2] Livy hints at (xlvii. 3–11 above), and Polybius XXIII. (XXIV.) iii. stresses the harm which the senate did by stimulating the vanity of Demetrius.
[3] Probably Marcius is meant (xlviii. 5 above).

throne, kept saying that his younger son was a greater burden to him than he wished.[1] He was displeased at times by the throngs of Macedonians who visited his son, and was indignant that while he lived there should be a second court. And there is no doubt that the young man had returned too much puffed up regarding himself,[2] relying somewhat on the judgments of the senate about him, and on the concessions made to him of what had been refused to his father; and whatever importance every reference to the Romans brought to him with the rest of the Macedonians, it brought him also exactly as much ill-will, not only with his brother but even with his father, especially after other[3] Roman commissioners came and Philip was compelled to evacuate Thrace and withdraw his garrisons and do other things in accordance with either the decisions of previous commissioners or the new arrangements of the senate. But, although it was with grief and lamentation, the more because he saw his son more frequently in the company of the commissioners than with himself, he nevertheless obeyed the Romans in everything, in order to give them no reason for immediately declaring war. Thinking also that their thoughts should be diverted from any suspicion of such designs, he led his army through the interior of Thrace against the Odrysae and Dentheleti and Bessi: he took the city of Philippopolis,[4] deserted by the flight of its citizens, who with their families had fled to the nearest mountains, and received in surrender the barbarians of the plain, after plundering their farms. Leaving a garrison in Philippopolis B.C. 183

[4] Probably in the territory of the Odrysae; not the town of the same name mentioned in xxv. 3 above.

A.U.C. 571 quod haud multo post ab Odrysis expulsum est,
oppidum in Deuriopo condere instituit—Paeoniae ea
15 regio est—prope Erigonum fluvium, qui ex Illyrico
per Pelagoniam[1] fluens in Axium amnem editur,
16 haud procul Stobis, vetere urbe: novam urbem
Perseida, ut is filio maiori haberetur honos, appellari
iussit.

LIV. Dum haec in Macedonia geruntur, consules
2 in provincias profecti. Marcellus nuntium praemisit
ad L. Porcium proconsulem ut ad novum Gallorum
3 oppidum legiones admoveret. Advenienti consuli
Galli sese dediderunt. Duodecim milia armatorum
erant: plerique arma ex agris rapta habebant; ea
4 aegre patientibus iis adempta, quaeque alia aut
populantes agros rapuerant aut secum attulerant.
De his rebus qui quererentur, legatos Romam mi-
5 serunt. Introducti in senatum a C. Valerio praetore
exposuerunt se superante in Gallia multitudine inopia
coactos agri et egestate ad quaerendam sedem Alpes
transgressos, quae inculta per solitudines viderent,
6 ibi sine ullius iniuria consedisse. Oppidum quoque
aedificare coepisse, quod indicium esset nec agro
nec urbi ulli vim adlaturos venisse. Nuper M.
Claudium ad se nuntium misisse bellum se cum iis,
7 ni dederentur, gesturum. Se certam, etsi non
speciosam pacem quam incerta belli praeoptantes

[1] Pelagoniam *Schaefer*: paeoniam ς.

---

[1] Cf. xxii. 6–7 and xlv. 6–7 above.

(it was expelled a little later by the Odrysae), he decided to found a city in Deuriopus—this is a district in Paeonia—near the Erigonus river, which flows from Illyricum through Pelagonia and empties into the Axius river not far from the ancient city of Stobi: to the new city he ordered the name of Perseis to be given, so as to show honour to his elder son. B.C. 183

LIV. While this was going on in Macedonia, the consuls departed for their provinces. Marcellus sent a messenger ahead to the proconsul Lucius Porcius, ordering him to move the legions to the new town of the Gauls.[1] On the arrival of the consul the Gauls surrendered. There were twelve thousand armed men: most of them had weapons picked up in the country; these were taken from them, to their great displeasure, and whatever else they had either carried off while ravaging the fields or had brought with them. They sent ambassadors to Rome to complain of this treatment. Introduced to the senate by Gaius Valerius the praetor, they explained that since the population of Gaul was too great, compelled by poverty and the unproductiveness of the soil, they had crossed the Alps in search of a home, and when they found a region which was untilled for lack of settlers, there they established themselves without injuring anyone. They had even, they said, begun to build a town, which was an indication that they had come with no design to harm either farm or city. Recently Marcus Claudius had sent a message to them that he would make war upon them if they did not surrender. Preferring an assured though unattractive peace to the uncertainties of war, they had entrusted them-

A.U.C. 571 dedidisse se prius in fidem quam in potestatem populi
8 Romani. Post paucos dies iussos et urbe et agro decedere sese tacitos abire, quo terrarum possent, in animo habuisse. Arma deinde sibi, et postremo omnia alia, quae ferrent agerentque, adempta.
9 Orare se senatum populumque Romanum, ne in se innoxios deditos acerbius quam in hostes saevirent.
10 Huic orationi senatus ita responderi iussit, neque illos recte fecisse, cum in Italiam venerint oppidumque in alieno agro, nullius Romani magistratus, qui ei provinciae praeesset, permissu aedificare conati
11 sint; neque senatui placere deditos spoliari. Itaque se cum iis legatos ad consulem missuros, qui si redeant unde venerint, omnia iis sua reddi iubeant, quique protinus eant trans Alpes, et denuntient Gallicis po-
12 pulis, multitudinem suam domi contineant: Alpes prope inexsuperabilem finem in medio esse: non utique iis melius fore quam qui[1] eas primi pervias
13 fecissent. Legati missi L. Furius Purpurio Q. Minucius L. Manlius Acidinus. Galli, redditis omnibus, quae sine cuiusquam iniuria habebant, Italia excesserunt.

LV. Legatis Romanis Transalpini populi benigne

[1] quam qui *Sigonius*: qui ϛ.

---

[1] Their situation is not unlike that of the Aetolians (XXXVI. xxvii. 8–xxviii. 6 and the notes).

[2] The eastern boundary of Cisalpine Gaul had never been defined, and the Gauls may have innocently supposed that the Romans did not intend to occupy this region. Roman ambitions, however, were now directed to Histria, and a colony at Aquileia was contemplated (lv. 4–6 below).

[3] That is, earlier Gallic invaders who had met defeat on Italian soil.

[4] Furius may have been one of the senators who received the *nota* (xlii. 5–6 above); the fragments of Cato's speeches

selves to the good faith rather than to the power of the Roman people.[1] When, a few days later, they were ordered to leave the town and the country as well, they had planned to go away in silence, wherever in the world they could. Then, they went on to say, their arms were taken from them, and finally everything else which they were carrying or driving. They begged the senate and the Roman people not to treat innocent persons who had surrendered more harshly than enemies. The senate ordered the reply to be given to this appeal, that neither had they acted properly when they came into Italy and attempted to build a town on others' land, without the permission of any Roman magistrate who was in charge of that province; [2] nor did it please the senate to despoil men who had surrendered. Accordingly, the senate would send with them ambassadors to the consul who would direct him, on condition that they would return whence they had come, to give back all their property, and who would then cross the Alps and warn the Gallic tribes to keep their population at home: the Alps were an almost insuperable boundary between them: in any case they would fare no better than those who had first made them passable.[3] The ambassadors who were sent were Lucius Furius Purpurio,[4] Quintus Minucius, Lucius Manlius Acidinus. The Gauls, having recovered all the property which they acquired without injuring anyone, left Italy. B.C. 183

LV. The Roman ambassadors were graciously answered by the Transalpine peoples. Their elders

against a Furius (the identification is not quite certain) seem to date from his censorship. If this is true, the embassy must have preceded the *lectio senatus*.

A.U.C. 571 responderunt. Seniores eorum nimiam lenitatem
2 populi Romani castigarunt, quod eos homines, qui gentis
iniussu profecti occupare agrum imperii Romani et in
alieno solo aedificare oppidum conati sint, impunitos
dimiserint: debuisse gravem temeritatis mercedem
3 statui. Quod vero etiam sua reddiderint, vereri ne
tanta indulgentia plures ad talia audenda impellantur.
4 Et exceperunt et [1] prosecuti cum donis legatos sunt.
M. Claudius consul Gallis ex provincia exactis His-
tricum bellum moliri coepit litteris ad senatum
missis, ut sibi in Histriam traducere legiones liceret.
5 Id senatui non placuit.[2] Illud agitabant uti colonia
Aquileia deduceretur, nec satis constabat utrum
Latinam an civium Romanorum deduci placeret.
Postremo Latinam potius coloniam deducendam
6 patres censuerunt. Triumviri creati sunt P. Scipio
Nasica C. Flaminius L. Manlius Acidinus.
Eodem anno Mutina et Parma coloniae civium Ro-
7 manorum sunt deductae. Bina milia hominum in
agro, qui proxime Boiorum, ante Tuscorum fuerat,
octona iugera Parmae, quina Mutinae acceperunt.
8 Deduxerunt triumviri M. Aemilius Lepidus T.
9 Aebutius Parrus [3] L. Quinctius Crispinus. Et
Saturnia colonia civium Romanorum in agrum Cale-
tranum est deducta. Deduxerunt triumviri Q.

[1] et ς: ita *M*.
[2] non placuit *Novák*: placuit ς.
[3] Parrus (*vel* Parus) *Buecheler*: carus ς.

---

[1] Since the territory of the Veneti had now been tacitly absorbed, the Histrians, living on the peninsula to the south of the modern Trieste, were near neighbours. There seems to be no evidence that they had given the Romans any cause to attack them at this time.

reproved the Roman people for their excessive lenience, because those men who had set out without the permission of their state and had attempted to occupy land belonging to the Roman empire and to build a town on others' soil had been let go unpunished: they should have been made to pay a heavy toll for their rash action. Moreover, as to the restoration of their property, the elders feared that such generosity might tempt more peoples to try the same venture. The ambassadors were both received and sent on their way with gifts. B.C. 183

Marcus Claudius the consul, having expelled the Gauls from the province, began to scheme for a war with the Histrians,[1] sending letters to the senate for permission to lead the legions into Histria. This did not please the senate. They were discussing the question of establishing a colony at Aquileia, but it was not generally agreed whether it should be a Latin colony or one of Roman citizens. Finally, the Fathers voted that a Latin colony rather should be founded. The three commissioners elected were Publius Scipio Nasica, Gaius Flaminius, Lucius Manlius Acidinus.

In the same year Mutina and Parma, colonies of Roman citizens, were established. Two thousand men in each case were settled on the land that had recently belonged to the Boi [2] and previously to the Etruscans, and the allotments at Parma were eight *iugera* each, at Mutina five. The board of three which founded them consisted of Marcus Aemilius Lepidus, Titus Aebutius Parrus, Lucius Quinctius Crispinus. Also, a colony of Roman citizens was established at Saturnia in the *ager Caletranus*.[3] The board of three

[2] Cf. XXXVI. xxxix. 3. [3] In Etruria.

A.U.C. 571 Fabius Labeo C. Afranius Stellio Ti. Sempronius Gracchus. In singulos iugera data dena.[1]

LVI. Eodem anno A. Terentius proconsul haud procul flumine Hibero, in agro Ausetano, et proelia secunda cum Celtiberis fecit, et oppida, quae ibi
2 communierant, aliquot expugnavit. Ulterior[2] Hispania eo anno in pace fuit[3] quia et P. Sempronius proconsul diutino morbo est implicitus, et nullo
3 lacessente peropportune quieverunt Lusitani. Nec in Liguribus memorabile quicquam a Q. Fabio consule gestum.

Ex Histria revocatus M. Marcellus exercitu
4 dimisso Romam comitiorum causa rediit. Creavit consules Cn. Baebium Tamphilum et L. Aemilium Paulum. Cum M. Aemilio Lepido hic aedilis curulis fuerat; a quo consule quintus annus erat, cum is ipse Lepidus post duas repulsas consul factus esset.
5 Praetores inde facti Q. Fulvius Flaccus M. Valerius Laevinus P. Manlius[4] iterum M. Ogulnius Gallus L. Caecilius Denter C. Terentius Istra.

6 Supplicatio extremo anno fuit prodigiorum causa, quod sanguine per biduum pluvisse in area Concordiae satis credebant, nuntiatumque erat haud procul Sicilia insulam, quae non ante fuerat, novam editam

[1] dena *H. J. Mueller* : decem *M* : *om.* ς.
[2] ulterior *Glareanus* : citerior ς.
[3] e.a.i.p.f. *ed. Frobeniana* 1535 : i.p.f.e.a. ς.
[4] P. Manlius *ed. Aldina* : p. aemilius ς.

---

[1] Lepidus was consul in 187 B.C. We are left to conjecture the number of defeats suffered by Paulus. Livy seems to dwell on the failures of Paulus, possibly for the contrast with his later brilliant career in Macedonia.

[2] His first praetorship was in 195 B.C. (XXXIII. xlii. 7). No reason is known for this unusual career.

which founded it consisted of Quintus Fabius Labeo, Gaius Afranius Stellio, Tiberius Sempronius Gracchus. Ten *iugera* were given to each colonist. B.C. 183

LVI. In the same year the proconsul Aulus Terentius, not far from the river Ebro, in the country of the Ausetani, both fought successful battles with the Celtiberians and captured a number of towns which they had fortified. Farther Spain that year was at peace, partly because Publius Sempronius the proconsul was suffering from a long illness, and with no one to provoke them the Lusitanians very fortunately remained quiet. Nor was anything worth recording done by the consul Quintus Fabius among the Ligurians.

Marcus Marcellus, recalled from Histria, disbanded his army and returned to Rome to hold the elections. He returned as consuls Gnaeus Baebius Tamphilus and Lucius Aemilius Paulus. The latter had been curule aedile with Marcus Aemilius Lepidus; this was the fifth year after the consulship of Lepidus, although Lepidus himself became consul after two defeats.[1] Next the praetors were chosen, Quintus Fulvius Flaccus, Marcus Valerius Laevinus, Publius Manlius (for the second time),[2] Marcus Ogulnius Gallus, Lucius Caecilius Denter, Gaius Terentius Istra.

At the end of the year there was a period of prayer by reason of the prodigies, because the Romans were well persuaded that there had been a shower of blood, lasting two days, in the precinct of Concord,[3] and because it was reported that not far from Sicily, a new island which had not been there before had

[3] Cf. also xlvi. 5 above and the note and XL. xix. 2.

A.U.C. 571

7 e mari esse. Hannibalem hoc anno Antias Valerius decessisse est auctor legatis ad eam rem ad Prusiam missis praeter T. Quinctium Flamininum, cuius in ea re celebre est nomen, L. Scipione Asiatico et P. Scipione Nasica.

risen from the sea. Valerius Antias says that Hannibal died this year, ambassadors having been sent to Prusias for this purpose, namely, Lucius Scipio Asiaticus and Publius Scipio Nasica,[1] in addition to Titus Quinctius Flamininus, whose name is best known in this connection. B.C. 183

[1] Again Livy appends an afterthought, inconsistent with his previous narrative.

LIBRI XXXIX PERIOCHA

M. Aemilius cos. Liguribus subactis viam Placentia usque Ariminum productam Flaminiae iunxit. Initia luxuriae in urbem introducta ab exercitu Asiatico referuntur. Ligures quicumque citra Appenninum erant subacti sunt. Bacchanalia, sacrum Graecum et nocturnum, omnium scelerum seminarium, cum ad ingentis turbae coniurationem pervenisset,[1] investigatum et multorum poena sublatum est. A censoribus L. Valerio Flacco et M. Porcio Catone,[2] et belli et pacis artibus maximo, motus est senatu L. Quinctius Flamininus, T.[3] frater, eo quod cum[4] Galliam provinciam consul obtineret, rogatus in convivio a Poeno Philippo quem amabat, scorto nobili, Gallum quendam sua manu occiderat sive, ut quidam tradiderunt, unum ex damnatis securi percusserat rogatus a meretrice Placentina cuius amore deperibat. Exstat oratio M. Catonis in eum. Scipio Literni decessit et, tamquam iungente[5] fortuna, circa idem tempus duo funera maximorum virorum, Hannibal a Prusia Bithyniae rege, ad quem victo Antiocho confugerat, cum dederetur Romanis, qui ad exposcendum eum T. Quinctium Flamininum miserant, veneno mortem consciit, Philopoemen quoque, dux Achaeorum, vir

[1] pervenisset *edd.* : perueni sed *codd.*
[2] *nomina corrupta correxerunt edd.*
[3] T. *edd.* : *om. codd.*
[4] cum *add. edd.*
[5] iungente *edd.* : lugente *NP.*

SUMMARY OF BOOK XXXIX

The consul Marcus Aemilius, having subdued the Ligurians, built a road from Placentia to Ariminum to connect with the Via Flaminia. The beginnings of luxurious living are said to have been introduced into the City by the army from Asia. All the Ligurians on this side of the Apennines were subdued. The Bacchanalia, a Greek rite celebrated by night, the breeding-ground of all crimes, since it had developed into a conspiracy of large numbers, were investigated and suppressed by the punishment of many. The censors Lucius Valerius Flaccus and Marcus Porcius Cato (the latter the greatest of men in the arts of both war and peace) expelled from the senate Lucius Quinctius Flamininus, the brother of Titus, on the ground that while he was holding the province of Gaul as consul, at the request of a Carthaginian, Philippus, a notorious degenerate whom he loved, he had, at a banquet, killed with his own hand a certain Gaul, or, as some say, that he had beheaded a man under sentence of death at the request of a courtesan of Placentia with whom he was desperately in love. The speech of Marcus Cato against him is extant. Scipio died at Liternum and, as if fortune were bringing them together, two deaths occurred about the same time of very great men—Hannibal, who committed suicide by poison when Prusias, king of Bithynia, with whom he had taken refuge after the defeat of Antiochus, was about to surrender him to the Romans who had sent Titus Quinctius Flamininus to demand him, and also Philopoemen, chieftain of the Achaeans and a very great man, who was poisoned

maximus, a Messeniis occisus veneno cum ab his in bello captus esset. Coloniae Potentia [1] et Pisaurum et Mutina et Parma deductae sunt. Praeterea res adversus Celtiberos prospere gestas et initia causasque belli Macedonici continet. Cuius origo inde fluxit quod Philippus aegre ferebat regnum suum a Romanis imminui et quod cogeretur a Thracibus aliisque locis praesidia deducere.

[1] Potentia *Sigonius*: polentia *codd.*

by the Messenians after they had captured him in war. The colonies of Potentia and Pisaurum and Mutina and Parma were founded. In addition the book contains the victories over the Celtiberians and the beginnings and causes of the Macedonian war. The origin of this was found in Philip's anger that his kingdom was diminished by the Romans and that he was compelled to withdraw his garrisons from Thrace and elsewhere.

INDEX OF NAMES

The References are to Pages)

INDEX OF NAMES

INDEX OF NAMES

INDEX OF NAMES

INDEX OF NAMES

Printed in Great Britain by Richard Clay (The Chaucer Press), Ltd., Bungay, Suffolk

MINUCIUS FELIX. Cf. TERTULLIAN.

OVID: THE ART OF LOVE and OTHER POEMS. J. H. Mosley. Revised by G. P. Goold.

OVID: FASTI. Sir James G. Frazer

OVID: HEROIDES and AMORES. Grant Showerman. Revised by G. P. Goold

OVID: METAMORPHOSES. F. J. Miller. 2 Vols. Vol. 1 revised by G. P. Goold.

OVID: TRISTIA and EX PONTO. A. L. Wheeler.

PERSIUS. Cf. JUVENAL.

PERVIGILIUM VENERIS. Cf. CATULLUS.

PETRONIUS. M. Heseltine. SENECA: APOCOLOCYNTOSIS. W. H. D. Rouse. Revised by E. H. Warmington.

PHAEDRUS and BABRIUS (Greek). B. E. Perry.

PLAUTUS. Paul Nixon. 5 Vols.

PLINY: LETTERS, PANEGYRICUS. Betty Radice. 2 Vols.

PLINY: NATURAL HISTORY. 10 Vols. Vols. I–V and IX. H. Rackham. VI.–VIII. W. H. S. Jones. X. D. E. Eichholz.

PROPERTIUS. H. E. Butler.

PRUDENTIUS. H. J. Thomson. 2 Vols.

QUINTILIAN. H. E. Butler. 4 Vols.

REMAINS OF OLD LATIN. E. H. Warmington. 4 Vols. Vol. I. (ENNIUS AND CAECILIUS) Vol. II. (LIVIUS, NAEVIUS PACUVIUS, ACCIUS) Vol. III. (LUCILIUS and LAWS OF XII TABLES) Vol. IV. (ARCHAIC INSCRIPTIONS)

RES GESTAE DIVI AUGUSTI. Cf. VELLEIUS PATERCULUS.

SALLUST. J. C. Rolfe.

SCRIPTORES HISTORIAE AUGUSTAE. D. Magie. 3 Vols.

SENECA, THE ELDER: CONTROVERSIAE, SUASORIAE. M. Winterbottom. 2 Vols.

SENECA: APOCOLOCYNTOSIS. Cf. PETRONIUS.

SENECA: EPISTULAE MORALES. R. M. Gummere. 3 Vols.

SENECA: MORAL ESSAYS. J. W. Basore. 3 Vols.

SENECA: TRAGEDIES. F. J. Miller. 2 Vols.

SENECA: NATURALES QUAESTIONES. T. H. Corcoran. 2 Vols.

SIDONIUS: POEMS and LETTERS. W. B. Anderson. 2 Vols.

SILIUS ITALICUS. J. D. Duff. 2 Vols.

STATIUS. J. H. Mozley. 2 Vols.

SUETONIUS. J. C. Rolfe. 2 Vols.

TACITUS: DIALOGUS. Sir Wm. Peterson. AGRICOLA and GERMANIA. Maurice Hutton. Revised by M. Winterbottom, R. M. Ogilvie, E. H. Warmington.

TACITUS: HISTORIES and ANNALS. C. H. Moore and J. Jackson. 4 Vols.

TERENCE. John Sargeaunt. 2 Vols.

TERTULLIAN: APOLOGIA and DE SPECTACULIS. T. R. Glover. MINUCIUS FELIX. G. H. Rendall.

TIBULLUS. Cf. CATULLUS.

VALERIUS FLACCUS. J. H. Mozley.

VARRO: DE LINGUA LATINA. R. G. Kent. 2 Vols.

VELLEIUS PATERCULUS and RES GESTAE DIVI AUGUSTI. F. W. Shipley.

VIRGIL. H. R. Fairclough. 2 Vols.

VITRUVIUS: DE ARCHITECTURA. F. Granger. 2 Vols.

Greek Authors

ACHILLES TATIUS. S. Gaselee.

AELIAN: ON THE NATURE OF ANIMALS. A. F. Scholfield. 3 Vols.

AENEAS TACTICUS. ASCLEPIODOTUS and ONASANDER. The Illinois Greek Club.

AESCHINES. C. D. Adams.

AESCHYLUS. H. Weir Smyth. 2 Vols.

ALCIPHRON, AELIAN, PHILOSTRATUS: LETTERS. A. R. Benner and F. H. Fobes.

ANDOCIDES, ANTIPHON. Cf. MINOR ATTIC ORATORS.

APOLLODORUS. Sir James G. Frazer. 2 Vols.

APOLLONIUS RHODIUS. R. C. Seaton.

APOSTOLIC FATHERS. Kirsopp Lake. 2 Vols.

APPIAN: ROMAN HISTORY. Horace White. 4 Vols.

ARATUS. Cf. CALLIMACHUS.

ARISTIDES: ORATIONS. C. A. Behr. Vol. I.

ARISTOPHANES. Benjamin Bickley Rogers. 3 Vols. Verse trans.

ARISTOTLE: ART OF RHETORIC. J. H. Freese.

ARISTOTLE: ATHENIAN CONSTITUTION, EUDEMIAN ETHICS, VICES AND VIRTUES. H. Rackham.

ARISTOTLE: GENERATION OF ANIMALS. A. L. Peck.

ARISTOTLE: HISTORIA ANIMALIUM. A. L. Peck. Vols. I.–II.

ARISTOTLE: METAPHYSICS. H. Tredennick. 2 Vols.

ARISTOTLE: METEOROLOGICA. H. D. P. Lee.

ARISTOTLE: MINOR WORKS. W. S. Hett. On Colours, On Things Heard, On Physiognomies, On Plants, On Marvellous Things Heard, Mechanical Problems, On Indivisible Lines, On Situations and Names of Winds, On Melissus, Xenophanes, and Gorgias.

ARISTOTLE: NICOMACHEAN ETHICS. H. Rackham.

ARISTOTLE: OECONOMICA and MAGNA MORALIA. G. C. Armstrong (with METAPHYSICS, Vol. II).

ARISTOTLE: ON THE HEAVENS. W. K. C. Guthrie.

ARISTOTLE: ON THE SOUL, PARVA NATURALIA, ON BREATH. W. S. Hett.

ARISTOTLE: CATEGORIES, ON INTERPRETATION, PRIOR ANALYTICS. H. P. Cooke and H. Tredennick.

ARISTOTLE: POSTERIOR ANALYTICS, TOPICS. H. Tredennick and E. S. Forster.

ARISTOTLE: ON SOPHISTICAL REFUTATIONS.
On Coming to be and Passing Away, On the Cosmos. E. S. Forster and D. J. Furley.

ARISTOTLE: PARTS OF ANIMALS. A. L. Peck; MOTION AND PROGRESSION OF ANIMALS. E. S. Forster.

ARISTOTLE: PHYSICS. Rev. P. Wicksteed and F. M. Cornford. 2 Vols.

ARISTOTLE: POETICS and LONGINUS. W. Hamilton Fyfe; DEMETRIUS ON STYLE. W. Rhys Roberts.

ARISTOTLE: POLITICS. H. Rackham.

ARISTOTLE: PROBLEMS. W. S. Hett. 2 Vols.

ARISTOTLE: RHETORICA AD ALEXANDRUM (with PROBLEMS. Vol. II). H. Rackham.

ARRIAN: HISTORY OF ALEXANDER and INDICA, 2 Vols. Vol. II 1983). New version P. Brunt.

ATHENAEUS: DEIPNOSOPHISTAE. C. B. Gulick. 7 Vols.

BABRIUS AND PHAEDRUS (Latin). B. E. Perry.

ST. BASIL: LETTERS. R. J. Deferrari. 4 Vols.

CALLIMACHUS: FRAGMENTS. C. A. Trypanis. MUSAEUS: HERO AND LEANDER. T. Gelzer and C. Whitman.

CALLIMACHUS, Hymns and Epigrams, and LYCOPHRON. A. W. Mair; ARATUS. G. R. Mair.

CLEMENT OF ALEXANDRIA. Rev. G. W. Butterworth.

COLLUTHUS. Cf. OPPIAN.

DAPHNIS AND CHLOE. Thornley's Translation revised by J. M. Edmonds: and PARTHENIUS. S. Gaselee.

DEMOSTHENES I.: OLYNTHIACS, PHILIPPICS and MINOR ORATIONS I.-XVII. AND XX. J. H. Vince.

DEMOSTHENES II.: DE CORONA and DE FALSA LEGATIONE. C. A. Vince and J. H. Vince.

DEMOSTHENES III.: MEIDIAS, ANDROTION, ARISTOCRATES, TIMOCRATES and ARISTOGEITON I. and II. J. H. Vince.

DEMOSTHENES IV.-VI: PRIVATE ORATIONS and IN NEAERAM. A. T. Murray.

DEMOSTHENES VII: FUNERAL SPEECH, EROTIC ESSAY, EXORDIA and LETTERS. N. W. and N. J. DeWitt.

DIO CASSIUS: ROMAN HISTORY. E. Cary. 9 Vols.

Dio Chrysostom. J. W. Cohoon and H. Lamar Crosby. 5 Vols.

Diodorus Siculus. 12 Vols. Vols. I.–VI. C. H. Oldfather. Vol. VII. C. L. Sherman. Vol. VIII. C. B. Welles. Vols. IX. and X. R. M. Geer. Vol. XI. F. Walton. Vol. XII. F. Walton. General Index. R. M. Geer.

Diogenes Laertius. R. D. Hicks. 2 Vols. New Introduction by H. S. Long.

Dionysius of Halicarnassus: Roman Antiquities. Spelman's translation revised by E. Cary. 7 Vols.

Dionysius of Halicarnassus: Critical Essays. S. Usher. 2 Vols. Vol. I.

Epictetus. W. A. Oldfather. 2 Vols.

Euripides. A. S. Way. 4 Vols. Verse trans.

Eusebius: Ecclesiastical History. Kirsopp Lake and J. E. L. Oulton. 2 Vols.

Galen: On the Natural Faculties. A. J. Brock.

Greek Anthology. W. R. Paton. 5 Vols.

Greek Bucolic Poets (Theocritus, Bion, Moschus). J. M Edmonds.

Greek Elegy and Iambus with the Anacreontea. J. M. Edmonds. 2 Vols.

Greek Lyric. D. A. Campbell. 4 Vols. Vol. I.

Greek Mathematical Works. Ivor Thomas. 2 Vols.

Herodes. Cf. Theophrastus: Characters.

Herodian. C. R. Whittaker. 2 Vols.

Herodotus. A. D. Godley. 4 Vols.

Hesiod and The Homeric Hymns. H. G. Evelyn White.

Hippocrates and the Fragments of Heracleitus. W. H. S. Jones and E. T. Withington. 4 Vols.

Homer: Iliad. A. T. Murray. 2 Vols.

Homer: Odyssey. A. T. Murray. 2 Vols.

Isaeus. E. W. Forster.

Isocrates. George Norlin and LaRue Van Hook. 3 Vols.

[St. John Damascene]: Barlaam and Ioasaph. Rev. G. R. Woodward, Harold Mattingly and D. M. Lang.

Josephus. 10 Vols. Vols. I.–IV. H. Thackeray. Vol. V. H. Thackeray and R. Marcus. Vols. VI.–VII. R. Marcus. Vol. VIII. R. Marcus and Allen Wikgren. Vols. IX.–X. L. H. Feldman.

Julian. Wilmer Cave Wright. 3 Vols.

Libanius. A. F. Norman. 3 Vols. Vols. I.–II.

Lucian. 8 Vols. Vols. I.–V. A. M. Harmon. Vol. VI. K. Kilburn. Vols. VII.–VIII. M. D. Macleod.

Lycophron. Cf. Callimachus.

LYRA GRAECA, J. M. Edmonds. 2 Vols.

LYSIAS. W. R. M. Lamb.

MANETHO. W. G. Waddell.

MARCUS AURELIUS. C. R. Haines.

MENANDER. W. G. Arnott. 3 Vols. Vol. I.

MINOR ATTIC ORATORS (ANTIPHON, ANDOCIDES, LYCURGUS, DEMADES, DINARCHUS, HYPERIDES). K. J. Maidment and J. O. Burtt. 2 Vols.

MUSAEUS: HERO AND LEANDER. Cf. CALLIMACHUS.

NONNOS: DIONYSIACA. W. H. D. Rouse. 3 Vols.

OPPIAN, COLLUTHUS, TRYPHIODORUS. A. W. Mair.

PAPYRI. NON-LITERARY SELECTIONS. A. S. Hunt and C. C. Edgar. 2 Vols. LITERARY SELECTIONS (Poetry). D. L. Page.

PARTHENIUS. Cf. DAPHNIS and CHLOE.

PAUSANIAS: DESCRIPTION OF GREECE. W. H. S. Jones. 4 Vols. and Companion Vol. arranged by R. E. Wycherley.

PHILO. 10 Vols. Vols. I.–V. F. H. Colson and Rev. G. H. Whitaker. Vols. VI.–IX. F. H. Colson. Vol. X. F. H. Colson and the Rev. J. W. Earp.

PHILO: two supplementary Vols. (*Translation only.*) Ralph Marcus.

PHILOSTRATUS: THE LIFE OF APOLLONIUS OF TYANA. F. C. Conybeare. 2 Vols.

PHILOSTRATUS: IMAGINES; CALLISTRATUS: DESCRIPTIONS. A. Fairbanks.

PHILOSTRATUS and EUNAPIUS: LIVES OF THE SOPHISTS. Wilmer Cave Wright.

PINDAR. Sir J. E. Sandys.

PLATO: CHARMIDES, ALCIBIADES, HIPPARCHUS, THE LOVERS, THEAGES, MINOS and EPINOMIS. W. R. M. Lamb.

PLATO: CRATYLUS, PARMENIDES, GREATER HIPPIAS, LESSER HIPPIAS. H. N. Fowler.

PLATO: EUTHYPHRO, APOLOGY, CRITO, PHAEDO, PHAEDRUS, H. N. Fowler.

PLATO: LACHES, PROTAGORAS, MENO, EUTHYDEMUS. W. R. M. Lamb.

PLATO: LAWS. Rev. R. G. Bury. 2 Vols.

PLATO: LYSIS, SYMPOSIUM, GORGIAS. W. R. M. Lamb.

PLATO: Republic. Paul Shorey. 2 Vols.

PLATO: STATESMAN, PHILEBUS. H. N. Fowler; ION. W. R. M. Lamb.

PLATO: THEAETETUS and SOPHIST. H. N. Fowler.

PLATO: TIMAEUS, CRITIAS, CLITOPHO, MENEXENUS, EPISTULAE. Rev. R. G. Bury.

PLOTINUS: A. H. Armstrong. 7 Vols. Vols. I.–III.

Plutarch: Moralia. 16 Vols. Vols I.–V. F. C. Babbitt. Vol. VI. W. C. Helmbold. Vols. VII. and XIV. P. H. De Lacy and B. Einarson. Vol. VIII. P. A. Clement and H. B. Hoffleit. Vol. IX. E. L. Minar, Jr., F. H. Sandbach, W. C. Helmbold. Vol. X. H. N. Fowler. Vol. XI. L. Pearson and F. H. Sandbach. Vol. XII. H. Cherniss and W. C. Helmbold. Vol. XIII 1–2. H. Cherniss. Vol. XV. F. H. Sandbach.

Plutarch: The Parallel Lives. B. Perrin. 11 Vols.

Polybius. W. R. Paton. 6 Vols.

Procopius. H. B. Dewing. 7 Vols.

Ptolemy: Tetrabiblos. F. E. Robbins.

Quintus Smyrnaeus. A. S. Way. Verse trans.

Sextus Empiricus. Rev. R. G. Bury. 4 Vols.

Sophocles. F. Storr. 2 Vols. Verse trans.

Strabo: Geography. Horace L. Jones. 8 Vols.

Theocritus. Cf. Greek Bucolic Poets.

Theophrastus: Characters. J. M. Edmonds. Herodes, etc. A. D. Knox.

Theophrastus: Enquiry into Plants. Sir Arthur Hort, Bart. 2 Vols.

Theophrastus: De Causis Plantarum. G. K. K. Link and B. Einarson. 3 Vols. Vol. I.

Thucydides. C. F. Smith. 4 Vols.

Tryphiodorus. Cf. Oppian.

Xenophon: Cyropaedia. Walter Miller. 2 Vols.

Xenophon: Hellencia. C. L. Brownson. 2 Vols.

Xenophon: Anabasis. C. L. Brownson.

Xenophon: Memorabilia and Oeconomicus. E. C. Marchant. Symposium and Apology. O. J. Todd.

Xenophon: Scripta Minora. E. C. Marchant. Constitution of the athenians. G. W. Bowersock.